Time Out

Miami

timeout.com/miami

Published by Time Out Guides Ltd, a wholly owned subsidiary of Time Out Group Ltd.
Time Out and the Time Out logo are trademarks of Time Out Group Ltd.

© Time Out Group Ltd 2006
Previous editions 1997, 2001, 2004.

10 9 8 7 6 5 4 3 2 1

This edition first published in Great Britain in 2006 by Ebury Publishing
Ebury Publishing is a division of The Random House Group Ltd,
20 Vauxhall Bridge Road, London SW1V 2SA

Random House Australia Pty Limited 20 Alfred Street, Milsons Point, Sydney, New South Wales 2061, Australia
Random House New Zealand Limited 18 Poland Road, Glenfield, Auckland 10, New Zealand
Random House South Africa (Pty) Limited Isle of Houghton, Corner Boundary
Road & Carse O'Gowrie, Houghton 2198, South Africa

Random House UK Limited Reg. No. 954009

Distributed in USA by Publishers Group West
1700 Fourth Street, Berkeley, California 94710

Distributed in Canada by Publishers Group Canada
250A Carlton Street, Toronto, Ontario M5A 2L1

For further distribution details, see www.timeout.com

To 31 December 2006: ISBN 1-904978-59-2
From 1 January 2007: ISBN 9781904978596

A CIP catalogue record for this book is available from the British Library

Colour reprographics by Wyndeham Icon, 3 & 4 Maverton Road, London E3 2JE

Printed and bound in Germany by Appl

Papers used by Ebury Publishing are natural, recyclable products made from wood grown in sustainable forests

Time Out Guides Limited
Universal House
251 Tottenham Court Road
London W1T 7AB
Tel + 44 (0)20 7813 3000
Fax + 44 (0)20 7813 6001
Email guides@timeout.com
www.timeout.com

Editorial
Miami Editor Lesley Abravanel
London Editor Lesley McCave
Listings Editor Courtney Recht
Proofreader Sylvia Tombesi-Walton
Indexer Anna Norman

Editorial/Managing Director Peter Fiennes
Series Editor Ruth Jarvis
Deputy Series Editor Lesley McCave
Business Manager Gareth Garner
Guides Co-ordinator Holly Pick
Accountant Kemi Olufuwa

Design
Art Director Scott Moore
Art Editor Pinelope Kourmouzoglou
Senior Designer Josephine Spencer
Graphic Designer Henry Elphick
Digital Imaging Dan Conway
Ad Make-up Jenni Prichard

Picture Desk
Picture Editor Jael Marschner
Deputy Picture Editor Tracey Kerrigan
Picture Researcher Helen McFarland

Advertising
Sales Director Mark Phillips
International Sales Manager Ross Canadé
International Sales Executive Simon Davies
Advertising Assistant Kate Staddon

Marketing
Group Marketing Director John Luck
Marketing Manager Yvonne Poon
Marketing & Publicity Manager, US Rosella Albanese

Production
Group Production Director Mark Lamond
Production Manager Brendan McKeown
Production Coordinator Caroline Bradford

Time Out Group
Chairman Tony Elliott
Managing Director Mike Hardwick
Financial Director Richard Waterlow
TO Magazine Ltd MD David Pepper
Group General Manager/Director Nichola Coulthard
TO Communications Ltd MD David Pepper
Group Art Director John Oakey
Group IT Director Simon Chappell

Contributors

Introduction Lesley Abravanel. **History** Tony Thompson, Lesley Abravanel. **Miami Today** Michael Sasser, Lesley Abravanel. **Latin Miami** Judy Cantor, Anne Tschida. **Miami Crime Lit** Andrew Humphreys, Lesley Abravanel. **Where to Stay** Lissette Fernandez. **Sightseeing Introduction** Andrew Humphreys, Lesley Abravanel. **The Beaches** Michael Sasser, Wendy Doscher-Smith. **Downtown** Michael Sasser, Wendy Doscher-Smith. **Coral Gables** Michael Sasser, Wendy Doscher-Smith. **Coconut Grove** Michael Sasser, Wendy Doscher-Smith. **Little Havana** Judy Cantor, Anne Tschida. **The Design District, Wynwood & Little Haiti** Nina Korman, Wendy Doscher-Smith. **North Miami & Beyond** Michael Sasser, Wendy Doscher-Smith. **South Miami & Beyond** Nina Korman, Wendy Doscher-Smith. **Restaurants & Cafés** Lesley Abravanel. **Bars & Pubs** Lesley Abravanel, Andrew Humphreys. **Shops & Services** Nina Korman, Brett Graff. **Festivals & Events** Gretchen Schmidt, Lesley Abravanel. **Children** Gretchen Schmidt, Brett Graff. **Film** Judy Cantor, Anne Tschida. **Galleries** Judy Cantor, Anne Tschida. **Gay & Lesbian** Tony Miro, James Cubby. **Music** Judy Cantor, Anne Tschida. **Nightclubs** Lesley Abravanel. **Sport & Fitness** Jacquelyn Powers, Courtney Recht. **Theatre & Dance** Mia Leonin, James Cubby. **Getting Started** Andrew Humphreys, Lesley Abravanel. **Fort Lauderdale & Palm Beach** Gretchen Schmidt, Lesley Abravanel. **The Everglades** Michael Sasser, Lesley Abravanel. **The Florida Keys** Andrew Humphreys, Lesley Abravanel. **Directory** Andrew Humphreys, Anne Tschida.

Maps JS Graphics (john@jsgraphics.co.uk).

Photography by Alys Tomlinson, except: pages 10, 13 Time Life Pictures/Getty Images; page 14 Bettmann/Corbis; page 17 Rex Features; page 25 Mario Anzuoni/Reuters/Corbis; page 30 AP Photo/Daniel Portnoy; page 160 Miami Bookfair International; page 163 Michael Katz; page 172 Imagenet; page 185 Julius Caesar; page 209 MagicalPhotos.com/Mitchell Zachs.

The following images were provided by the featured establishments/artists: pages 154, 159.

The Editors would like to thank Magnus Andersson, Jenny Gannaway, James Mitchell and all contributors to previous editions of *Time Out Miami*, whose work forms the basis for parts of this book.

Contents

Introduction

Ask anyone who lives here and they'll likely agree that Miami is one of the oddest yet most compelling cities in the world. What some used to call Heaven's Waiting Room, thanks to the scads of blue-haired women and white haired- (and -shoed) men playing gin rummy in fold-out chairs in front of their rickety old folks' home, has transformed quickly into a jetset hotspot where some of the aforementioned old folk can still be seen boozing it up next to Beyoncé at the Forge restaurant on Wednesday nights.

There are many dichotomies that make Miami fascinating and frustrating at the same time. The top one per cent of wealthy people who live and play here never have to work harder than climbing into their Bentleys to cruise to Prime 112 for a $20 Kobe beef hot dog. But that's work, really. Getting coiffed, dressed, bejewelled and bedazzled has become a major part of the Miami way of life. Don't be dismayed, though. Thanks to the booming development of the arts and nightlife scene in grittier parts than South Beach, a cash crop of arty, indie and – lo and behold – intellectual people have given Miami the fix of substance it was so sorely lacking during the so-called halcyon days of the late '80s and early '90s. From hipsters to hip hop, Miami has become, whether we like to admit it or not, an influential city of the 21st century. Sure, you can still slam candy-coloured cocktails while gawking at the likes of Paris Hilton in the clubs, but at the same time you can avoid them if you really want to. Clubland is no longer holding a monopoly on the city. It's important, yes, and if ever the club scene completely faded away Miami might be at a major loss, but, as proven over the years, this city has had more comebacks than Madonna. It's just that, right now, the city has other things on its mind.

Firstly, not too far from South Beach, there's that pesky real-estate thing going on, where nearly 50,000 condo units are being built to house what developers hope is a lot more than ego and hot air. And a city that was once devoid of the arts is about to receive a multi-multi-million-dollar Cesar Pelli-designed temple devoted to them, in the form of the Miami Performing Arts Center. Art Basel, which was once dismissed as an excuse for the chilly Swiss to take a spring break, has become a mega-watted annual event too. And Miami's even child-friendly now as well. No need to cover the kids' eyes in fear of topless bathing beauties or sexually confused characters prancing around in the opposite sex's night clothes any more. The Miami Children's Museum, among other spots, is a safe haven in which to carefully shelter the young ones before you and yours hit the town.

Miami isn't all sparkly and glittery, of course. Just like any major metropolis, there is a darker underbelly that's speckled with everything from immigration tensions brought on by boatfuls of desperate Haitian and Cuban immigrants to less frequent than before but still not uncommon drugs busts at the port and airport.

Basically, Miami is what you want it to be. Either a stunning, vacuous supermodel that just looks good on the surface or, if you dig further down into the sand, a smart, sassy and ever-evolving character that only gets better (and deeper) with age.

ABOUT TIME OUT CITY GUIDES

This is the fourth edition of *Time Out Miami*, one of an expanding series of Time Out guides produced by the people behind the successful listings magazines in London, New York and Chicago. Our guides are all written by resident experts who have striven to provide you with all the most up-to-date information you'll need to explore the city or read up on its background, whether you're a local or a first-time visitor.

THE LOWDOWN ON THE LISTINGS

We have tried to make this book as easy to use as possible. Addresses, phone numbers, bus information, opening times and admission prices are all included in the listings. However, businesses can change their arrangements at any time. Before you go out of your way, we'd strongly advise you to phone ahead to check opening times and other particulars. While every effort and care has been made to ensure the accuracy of the information contained in this guide, the publishers cannot accept responsibility for any errors it may contain.

THE LIE OF THE LAND

The majority of Miami's street layout is easy to understand. Miami Beach and much of the mainland both use variants on the grid system common to so many US cities. However, there are enough quirks and idiosyncracies to confuse even the most seasoned explorer – especially in Coral Gables and Coconut Grove, where the numbered grid system goes right out of the window – and a map is a must. For more on Miami's street layout, *see p249*.

To make the city easier to navigate, we have divided it into areas. Although these areas are a simplification of Miami's geography, we hope they will give you a useful means of understanding the city's layout and finding your way between sights. The areas are used in addresses throughout the guide. See p59 for a summary of these areas.

ESSENTIAL INFORMATION
For all the practical information you might need for visiting the area – including visa and customs information, details of local transport, emergency numbers, information on local weather and a selection of useful websites – turn to the Directory, which starts on page 246.

PRICES AND PAYMENT
We have noted where venues such as shops, hotels, restaurants and theatres accept the following credit cards: American Express (AmEx), Diners Club (DC), Discover (Disc), MasterCard (MC) and Visa (V). Many will also accept travellers' cheques, and/or other cards such as Carte Blanche.

The prices we've listed in this guide should be treated as guidelines, not gospel. If prices vary wildly from those we've quoted, ask whether there's a good reason. If not, go elsewhere. Then please let us know. We aim to give the best and most up-to-date advice, so we want to know if you've been badly treated or overcharged.

TELEPHONE NUMBERS
Miami has two area codes: 305, which the vast majority of Miami numbers take, and the relatively new 786. When dialling a Miami number from within Miami, dial the code (305 or 786) and then the seven-digit number. When calling from elsewhere in the US, prefix this ten-digit number with 1. And when phoning from

abroad, prefix this 11-digit number with your country's international access code (from the UK it's 00). For more on phones and codes, *see p258*.

MAPS
We provide a map reference for all places listed in central Miami and Miami Beach, indicating the page and grid reference at which an address can be found on our street maps, which start on page 272. They also pinpoint the locations of hotels (**❶**), restaurants and cafés (**❶**) and bars and pubs (**❶**) featured in the relevant chapters.

LET US KNOW WHAT YOU THINK
We hope you enjoy *Time Out Miami*, and we'd like to know what you think of it. We welcome tips for places that you consider we should include in future editions and take note of your criticism of our choices. You can email us at guides@timeout.com.

There is an online version of this book, along with guides to over 100 international cities, at **www.timeout.com**.

bumpy boat ride at the
seaport where you lost
your wallet: $45

(not feeling queasy: priceless)

Don't worry. MasterCard Global Service™ is available wherever
you travel, in any language you speak. So just call the local toll-free
number and we'll rush you a new card most anywhere in the world.
For a complete list of toll-free numbers, go to www.mastercard.com.

AUSTRALIA	1800-120-113	ITALY	800-870-866
BRAZIL	0800-891-3294	MEXICO	001-800-307-7309
CANADA	1-800-307-7309	PUERTO RICO	1-800-307-7309
FRANCE	0-800-90-1387	SPAIN	900-97-1231
GERMANY	0800-819-1040	UK	0800-96-4767
HONG KONG	800-966677	USA	1-800-307-7309

From all other countries call collect:
1-636-722-7111

there are some things money can't buy for peace of mind there's MasterCard®

In Context

Features

History

There's sometimes trouble in paradise, but Miami always manages to weather the storm.

Despite the fact that Florida has been inhabited for at least ten centuries, little is known about the lives of the earliest settlers, descendants of Central and South American Indians. But thanks to the discovery in 1998 of artefacts in downtown Miami dubbed the Miami Circle, they are known to include the Calusa (or, more commonly, Tequesta) tribe, whose origins date back 2,000 years. However, detailed records began only with the arrival of one of Spain's greatest explorers. Juan Ponce de León had sailed with Christopher Columbus on his second voyage to the Americas in 1493 and later conquered Puerto Rico for Spain. His reward was to be made governor of the island in 1510, but the spirit of adventure never left him.

During de León's term as governor, he constantly heard tales from Puerto Rico's Native American inhabitants about a mythical island called Bimini, believed to be somewhere north of Cuba (which de León had surveyed with Columbus). Bimini was said to be teeming with gold reserves and to possess a magical spring whose waters had the power to restore youth and heal the sick. Seduced by the tales, de León repeated them to King Ferdinand V of Spain in 1512. Within days, he had been provided with a boat, a crew and orders to find, conquer and colonise Bimini.

When his expedition eventually sighted land on 27 March 1513, de León believed he had succeeded. Landing just north of what is now St Augustine, on Florida's north-eastern coast, he made a claim in the name of the king and, because he had first seen land on Easter Sunday, known in Spanish as *Pascua Florida* ('Festival of Flowers'), decided to name the region Florida. Believing that he had discovered an island, de León tried to circumnavigate it, looking for the fountain and the gold; finding neither, he eventually gave up and returned to Puerto Rico in 1514.

Many Indian tribes inhabited Florida and the surrounding area. Some, like those in Cuba, had welcomed the Spanish colonists with open arms, but other tribes fiercely resented the invaders, and when de León returned to Florida in 1521 with two shiploads of horses, cattle, tools, seeds and people to start a new Spanish settlement, he came under attack. Badly wounded, he was forced to flee, and died in Cuba soon after.

The legend of Florida, however, lived on. During the next few years, a host of young Spaniards tried and failed to establish a permanent settlement, chiefly in the hope of finding the rumoured reserves of gold. All were beaten back by the Indians, and by the 1560s interest was starting to wane. But when a massive French force, led by Jean Ribaut, arrived in 1562 to claim the new territory for France, the Spanish realised they had to take action or risk losing Florida altogether.

POWER STRUGGLES

Pedro Menéndez de Avilés, captain-general of the Spanish fleet, was ordered to destroy the French colony of Fort Caroline. In 1565 Ribaut and his followers were captured and executed, leaving Menéndez free to establish St Augustine, the oldest continuous European settlement in the US. The French tried but failed to retake the town, and it became a key trading centre.

> ### 'The Americans' intention was to remove the Indians completely and take control of the region.'

However, the bloodshed didn't stop. In 1586 Britain attempted to get in on the act, sending Sir Francis Drake on a naval bombardment that razed St Augustine. For the next 150 years, the English, Spanish and French all vied with the Indians for control of the 'New World'. Spain had the upper hand until the Seven Years War (1757-63, also known as the French and Indian War) between Britain and France, in which Spain sided with France. In the First Treaty of Paris, which ended the war, the Spanish ceded Florida in return for the strategically important port of Havana, which the British had captured in 1762.

Under British rule, Florida was divided into two separate colonies, East and West, leaving the surviving Indian tribes, who had joined forces with the Creek Indian tribes that had been pushed down into Florida after repeatedly losing out to the might of the American army, undisturbed in the inland area. Collectively, the

new Indians called themselves the Seminole (meaning 'wild one' or 'runaway') and would soon prove to be a force to be reckoned with. The British held on to the area during the American War of Independence (1775-83), but the Second Treaty of Paris, which brought peace, also handed Florida back to Spain.

THE US TAKES OVER

From around 1814, American troops made a series of raids into Florida, claiming they were attempting to capture escaped slaves from the neighbouring state of Georgia. They left the Spanish well alone, but killed hundreds of Indians, who regularly gave refuge to escaped slaves and had begun to intermarry. The scale of the slaughter matched that seen elsewhere in the newly united States, with the Indians slowly being wiped out.

The Americans' true intention, of course, was to remove the Indians completely and take control of the region in order to wrest it from the Spanish. The conflict became known as the First Seminole War. Led by General (later President) Andrew Jackson, the US troops captured the city of Pensacola in May 1818 and deposed the Spanish government. Spain formally ceded Florida to the US in 1819.

Thousands of colonists soon began to arrive from the north, pushing the native Indians ever further south. In 1830 the American Congress passed the Removal Act, a piece of legislation that is described in TD Allman's *Miami: City of the Future* as being reminiscent of the later policies of apartheid South Africa and Nazi Germany. In accordance with this new law, the Indians were told they would have to move to a new territory in the barren lands west of the Mississippi. Their chief, Osceola, refused, thrusting his knife into the unsigned treaty as a show of defiance. A few weeks later, 110 US soldiers on patrol were killed by the Indians and runaway slaves who had joined them, sparking the Second Seminole War.

The cost to both sides, financially and in lives, was enormous. In 1837, the US agreed to negotiate, and Osceola entered one of their camps under a flag of truce. It was a ruse. He was captured and imprisoned, but still the war raged on. In the end, the US spent more than $40 million and lost 2,500 soldiers before the majority of the Seminoles – around 4,000 of them – finally relented and moved to Arkansas. A few, though, refused to leave, fleeing to the Everglades, where they remain today.

MIAMI TAKES SHAPE

In 1845, Florida became the 27th state to join the Union and, for a short time, there was peace. It was also around this time that what would eventually become the city of Miami began to take shape. During the war the US had established Fort Dallas, a limestone fortress on the north bank of a river that flowed through southern Florida. When the soldiers left, the fort became the base for a tiny village established by William H English, which he called Miami (from the Indian word 'mayami', meaning 'big water'; the main Tequesta Indian settlement was by the Miami River; *see also p10*.)

In the meantime, railroads and steamboats had appeared in the north of the state, bringing prosperity and better links with the rest of the Union. William D Moseley was elected state governor and took control of a population that numbered 87,445, of which 39,000 were black slaves. The vast majority of the white population considered slavery acceptable,

and the newly accepted state began to feel increasingly isolated as dissent about the use of slaves led to the formation of the Republican Party (trading in slaves had already been abolished in 1808).

When Abraham Lincoln became the first Republican president in 1860, Florida responded by withdrawing from the Union and joining other southern slave states in the Confederacy. Though the Civil War hardly touched south Florida, most of the major towns in the north – with the exception of Tallahassee – were captured by the Union early in the war. There was only one large-scale engagement: the Battle of Olustee in February 1864, which proved to be one of the last Confederate victories. On 10 May 1865, federal troops entered Tallahassee and the US flag flew

Gone with the wind

Watching the condensation drip languidly down the side of the glass that holds your magenta Mai Tai as you stretch out by the beach on another sun-drenched day, it's hard to believe some of the nastiest storms on earth have slammed into the shore right where you're lounging. But of more than 160 hurricanes that struck the US between 1900 and 2000, over a third hit Florida. In other words, more often than every two years – during hurricane season, June to November – Floridians board up their windows, tie up their boats and get the hell out of the way.

A hurricane is a type of tropical cyclone, itself the general term for all circulating weather systems over tropical waters. There are three levels of tropical cyclone, of which hurricanes, intense systems with winds above 73 miles per hour, are the nastiest. Hurricanes are given names, dubbed in alphabetical order – the first storm of the year has a name beginning with A, the next with B and so on – which helps to avoid confusion when more than one hurricane is being tracked simultaneously. Hurricanes, too, are ranked on a scale of one to five. Category one hurricanes are the weakest, while category five storms are catastrophic, with winds in excess of 155 miles per hour. Luckily, the nastiest hurricanes are extremely rare, with only a few having occurred in the last century.

In the first major storm of 1992, south Florida experienced one of nature's furies: a category four hurricane. Andrew swept across the area with winds of more than 145 miles

per hour. At least 15 people were killed, hundreds were injured, over 250,000 were left homeless and entire swathes of land – particularly in Homestead – were annihilated, causing $30 billion of damage. But despite its ferocity, Andrew was not the deadliest hurricane in the city's history. That honour rests with a nameless – hurricanes weren't consistently given names until the 1950s – category five storm that slammed into the city on Labor Day 1935, killing 400 people.

Since Hurricane Andrew, Florida has been battered regularly, but by far less devastating hurricanes. The Panhandle area around Pensacola, in particular, seems to have been targeted by Mother Nature for special misery in recent years. But none has been as strong as Andrew. And in any case, Florida residents barely raise an eyebrow at anything smaller than a category three.

If it's any comfort, there is something standing between you and nature: the US National Hurricane Center, based at Florida International University in Miami. The NHC closely monitors tropical cyclones, decides which threaten US coastlines, determines which areas are most likely to be hit, and issues hurricane watches (one is expected to threaten the vicinity) and warnings (hurricane conditions expected in the immediate area). These are designed to give you time to hit the road. Hurricanes, you see, are far more fun when watched on the news from the comfort of a faraway sofa than as they roar in around you, as if belched out by God after a few too many cold ones.

Sinatra struts his stuff at the Fontainebleau, 1968. *See p18.*

once more. Slavery was abolished, a new state constitution adopted, and Florida was readmitted to the Union in 1868.

THE RAILWAY APPROACHES

The 1862 Homestead Act promised 160 acres of land free to any citizen who would stay on it for at least five years and, during that period, effect some improvement. Among the early takers was Edmund Beasley, who, in 1868, moved into the bayside area now called Coconut Grove. Two years later, William Brickell bought extra land on the south bank of the Miami River and Ephraim Sturtevant acquired the area known as Biscayne. In 1875, his daughter, Julia Tuttle, visited him and fell in love with the area, but it would be 16 years before she returned.

Although it had the beginnings of a small community, Miami would never have become the major city it is now had it not been for one of the country's greatest entrepreneurs. Henry Flagler, who had made his $50 million-plus fortune as an associate of John Rockefeller in the Standard Oil company, first came to Florida in the 1880s because he felt the year-round good climate would help his wife's frail health. After moving to the area, he decided to enter the railroad and hotel business and, starting in St Augustine, built a new railroad.

Flagler and his teams slowly worked their way down the east coast, stopping at each major town to build a plush hotel. With the newspapers extolling Florida's weather – so

warm that citrus fruits could be grown – it soon became a major tourist destination for the wintering rich. When another railway magnate, Henry Plant, began building the Atlantic Coastline Railroad on the opposite coast, from Jacksonville right down to Tampa, still more investors and settlers began to flood in.

ONE WOMAN'S VISION

At the end of the 1880s, the area around Miami comprised nothing more than a few plantations and trading posts. The first proper community, some way south of the Miami River, was Coconut Grove, but it was only after Julia Tuttle's husband died, in 1886, and she decided to relocate from Cleveland to a plot of land north of the river, that things really started to move. Tuttle approached Plant and asked him to extend his railroad to Miami. When she was turned down, she went to Flagler, whose own railway line stopped at Palm Beach, just 66 miles to the north. He kindly explained that he could see no benefit in extending his line to Miami because there was simply nothing there.

Tuttle knew all too well that without the railroad, the tiny settlement would be too isolated to ever become prosperous. For example, the simple act of sending a letter from Palm Beach to Miami took at least two months: the letter went to a lighthouse community at Jupiter, then by Indian river steamer to the railhead at Titusville, then by train to New York, then by steamer to Havana, and finally

Mariel Boatlift from Cuba. *See p19.*

by a trading schooner that docked at the mouth of the Miami River, all for a total journey of 3,000 miles. Nature, though, soon intervened.

In the winter of 1894-5, a killer frost devastated most of the orange crop in the north of the state, but Miami, further south and well within the 'tropical zone', escaped the freeze. According to popular legend, Julia Tuttle sent Flagler a handful of orange blossoms to show that her crop was unaffected. When she agreed to give Flagler half her land (some 300 acres), along with some of William Brickell's, the hard-nosed businessman finally agreed to begin work on the railway.

When the first locomotive arrived in Miami on 15 April 1896, all 300 residents turned out to greet it. Some of the old-timers, though, had never seen a train before and fled to the woods at its approach. Thousands of new settlers and investors flocked down in anticipation of the boom that would surely follow. Tuttle's dream was about to come true.

BIRTH OF A CITY

The shallowness of Biscayne Bay had hindered the growth of the area, but the extension of the railroad meant that machines, supplies and people could easily get to Miami now. A month after the railroad arrived, Miami's first paper, the *Miami Metropolis*, rolled off the presses; in

July Miami was granted city status; in September the first school opened. Flagler used some of his newly acquired land to build the enormous, plush Royal Palm Hotel, with the intention of encouraging visitors to spend money. More and more tourists began to visit, responding to advertisements in newspapers and magazines that described Miami as 'the sun porch of America', 'where winter is turned to summer'.

> **'One soldier wrote home: "If I owned both Miami and Hell, I'd rent out Miami and live in Hell."'**

Considering Florida's earlier attitude to slavery, it's ironic that blacks became so tied to Miami's history. The first shovel of earth that began construction of the Royal Palm Hotel was dug up by the Reverend AW Brown, who was black, as was WH Arston, who signed the original city charter. When the city was incorporated, a third of the original voters were former slaves, despite the fact that blacks had few rights elsewhere in Florida. However, right after incorporation, the city's blacks were disenfranchised.

To ensure growth took place in an organised fashion, the city's founders laid out a basic grid plan to the north and south of the river, only to see most of the wooden buildings destroyed in a fire in December 1896. Perhaps it was the shock of seeing her dream go up in flames, but Julia Tuttle died unexpectedly soon afterwards, aged just 48. Miami's founding mother was gone, but the city was quickly rebuilt and attracted ever-growing numbers of tourists. However, they were joined by some less welcome visitors.

During the ten-week Spanish-American War in 1898, 7,000 US troops were stationed in Miami, waiting to be shipped down to Cuba. They amused themselves by using coconuts for target practice and swimming naked in the bay, much to the chagrin of local residents, who did their best to make them feel unwelcome. The church-going black community was a target and, on more than one occasion, tensions escalated into violence. It seems that between the residents and the mosquitoes, the soldiers were indeed made miserable. One wrote home: 'If I owned both Miami and Hell, I'd rent out Miami and live in Hell.'

THE 20TH CENTURY

With the new century came new settlers. Both the population and the town began to grow rapidly; a business district, banks, movie theatres and a rival newspaper, the *Miami Evening Record*, were set up. There were also so many drinking dens and gin houses that the main thoroughfare became known as Whiskey Street, prompting the arrival of Carry Amelia Moore Nation, 'the Kansas Cyclone'. A six-foot-tall, powerfully built woman and the wife of a chronic alcoholic, she saw it as her task to rid the world of the evil of alcohol, seeing her name – Carry A Nation – as divine providence. She stormed into Miami in 1908 and sold copies of her newsletter, 'Smasher's Mail', but was prevented from doing much 'good work' by concerned citizens.

Even then, law enforcement was hardly Miami's strong point. The city's first marshall was Young F Gray, a bandy-legged Texan who was frequently so drunk that he needed help to mount his bicycle. As well as being the city's first cop, he was also the first to be suspended after being found drunk on duty once too often.

THE FIRST BOOM

Governor Napoleon Bonaparte Broward, in office from 1905 to 1909, was the first to begin major drainage of the Everglades in order to reclaim land for development. By 1913, 142 miles of canals had been constructed, and Henry Flagler had finally extended his railroad

all the way to Key West. Government Cut, later to become the Port of Miami, was dug across the lower end of the future Miami Beach to improve access to the harbour, creating Fisher Island in the process.

John Collins, a visionary rather than a businessman, saw potential in the area and borrowed money to build a bridge from Miami to the beach. His money ran out halfway through, but he was bailed out by Carl Fisher, who had made a fortune by inventing a new kind of car headlight; in return, Fisher was given much of the land on the beach. By the start of World War I, Miami was in the middle of one of its most rapid periods of growth.

Fisher could see the true potential of the beach and began removing its trees and dredging the sea around it, creating his vision of perfection. Within a year, the area had its first hotels, swimming pools, restaurants and casinos. It was the ultimate playground of the rich. Elsewhere in Miami, many of the wealthy visitors who had spent winters in the city decided to move there permanently, building fabulous waterfront estates such as James Deering's opulent Vizcaya.

THE ROARING '20S

Miami's population doubled between 1920 and 1923. Some of the newcomers were drawn by slick advertising campaigns promoting equally slick community developments, such as the 3,000-acre Coral Gables. Described by its developer George Merrick as the City Beautiful,

Merrick House, childhood home of city founder George Merrick. *See p84.*

Living the high life

The local politicians, chambers of commerce and flag-wavers for the 'Magic City' would like to scratch it from collective memory. But whether they like it or not, Miami's history is inexorably tied to illegal activity in general, and drugs in particular.

Miami's hedonistic reputation took off in the 1920s, when the city's first fully fledged boom was fuelled not just by its beachfront location but also by gambling – and the fact that the locals turned a blind eye to Prohibition. Miami was the largest import point for alcohol on the East Coast, and rum runners were seen as Robin Hoods doing the community a service. In 1928 Al Capone purchased a mansion on exclusive Palm Island, and by the 1950s gamblers and gangsters had infiltrated Miami Beach, as the city enjoyed another boom.

A new economy emerged in the early 1980s: drugs. Thanks to its easy sea access to South America, the city gained prominence as the major East Coast entry port for the dealers. Cocaine cowboys came to town with absurdly large sums of money that they needed to both launder and spend. The local economy was revitalised as the drug lords funnelled hundreds of millions of cocaine dollars into real estate, construction and securities investments.

Just how dirty was Miami? In his book *Miami: City of the Future*, TD Allman claims that by 1985, statistically speaking, every man, woman and child in the Miami area had not only had drug money, but drugs on their hands. When a local pharmacologist tested several bundles of currency chosen from the deposits of seven of the city's most respectable banks, he found large amounts of cocaine on all of them. You could refuse to take drugs, you could refuse to associate with people who took drugs; but whatever you did in Miami, drugs would be part of your life.

But with the economic prosperity came an increase in crime and the rise to notoriety of figures like Conrado Valencia Zalgado, better known as 'El Loco'. The original cocaine cowboy, El Loco was the maniac who hung from a speeding Audi and fired a machine gun at rival dealers on the Florida Turnpike. When the cops caught up with him, they found a dead Colombian in the car trunk. El Loco made Al Pacino's Scarface look like the Hamburglar by comparison.

The police, the coast guard, the border patro, the Drug Enforcement Agency and the FBI came together to try and stop the influx of drugs and crime, inspiring the TV show that would eventually bring Miami to the tip of everyone's tongues. *Miami Vice* (*photo right*) glamorised criminal life in the city, and by the late 1980s, people all over the world had begun to rediscover Miami. Fashion shoots brought hordes of models to the Beach, and celebs moved into palatial homes on Star Island. The Deco District underwent a major renovation, and a new tourist boom was born.

But despite its newfound fabulousness, the city was still rife with drugs. While Miami rebuilt its tourism industry, South Beach

the Gables was designed as a vision of paradise on earth and carefully regulated by an array of local laws and directives – still in place today – to stay that way.

But not all of the new residents were quite so well-to-do. Prohibition and its 'anti-saloon laws' never really worked in Miami. With rum runners able to smuggle freely along the impossible-to-patrol coast, it wasn't long before everyone in the US knew of the supposed haven. The city became overrun by mobsters and illegal liquor, giving rise to its nickname as 'the leakiest spot in America'. Things got so bad that the old courthouse, once the venue for public hangings, had to be replaced in 1926 by a larger building. So large, in fact, that for the next 50 years the Dade Country Courthouse was Miami's tallest building.

Meanwhile, Miami was in the midst of a building boom. Some of the growth was 'controlled' by a plan to divide the city into four geographic sections and rename some of the districts and streets, a move deemed necessary when the US Post Office threatened to stop delivering mail because of the city's outdated street system. Prices rocketed as people rushed to be part of the latest land boom (which was satirised in the Marx Brothers' first movie, *The Cocoanuts*). Hotels, airports and other amenities sprang up. Miami Beach alone suddenly found itself with more than 15,000 residents.

Everyone was so busy making money and plans that when the *Miami Tribune* warned, in early September 1926, of an impending tropical storm, few people paid much attention.

became known as a party destination with world-class clubs, bars... and drugs. Ecstasy, ketamine, GHB, methamphetamine and Rohypnol all gained in popularity as people came to indulge. It was only in the late '90s that the clampdown started, and drug raids closed several popular hotspots.

South Beach politicians now have an uneasy relationship with the nightlife industry.

While they know the clubs are a major draw for tourism, especially the after-hours hangouts, they don't want to be seen to be encouraging drug use. But just as South Beach tried to harden its stance, so the City of Miami started issuing 24-hour licences to Downtown clubs. The message to the Beach was clear: if you don't want the business, we'll have it.

How they wished they had. The hurricane hit in the middle of the night of 26 September, when winds of up to 128 miles per hour smashed their way through the city. More than 100 people died and thousands more were left homeless, with most bayside developments suffering terrible floods.

The hurricane damage was just being mended and the economy had barely recovered when the Great Depression and a state-wide recession brought on by the 1929 Wall Street Crash descended. As if that wasn't enough, the northern part of Florida was invaded by Mediterranean fruit flies, which destroyed more than 60 per cent of the citrus groves. It seemed that the city was finished, a sentiment echoed by newspaper headlines that screamed: 'Miami is wiped out!'

MIAMI RISES AGAIN

Many of the millionaires who had profited during the boom years, including George Merrick and one-time mayor John 'Ev' Sewell, were destroyed by the fall in real-estate prices. But, even though the founding financiers had gone, the mix of beautiful beaches, a fantastic climate and seemingly endless potential remained, so new money soon flowed in and was warmly received.

A group of mostly Jewish developers began building small, Modern-style hotels on Miami Beach along Collins Avenue and Ocean Drive, adding to Miami's fast-growing Jewish community and creating what would later become the Art Deco District. With the hotels came tourists, and with the tourists came renewed prosperity. Pan American Airways launched a service connecting Miami with dozens of other major cities, including many in South America. Miami was soon established as one of the country's key 'gateways to Latin America' and the population grew steadily.

After Franklin D Roosevelt came to power in 1933 – just weeks after he survived an assassination attempt in Miami's Bayfront Park, in which Chicago mayor Anton Cermak perished – he launched the New Deal, a package of reconstruction programmes designed to better the lives of many Americans. Young men and not-so-young war veterans were drafted to build parks and new public buildings, which, in Miami, included fire stations, highways, public housing and social clubs. A hurricane struck on Labor Day 1935, killing 400 people and wiping out much of the new construction work, but, once again, Miami found the will to rebuild the damage and continue. There was, however, resentment about Jewish involvement in southern Miami Beach. Slowly, the Beach became segregated: 'Gentiles Only' signs appeared in the northern part, just as the tide of anti-Semitism began to rise across the Atlantic.

WORLD WAR II
The battles in Europe and the Far East seemed a long way off until the US naval base at Pearl Harbor was bombed without warning by the Japanese on 7 December 1941. The US entered the war, and no one was sure what would happen next. Florida's coastline was seen as a weak link in the US's defence, and tourism, by then the mainstay of Miami's economy, dropped off dramatically. Everyone's worst fears were confirmed in February 1942 when, in full view of thousands of horrified Miami residents, a fleet of German submarines attacked and sank four tankers in a torpedo attack just off the main harbour. More attacks quickly followed: with most of the US Navy's major ships out in the Pacific Ocean, German U-boats found they could attack Florida virtually at will. While the US never had to face the equivalent of the Blitz, the submarines ensured that those who lived in Miami would never feel the war was more than a few hundred feet away, and what little tourism remained quickly died away.

Ironically, the war would later save Miami. The warm climate was deemed perfect for training new soldiers, and by the end of 1942, nearly 150 hotels had been converted into barracks, with others turned into temporary hospitals for the wounded. By the time World War II was over, one-quarter of all officers and a fifth of enlisted men in the US Army Air Corps had passed through Miami.

The shortage of manpower brought about by the war improved the lot of Miami's growing black community. In the late 1940s, the first black police officer was appointed to patrol the 'coloured district', and an all-black municipal court was set up. The city's first black judge was also appointed, and, for the first time, blacks were allowed into the Orange Bowl Stadium, albeit restricted to sitting in the end zone. Beaches remained segregated, however, adding to the underlying racial tensions that occasionally exploded into violence. In 1951, Carver Village, a black housing project in a formerly white neighbourhood, was repeatedly bombed. Several synagogues and a Miami Shores church were attacked because of their pro-black sympathies and activities.

Around this time, gangsters returned to Miami. No one was sure how they managed to evade the law until the publishers of the *Miami Herald* and *Miami Daily News* got together to launch a campaign to drive them out. In July 1950 the Crime Commission of Greater Miami held live television hearings of court cases. Corruption was discovered at every level of government and eventually the county sheriff was removed from office. But the most welcome post-war change was that thousands of soldiers who had trained there returned with their families. Once again, Miami was on the up.

COME FLY WITH ME
The 1950s saw southern Florida, and Miami in particular, gain renown as the playground of America. Air travel made the place accessible to New Yorkers for quick weekends. Miami Beach gained a new strip of fabulous hotels, notably the Diplomat, the Eden Roc and, the luxe of the luxe, the Fontainebleau. Designed by architect Morris Lapidus, the Fontainebleau was a stage set of a hotel, the kind of place in which to put on a Busby Berkeley number. It gave its patrons everything they'd ever dreamed of, and then some. It catered to the big shots and was the celebrity magnet of its day. The entertainment manager, Joe Fischetti, was a cousin of Al Capone and a friend of Frank Sinatra, who played a series of engagements at the hotel. Sinatra and the hotel also hosted Elvis Presley's first post-army performance, an hour-long special made for ABC, and the Fontainebleau was also the setting for *The Bellboy*, directed by and starring Jerry Lewis. By the mid '50s two and a half million tourists were coming to Miami every year. The city's public relations director claimed that more hotels had been built on Miami Beach since the end of World War II than in the rest of the world combined.

When Havana, the East Coast's premier party spot, was closed down by revolution in 1959, Miami cleaned up, offering its alternative vision of surf, sun, flesh and flash. Chat show host Ed

Sullivan moved down to broadcast from the Beach and secured the first performance by the Beatles on their US tour, at the Deauville hotel.

RISING TENSIONS

The 1959 Cuban revolution changed Miami in other, more significant ways. The city became home to thousands of anti-Castro immigrants. What started as a trickle became a flood as daily flights brought nearly 100,000 Cubans to the city within a few months. Although the first wave was mostly from Cuba's affluent middle classes, later arrivals were far less wealthy and found themselves competing with Miami's poorest blacks for jobs and housing. When a recession hit in the 1970s, the worst for 40 years, unemployment soared and violent, race-related confrontations became the norm, though this did little to stop the flow of Cubans to the city. By 1973 there were more than 300,000 in Miami (for more on the Cuban influx, *see pp27-29*). The Jewish community also grew rapidly in the mid 1970s, ultimately matching the Cuban population and becoming one of the largest concentrations of Jews in the US outside New York. Miami became particularly attractive to the older Jewish generation: 75 per cent of those living there were aged over 60.

Racial tensions, however, remained. In the summer of 1980, an all-white jury in Tampa,

on the west coast of Florida, acquitted a white policeman of beating to death black insurance agent Arthur McDuffie. The anger of Miami's incensed African-American community boiled over into a riot that claimed 18 lives and levelled parts of Liberty City. The disruption lasted for three days and caused damage worth $80 million. The following week – as thousands of 'boat people' began to arrive from Haiti, fleeing their own dictatorship and attracted by the success of the Cuban immigrants – *Time* magazine ran a cover story about Miami headlined 'Paradise Lost?'

'Two years later, Miami had become safe enough for the Pope to visit.'

The Mariel Boatlift in 1980 brought 125,000 Cuban refugees to Miami, including thousands of criminals and mental patients, part of a plan by Castro to unload the dregs of society. Cubans soon established themselves as the premier drug dealers in the area, not hesitating to shoot rivals out of business. Miami became Murder Capital USA, with 621 violent deaths in the city in 1981 alone, most of them narcotics related: *see p16* **Living the high life**.

Miami's historic **Art Deco District** is a huge draw for tourists. *See p17*.

NEWFOUND FAME AND FORTUNE

With international attention focused on the area, the city councillors realised something had to be done to prevent Downtown and South Beach from being overrun by dealers and down-and-outs. The Art Deco District received federal protection, a new transport network was developed, and fashion photographers began staging shoots in South Beach, sparking its transformation into a hip, happening area buzzing with clubs, restaurants and bars. Xavier Suarez became Miami's first Cuban-born mayor in 1985, and it seemed that someone was working to reduce racial tensions. Two years later, the city had become safe enough for the Pope to visit. The latest boom was in full flow. Even 1992's Hurricane Andrew, which left more than 150,000 homeless, failed to halt the rise. It spared the city of Miami but hit South Dade, causing damage totalling $30 billion.

In 1999 Miami was thrust into the spotlight again, this time because of a six-year-old Cuban boy named Elián González, who washed ashore in an inner tube on Thanksgiving Day, the rest of the group of would-be exiles having perished at sea. (Elián was eventually returned to his homeland.) The 2000 presidential election fiasco again put Miami and south Florida back in the headlines for all the wrong reasons as the eyes of the world focused critically on the state's inability to vote or count properly. But the city bounced back with a resilience comparable only to Madonna's. Not only did it prove it could count, but after the tragedy of 9/11, it proved that it could be counted on as an Eden-istic escape from harsh reality. Tourism continued to boom, as it does today. Major events such as the Latin Grammy Awards, the Grand Prix of the Americas and the controversial Free Trade Area of the Americas convention chose Miami as central command for business as (un)usual. As South Beach boomed in the early 1990s, the once-desolate, *Bonfire of the Vanities*-esque area of Downtown is now beginning to experience a similar renaissance, turning an urban wasteland into an urban paradise. But there may be dark clouds forming on the horizon: in 2005 Miami's condo and construction boom reached an all-time high, leaving sceptics fearing the bubble will eventually burst, resulting in dozens of empty and unfinished apartment buildings. But as has happened so many times in the past, Miami is sure to recover in the long term.

Key events

3,000 BC Tequesta Indians, early Miami inhabitants, appear as a culture.
1513 Juan Ponce de León lands in Florida, claiming it for Spain.
1763 Spain cedes Florida to Britain.
1783 The Spanish gain control again.
1817-9 The First Seminole War.
1819 Spain hands Florida to the US; it becomes a US territory in 1821.
1835-42 The Second Seminole War.
1845 Florida joins the Union, then withdraws during the American Civil War. It is eventually readmitted in 1868.
1855-8 The Third Seminole War.
1896 Henry Flagler's railroad arrives in April. Miami is granted city status in July.
1905-13 The Everglades are drained to provide land for building; Miami Beach grows.
1921 George Merrick begins building the city of Coral Gables.
1926 A hurricane destroys much of the city, and Miami slides into recession, exacerbated by the Wall Street Crash of 1929.
1930s Hundreds of art deco hotels are built on Miami Beach.
1935 A Labor Day hurricane wrecks the city, killing 400.

1941 US joins World War II; thousands of US troops train in Miami.
1959 Fidel Castro takes power in Cuba; 100,000 Cubans flee to Miami.
1961 Kennedy attacks the Bay of Pigs.
1962 The Cuban Missile Crisis.
1980 The Liberty City riots tear the city apart; the Mariel Boatlift backfires.
1984 *Miami Vice* begins airing on US TV.
1992 Hurricane Andrew hits south Florida, leaving 150,000 people homeless.
1994 The Summit of the Americas is held at the Biltmore Hotel.
1996 Miami celebrates its centennial by going bust.
1997 A referendum is held on the continued existence of the City of Miami.
1998 Madonna puts her Miami manse up for sale, sparking a mass celebrity exodus.
1999 Elián González washes up on shore.
2000 Bush wins the presidential election, but only after multiple recounts.
2003 The Florida Marlins win the baseball World Series.
2004 Bush wins the presidential election again. Brother Jeb celebrates in Florida's State Capitol.

Downtown skyline, *à la Miami Vice.*

Miami Today

Joni Mitchell was close – only in Miami, they're paving paradise and putting up condos, not parking lots.

Miami and its vibrant nightlife are still hot – just ask Paris Hilton, who said, simply, 'Miami's hot', and continues to bring her gaggle of glam girls down to party and live life like an heiress should. Despite the Hollywoodisation of Miami, the city is not solely about all things trendy anymore. Other areas, including the bustling financial/Downtown district, are coming into their own, not because Britney Spears stayed at the swank Four Seasons there, but because of these newer places themselves: as well as the Four Seasons, there's the Conrad and the Mandarin Oriental, which are joined by a never-ending list of upscale restaurants and million-dollar condominiums. Residents and visitors alike who have complained about the city's dearth of cultural options are finally able to rejoice over the new multi-million-dollar performing arts centre that's just five minutes

away from the aforementioned hotels (construction had lingered on, but the grand opening was scheduled for October 2006). As for art snobs, just mention two magical words – Art Basel – and all is right in the world.

Just a handful of years ago, however, the city did not have the greatest international standing. There was 2000's 'can't count/won't count' presidential election controversy; a mayor was removed from office after an election featured dead men (and women) voting; and then there were the dreadful images of stormtrooping police facing off against a terrified little boy and his tearful elderly relatives in the international custody battle over Cuban tyke Elián González. The glitz and glamour that legitimately defined Miami started to tarnish – briefly.

Fast forward a few years, and all of a sudden Miami, while still totally out of sync with reality (a quality that practically defines the city), doesn't seem as harsh. Reviews of that wonky election count (which, remember, led to the Florida governor's brother becoming president) revealed that the eventual results were debatably accurate. Then, not long after the US handed Castro a victory in the custody battle over little Elián, 'the Beard', as the Cuban leader is often referred to in Miami (just as back home), engaged in a fresh round of murder, incarceration and oppression of political dissidents. (Many commentators took this as proof that returning a child to a country where the constitution claims that all children are the property of the state might not have been the most humane thing to do.)

'The nice part about living in Miami is how close it is to the United States.'

Politically, there have also been major shifts in Miami. Once upon a time, corruption here was as refreshingly straightforward as in any Third World kleptocracy: you wanted something, you paid off the right officials and you got it. But after years of contentious leadership and seemingly unceasing public corruption probes, in November 2001 Miami elected a mayor, Manuel A Diaz, who united the city's diverse community leadership in its praise. By and large, Miami today has more stable and honest leaders. Corruption hasn't been completely eliminated – the head of the teachers' union was busted for his Enron-esque lifestyle at the expense of union members, including using union funds for holidays, gifts and the occasional sex toy. But still, this is a far cry from the last decade's antics, when city leader Joe Gersten fled the country in light of a crack and hooker controversy.

So what gives all of a sudden? Is it just that the city's humidity makes it slower to adapt to change? Not really. The bottom line is that Miami, while definitely a late bloomer, is maturing thanks to the fact that the people who settled into the city in the late '80s and early '90s – drawn by the exploding nightlife scene, Madonna sightings and high energy, hedonistic lifestyle – are a bit older now and looking not necessarily to settle down, but perhaps to slow down with a brand of sophistication not found inside the velvet ropes. Whether we like it or not, the city's growing up – and so are we.

IN THE MIX

One of the things residents of all stripes tend to appreciate (or abhor) is that Miami will never be anything like any other US city. The fact is,

Miami is and will always be as much (or more) a part of the Caribbean and Latin America as it is a part of the United States. Or, as local Miami boosters like to say, the nice part about living in Miami is how close it is to the United States.

To comprehend what makes Miami so very different from other American cities, one has to understand what real 'multiculturalism' is. The term has been devalued through constant use in political soundbites calculatingly deployed to target minority votes. Miami's civic leaders also like to toss around the terms 'diversity' and 'multiculturalism', the difference being that here they really mean something. Diversity is not a goal in Miami, it's a long-term fact of life. According to George Wilson, a University of Miami sociologist whose area of study includes the development of immigrant populations, Miami has the most diverse population in the US. It's made up of approximately 66 per cent Hispanic and 20 per cent each black and Anglo. Even these figures fail to recognise the extent of the mix, since Hispanics are lumped into one group despite great ethnic differences; hop into a taxi and your Latino driver could be Cuban, Colombian, Chilean, Haitian, Honduran, Puerto Rican, Nicaraguan or Venezuelan.

Miami wasn't always rainbow-coloured. Well into the mid 20th century, it was little different from many other southern American cities. There were some black islanders from the Caribbean but they had little engagement with the overwhelmingly white leaders. The change came when Castro seized power in Cuba in 1959, and hundreds of thousands fled the island to make Miami their home – and the de facto capital of exiled Cubans. But these immigrants did not follow the pattern of virtually every other group of 'new Americans'. Prosperity was not a generation or two away. By conducting commerce among themselves and adhering to the particular Cuban appreciation of education and work ethics, Miami's Cuban-Americans became a power to be reckoned with almost immediately – today they remain the dominant political and social force in the city.

The Latinisation of Miami didn't go down well with the southern white politicians. Nor was the old power structure thrilled when the city's rep as a haven for immigrants began to attract other new arrivals. In the 1980s and '90s, the largest group of new arrivals was Haitian, while in the run-up to Great Britain's handover of Hong Kong, the soon-to-be-Chinese island's wealthy residents came purchasing property in Miami as a bolt hole should things turn nasty post-regime change. Since the collapse of the Soviet Union, a sizeable Russian presence has emerged in northern Miami Beach, and, most recently, economic disaster in South America,

Hangin' on South Beach.

particularly Argentina, has further swollen and added even greater diversity to Latin Miami. Should New York ever tire of its famed Statue of Liberty and her 'Bring me your huddled masses' exhortation, there's a strong case to be made for shipping the big lady down to Biscayne Bay.

PUTTING IT TOGETHER

Those naysaying white politicians with their jitters about immigration did have a point. Taking a sleepy southern town and adding an epic influx of immigrants from across the Americas – and much of the rest of the world – was never going to be easy. Devoid of any real form of industry and founded in large part on land scams and similar foolishness, Miami struggled to absorb the massive number of newcomers. Crime in the 1980s was rampant, the city was broke in all senses of the word, and the friction between the newly arrived and unsettled elements regularly sparked into riots and resulting racial isolation.

The troubles started to abate when the city's economy began to turn around – slowly at first, and then at breakneck speed. Miami became the centre of a booming import-export business, a hub of international banking and the meeting point for hemisphere businesses as the capital

of Latin America and the Caribbean. City fathers tried to obscure the truth, but as much as planning and good luck helped Miami turn around, so too did the drugs trade. The cocaine boom of the 1980s washed up millions and millions of illicit dollars in Miami. To call the new Miami 'the city that drug money built' would not be far from the truth.

In the longer term, however, it is tourism that has ultimately proved to be the engine powering the city's economic regeneration. Once again, city fathers tend to take the credit, but the boom that made Miami was actually the result of a television series – itself inspired by drugs and crime. When Michael Mann's *Miami Vice* introduced the world to the flamingo-pink sunsets, topaz-blue waterfront, salsa-tinged heartbeat and candy-coloured architecture, it would forever change the face of the city. Overnight the place was reinvented as exotic, seedy and oh-so-hip. The brazen cocaine cartels, periodic SWAT raids and shoot-outs on the street only added to the allure.

With the trail blazed by *Miami Vice*, Hollywood and the fashion industry woke up to the city's palm-fringed, white powder-tinged allure, and Miami became the nation's winter modelling and entertainment capital. Celebrities ranging from Madonna to Sly Stallone to Oprah

Ocean drive

Rent an Alamo car in Florida and as **Time Out readers**, you'll enjoy up to **20% discount** on our fully inclusive rates. Plus, we're offering free additional driver cover, **saving you up to $49** per week, per driver.

With a great choice of cars including convertibles and SUVs, at locations throughout Florida, we've got it covered.

So just book it, relax and enjoy the drive.

Click on the latest deals at
www.alamo.co.uk/offer/timeout
or call **0870 400 4565** quoting TIMEOUT

Up to 20% Time Out discount

Cel-ebb and flow

Paris Hilton.

While the Miami club scene still thrives at places like Opium, Privé, Mansion and Space, a kinder, gentler brand of boozy sophistication can be found in hotel lounges and restaurants, where the theme of cocktail conversations have matured from 'Where are you going after this?' to 'Where are you buying after this?', referencing the inevitable, explosive condo boom taking place in 21st-century Miami.

While Los Angeles and New York still reign supreme in the celeb stakes, Miami has become a haven for stars and starlets who consider the city a working holiday, and now, thanks to the ubiquitous trend of condo hotels, a home away from home. *Scarface* and *Miami Vice* may have kick-started the celeb movement, but as the South Beach renaissance revved into high gear in the

'90s, LA-based location scouts started looking south, using Miami as the backlot for what were mostly mediocre to downright awful films. But, boy, didn't they look good. And bad or not, the filming still brought the stars to town, especially when Madonna staked her claim on a Coconut Grove waterfront manse, creating a paparazzi frenzy that hadn't been seen in the city since the Mariel Boatlift. Like a fabulati magnet, Madge attracted everyone to town, including Prince, Will Smith, John Travolta, Oprah Winfrey, Rosie O'Donnell, Jack Nicholson, Harrison Ford and so on and so on.

Whereas pink or orange may be the new black, lounges and restaurants are the new clubs – at least for the population who has been there and done that already. Places like the Setai, the extravagant Asian-flaired hotel and condo, where drinks cost upwards of $25 a pop, is packed with a motley mix of ageing socialites, young professionals, hipsters and celebrities of the George Hamilton ilk. Over at the Sagamore hotel's Social Miami, you're likely to run into a Fortune 500 CEO sipping cocktails next to a Hilton sister while waiting for Beyoncé and Jay-Z to vacate their table at Nobu. We could go on rolling out an exhaustive string of names, but it's undoubtedly more entertaining to experience your own brief celebrity encounter, a distinct possibility in this town.

The greatest number of celebrity sightings are to be had at the aforementioned hotspots and all over South Beach (*see p62* **Celebrity stares**). Other celebs keep a low profile, and will be hard to find. Ricky Martin has been spied, appropriately enough, hanging in Little Havana, while Bill Clinton occasionally indulges in fore-play on the greens at the Biltmore Hotel in Coral Gables. Sometimes celebs pop up where you least expect: Yoko Ono at Club Space in Downtown was a good one.

But there's nothing better than spying a celebrity at a party hawking the latest zillion-dollar condo. That's all the rage these days. These are extravagant, elaborate soirées designed to attract potential buyers into the market everyone's so afraid will burst. When actor Hugh Jackman attended one of these parties, he had no idea he was supposed to bring his chequebook. 'Maybe the developer will give me a discount,' he laughed. Well, maybe, just maybe.

Winfrey and (seemingly) half the Arab royalty of the Middle East came calling, with all the attendant lights, cameras and action. Madge and co may have moved on, but the glamour stuck, and Miami remains celeb city; *see p25* **Cel-ebb and flow**. And, of course, enter *Miami Vice* the movie in 2006, focusing attention once again on this city of movers, shakers and the sexcapades of Colin Farrell. In fact, today the city has never been more glamorous, the object of affection of moguls, jet-setters and pretty much everyone who matters to those who pay attention to that sort of thing.

This economic turnaround has resulted in the end of the old Miami era. All vestiges of the sleepy southern town were wiped away. In its place was something completely new and different. Prosperity turned out to be a very effective salve for the wounds incurred by unprecedented population shift.

> **'Tourism has climbed again, helped by the growth of domestic travel as Americans avoid the terror that is "abroad".'**

FUTURE PERFECT?

Challenges remain. Despite the surge at the end of the 20th century, the City of Miami remains the poorest urban region in the United States. The national economic downturn from early 2000 to mid 2003 hurt, and the collapse of the high-tech/internet industry struck a particular blow to a south Florida that was well on the way to justifying its catchy new moniker of 'Cyber Beach'.

And then there was the terrorist strike of 11 September 2001. It may have targeted New York, but the outpouring of emotion swelled all the way down to southern Florida where, for the first time since perhaps World War II, it served to unite all the diverse communities. Haitian children stood in their front yards waving American flags. Spanish-language radio let Miami's largest community vent its hurt and anger. Historians might reflect back on south Florida history and point to this tragic event far to the north as the moment things ironically, even perversely, began to turn around; a diverse, fractioned community came together to gain a combined strength that might well have been the impetus for political reform and ethnic détente.

Still, the World Trade Center attack cost Miami financially, perhaps more so than any other US city outside New York. Tourism

stopped dead. It has climbed again since, helped by the growth of domestic travel as Americans avoid the terror that is 'abroad'.

Indeed, at this point, tourism has been surpassed as the driving force of the new Miami economy. Real estate and building have taken over. Development in the City of Miami proper – particularly in the Downtown area, along the Miami River and an area now dubbed Midtown, north of Downtown – has exploded. Forward-thinking developers are racing to cater for a new-found demand for luxury condo units and other housing in and around Miami's urban core; *see p79* **Downtown top ranking**. These developments represent the most significant trend in Miami today and likely hold the future of the city and its economic well-being.

The result of the economic turnaround was the end of the old Miami era. All vestiges of the sleepy southern town were wiped away. In its place was something completely new and different. Prosperity turned out to be a very effective salve for the wounds incurred by unprecedented population shift.

And what of all that vice that made the city so famous? Well, crime in Miami is far removed from the pastel-suited cocaine cowboys of the 1980s. But just because it is not as hip to be crime-ridden does not mean it doesn't exist. Major initiatives by local police departments have helped the Beach better safeguard visitors, while on the mainland they've done a remarkably good job of making areas such as Biscayne Boulevard – once a strip of cheap flophouses and crack dens – safe for the public. There had been a strong trend for residents to flee South Beach prices and move into Downtown, with businesses and services following close behind. In neighbourhoods like the Design District and Wynwood, once characterised by visible poverty and despair, there are now boutique shops, antiques dealers, gourmet food markets and stylish restaurants.

By comparison with what has already gone before, the challenges facing Miami these days don't seem particularly daunting. Been there, done it, outgrown the T-shirt. As headlines in the US media declare that over the next 50 years ethnic Americans will exceed the number of American-born Anglos, Miami offers a collective shrug, as this is already the case here and has been for years. So, those challenges America frets over having to meet in the years to come have already been met here in south Florida. More than anything else, this qualifies Miami as either the cutting-edge model American city for the 21st century, or a post-modern urban poster child warning for other less diverse American cities.

Playing dominoes in **Little Havana**.

Latin Miami

The Cubans – and Mexicans, and Argentinians, and Venezuelans and Brazilians – are coming.

Walk into any store or restaurant in Miami and you're more likely to be greeted with '*buenas tardes*' than 'good afternoon'. Seventy-five per cent of the city's residents speak a foreign language, usually Spanish. No wonder Miami is often referred to as 'the Capital of the Americas', a title the city's Hispanic officials bandy about with pride.

While Miami is best known as the exile home for Cubans, it is actually pan-Latin, with citizens from many other Latin American countries contributing to the Spanish-speaking mix. Similar to the Cubans, who for over 40 years have sought refuge here from political and economic circumstances on their native island, other immigrants come to Miami to escape problems at home.

From a general point of view, the city's population reflects the state of play to the south. Migrant workers from Mexico, Guatemala and El Salvador have found work in the fields of southern Dade County for decades. In recent years the city has seen an increase in its Argentinian population, as the economy there foundered. Colombians now make up one of the largest Hispanic groups, having fled decades-

long turmoil, while affluent Venezuelans have come in large numbers since leftist President Hugo Chávez took office. And a steady stream of Brazilians continues to arrive, looking for an alternative to the economic and social woes in their country. Peruvians and Nicaraguans also have long-established communities in Miami.

But the city's Latin cultures do not mix easily. Immigrants from each country tend to stake out their own turf: in addition to Little Havana, there is now a Little Buenos Aires in Miami Beach, and a few blocks away is Little Brazil. With so many different Spanish accents and dialects being spoken, Miami often feels more like a Tower of Babel than a melting pot.

LITTLE CUBA

Despite all this, the Cubans hold the longest claim to Miami and still make up the majority of its Spanish-speaking residents. The first large influx of immigrants from the island arrived soon after Fidel Castro took power on New Year's Day 1959. Twice-daily freedom flights began bringing thousands of Cubans to Miami; by the time they ended in 1973, the city's Cuban population had reached 300,000.

Meat and greet

One big, fat, juicy benefit from all the recent Latin immigration: the proliferation of the Argentinian steak. Actually, the steak is just one part of the *parrillada*, which means mixed grill but is also what many people call any Argentinian grill joint.

In Argentina beef is king, and steaks are the crown. The strip, skirt, New York or flat steaks – huge portions of which are marinated and then thrown on the grill – are the culinary achievement of these *parrilladas*. They are usually more thinly cut than their American counterpart, and quite tender; sometimes the slab is so big it's folded over to fit on the plate. Traditionally, Argentinian cows graze only on grasses, and their meat is far leaner, giving the steaks a superior flavour. But in reality it will turn out to be the style of cooking rather than the origin of the meat that you will taste, as most of it comes from the US.

Unlike a classic North American steakhouse, these *parrilladas* are usually small, family-run, neighbourhood-oriented eateries – and they have popped up on every other corner in Miami. And although prices have risen somewhat with the *parrillada*'s popularity, these are still some of the most affordable meals in town – and never skimpy.

First, don't plan your trip to a *parrillada* a half-hour before your movie. In true Latin style, your meal should take a little longer (and it may do anyhow, against your wishes). It usually starts with a bottle of house red wine (some places don't even offer white). Argentinian wines have taken off as well in recent years, and are still inexpensive.

Then, enjoy some *empanada* appetisers, those little pastries usually filled with meat, cheese or spinach. They are sometimes just an excuse to have something to dip into the delicious green *chimichurri* (chilli and herb sauce), which includes lots of garlic, chillies, olive oil, parsley and coriander, and which accompany the later meats as well. Or try the grilled cheese (once in a while even a vegetarian can score in a *parrillada*).

Meanwhile, the tables around you will start to fill up with large groups of families or friends, who are likely to be there long after you're gone. If sitting outside, the music will be turned up; if inside, the TV screen will be blaring, as an all-important Argentinian *fútbol* game will be on (maybe even between intense rivals Boca Juniors and River Plate), or failing that, Latin music videos. There's often a party-like atmosphere, as Argentinians find a homely place far from home.

Aside from the steak, there's the mixed grill plate itself, which can include chorizo, pork, chicken, ribs and all those organ delicacies. Most menus also feature some pasta dishes, as Argentinian culture has been profoundly influenced by its huge Italian immigration. Which means that, all the wine bottles empty, it's time to top it all off with an espresso.

Here are some helpful *parrillada* phrases:
Carne: meat (in this case, beef)
Mollejas: sweetbreads
Riñones: kidneys
Vino tinto: red wine
No más, por favor: no more, thanks – that was almost a whole cow

---

These new arrivals had made up Cuba's society class before the Revolution, when their land and businesses were confiscated by the communist government. The upper-class refugees had already travelled frequently to the States for study, vacation or business, and they tended to speak fine English. They quickly set about making their fortunes in Miami.

In 1980 the Mariel Boatlift brought a further 125,000 political émigrés to south Florida. These Cubans were quite different from the founders of Miami's Cuban community. They came with little means, and possibly as many as 25,000 were ex-cons and mental patients who Castro had spitefully released to sail on the refugee boats to America. Some of those so-called mental patients were homosexuals, who fled in large numbers during the boatlift. One of

Cuba's leading writers, Reinaldo Arenas, was part of the exodus: in 2000 his great memoir *Before Night Falls* was made into a hit movie starring Javier Bardem.

The newly arrived Cubans did not adapt quickly to their new life, nor did they start building for the future. At first they simply struggled to survive (one example of that struggle is in the film *Scarface*, in which the Al Pacino character, Tony Montana, is a Marielito).

In 1994 Miami again took in thousands of Cubans who rafted their way to south Florida's shore; many more drowned in the attempt. Cuban-born, Miami-bred playwright Nilo Cruz told a lyrical and moving account of three such *balseros* in his play *A Bicycle Country* (1999). A few years later, in October 2002, Cruz's Pulitzer Prize-winning play *Anna in the Tropics* debuted at the New Theatre in Coral Gables. The rafters' exodus focused international attention on Cuba; it also changed the face of Miami's Cuban community, since many of these refugees were black. For the first time, a large black Cuban community in Miami was formed, centred in the working-class neighbourhood of Allapattah. It is significant to note that, as in Cuba in the 1950s, the majority of black Cubans in Miami live at a remove from the more well-to-do 'white' Cubans.

Yet for all the tensions that these later immigrations initially created, Miami's cultural community only prospered – they now make up many of the leading lights in music, the visual arts and dance.

'New visa requirements have almost put an end to Cuban concert tours in Miami.'

Cuba may only be 90 miles from Key West, but until the 1990s few exiles ever went back. Instead, they maintained links to the homeland in nostalgic trips to Miami's many Cuban restaurants and stores stocked with artefacts and ephemera relating to the glamorous lives left behind. The US embargo against Cuba forbids Americans from spending money on the island and, by extension, travel there is not permitted. But by the early '90s both the Cuban and American governments had allowed several charter companies to operate flights between Miami and Havana (as well as New York and Havana). After the fall of the Soviet Union, Cuba was left without financial support, and officials were eager for American dollars to boost the island's miserable economy (although the dollar is now once again banned there).

While some exiles still refuse to return to Cuba while Castro is in power, many others have made regular trips there over the last decade. Thousands of other Americans travelled to Cuba, taking advantage of the Clinton administration's support of cultural exchange as a means of détente between the two countries.

Not everyone was happy about this new cultural freedom, however. Conservative exile groups consider anyone who lives in Cuba – from government officials to trumpet players – to be a 'soldier of Castro'. The exile experience has often been characterised by extremism, and sometimes violence. In 1999 police in riot gear were called in to control thousands of exile demonstrators at a concert by the popular Cuban dance band Los Van Van. The conflict made headlines around the world, but in Miami it was just one more episode in the city's long history of intolerance against anyone perceived to sympathise with the Castro regime.

BUSH'S BACKLASH

The artistic flow between Miami and Havana proved to be only a cultural Camelot, a brief but shining moment for Cuban culture and co-operation. After 9/11 the Bush administration classified Cuba as a terrorist country, viewing its citizens as potential threats until proven otherwise. New, stringent visa requirements have almost put an end to Cuban concert tours and other performing arts events in Miami and all over the United States.

The Bush administration has also clamped down on Americans travelling to Cuba. Travel agencies that organised group tours to events such as the Havana Art Biennial and the Havana International Jazz Festival have had their licences revoked. Journalists and academic researchers, as well as anyone with relatives in Cuba, though even the latter are now allowed to go back only once every three years, for a maximum of two weeks.

But the historic breakthroughs made in the '90s have made a lasting impression in Miami. A wide selection of albums recorded in Cuba are still commonly sold here, films from Cuba are screened regularly, and galleries often feature work by Cubans living on the island.

Miami has become a more tolerant place, in large part because its population has changed. Younger generations of Cuban-Americans – removed from the pain of exile felt by their parents and grandparents – embrace Cuban culture from both sides of the Straits. Recent immigrants from Cuba, who include musicians, artists and intellectuals, have brought a vision of the Cuban experience that significantly differs from that of the Cuban-Americans.

And the rest of the city's Latin population, largely drawn from countries formerly under right-wing dictatorships, either admires the contemporary Cuban system or simply doesn't understand what all the fuss is about. Though it would seem impossible to most Cubans, some people are not interested in Cuban culture.

With multinational banking, Spanish-language TV channels and magazines, record labels and other companies setting up headquarters here, Miami looks much further than across the water to Cuba. Cable channels like MTV Latin America, along with ad agencies and Spanish-language internet companies, have brought a mass of young, creative South American professionals with plenty of style.

Just stroll down South Beach's Lincoln Road to feel today's hip Latin metropolis. You'll see the typical mix of fashionistas, executives, young families, and probably a few pregnant women in midriff-bearing tops, all moving to the unhurried, tropical rhythm of the city, accompanied by a symphony of Spanish conversation.

Edna Buchanan – she means business. *See p31.*

Miami Crime Lit

A weird and wonderful bunch, Miami's penmen are perfectly suited to capture the craziness of south Florida.

New York boasts Paul Auster, Brett Easton Ellis, Jonathan Lethem, Jay McInerney and Tom Wolfe. San Francisco has Ethan Canin, Michael Chabon, Dave Eggers, Armistead Maupin and Amy Tan. And Miami? Try Edna Buchanan, James W Hall, Carl Hiaasen, John D MacDonald and Charles Willeford. If none of these names raises a glimmer of recognition, that's hardly surprising. Aside from Carl Hiaasen, whose books regularly feature on the bestseller lists, these are writers who rarely, if ever, trouble the literary pages of the world's newspapers and journals. It's not that their work isn't deserving of attention (on the contrary, it's read plenty out in the studio lots of LA, where books by Buchanan, Hiaasen, MacDonald and Willeford have all been made into movies), it's just that there's a certain literary prejudice against the kind of fiction they write: genre fiction, or – to be more specific – crime fiction.

Crime writing is Miami's greatest contribution to the American literary scene. There's no doubt that these days Miami

supports more crime, thriller and mystery writers per capita than any other US city, yet the genre didn't begin here. The greatest early exponents of the field, Raymond Chandler and Dashiell Hammet, were both southern Californian writers who had their gumshoes treading leather and trading bruises in the canyons round Los Angeles and valleys of San Francisco. But over the last three decades, no city has done crime writing as well as Miami. The reasons for this aren't hard to fathom: over the last three decades no city has done crime as well as Miami.

Since the 1970s the city has virtually made an art of murder. Its recent history is as a late 20th-century frontier town with an explosive mix of immigrants from all 50 states and the whole of Latin America. The resulting violent racism, political unrest, drug trafficking and organised crime, combined with the hedonistic lifestyle of the wealthy and the desperate needs of the poor, make for a volatile mix. Add semi-tropical heat, step back and wait for it to explode.

Whenever it did explode, more often than not first on the scene to witness the aftermath was a big-haired, fast-talking lady named **Edna Buchanan**. A native of New Jersey but a life-long convert to the charms of south Florida, Buchanan spent most of her working career covering the crime beat for the *Miami Herald*, winning a Pulitzer Prize along the way. Her autobiographical account of those years, *The Corpse Had a Familiar Face*, makes for lurid and sensational reading. The Haitian who was knitted to death in a Hialeah factory. The father who murdered his comatose daughter in her hospital bed. The naked man who threw his girlfriend's severed head at a young cop – who threw it back. During Buchanan's time on the paper, Miami broke all prior records for violence, and in 1980-81 its murder rate skyrocketed to number one in the nation. Killings in one particular nightclub became such a regular fixture that staff just dumped the bodies out in the parking lot with the trash. Police beatings set off riots that burned whole city neighbour-hoods. Bodies were stacked so high at the city's Jackson Memorial Hospital morgue that the authorities had to rent a refrigerated trailer from Burger King to cope with the overflow.

'What appears to be political farce often turns out to be grounded in political fact.'

Since quitting the newsroom in the late '80s, Buchanan has taken up mystery writing, penning a series of novels starring Britt Montero, who is – what else? – a spunky lady crime reporter. The trouble is, Buchanan's fiction can't begin to compete with the reality.

Perhaps no crime in Miami history better represents the city's turbulent times than the one that screamed across headlines worldwide on 11 April 1986. That morning, FBI agents were staking out a traffic corridor off US 1 in tony Pinecrest, looking for a gang of robbers who had been terrorising the area's banks. Spotting the suspects driving by, the agents forced them to stop, but the thieves came out firing. For several minutes, a high-intensity shootout erupted at the intersection of SW 183rd Street and SW 22nd Avenue, just feet from south Miami's major artery. Hundreds of rounds of ammunition were expended on both sides. Despite being badly wounded, the two bandits staggered up to FBI special agents Jerry Dove and Benjamin Grogan and callously executed them at close range.

With that kind of communal exchange going on in the 'burbs, most sane people's reaction

would be '*adiós*'. But when, shortly before his death in 1988, **Charles Willeford** was asked by the *Miami Herald* why he preferred to live in Miami, the answer he gave was 'because of the high crime rate'. Willeford was the writer who launched the modern era of Miami crime fiction. Although it was another writer, **John D MacDonald** (remembered now, if at all, for writing the novel that was later filmed – twice – as *Cape Fear*), who had put the city on the mystery map far earlier with his Travis McGee books, that was in the 1960s, when it was an older, sleepier south Florida. Willeford sparked off the whole weird crime thing with his own peculiar brand of what isn't so much hard-boiled fiction as just crotchety. A former flea circus barker, professional boxer, soft-porn writer and decorated tank commander, he had a way with titles (*The Burnt Orange Heresy*; *The Shark-Infested Custard*), although his breakthrough came with something called simply *Miami Blues* – his publishers choosing the title in the hope of getting a free ride on the coat tails of hit TV show *Miami Vice*. Published in 1984, this and the three subsequent novels in the series featured a cop with ill-fitting false teeth and a poor dress sense named Hoke Moseley adrift in a Miami in transition. 'Miami Blues launched the modern era of crime fiction,' says Mitch Kaplan, owner of Miami's popular trio of independent bookstores, Books & Books. Willeford was big on absurdities. In the opening scene of *Miami Blues* (filmed in 1990 with Alec Baldwin), Freddy Frenger, a haiku-writing psychopath, wards off a Hare Krishna at Miami Airport by casually breaking his finger; the Krishna collapses in shock and dies of a heart attack. The hard-living Willeford himself died of a heart attack, although in his case it was largely brought on by heavy drinking and smoking.

If Charles Willeford pioneered a particularly skewed Miami take on crime writing, it was sold to the mainstream by **Carl Hiaasen**. Another former *Miami Herald* crime reporter, now its star columnist, Hiaasen has what has been described as a 'gleefully wicked mind'. A twisted Mark Twain, he writes satires that paint the Sunshine State as a paradise screwed (which is, incidentally, the title of a volume of his collected *Herald* columns). The screwing in his view has been done by a toxic mix of rapacious developers, hand-in-the-till councillors, craven administration and toss-the-trash-out-the-window tourists. For Hiaasen, who these days lives in the Keys, writing is a way of getting his own back at what he sees as the devastation of south Florida's natural environment. He's an author who will write about a blue-rinse retiree getting eaten by a crocodile and have you rooting for the crocodile. In May 2006 the big-screen version of Hiaasen's *Hoot*, an entertaining piece of crime fiction aimed at an adolescent audience, was released. Producers included Jimmy Buffett, and the film was shot in Fort Lauderdale: clearly Hiaasen likes to keep his stuff in the South Florida family.

Fellow author **James W Hall**, originally from Kentucky but a long-time resident of south Florida, began his thriller writing (with 1986's *Under Cover of Daylight*) in the same vein as Hiaasen, mixing conservation battles with ruthless semi-competent hitmen and a healthy dose of thinly disguised authorial outrage at the destruction and desecration he saw around him. However, over the course of ten or so books, Hall has mellowed and his thrillers are now more straightforward tales of local psychos on the loose. But Hall doesn't come close to Hiaasen when it comes to upping the ante on the wackos. The hitman in Hiaasen's 1989's *Skin Tight*, for example, is a six-foot-nine victim of plastic surgery gone wrong left with a face that looks like it's covered in Rice Crispies. He also has a rotor-stripper attached to the stump of his right hand.

But what appears in his fiction to be political farce often turns out to be grounded in political fact. Hiaasen admits that much of what seems like the product of a warped imagination comes right out of the newspapers. 'Florida is kind of the superkingdom for bad behaviour and, frankly, it's hard for a novelist to stay ahead of the weirdness curve. There are times when I've written something that I think is about as sick as it gets and the next day in the *Miami Herald* there's a headline that just makes me weep that I didn't think of it first.'

Hiaasen, in common with many other crime writers, is one of the most astute chroniclers of America today and, for any visitor to south Florida, any novel by him makes for a first-class primer. In fact, his first novel, *Tourist Season* (1986), was named by *GQ* magazine as 'one of the ten best destination reads of all time'. Hiaasen, though, would disagree: he's on record as saying that the best book ever written about Miami, or more specifically, South Beach, is *La Brava* by **Elmore Leonard**.

You may have heard of Leonard. According to online magazine *Salon*, he's the 'world's coolest crime writer'. Even people who don't read have heard of Leonard, thanks to a string of highly successful movies, including *Get Shorty* (1995), *Jackie Brown* (1997) and *Out of Sight* (1998), all adapted (quite faithfully, as it happens) from his books. Unlike the writers already mentioned, who, if not Miami-born and bred at least have called the city home, Leonard has lived in the northern state of Michigan for most of his life. His first crime novels (he wrote

westerns early in his career) were set in and around Detroit. Yet, like so many Americans, he grew up holidaying down south. He was quick to see the potential in the freakiness of south Florida and spread some of the action of 1980s *Gold Coast* down to Fort Lauderdale. He followed up with a string of novels all utilising Sunshine State locales. His breakthrough came with *Stick* (1983), which assembled the combination that caught the public's attention of Miami, Marielitos, movies and drugs. Leonard's characters are supremely suited to Miami life. The people on the side of the law (cops, judges, lawyers) are frequently dirty themselves, while the criminals are often smart talkers full of bullshit and charm – John Travolta's hustling enforcer Chili Palmer in *Get Shorty* is a classic Leonard character and, at the same time, the kind of guy you might run into twice a day lounging behind shades at the News Café on Ocean Drive.

Leonard's research – which he pays somebody to do for him – is meticulous. Characters drop by Wolfie's deli on North Beach for takeout Jell-O; they lunch on claws at Joe's Stone Crab in South Beach; they size up prey from the front porch of Ocean Drive's Cardozo Hotel. You can read Leonard with a map of Miami spread open, plotting the course of the action.

If it seems odd that the best-known practitioner of Miami crime lit has never lived in the city, consider this: the best-known Miami thriller writer has never written about Miami. **Thomas Harris**, the man who has scared the bejesus out of millions courtesy of his fictional creation Hannibal Lecter (presented to the public in the novels *Red Dragon*, *The Silence of the Lambs* and *Hannibal*), is a resident of the exclusive enclave of Golden Beach, the northernmost community on Miami Beach. Harris is a permanent fixture on the South Beach A-list, sporting his trademark straw hat and a beard that may disguise his inner demons. We have a theory about why he's never set any of his writing in the weirder-than-fiction city in which he lives, which is that if dear old Hannibal were to venture down to the South Beach of Willeford, Hiaasen, Leonard, et al, the freaks down there would eat him alive.

It's no shock that some experts even consider crime lit Miami's only real genre of fiction. 'Right now this is a wide-open, wild and woolly town. Anybody who's writing about this place and who we are would rightfully be talking about crime and punishment,' said Les Standiford, author of several Miami crime lit books including *Raw Deal* and *Deal with the Dead*. 'Imagine trying to put out *New Times* every week in Kansas City – what the hell would you be writing about?' Scary, but true.

Where to Stay

Where to Stay

As they say, the winters get you to Miami, but the hotels get you to stay.

In Miami, to say 'you are where you stay' would be the understatement of the century. Especially since more and more hotels in the city are turning into condo-hotels and making permanent residents out of their guests (*see p52* **Room service!**). More stock is put into a hotel's name, reputation, services and amenities than a banker's portfolio, and the competition among Miami hotels fighting for your money is legendary. On the constant stream of press releases, not a single word is missed to communicate that a hotel has a more manicured lawn, shimmering infinity pool, relaxing rooftop spa, privileged beach access, celeb-filled bar, name-chef restaurant, whim-catering amenities or art-laden lobby than its adversary. Hoping to be the place that puts everyone from dignitaries to Mr & Mrs Beckham on their VIP list, a hotel opening (or reopening) is met with more press and fanfare than a World Cup football final.

Just look at the crop of the city's rookie hotels, such as the new **Standard** (*see p38*), **Sanctuary** (*see p43*) or **Setai** (*see p37*). All tout luxurious spas, sparkling pools, A-list celebrities and plenty more of those amenities we just mentioned – and they deliver. But the lower end of the market has some choice offerings too: the old Vagabond motel on Biscayne Boulevard is being brought back to life – with the help of $4 million – by two Cuban brothers aiming to restore it to its 1950s glory, along with flat-screen TVs and other modern amenities designed to attract the area's newly gentrified young hipsters.

Unless you are in town for Art Basel (*see p175*) or the Miami Wine & Food Festival (*see p128* **Whining and dining**), you'll be spending most of your time lounging, lazing and lolling, quite possibly in or around your hotel. More than in perhaps any other US city, your choice of lodgings can make or break a stay. So when it comes to accommodation, this is a place to go for bust: book into the choicest you can afford and then make sure you wear the hell out of that complimentary bathrobe, scarf all the bar snacks and never leave the restaurant without a doggy bag.

LOCATION
Without question, where you want to be is among the palms and deco of South Beach. Preferably, it should be Ocean Drive or Collins Avenue, although Washington will do at a push, and it should be between 5th Street and 20th. Go north of 20th Street, especially up on Mid Beach and North Beach, and it all starts to go a bit quiet. This may be what you prefer. However, a car is necessary to get around, especially since the fledgling Design and Performing Arts Districts across the causeway are worthy of the reputations they have quickly inherited. Granted, you still need a very good reason to justify staying over on the mainland, in **Downtown**, **Coral Gables** or **Coconut**

The best Hotels

For channelling your outermost hedonist
The **Standard**. *See p38.*

For escaping the fray
Miami River Inn. *See p53.*

For recharging your batteries
Grove Isle Hotel & Spa. *See p54.*

For going topless
The **Shore Club**. *See p38.*

For going incognito
The **Delano**. *See p35.*

For going broke
The **Setai**. *See p37.*

For the inspired artiste
Sagamore. *See p37.*

For your other personality
Pelican. *See p43.*

For fore play
The **Biltmore**. *See p53.*

For sand in the city
The **Mandarin Oriental Miami**. *See p53.*

---

❶ Green numbers given in this chapter correspond to the location of each hotel on the street maps. *See pp272-277.*

The **Raleigh**. *See p37*.

Grove. Some of the hotels are grand (we're thinking the **Four Seasons**, *see p52*, the **Mandarin Oriental**, *see p53*, and, of course, the **Biltmore**, *see p53*), but they are a long way from anywhere. These are primarily business and conference venues.

The one drawback to South Beach is that it contains far too many cars and far too few parking spaces. If valet parking is available at your hotel, use it and swallow the often-obscene cost and the eternal waiting line. Rates are for the day, so you can come and go as you please, saving you from having to feed a meter. The alternative option for the more budget-conscious and impatient: ask your concierge if they sell Miami Beach Parking Cards. Most parking meters now take reusable and refundable parking meter cards that actually refund time not spent on the meter back to your card. Finally, it might just be easier to do away with the car altogether. A cab ride from Miami International Airport to most of the hotels on South Beach will cost you, on average, about $30, and a pair of comfy flip flops (Burberry, natch) should get you everywhere you need to go in South Beach.

PRICES
Rates for rooms in Miami and Miami Beach hotels vary wildly. Peak season, which runs from November to the end of April, is the most expensive. Prices are often sneakily hiked up for happenings like Art Basel or the Boat Show (*see p163*).

Hotels in this chapter have been organised by area and price, based on the price of a double room or equivalent during peak season. We have tried to be as specific as possible, but, again, rates vary hugely depending on type of room and time of year. Remember: these are the rack (official) rates quoted by the hotels during peak season. At other times you can pay considerably less, for instance, during the summer, when prices may be reduced by as much as 50 per cent. It's also worth checking out websites such as Expedia and Lastminute for late bargains. Bear in mind that the rates we quote were correct at the time of going to press, but hotels can, and will, change them at any time. Also, note that the rates below do not include sales tax, which adds another budget-busting 13 per cent to the bill.

The Beaches

South Beach

Deluxe

Delano
1685 Collins Avenue, at 17th Street (reservations 1-800 697 1791/front desk 305 672 2000/fax 305 532 0099/www.delano-hotel.com). Bus C, G, H, L, M, S. **Rates** $300-$1,000 single/double; $500-$1,600 suite; $950-$3,500 bungalow. **Credit** AmEx, DC, Disc, MC, V. **Map** p273 A3 ❶

Though no longer topping everyone's A-list in the way that it so recently did, for our money the Delano remains the Mount Olympus of Miami Beach hotels. The lobby is a temple to cool Starck minimalism, with a procession of lofty portals hung with billowing gauzy white curtains. To the rear is the billiard table of the tiny house watering hole, the Rose Bar (*see p138* **Walk on**), alongside the Blue Door (*see p115*), the fabulous patio restaurant overlooking the Delano's coveted bungalows and palm-colonnaded infinity pool. It's a celestial setting for celestial bodies that – for as long as hip hotelier Ian Schrager remains at the helm – will continue to draw the celebs. Mere mortals should try bluffing their way to the bar. *Bars (2). Business centre. Concierge. Disabled-adapted rooms. Gym. Internet. No-smoking floors. Parking ($30/day). Pool (outdoor). Restaurants (2). Room service (24hrs). Spa. TV.*

Loews Miami Beach

1601 Collins Avenue, at 16th Street (reservations 1-800 235 6397/front desk 305 604 1601/fax 305 531 8677/www.loewshotels.com). Bus C, H, K, W, South Beach Local. **Rates** $289-$499 double; $550-$1,000 suite. **Credit** AmEx, DC, MC, V. **Map** p273 A3 ❷

South Beach's massive convention hotel is peppered with many a name-tagged conventioneer, but if you like big, it's got your name on it too: 800 rooms, including 57 suites featuring bay, city and ocean views. Its six restaurants and bars include Emeril's, where hot chef Emeril Lagassee flaunts his nouveau New Orleans cuisine. On top of that, there's a gigantic fitness centre, an oceanfront swimming pool and 20 butler-serviced cabanas, plus ballrooms and meeting rooms galore. But as huge as it is, the Loews hasn't obliterated every historic structure in its path. Attached to the property is the streamline Modern St Moritz Hotel, first designed in 1939 by architect Roy France and now restored to its former glory. *Bar. Beauty salon. Business centre. Concierge. Gym. Internet. No-smoking floor. Parking ($30/day). Pool (outdoor). Restaurants (2). Room service (24hrs). TV.*

Raleigh

1775 Collins Avenue, at 18th Street (reservations 1-800 848 1775/front desk 305 534 6300/fax 305 538 8140/www.raleighhotel.com). Bus C, G, H, L, M, S. **Rates** $295-$375 single/double; $650-$1,000 suite. **Credit** AmEx, DC, MC, V. **Map** p272 C3 ❸

Following a renovation a few years ago, the Raleigh is finally having its day in the sun. This 1940 L Murray Dixon-designed structure now boasts all mod cons, down to bedside buttons controlling everything from light to room temperature. Sleek furniture matches the new clientele – primarily fashion-industry types. The scalloped beachfront pool with DJs and lifeguards has maintained its Sunday night status as the place to be for hipsters ahead of the old-school alternatives like Nikki Beach Club. For a quieter time, head for the intimate terrace bar and sample what some claim to be the best Martini in town. **Photo** *p35.*

Bars (2). Business centre. Concierge. Disabled-adapted rooms. Gym. Internet. No-smoking rooms. Parking ($30/day). Pool (outdoor). Restaurant. Room service (24hrs). TV.

Ritz-Carlton South Beach

1 Lincoln Road, at Collins Avenue (786 276 4000/fax 786 276 4001/www.ritzcarlton.com). Bus C, G, H, L, M, S. **Rates** $319-$519 single/double; $479-$2,500 suite. **Credit** AmEx, DC, Disc, MC, V. **Map** p273 A3 ❹

This is not your grandfather's Ritz. The former deco landmark is a deluxe addition to South Beach and for a chain hotel it feels young, heck, even vibrant. A whopping $200 million was thrown into the restoration, and it shows: custom-designed contemporary Venetian glass and stainless-steel light fixtures, a curved wall of polished cherry wood, original black terrazzo floors: it's gorgeous. All the big pluses that you expect from any establishment bearing the name 'The Ritz' are here: exceptional service, comfortable yet elegant rooms and every possible amenity that you can think of. Added to which, that's Miami Beach right outside your room. If South Beach is too manic for your tastes and you prefer a more laid back, albeit luxurious, Caribbean-style escape, the Ritz-Carlton Key Biscayne (455 Grand Bay Drive, 305 365 4500) is a beachfront haven for the likes of Brad Pitt, John Travolta and anyone else who wants to escape the blinding bulbs of the South Beach paparazzi. *Bars. Business centre. Concierge. Disabled-adapted rooms. Gym. Internet. Parking ($25/day). Pool (outdoor). Restaurant. Room service (24hrs).*

Sagamore

1671 Collins Avenue, at 17th Street (305 535 8088/fax 305 535 8185/www.sagamorehotel.com). Bus C, G, H, L, M, S. **Rates** $215-$525 suite; $635-$1,050 bungalow. **Credit** AmEx, DC, Disc, MC, V. **Map** p273 A3 ❺

One of New York's finest hotels, 60 Thompson, has gone on vacation and landed in South Beach. With generously sized, apartment-like accommodations, the Sagamore houses a quietly hip crowd who could not care less about what's going on next door at Delano's pool. The hotel lobby doubles as a brilliant modern art gallery (including work by Danish-born artist Olafur Eliasson), while its newest addition is Social Miami, an artful eatery co-created by chefs Michelle Bernstein and Sean Mohamed (*see p109*). For maximum luxury, there are whirlpool bath/showers in every room, and an oceanfront infinity pool. *Bar. Business centre. Concierge. Disabled-adapted rooms. Internet. Parking ($30/day). Restaurants. Room service (24hrs). Spa. Pools (1 indoor, 1 outdoor). TV.*

Setai

2001 Collins Avenue, at 20th Street (305 520 6000/fax 305 520 6600/http://www.setai.com). Bus C, G, H, L, M, S. **Rates** $900-$1,100 single/double; $2,000-$6,000 suite. **Credit** AmEx, DC, Disc, MC, V. **Map** p272 C3 ❻

Take a ride in the elevator to the top floors of the Setai and you may very well find yourself stumbling into Lenny Kravitz's state-of-the-art music studio. Take a walk into the lobby and you may very well find yourself hob-nobbing with other celebrities, socialites and millionaires. The Setai is the most luxurious hotel to open in Miami in years. And, if you can get past the slightly self-indulgent $25 cocktails at the beachside bar, it's also one of the most beautiful and understated places to stay. The Asian-influenced hotel now stands in the shoes of the 1930s' Dempsey Vanderbilt Hotel. The rooms are simple, neat and elegant to the core, with expensive appliances and Asian-inspired decor. The huge bathrooms feature rainshower heads in the shower, as well as luxurious Acqua di Parma products. And if the price of that cocktail didn't scare you away, dining in the restaurant or Champagne, Crustacean and Caviar Bar is a must. **Photos** *p39.*
Bars. Beauty salon. Business centre. Concierge. Disabled-adapted rooms. Gym. Internet. No-smoking rooms. Parking ($30). Restaurants (2). Spa. Pools (3, outdoor). Room service (24hrs). TV.

The chain gang

Aside from the hotels listed elsewhere in this section, there are a great many chains present in the Miami area. Call their central numbers below or check their websites for exact locations.

Deluxe/expensive

Hilton 1-800 445 8667/www.hilton.com.
Sheraton 1-800 233 1234/www.hyatt.com.

Moderate

Holiday Inn 1-800 465 4329/ www.basshotels.com/holiday-inn.
Howard Johnson 1-800 654 2000/ www.hojo.com.
Marriott 1-800 228 9290/www.marriott.com.
Radisson 1-800 333 3333/www.radisson.com.

Budget

Best Western 1-800 528 1234/ www.bestwestern.com.
Comfort Inn 1-800 228 5150/ www.comfortinn.com.
Days Inn 1-800 325 2525/www.daysinn.com.
Motel 6 1-800 466 8356/www.motel6.com.
Super 8 1-800 800 8000/www.super8.com.
Travelodge 1-800 578 7878/ www.travelodge.com.

Shore Club

1901 Collins Avenue, at 19th Street (305 695 3100/ fax 305 695 3299/www.shoreclub.com). Bus C, G, H, L, M, S. **Rates** $345-$2,200 single/double/suite. **Credit** AmEx, DC, Disc, MC, V. **Map** p272 C3 ❼
The Shore Club is still hip, but thanks to the 2005 shooting of rap mogul Suge Knight there, it has, finally, got a bit of street cred too. The 325 spacious rooms and 75 astronomically priced suites have been given a fashionably minimalist but colourful makeover by Brit architect David Chipperfield. Those with the necessary lucre also have the option of the Beach House, a private oceanside bungalow with gated pool. Added swoon factor comes courtesy of the in-house restaurants – which include Robert de Niro's Nobu (*see p109* – and the Sky Bar (*see p138* **Walk on**), four Moroccan-chic bars that sprawl over 10,000sq ft, all packed out nightly with everyone from demi celebs to cigarette girls selling lollies. **Photo** *p40.*
Bars (2). Beauty salon. Business centre. Concierge. Disabled-adapted rooms. Gym. Internet. No-smoking rooms. Parking ($30/day). Pools (2, outdoor). Restaurants (2). Room service (24hrs). TV.

Standard

40 Island Avenue, at the Venetian Causeway (305 673 1717/fax 305 673 8181/www.standardhotel. com). Bus A. **Rates** $195-$750. **Credit** AmEx, DC, Disc, MC, V. **Map** p272 C1 ❽
Looking for the newest hotspot to sun and be seen on the beach? Then don't go to the beach at all. André Balazs, owner and proprietor of the newly renovated Dilido Spa Hotel, now the Standard, will tell you that it's really Biscayne Bay's Intercoastal that's hot. And the many Miami Beach residents who pay for membership and the privilege to sun-worship poolside at the Standard would most certainly agree. But while the pool draws its fair share of locals and travellers alike, you're more likely to find most of them socialising in the chic new spa, the coolest thing to hit the Intracoastal in a long time. As well as standard (no pun intended) massages, facials and scrubs, there are Chinese medicine baths, hydrotherapy and 'moon-phase' treatments, plus steam, water and mud treatments. *The* place to see and be seen. **Photo** *p40.*
Bars (2). Beauty salon. Business centre. Concierge. Disabled-adapted rooms. Gym. Internet. No-smoking rooms. Parking ($22). Pool (outdoor). Restaurants (2). Room service (24hrs). Spa. TV.

Tides

1220 Ocean Drive, at 12th Street (reservations 1-800 439 4095/front desk 305 604 5070/fax 305 503 3275/www.thetideshotel.com). Bus C, H, K, W, South Beach Local. **Rates** $245-$3,000 suites. **Credit** AmEx, DC, MC, V. **Map** p273 C3 ❾
This self-anointed 'Diva of Ocean Drive' is still the shiniest, loveliest thing on the beachfront strip. An L Murray Dixon creation, it features porthole windows, abundant stainless steel and frosted glass, with the curves and lines of a golden-era cruise ship. Designer Kelly Wearstler has been busy with renovations recently, updating the hotel's handsome

Scale the heights of luxury at the **Setai**. *See p37.*

Front Terrace restaurant by adding crisp, geometric motifs, as well as adding her touch to the lobby, the 45 lovely stunningly white suites (which all face the ocean) and the three penthouses that are the high points (in both senses of the phrase) of Ocean Drive, boasting sundecks and stunning ocean views. The pool deck on the mezzanine level is set to receive improvements as well, with a new full-service bar by Wearstler, as well as private cabanas. With all of these tweaks, however, don't forget to check out 1220 at the Tides (*see p116*), the hotel's posh restaurant. And millionaires take note: you can 'buy' the hotel for two nights for a mere $1 million. **Photos** *p47.*
Bars (2). Business centre. Concierge. Disabled-adapted rooms. Internet. No-smoking floor. Parking ($30/day). Pool (outdoor). Restaurant. Room service (24hrs). TV.

Hotel Victor

1144 Ocean Drive, at 11th Street (305 428 1234/ fax 305 421 6281/www.hotelvictorsouthbeach.com). Bus K, W. **Rates** $399-$625. **Credit** AmEx, DC, Disc, MC, V. **Map** p273 D3 ⑩

Adjacent to the famed Versace Mansion, the Victor is every bit as rich and opulent as the designer label itself. Another designer, however, Jacques Garcia (the man behind Paris's Hotel Costes), is responsible for beautifully adapting the 1930s into the Victor's modern structure. He based the interiors on warm beige tones and distinctly accented the lobby and rooms with bold ox blood, magenta and emerald furnishings. Guest rooms are similarly luxurious and striking, with a touch of boudoir about them, plus infinity bathtubs and huge walk-in showers. And with generous-sized mini bars, CD players and plasma-screen TVs, you'll never want to step outside. But you must – the hotel's other areas are equally designed for play, from the gorgeous mosaic-tiled pool to the spa (with hammam) to the Vix restaurant, Vue outdoor ceviche bar and decadent V Bar & Lounge, complete with musical live jellyfish tank and bird's-eye view of Ocean Drive. What fun!
Bars (3). Beauty salon. Business centre. Concierge. Disabled-adapted rooms. Gym. Internet. No-smoking rooms. Parking ($30). Pool (outdoor). Restaurant. Room service (24hrs). Spa. TV.

Expensive

Hotel Astor

956 Washington Avenue, at 10th Street (reservations 1-800 270 4981/front desk 305 531 8081/fax 305 531 3193/www.hotelastor.com). Bus C, H, K, W, South Beach Local. **Rates** $175-$290 single/double; $310-$500 suite. **Credit** AmEx, DC, MC, V. **Map** p273 D2 ⑪

A suave 1936 streamline hotel buffed up and polished for 21st-century consumption. The intimate lobby is softly illuminated and decorated in sand and willow-green hues, while the 42 elegant bedrooms come equipped with European king-size beds, imported cotton sheets and fleecy robes hanging on

Shore Club – wake me up when it's time to turn over. *See p38.*

the doors to the marble bathrooms. All rooms are double-insulated against the hustle of Washington Avenue. The Metro Kitchen & Bar (*see p115*) is an ace little cocktail venue with attached dining room (overstuffed chairs and blond-wood furniture resting on terrazzo floors) serving excellent Asian, French and Italian twists on modern American fare. *Bar. Business centre. Concierge. Disabled-adapted rooms. Internet. No-smoking rooms. Parking ($25/day). Pool (outdoor). Restaurant. Room service (7.30am-11pm). TV.*

Catalina Hotel & Beach Club

1732 Collins Avenue, at 17th Street (305 674 1160/ fax 305 672 8216/www.catalinahotel.com). Bus C, G, H, L, M, S. **Rates** $163-$237. **Credit** AmEx, DC, MC, V. **Map** p272 C3 ⑫

The newest member of the South Beach Group stable (which also owns the Chelsea, *see p45*, the Whitelaw, *see p48*, and the Lily Leon, *see p46*), the Catalina lives up to its 'cheap-chic' billing. Prices are good for the location, the small pool area is tropical and lovely, and the new restaurant and Spy Bar (*see p135*) look promising. Rooms are a riot of white, with funky light fittings and Tempur-Pedic mattresses. Things can be a little rough around the edges (the free breakfast is spartan, and the staff aren't always as friendly as they could be), but for party people this place is hard to beat. Free evening cocktails, reduced-price entry to the gym at the Delano hotel over the road and complimentary airport shuttle transfers are further draws.

Bar. Concierge. Disabled-adapted rooms. Internet. No-smoking rooms. Parking ($26/day). Pool (outdoor). Restaurant. TV.

Hotel

801 Collins Avenue, at 8th Street (305 531 2222/fax 305 531 3222/www.thehotelofsouthbeach.com). Bus C, H, K, W, South Beach Local. **Rates** $195-$425. **Credit** AmEx, DC, MC, V. **Map** p273 E2 ⑬

The Hotel was designed in 1939 by architect L Murray Dixon, and redecorated by clothing designer Todd Oldham in 1998. Formerly known as the Tiffany, it was forced to change its name by the litigious jewellery giant. Ya, boo, sucks, it's still one of the coolest joints on South Beach and still au courant. Ever-trendy are the mosaic-tiled bathrooms and tie-dye robes, which lend a whimsical feel to the small but avant-garde rooms. The cosy lobby shows off with polished terrazzo floors and couches upholstered in emerald, gold and ruby velvet. The couture touches extend to stellar house restaurant Wish (*see p117*). The octagonal rooftop pool and Spire Bar afford spectacular beach views.

Bars (2). Business centre. Concierge. Disabled-adapted rooms. Gym. Internet. Parking ($18/day). Pool (outdoor). Restaurant. Room service (7am-11pm). TV.

Hotel Impala

1228 Collins Avenue, at 12th Street (reservations 1-800 646 7252/front desk 305 673 2021/fax 305 673 5984/www.hotelimpalamiamibeach.com). Bus

C, H, K, W, South Beach Local. **Rates** $145-$195 single; $195-$225 double; $325-$425 suite. **Credit** AmEx, DC, MC, V. **Map** p273 C2 ⓮
Synonymous in Miami with Mediterranean villa charm, the Impala is where Floridians stay when they don't have time to vacation in Europe. Greco-Roman frescoes and a perfumed garden are welcome respite from the art deco barrage on Collins Avenue. The rooms are the definition of comfort, with inviting sleigh beds, cotton linens, custom-made wrought-iron fixtures, rich wood furniture and bathrooms done up in coral rock and stainless steel. Surprisingly private, the Impala has been a hideaway for numerous celebrities whose identities the management, of course, would never divulge.
Bar. Business centre. Concierge. Disabled-adapted room. Internet. No-smoking rooms. Parking ($25/day). Restaurant. Room service (24hrs). TV.

Marlin

1200 Collins Avenue, at 12th Street (reservations 1-800 688 7678/front desk 305 604 3595/fax 305 673 9609/www.marlinhotel.com). Bus C, H, K, W, South Beach Local. **Rates** $175-$995 suite. **Credit** AmEx, DC, MC, V. **Map** p273 C2 ⓯
The design team at the Marlin has just performed a much-needed makeover on this historic hotel. One wonders if they were drinking (and drinking, and drinking) when they did it. And that's a good thing. This gorgeous building (architect L Murray Dixon, 1939) contains several intoxicating design touches. Almost immediately upon entering, the cool lot of bartenders behind the lobby bar entice guests to pick their poison. Behind them, rows of Jim Beam bourbon whiskey bottles sit as shelf art. You're encouraged to enjoy your libations in the sunken VIP-esque lounge area adjacent to the bar and the seldom-empty DJ booth. Look closely: cleverly disguised peepholes double as wall art behind the comfy red booths. The Marlin promises that in any of the 12 oversized suites or eight spacious designer-appointed studio suites you'll find the in-room bar stocked with your favourite spirits. Now that's something we just have to check out.
Bar. Business centre. Concierge. Disabled-adapted room. Internet. Restaurant. Room service (9am-5pm). TV: web TV (selected rooms).

Hotel Nash

1120 Collins Avenue, at 11th Street (reservations 1-800 403 6274/front desk 305 674 7800/fax 305 538 8288/www.hotelnash.com). Bus C, H, K, W, South Beach Local. **Rates** $169-$300 single/ double; $495-$1,400 suite. **Credit** AmEx, DC, MC, V. **Map** p273 D2 ⓰
While not buzzing with vibe like most of its neighbours on South Beach, the Nash is nonetheless a lovely place to stay. An $8-million renovation several years ago resulted in a lobby exuding jasmine and bougainvillea scents, and three small outdoor pools – freshwater, saltwater and mineral water – creating a Calistoga spa-like environment. Classy rooms have a European feel with amenities that are 21st century. Streetfront rooms overlook the

observatory of the infamous Versace mansion. Chef Mark Militello does a superb job at house restaurant Mark's South Beach *(see p115).*
Bar. Concierge. Disabled-adapted rooms. Internet. No-smoking rooms. Parking ($25/day). Pool (outdoor). Restaurant. Room service (7am-11pm). TV.

Hotel Ocean

1230 Ocean Drive, at 12th Street (305 672 2579/fax 305 672 7665/www.hotelocean.com). Bus C, H, K, W, South Beach Local. **Rates** $230-$360 single/ double; $360-$750 suite. **Credit** AmEx, DC, MC, V. **Map** p273 C3 ⓱
One of the first boutique-style hotels on the Drive, the Ocean deploys experience to its advantage. It has a Mediterranean feel, with rooms distinguished by their airy capaciousness and relaxing decor (including hand-picked antiques). After finishing your complimentary newspaper and breakfast, ask the concierge for a beach towel and chaise on the sand. For dinner, reserve a table on the bustling sidewalk at Hosteria Romana, one of the only restaurants in Miami serving authentic Roman-Jewish cuisine, where from time to time you'll see a waiter or two decked out in ghastly Coliseum garb. Quick, grab the camera!
Bar. Concierge. Disabled-adapted rooms. Internet. Parking ($25/day). Restaurant. Room service (7.30am-11.30pm). TV.

Palms

3025 Collins Avenue, at 30th Street (reservations 1-800 550 0505/front desk 305 534 0505/fax 305 534 0515/www.thepalmshotel.com). Bus C, G, H, L, M, S. **Rates** $129-$479 single/double; $269-$999 suite. **Credit** AmEx, Disc, MC, V. **Map** p272 A4 ⓲
If Indiana Jones and Ernest Hemingway had opened a resort in Miami together, this would've been it. As you walk into the busy lobby, lazy ceiling fans with palm-tree blades twirl overhead. Past the rich, dark furniture with comfortable bamboo-coloured cushions and elephant table lamps is the check-in. Next, make a beeline for the Veranda Bar or the dining room that's called, funnily enough, the Dining Room. Not just clever names, but actual locations within the resort that cater to every thirst-quenching and culinary whim you may have. Stomach full, you retire to one of the 242 rooms. Bliss!
Bars. Beauty salon. Business centre. Concierge. Disabled-adapted rooms. Gym. Internet. No-smoking rooms. Parking ($19). Pool (outdoor). Restaurant. Room service (6.30am-11pm). Spa. TV.

Park Central

640 Ocean Drive, at 6th Street (reservations 1-800 727 5236/front desk 305 538 1611/fax 305 534 7520/www.theparkcentral.com). Bus C, H, K, W, South Beach Local. **Rates** $115-$300. **Credit** AmEx, DC, MC, V. **Map** p273 F2 ⓳
Tony Goldman, the man largely responsible for the South Beach renaissance in the late 1980s/early '90s, renovated this 1937 Henry Hohauser hotel by taking its old deco glory and infusing it with sleek, modern touches such as octagonal, etched-glass windows.

The Standard. *See p38.*

Ceiling fans, tropical-print carpets, plump beds and period furnishings fill the 115 rooms. The rooftop sundeck provides patrons with an alternative to sand between the toes. The lobby bar is no longer as hip as it was, but it still attracts a decent crowd.
Bar. Business centre. Concierge. Disabled-adapted rooms. Gym. Internet. Parking ($25/day). Pool (outdoor). Room service (7.30am-midnight). TV.

Pelican

826 Ocean Drive, at 8th Street (reservations 1-800 773 5422/front desk 305 673 3373/fax 305 673 3255/www.pelicanhotel.com). Bus C, H, K, W, South Beach Local. **Rates** $170-$500. **Credit** AmEx, DC, MC, V. **Map** p273 E2 ⑳

One of the most whimsical hotels in Miami, the Diesel-owned Pelican is also one of the most energetic. Swedish designer Magnus Erhland was given absolute creative liberty to design the 30 rooms. And liberty he took. Rooms include the 'Viva Las Vegas' (complete with bikini-babe bed headboard), 'Best Whorehouse' (red walls, heart-backed love chairs) and 'Me Tarzan, You Vain' (African sculptures, jungle fittings). The front desk selects rooms to fit a guest's profile, or you can make requests – each room is visitable on the hotel's website. Unique, and a real hoot to boot.
Bar. Business centre. Concierge. Disabled-adapted room. Internet. Parking ($18/day). Pool (outdoor). Restaurant. Room service (7am-midnight). TV.

Sanctuary

1745 James Avenue, at 17th Street (305 673 5455/ fax 305 673 3113/www.sanctuarysobe.com). Bus A, M, R, S. **Rates** $250-$550. **Credit** AmEx, DC, Disc, MC, V. **Map** p272 C3 ㉑

Though located in the heart of Miami Beach, by day this sleepy little all-suite hotel prides itself on making its guests feel worlds away. No doubt this is due in part to the central and serene bamboo-garden courtyard, full-service spa and possibly the most relaxing rooftop pool oasis in the whole of Miami. After the sun goes down, however, it's a brand-new world. The rooftop trades in its Zen-like oasis for some of the best and, rumour has it, most outrageous parties in town, and the resident restaurant, Sugo, is never empty. **Photo** *p48*.
Bars. Beauty salon. Business centre. Concierge. Disabled-adapted rooms. Internet. No-smoking rooms. Parking ($25). Pool (outdoor). Restaurant. Room service. Spa. TV.

Townhouse

150 20th Street, at Collins Avenue (reservations 1-800 534 3800/front desk 305 534 3800/fax 305 534 3811/www.townhousehotel.com). Bus C, G, H, L, M, S. **Rates** $110-$395. **Credit** AmEx, DC, Disc, MC, V. **Map** p272 C3 ㉒

This small boutique hotel is a first-rate knock-off. It was opened in 2000 by Jonathan Morr, and the Stark-Schrager influence is obvious. Stylish and minimalist decor (from designer India Mahdavi)? Check. Eye-candy staff? Check. A trendsetting bar serving sushi (the Bond St Lounge; *see p138* **Walk on**)?

Check. DJs spinning slick tunes on the crowded rooftop? Check. The difference is in the price. A room at the Townhouse will set you back a fraction of what you'd drop at the neighbouring Shore Club or Delano. Space doesn't allow for a pool, but the rooftop terrace does offer relaxing lounges, playful waterbeds and shade umbrellas to keep guests cool. Although, if they're staying here, their coolness is not in doubt. **Photo** *p49*.
Bar. Concierge. Disabled-adapted rooms. Internet. No-smoking floors. Parking ($25/day). Room service (6am-11pm). TV.

Moderate

Avalon Hotel

700 Ocean Drive, at 7th Street (reservations 1-800 933 3306/front desk 305 538 0133/fax 305 534 0258/www.southbeachhotels.com). Bus C, H, K, W, South Beach Local. **Rates** $129-$209. **Credit** AmEx, DC, MC, V. **Map** p273 E2 ㉓

The streamline-styled architecture of this classic deco hotel is more interesting than the rooms themselves, which are simply small and tidy. But that doesn't hurt its popularity among those looking for a clean, friendly and functional place to stay in a prime location. Although not all of the 105 rooms have ocean views, A Fish Called Avalon, the hotel's fun and casual restaurant, sits right on Ocean Drive among all the babble and glitz.
Bar. Business centre. Concierge. Disabled-adapted rooms. Internet. Parking ($20/day). Restaurant. TV.

Cardozo

1300 Ocean Drive, at 13th Street (reservations 1-800 782 6500/front desk 305 535 6500/fax 305 532 3562/www.cardozohotel.com). Bus C, H, K, W, South Beach Local. **Rates** $205-$460. **Credit** AmEx, MC, V. **Map** p273 C3 ㉔

The Cardozo is a bit of a movie star. The hotel debuted in the 1959 Frank Sinatra film *A Hole in the Head* and has since been featured in Joel Schumacher's *8MM* and the Farrellys' *There's Something About Mary*. Now owned by Gloria Estefan, it was built in 1939 by Henry Hohauser, whose architectural firm was responsible for over 300 buildings in the Miami area. The keystone façade is a classic of streamline design. Inside it's Dali meets deco, with a whimsical modern feel, wrought-iron furniture and 44 rooms with glossy cherry-wood floors. The four apartment-sized suites feature breakfast nooks, king-size beds and delicious whirlpool baths.
Bar. Concierge. Disabled-adapted rooms. Internet. No-smoking rooms. Parking ($17/day). Pool (outdoor). Restaurant. Room service (7am-midnight). TV.

Century

140 Ocean Drive, at 1st Street (reservations 1-888 982 3688/front desk 305 674 8855/fax 305 538 5733/www.centurysouthbeach.com). Bus H, M, W. **Rates** $95-$215 single/double; $190-$350 suite. **Credit** AmEx, DC, MC, V. **Map** p272 F3 ㉕

Sleek, stylish and preserved to perfection. To prove it, this 1939 Hohauser gem has received awards, including the Miami Design Preservation League's award for outstanding façade preservation. Designed in the streamline style, it has several classic features, such as a low porch wall punctured by portholes. Hardwood floors, marble baths and sleek contemporary furniture adorn the rooms; amenities stretch to temperature control. Rumour has it that actor Danny DeVito has purchased the old Joia restaurant next to the hotel and is turning it into, well, a celebrity-owned Italian eaterie. Watch this space.

Business centre. Internet. No-smoking rooms. Parking ($20/day). Restaurant. Room service (7am-11pm). TV.

Hotel Chelsea

944 Washington Avenue, at 9th Street (305 534 4069/fax 305 672 6712/www.thehotelchelsea.com). Bus C, H, K, W, South Beach Local. **Rates** $115-$165 double; $120-$195 suite. **Credit** AmEx, DC, MC, V. **Map** p273 D2 ㉖

This 42-room boutique hotel has mastered the art of feng shui without forcing it on guests. The bamboo floors and amber lighting relax and refresh, while serene rooms with low, Japanese-style beds are designed simply for a good night's sleep. The hospitality, too, is reserved yet attentive. Lightly publicised but heavily consumed is the free cocktail hour for guests in the lobby every night. While the name doesn't fit the space, the Chelsea is arguably the best little Asian-inspired hotel on the Beach. Note that the hotel also offers free airport pick-up.

Bar. Business centre. Concierge. Disabled-adapted rooms. Internet. No-smoking rooms. Parking ($18/day). Restaurant. Room service (11am-10pm). TV.

Clevelander

1020 Ocean Drive, at 10th Street (reservations 1-800 815 6829/front desk 305 531 3485/fax 305 534 3953/www.clevelander.com). Bus C, H, K, W, South Beach Local. **Rates** $89-$235. **Credit** AmEx, DC, MC, V. **Map** p273 D3 ㉗

The Clevelander is best known for its Ocean Drive poolside glass-block and neon bar (*see p134*). Fuelled by fun drinks, the scene here is boosted by live entertainment and a 10ft TV screen for special sporting

---

Liquid assets

Because most Miami hotels don't have the luxury of a sandy backyard, they value their swimming pools like a stockbroker values his portfolio. Miami's pools range in size from the tiny, wading-only variety at the **Hotel Nash** (*see p41*) to the Olympic-size cistern at the **Biltmore** (*see p53*). For something in between, try the pool at the Delano or the Shore Club. The infinity pool at the **Delano** (*see p35*) is surrounded by white-clothed cabanas by day. By night, patrons are invited to roll up their pant legs to wade to the cocktail table, complete with romantic candlelight, in the shallow end. The pools at the **Shore Club** (*see p38*) make for a great place to see and be seen – especially the more private pool behind the back bar, which usually has a floating celeb (or two).

Fed by a wall of water and illuminated by night, the pools at the **Four Seasons** (*see p52*) are perfect for posing in your Burberry bikini bottoms – in Miami, almost every pool is top-optional.

Hollywood glamour emanates from the curvy body of water behind the **Raleigh** (*see p37*), as it has ever since it was opened in the 1940s by voluptuous waterbabe Esther Williams. Nautical types who'd rather sail the high seas than stick around on land can dive into the pool at the **Ritz-Carlton South Beach** (*see p37*) where the entire pool area has

been mocked up to resemble the deck of a luxury liner. Overlooking Biscayne Bay, the pool at the **Mandarin Oriental** (*see p53*) boasts an infinity edge, making you feel as if you're about to swim off the edge of the universe. Back on South Beach, up on the rooftop of the **Hotel** (*see p40*) is a gem-shaped pool with a view of endless blue sky and white sandy beaches.

The **Hotel**.

events. In terms of accommodation, think firm beds, dark shades and cold air-conditioning. This is home away from the frat house for many a college student, although it's worth noting that the all-around party vibe means that staff limits guests to those over 21.
Bar. Concierge. No-smoking rooms. Pool (outdoor). Restaurant. TV.

Clinton Hotel

825 Washington Avenue, at 8th Street (305 938 4040/fax 305 538 1472/www.clintonsouthbeach. com). Bus C, H, K, W, South Beach Local. **Rates** $129-$400. **Credit** AmEx, Disc, DC, MC, V. **Map** p273 E2 ❷

The grot of Washington Avenue is immediately forgotten on stepping into the Clinton's lobby. Designed by French architect Eric Raffi, it's a swellegant combination of cool and warmth, with rich dark-wood accents and rainbow-blue hues. In fact, it's downright sexy. This carries through to the bedrooms – naturally – which, complete with flat-screen TVs, down-filled duvets and pillows, internet access and designer bath products, are little cocoons of chic. A select few also have whirlpool baths and terraces. Lounge by the pool or slump on overstuffed cushions at low tables for breakfast and light lunch served by the house restaurant, 8½.
Gym. Internet. Parking ($23/day). Pool (outdoor).

Kent

1131 Collins Avenue, at 11th Street (reservations 1-866 826 5268/front desk 305 604 5068/fax 305 531 0720/www.thekenthotel.com). Bus C, H, K, W, South Beach Local. **Rates** $79-$175; $350 suite. **Credit** AmEx, DC, MC, V. **Map** p273 D2 ❷

The Kent certainly didn't skimp on decor or personality during its renovation a few years back. The lobby is like a metallic candy box, with orange, pink and purple accents splashed on to steel fixtures. The 54 rooms and two suites retained their original wood features, but now have lilac and steel to throw the Kent into the future. Not to be missed is the Barbarella-esque suite, with its lucite fittings. There's no pool or sundeck, but thankfully the beach is close by. All in all, a funky choice for the budget-conscious younger traveller.
Business centre. Internet. No-smoking rooms. Parking ($30/day). TV.

Lily Leon

841 Collins Avenue, at 8th Street (reservations 1-877 762 3477/front desk 305 535 8284/fax 305 535 0077/www.southbeachgroup.com/lily/lily.shtml). Bus C, H, K, W, South Beach Local. **Rates** $125-$250 single/double; $295-$395 suite. **Credit** AmEx, DC, MC, V. **Map** p273 E2 ❸

In 2005 the Lily Hotel and the Leon Hotel teamed up to become the breezy and whimsical Lily Leon, which combines original 1929 woodwork with modern furnishings and bright hues. If you like sand in your toes, then you'll love the penthouse suite, which prides itself on its sand-floored tiki hut. (Don't worry, there's an outdoor shower to rinse the sand off when you're ready to go back inside.) The hotel

is part of the South Beach Group (as are the Hotel Chelsea, *see p45*, the Catalina, *see p40*, and the Whitelaw, *see p48*), and, in keeping with SBG policy, it offers guests free drinks during cocktail hour (7-8pm) and free airport transfers.
Bar. Business centre. Concierge. Disabled-adapted room. No-smoking rooms. Parking ($30/day). Restaurant. Room service (11am-11pm). TV.

Royal Hotel

758 Washington Avenue, at 8th Street (reservations 1-888 394 6835/front desk 305 673 9009/fax 305 673 9244/www.royalhotelsouthbeach.com). Bus C, H, K, W, South Beach Local. **Rates** $99-$119 double; $169-$199 suite. **Credit** AmEx, DC, MC, V. **Map** p273 E2 ❸

The Royal condo hotel is a real treat. Designer Jordan Mozer took its 42 hyper-hued guest rooms and transformed them into super-futuristic sleeping quarters. Curvy white plastic beds boast headboards with dual use: they're also bars, complete with stools for two. Shades of lilac, powder blue, mint and tangerine accent the stark white. High-tech chaises longues have computer and TV connections; small pets are allowed too.
Bar. Concierge. Disabled-adapted room. Internet. No-smoking rooms. Parking ($18/day). TV.

Budget

Aqua

1530 Collins Avenue, at 15th Street (305 538 4361/ fax 305 673 8109/www.aquamiami.com). Bus C, H, K, W, South Beach Local. **Rates** $129-$750. **Credit** AmEx, DC, MC, V. **Map** p273 B3 ❷

This place has an attitude that's friendly verging on frisky (its tagline is 'sleep with me…'). The Aqua advertises itself as '*Jetsons* meet *Jaws*', a description that's not a million miles off the mark in terms of the funky decor. The rooms here are basic but big, and the ambience reeks of budget cool. Unusually for Miami boutique hotels, the hospitality extends to guests' pets. Other welcome touches include a small bar in the lobby and an outdoor whirlpool bath in the courtyard.
Bar. Business centre. Concierge. Internet. TV.

Beachcomber Hotel

1340 Collins Avenue, at 14th Street (reservations 1-888 305 4683/front desk 305 531 3755/fax 305 673 8609/www.beachcombermiami.com). Bus C, H, K, W, South Beach Local. **Rates** $80-$160. **Credit** AmEx, DC, MC, V. **Map** p273 C2 ❸

The immaculate white exterior of this hotel houses an inviting porch and a sunny lobby, where breakfast is served. There are few luxuries here, but the beach is a block away, bars can be found in every direction and there's a 24-hour launderette just around the corner. Rooms are small, functional and well scrubbed, the staff is friendly, and the Sushi Rock Café across the street serves some of the freshest fish on the Beach.
Business centre. Concierge. Internet. TV.

The **Tides**. *See p38.*

Naughty by night: the **Sanctuary**. *See p43.*

Greenview

1671 Washington Avenue, at 16th Street (reservations 1-877 782 3557/front desk 305 531 6588/fax 305 531 4580/www.rubellhotels.com). Bus C, H, K, W, South Beach Local. **Rates** $79-$155 single/double; $119-$189 suite. **Credit** AmEx, DC, MC, V. **Map** p273 A2 ③④

The Greenview is a simple and serene little hotel in the middle of South Beach. The building is a Hohauser construction from 1939, renovated by Parisian Chahan Minassian in 1995. The interiors are clean, uncomplicated and furnished with light-wood furniture by Juan Pompanes. The location's great, too, just steps from the cafés and restaurants on boutique-central Lincoln Road and the Miami Convention Center.

Bar. Gym. No-smoking rooms. Restaurant. Room service (6am-10pm). TV.

Indian Creek Hotel

2727 Indian Creek Drive, at 27th Street (reservations 1-800 491 2772/front desk 305 531 2727/fax 305 531 5651/www.indiancreekhotel.com). Bus C, G, H, L, M, S. **Rates** $90-$260. **Credit** AmEx, DC, MC, V. **Map** p272 B4 ③⑤

This painstakingly restored hotel is a gem. The lobby transports you back to the 1930s, with immense planters, deco-style chandeliers and oversized uphol-stered chairs. The owner trawls the flea markets on weekends for vintage pieces. Pleasant rooms offer tasteful touches such as writing desks, bathrooms are

spotless, and the efficient staff make guests feel at home. Mrs Ira Gershwin stayed here in 1937, and like today's guests she handed her key to the front desk when she left for the evening. That's right – there are no credit card keys at Indian Creek. Instead, staff lovingly attach your good old-fashioned key to a toy alligator whenever you leave the hotel. It doesn't get more retro than that these days. Not so retro, thank goodness, is Creek 28, the hotel's Tuscan cuisine restaurant. **Photos** *p51.*

Bar. Business centre. Concierge. Disabled-adapted rooms. Internet. No-smoking rooms. Parking ($6.42/day). Pool (outdoor). Restaurant. Room service (6am-11pm). TV.

Whitelaw Hotel

808 Collins Avenue, at 8th Street (305 398 7000/ fax 305 398 7010/www.whitelawhotel.com). Bus C, H, K, W, South Beach Local. **Rates** $150-$165. **Credit** AmEx, DC, MC, V. **Map** p273 E2 ③⑥

How can you resist a hotel whose motto is 'clean sheets, hot water, stiff drinks?' Those sheets are luxe Belgian and, like almost everything else in the hotel, they're pristine white – a stark aesthetic that just about stays the right side of insane asylum, cour-tesy of fun touches like the groovy lobby furnish-ings. Staff are ultra friendly and well plugged into the Beach scene (guests get free access to certain clubs). The party vibe is helped along by 808, the lobby's vodka bar, which, like the bars at the other South Beach Group hotels (the Catalina, *see p40,* Chelsea, *see p45,* and the Lily Leon, *see p46),* offers free cocktails to guests each evening from 6pm to 7pm. That'll be those stiff drinks, then.There are also free transfers to the airport.

Bar. Business centre. Concierge. Disabled-adapted rooms. Internet. No-smoking rooms. Parking ($18/day). TV.

Hostels

Clay Hotel & International Hostel

1438 Washington Avenue, at Española Way (reservations 1-800 379 2529/front desk 305 534 2988/fax 305 673 0346/www.clayhotel.com). Bus C, H, K, W, South Beach Local. **Rates** $55-$64 standard; $68-$89 deluxe. **Credit** MC, V. **Map** p273 B2 ③⑦

Budgeteers got it good. The Clay's location – on the corner of Washington and the café-lined European plaza known as Española Way – is excellent: all the best bars and clubs are nearby, as are Lincoln Road Mall and the beach. The Mediterranean-style build-ing was formerly the headquarters of Al Capone's gambling syndicate and, later, a favourite location for the producers of *Miami Vice*. These days it attracts adventurous nomads in search of a good room deal. In addition to the cut-rate dorms, there are also private or single-sex rooms. Lodgings are basic but clean and brightly decorated.

Cooking facilities. Laundry. Parking ($10/day). TV.

Miami Beach International Travellers Hostel

236 9th Street, at Washington Avenue (305 534 0268/fax 305 534 5862/www.sobehostel.com). Bus C, H, K, W, South Beach Local. **Rates** $14-$20 dorm; $36-$99 private room. **Credit** MC, V. **Map** p273 E2 ③⑧

Utility at its finest. This is the place to stay if you've got a lot of cash to spend on drinks and none to spend on living quarters. Lodgings range from dorms for four to private rooms. Bathrooms are all en suite. What's more, the location is phenomenal. What more do you really need?
Cooking facilities. Internet. Laundry. TV.

Mid Beach

Deluxe

Fontainebleau Resort

4441 Collins Avenue, at 44th Street (reservations 1-800 548 8886/front desk 305 538 2000/fax 305 673 5351/www.fontainebleau.com). Bus G, H, L, S. **Rates** $199-$299 single/double; $500-$800 suite. **Credit** AmEx, DC, MC, V.

Catering to the wealthy and their progeny, this compound is the Las Vegas casino resort of Miami Beach. Stretching over 20 acres, it has 1,000 employees and rooms for triple that number of guests. Built in garish Hollywood style by architect Morris Lapidus, this grande dame has, appropriately enough, starred in dozens of movies and TV shows including Jerry Lewis's *The Bellboy*, Frank Sinatra's *Tony Roma*, the Bond romp *Goldfinger*, the Elmore Leonard adaptation *Stick*, warble fest *The Bodyguard* and, most recently, an episode of *The Sopranos*. The hotel boasts its very own water playpark (*see p169*), plus Club Tropigala (*see p190*).
Bar. Beauty salon. Business centre. Concierge. Disabled-adapted rooms. Gym. Internet. No-smoking floors. Parking ($18/day). Pool (outdoor). Restaurant. Room service (24hrs). TV.

Expensive

Eden Roc Resort & Spa

4525 Collins Avenue, at 45th Street (reservations 1-800 327 8337/front desk 305 531 0000/fax 305 674 5555/www.edenrocresort.com). Bus G, H, L, S. **Rates** $159-$299 standard; $164-$294 deluxe; $234-$315 oceanfront. **Credit** AmEx, DC, Disc, MC, V.

Since 1956, this Morris Lapidus-designed hotel has been attracting Hollywood's A-list. Everyone from Lucille Ball and Desi Arnaz to Lena Horne, Jerry Lewis and Elizabeth Taylor have stayed, performed and partied at the Eden Roc. In the past five years more than $35 million has been spent on renovations, with everything from the physical structure to the pillowcases receiving a facelift. The decor remains true to its 1950s roots, but adds all the con-veniences and amenities one might expect from one of Miami's premier resorts. Rich jewel tones and mahogany rule in the vast lobby, and ample rooms sport luxe sheets and tropical prints bedspreads. An esteemed oceanfront spa offers pampering. Pool sharks can check out the swimmers through an underwater 'porthole' window.
Bar. Beauty salon. Business centre. Concierge. Disabled-adapted rooms. Gym. Internet. No-smoking floors. Parking ($20/day). Pools (2, outdoor). Restaurants (2). Room service (24hrs). TV.

North Beach

Budget

Best Western on the Bay Inn & Marina

1819 NE 79th Street Causeway, at Normandy Drive, North Bay Village (reservations 1-800 624 3961/front desk 305 865 7100/fax 305 868 3483/www.bestwestern.com). Bus L. **Rates** $60-$85. **Credit** AmEx, DC, MC, V.

Which way to the **Townhouse**? *See p43.*

This is a typical outpost of the Best Western chain, conveniently located halfway between Downtown and Miami Beach in sedate North Bay Village. Rooms are spic and span, and some are equipped with kitchenettes. One thing that sets this place apart from its sister establishments is the breathtaking sunset view from Shuckers bar (*see p137*) downstairs. Relaxed locals even arrive by boat at this popular joint, home of beach volleyball, raw and alcohol bars and, at times, live reggae. The hotel offers free transfers to the airport and sea port.
Bar. Business centre. Dataport (selected rooms). Disabled-adapted rooms. Internet (selected rooms). No-smoking rooms. Parking (free). Pool (outdoor). Restaurant. TV.

Surfside to Golden Beach

Deluxe

Acqualina, A Rosewood Resort

17875 Collins Avenue, at 178th Street, Sunny Isles (reservations 1-888 767 3966/front desk 305 918 8000/fax 305 918 8100/www.rosewoodhotels.com). Bus E, K, S, V. **Rates** $425-$950 single/double; $775-$2,200 suite. **Credit** AmEx, DC, MC, V.
Modelled after a grand European piazza, this magnificent oceanfront property welcomes guests with stately architectural features like iron gates, sculpted archways, baroque fountains and a porte-cochere with a domed cupola. The 51-storey Mediterranean-inspired tower features 97 ultra-luxurious rooms and 188 lavishly appointed residences, all with private terraces and breathtaking views of either the Intracoastal Waterway or the Atlantic. Kids can learn about marine biology on the specially designed AcquaMarine Program. Adults, meanwhile, will be more than happy with the huge ESPA spa, the first US location for the renowned UK-based spa authority, complete with Jacuzzi and freshwater pool. With all this, you mustn't forget to make reservations well in advance for Il Mulino New York. That's right – the same Il Mulino that's won rave reviews for decades in the Big Apple is now available here.
Bars (2). Beauty salon. Business centre. Concierge. Disabled-adapted rooms. Gym. Internet. No-smoking rooms. Parking ($25/day). Pool (outdoor). Restaurants (3). Room service (24hrs). TV.

Budget

Bay Harbor Inn & Suites

9660 East Bay Harbor Drive, at 97th Street, Bay Harbor Islands (305 868 4141/fax 305 867 9094/www.bayharborinn.com). Bus G, H, K, V. **Rates** $79-$99 single/double; $89-$119 suite. **Credit** AmEx, DC, MC, V.
This is actually a complex of two modest buildings across the street from each other in a quiet area near Bal Harbour; one modern, one traditional. The modern building has a pool at the back and faces the Intracoastal Waterway. The traditional structure contains bigger rooms at a lower price. Rooms are comfortable, and many are reserved a year in advance by a clientele that returns every season. King-size canopy beds, living rooms with full-size sofa sleepers, dataports and refrigerators are in all of the suites. For dinner, try your luck at the Inns London Tavern, which is run by students at the Johnson & Wales Culinary Institute.
Bar. Business centre. Concierge. Dataport (selected rooms). Disabled-adapted rooms. Gym. Internet. No-smoking rooms. Parking (free). Pool (outdoor). Restaurant. TV.

Sea View

9909 Collins Avenue, at 99th Street, Bal Harbour (reservations 1-800 447 1010/front desk 305 866 4441/fax 305 866 1898/www.seaview-hotel.com). Bus H, K, S, T. **Rates** $180-$235 single/double; $315-$350 suite. **Credit** AmEx, DC, MC, V.
On the beach in sleepy, ritzy Bal Harbour, the Sea View attracts a conservative clientele and celebrities in temporary hermitage. These are people who want to be on the beach, not the Beach. The lobby is an understated mix of antique and contemporary furniture. Not so subtle, however, is the massive chandelier hanging in the entrance. The 220 commodious and tasteful rooms face the ocean or Biscayne Bay. The beach is out the back door, and the swanky shops of Bal Harbour are out the front.
Bar. Beauty salon. Business centre. Concierge. Disabled-adapted rooms. Gym. Internet. No-smoking floors. Parking ($10/day). Pool (outdoor). Restaurant. Room service (7am-11.30pm). TV.

Key Biscayne

As this guide went to press, the **Sonesta Beach Resort** (350 Ocean Drive, Key Biscayne, 305 361 2021) was about to go under wraps for a massive $300-million redevelopment that will bring it in line with its more luxe neighbours, such as the **Ritz-Carlton Key Biscayne** (*see p37*).

Expensive

Silver Sands Beach Resort

301 Ocean Drive, Key Biscayne (305 361 5441/fax 305 361 5477/www.silversandsmiami.com). Bus B. **Rates** $129-$189 mini suite; $279-$329 cottage. **Credit** AmEx, DC, MC, V.
Staying on fabulous Key Biscayne doesn't have to cost you an arm and a leg. Silver Sands, the oldest hotel in Key Biscayne, will just take the arm. Built in the 1950s as a bungalow hideaway, it closed due to Hurricane Andrew in 1992. Back in business since 1995 after a complete restoration, it still relies on its great beach location. Mini suites have two double beds; cottages can accommodate up to two adults and four children. A tropical theme pervades in the rooms, some of which have mini kitchens.
Disabled-adapted rooms. Internet. Kitchenette (selected rooms). Parking (free). Pool (outdoor). TV.

Indian Creek Hotel – don't worry, the keys don't bite. *See p48.*

Room service!

Ever fantasise about not having to make your bed? Do your dishes? Look for a parking space? Have you ever speed-dialled your favourite pizza delivery place, only to realise that it closed an hour ago? Have you ever been running so late you wish you had your own private elevator so you didn't have to wait for anyone else? Can you imagine never running out of toilet paper, toothpaste or deodorant because the secret room fairy noticed you were running low and replaced it? What we're trying to ask is: have you ever craved all of the amenities of a hotel at home? Yeah, us too. Clearly there's only one thing to do to satiate our appetites.... move to Miami.

There's a growing trend happening in Miami: the condo-hotel. That's right: 24-hour room service – at home! Establishments known for decades as the pinnacle of service, offering the finest in hospitality and whim-catering in the hotel market, are finally getting into the real-estate one. In the past several years, Miami has seen the likes of five-star hotels like the **Ritz-Carlton** (*see p37*), the **Four Seasons** (*see below*) and the **Setai** (*see p37*) open their doors to more permanent guests. And while some hotels cater to a second-homeowner and have been supplementing their condo owners' mortgages for quite some time, others, like the Miami outpost of the **W** chain (which is set to open late 2006/early 2007) and the **Doral Resort & Spa** (2007), are just getting in on the act. Even smaller boutique establishments such as the **Royal Hotel** (*see p46*) and the **Sanctuary** (*see p43*), with just 30 apartment

suites, are using their advertising to market to second-homebuyers, not travellers. Clearly, it pays to buy into a condo-hotel as a chic alternative to a second home. But don't even think about laying out the welcome mat somewhere like the Ritz or the Setai without shelling out seven figures first.

There's just one thing we can't figure out... with all of those aforementioned amenities, why on earth *would* you live anywhere else?

The Mainland

Downtown

Deluxe

Four Seasons Hotel Miami

1435 Brickell Avenue, at SW 15th Street (reservations 1-800 819 5053/front desk 305 358 3535/fax 305 358 7758/www.fourseasons.com/ miami). Bus 24, 48, B/Metromover Financial District. **Rates** $275-$475 single/double; $475-$1,150 suite. **Credit** AmEx, DC, Disc, MC, V.
A high-flyer (70 storeys high, to be exact) in the Downtown financial district, the Four Seasons could be mistaken for an office building. But beyond the façade and the utilitarian lower lobby, it's pure palatial chic. Marble-lined public areas double as gallery space for an impressive modern art collection, anchored by three massive Botero sculptures. The 221 rooms, including 39 suites, all boast terrific views over Biscayne Bay, to be enjoyed from padded window-ledge love seats. Amenities include an enormous spa and sports club, plus a huge business centre. Of the several house restaurants, the north Italian Acqua is excellent. The Beach is a 15-minute drive across the MacArthur Causeway, but the Latin-themed Bahia bar (*see p137*) is a more-than-adequate substitute; after a hard day's slouching, nothing beats a tropical breeze and a $12 Mojito (that's cheap in Miami).
Bars (2). Beauty salon. Business centre. Concierge. Disabled-adapted rooms. Gym. Internet. No-smoking rooms. Parking. Pools (3, outdoor). Restaurants (4). Room service (24hrs). Spa. TV & DVD.

Mandarin Oriental Miami

500 Brickell Key Drive, at Brickell Avenue (reservations 1-866 888 6780/front desk 305 913 8288/fax 305 913 8300/www.mandarin-oriental.com/miami). No public transport. **Rates** *$298-$629 single/ double; $525-$1,250 suite.* **Credit** *AmEx, DC, MC, V.* **Map** *p274 F4* ❸❾

Certain members of the bling dynasty – Will Smith and Mary J Blige, to name but two – apparently count the Mandarin as one of their favourite places to chill. It's far from low-key, however: well over $100 million was needed to construct the hotel on a small island adjacent to the city's financial district. Rich fabrics and modern furnishings decorate the rooms, many of which have balconies overlooking the Atlantic, Biscayne Bay or the Miami skyline. Bathrooms are clad in Spanish marble, and some of the suites have their own kitchen. An expansive spa, a state-of-the-art fitness centre and a beach club contribute to the lavishness. There are two restaurants, Café Sambal and Azul, plus the lovely M-Bar (*see p139*).
Bar. Business centre. Concierge. Disabled-adapted rooms. Gym. Internet. No-smoking rooms. Parking ($24/day). Pool (outdoor). Restaurants (2). Room service (24hrs). TV.

Expensive

Hotel Inter-Continental Miami

100 Chopin Plaza, at Biscayne Boulevard (reservations 1-800 424 6835/305 577 1000/fax 305 577 0384/www.miami.interconti.com). Metromover Bayfront Park. **Rates** *$189-$359 double; $429-$749 suite.* **Credit** *AmEx, DC, MC, V.* **Map** *p274 E4* ❹❶

The pool at the Inter-Continental is desolate between the hours of 9am and 5pm. That's because all the guests are in a meeting. This hotel has been designed almost exclusively with the business traveller in mind. Constructed from honey-coloured marble, it is lightened by a three-storey lobby with a bright skylight, casual wicker furniture and countless plants. Decorated in sombre shades of beige and grey, rooms are well appointed, and many have views of the bay. Amenities are standard rather than exceptional but, nonetheless, this 600-room structure is still a convenient place if you're doing business in Downtown.
Bar. Beauty salon. Business centre. Concierge. Dataport (selected rooms). Disabled-adapted rooms. Gym. Internet (selected rooms). No-smoking floors. Parking ($20/day). Pool (outdoor). Restaurant. Room service (24hrs). TV.

Moderate

Miami River Inn

118 SW South River Drive, at SW 4th Avenue (reservations 1-800 468 3589/front desk 305 325 0045/fax 305 325 9227/www.miamiriverinn.com). Bus 8. **Rates** *$79-$199.* **Credit** *AmEx, DC, Disc, MC, V.*

Though its website proudly proclaims 'fresh squeezed paradise', it's doubtful that you'll find a Miamian who's able to testify on the Miami River

Inn's behalf. And yet this B&B close to Downtown is seeped in history. Actually a compound made up of five restored clapboard buildings built between 1906 and 1910, the Inn looks as if it was transported from New England. The rooms are furnished in traditional style with wood-plank floors, brass beds, flowered wallpaper, wicker chairs and wood panelling. Bathrooms are tidy. The Inn is now listed on the National Register of Historic Places.
Disabled-adapted rooms. Internet. No-smoking rooms. Parking (free). Pool (outdoor). TV.

Budget

Holiday Inn – Port of Miami

340 Biscayne Boulevard, at NE 3rd Street (reservations 1-800 315 2621/front desk 305 371 4400/fax 305 372 2862/www.holidayinn.miami. ichotelsgroup.com). Metromover Bayfront Park. **Rates** *$99-$142.* **Credit** *AmEx, DC, MC, V.* **Map** *p274 D3* ❹❶

Everything you'd expect from one of the largest and most reputable budget hotel chains. No frills, but plenty of friendly staff, clean rooms and a great location. Situated across the street from Bayside Marketplace and overlooking the American Airlines Arena and the Biscayne Bay, this Holiday Inn really allows you to enjoy your holiday. Within walking distance of the Port of Miami, it's convenient for travellers coming to Miami as a cruise departure city as well. This hotel also offers a bonus for international travellers: the staff speaks English, French, Italian, Portuguese and, of course, Spanish.
Business centre. Concierge. Disabled-adapted rooms. Gym. Internet. Kitchenette. No-smoking rooms. Parking ($10/day). Restaurant. Pool (outdoor). Room service (6.30-11am; 5.30-10pm). TV.

Coral Gables

Deluxe

Biltmore

1200 Anastasia Avenue, at Granada Boulevard, (reservations 1-800 727 1926/front desk 305 445 1926/fax 305 913 3159/www.biltmorehotel.com). Bus 72. **Rates** *$279-$359 single/double; $479-$609 suite.* **Credit** *AmEx, DC, MC, V.* **Map** *p276 D2* ❹❷

A majestic monument to the Gables of the Florida boom years, the Biltmore boasts a landmark 300ft bell tower modelled after that of the Giralda in Seville, as well as the largest pool in the continental US. It's worth checking in for the history alone (*see p85* **Gimme Biltmore**), although the modern-day experience is also something to savour. The lobby has an intricate hand-painted vaulted ceiling with French and Spanish furniture and large wooden aviaries containing songbirds. Marble floors, oriental rugs, 25ft columns, oversized arches and blue and white porcelain planters add to the grandiose splendour. On a comfort level, period reproduction furniture, Egyptian cotton duvets and wonderfully plump

feather beds make the rooms eminently inhabitable. To top it off, there's an adjacent world-class golf course, a spa, a wine club and sumptuous Sunday brunches. The only drawback is the rather lonely location: it's a 20-minute walk to get to central Coral Gables, or a 20-minute drive to Miami Beach.
Bar. Beauty salon. Business centre. Concierge. Disabled-adapted rooms. Gym. Internet. No-smoking floors. Parking ($24/day). Pool (outdoor). Restaurants (2). Room service (24hrs). TV.

Expensive

Colonnade Hotel

180 Aragon Avenue, at Ponce de León Boulevard, (reservations 1-866 770 9877/front desk 305 441 2600/fax 305 445 3929/www.colonnadecoral gables.com). Bus 24, 40, 72, Coral Gables Circulator. **Rates** $179-$229. **Credit** AmEx, DC, MC, V. **Map** p276 B4 ⑬
Once the offices of Coral Gables' founder George Merrick, this building later housed the Florida National Bank for almost 40 years. In the mid 1980s, it was renovated and turned into an elegant hotel, designed to cater to a largely business clientele. The immense entrance is a two-storey rotunda with Corinthian columns, hand-blown crystal chandeliers and a fountain in the centre of the inlaid marble floor. Rooms are equally plush, with marble vanity tops, brass fixtures and rich mahogany furniture. It'll come as no surprise to hear, then, that champagne is served on arrival.
Bar. Business centre. Concierge. Disabled-adapted rooms. Internet. No-smoking floors. Parking ($14/day). Pool (outdoor). Restaurant. Room service (24hrs). TV.

Budget

Best Western ChateauBleau Hotel

1111 Ponce de León Boulevard, at Antilla Avenue, (reservations 1-800 780 7234/front desk 305 448 2634/fax 305 448 2017/www.hotelchateaubleau. com). Bus 42, J, Coral Gables Circulator. **Rates** $84-$134. **Credit** AmEx, DC, MC, V. **Map** p276 A4 ⑭
Don't let the name fool you: this modest Best Western affiliate is a long way short of *la vie de château*. It is, however, very good value for the location, just around the corner from Miracle Mile, the Gables' shopping and dining district. All rooms are spacious, neat and comfortable, and, given the very urban location, the heated pool is a welcome boon. House restaurant Mylos is well regarded, and the hotel also offers free airport transfers.
Bar. Disabled-adapted rooms. Internet. Kitchenette (selected rooms). No-smoking rooms. Parking (free). Pool (outdoor). Restaurant. Room service (7am-midnight). TV.

Hotel Place St Michel

162 Alcazar Avenue, at Ponce de León Boulevard (305 444 1666/fax 305 529 0074). Bus 56, 73. **Rates** $125-$165 single/double; $160-$200 suite. **Credit** AmEx, DC, MC, V. **Map** p276 B4 ⑮

This hotel, built in 1926 and refurbished in 1995, is a tiny, European-style gem in the heart of Coral Gables. Fresh flowers and fans adorn the cosy lobby. The distinctive rooms have wood floors, dark panelled walls, lovely antique furniture and a fruit basket. Room rates include continental breakfast; for dinner, the Restaurant Place St Michel (*see p127*) downstairs serves contemporary American fare with light French influences.
Concierge. No-smoking rooms. Parking ($7/day). Restaurant. Room service (7am-9pm). TV.

Coconut Grove

Deluxe

Grove Isle Hotel & Spa

Grove Isle Drive, off S Bayshore Drive (reservations 1-800 884 7683/front desk 305 858 8300/fax 305 858 5908/www.groveisle.com). No public transport. **Rates** $199-$499 single/double; $269-$799 suite.
Credit AmEx, DC, Disc, MC, V.
Set in lushly tropical landscaped gardens, the Grove has a rather peachy view over Biscayne Bay. Rooms are pleasant with terracotta floors; some have canopy beds shrouded in butterfly netting. But although secluded, the hotel has its fair share of Miami eccentricity – garish palm-tree columns, paintings of monkeys and fixtures made of pineapples. Not to mention Havana Nights, a salute to Latin cuisine (Thursdays, 8-11pm) in Baleen, the resident restaurant (*see p129*), which is one of the best in the Grove.
Bar. Disabled-adapted rooms. Gym. Internet. Parking ($17/day). Pool (outdoor). Restaurant. Room service (7am-11pm). TV.

Expensive

Wyndham Grand Bay Coconut Grove

2669 S Bayshore Drive, at SW 27th Avenue (reservations 1-877 999 3223/front desk 305 858 9600/fax 305 859 2026/www.wyndham.com). Bus 48. **Rates** $118-$289 single/double; $649-$929 suite. **Credit** AmEx, DC, MC, V. **Map** p277 B4 ⑯
Signposted by an enormous red tubular sculpture at the foot of the driveway, this top-line luxury hotel has been the choice of a great many visiting celebs: years ago, management redecorated the presidential suite to Wacko Jacko's specifications, and George Michael filmed his 'Careless Whisper' video here. With amenities such as high-speed internet access, computer facilities, Herman Miller Aeron ergonomic chairs and dual-line cordless phones in every room, the hotel's also a shoe-in for the business traveller. Some rooms have terraces where you can take in the bay views. House restaurant Bice, serving haute Italian cuisine, is worth a look.
Bar. Business centre. Concierge. Disabled-adapted rooms. Gym. Internet. No-smoking rooms. Parking ($15/day). Pool (outdoor). Restaurants (2). Room service (7am-11pm). TV: pay movies.

Sightseeing

Introduction

The lie of the land (and the sea).

If you're looking for charming cobblestone streets and vestiges of history, what are you doing here? Miami's still a foetus compared to most cities. Still in its infancy as late as the 1920s (and, depending on who you talk to, it's yet to reach maturity), its major period of growth coincided with the rise of the motor car. The car, therefore, dictated development: hence, Miami is a city that sprawls over vast areas. In fact, the metropolitan area covers some 1,945 square miles of Dade County, comprising no fewer than 29 separately governed cities. The Downtown business district is several miles from the admin centre and site of Miami City Hall in Coconut Grove to the south, while the entertainment district of Miami Beach is several miles out to sea, tethered to the mainland only by a series of spindly causeways.

For visitors used to European cities that have grown organically around some central feature, typically a market square, the effect can be disorienting. For the fact is that Miami has no centre at all. Instead, it has a collection of enclaves, each of which has its own local centre of commerce, entertainment and colour. While that could equally be said of London, Paris or Madrid, the difference with Miami is that its neighbourhoods tend to be separated by vast swathes of no-man's-land. In keeping with its unflattering distinction of being one of the poorest cities in the US, Miami has a highly visible degree of urban decay and poverty. Only broad strips of highway with safely fast-moving traffic make it possible to get from one white, wealthy (in other words, visitor-friendly) area to another. It's not quite Johannesburg, but it's definitely not a city for exploring on foot.

However, this is not an issue if you decide, as many do, to spend all your time on South Beach (by day it's got the beaches and cafés; by night it's buzzing with restaurants, bars and clubs). This is the one truly pedestrian-friendly part of the city and, given the difficulties of finding parking (see p248), it could even be classified as anti-car. But if you want to see more of the other neighbourhoods, you'll almost certainly need to rent a car. There is a public transport system, but to get almost anywhere from South Beach involves taking one of the infrequent C or K buses over to Downtown for the first of anything up to two or three changes, depending on where you want to get to. (Talk of improving links by extending the light rail Metromover service across the causeway has been stymied by

Miami Beach officials worried about attracting the wrong kind of people.) For those who choose not to rent a car, we give full public transport details throughout this guide wherever relevant, including at the beginning of each sightseeing chapter. For more general information on getting around Miami, *see pp246-248*.

Tours

Air tours

Dean International (305 259 5611, www.fly miami.com) operates out of Tamiami airport: $156 will get a one-hour tour of Miami Beach, Downtown and Coral Gables for three people. **Action Helicopter Tours** (305 858 1788), at Watson Island, offers daily tours lasting about 40 minutes, costing $150 per person. Depending on which option you choose, your flight will take you over South Beach, the Port of Miami, Coconut Grove and up to Bal Harbour.

Boat tours

Many boats depart from the marina at Bayside Marketplace (*see p80*). Ninety-minute dinner cruises on the yachts **Celebration** and **Friendship** (305 373 7001) cost $34.50 per person. **Island Queen**, **Island Lady** and **Pink Lady** (call Island Queen Cruises on 305 379 5119, or see www.islandqueencruises.com) tour waterfront estates at Millionaires' Row and the private islands of Miami Beach for $14 per person ($8 for children); the cruises last 90 minutes. The **Heritage of Miami** (305 442 9697, www.heritageschooner.com), an 85-foot, two-masted schooner, tours Biscayne Bay from September to June; two-hour daytime trips cost $20 per person ($15 kids), or there's a night-time cruise lasting one hour that costs $15 ($10 kids). And **Dade Heritage Trust** (305 358 9572, www.historicmiami.com) offers two-and-a-half hour tours of the Miami River for $55.

Walking, cycling & other tours

The **Art Deco District Welcome Center** organises various walking tours of South Beach's Deco District; for details, *see p66*. Local historian Dr Paul George is well known for his walking, boat and cycling tours of Greater Miami, including the Downtown/ Miami River Walking Tour and the Murder and Mayhem Coach Tour. Run in association with the **Historical Museum of Southern Florida** (*see p79*), the tours cost from $15 to $40 and last between two and three hours; call 305 375 1621 for an up-to-date schedule and reservations.

NATURE TOURS

Naturalist tours, including wading tours off Key Biscayne, kayak and canoe trips through Coral Gables waterways and a Key Biscayne sunset canoe trip, are offered by **Miami-Dade Parks & Recreation Department** at the Crandon Park Visitors' Center (4000 Crandon Boulevard, 305 361 5421). Walks and wading tours take one to three hours and cost $10 for adults ($8 for children); canoe and kayak trips last up to five hours and cost $20-$30 per person. Call 305 361 6767 or 305 667 7337 for details. **Dragonfly Expeditions** (305 774 9019, www.dragonfly expeditions.com) offers various tours, from bus tours of Coral Gables to walking tours of the Deco District, plus more adventurous nature ecotours in the Everglades and Cabbage Key.

The best Sightseeing

For a *Sex and the City* moment
Segafredo, SushiSamba Dromo et al – it's got to be the **Lincoln Road Mall**. *See p69.*

For a Fritz Lang circa *Metropolis* moment
Driving north on the **MacArthur Causeway** – but keep your eyes on the roads, not the cranes! *See p74* **Islands and causeways**.

For channelling your inner child
The **Miami Children's Museum** – whatever you really wanted to be when you grew up, you can be it here. *See p165.*

For artful dodging
Forget Romero Britto's pop schlock: the **Design District** is for serious art and design types who know the difference between Impressionism and knock-offs. *See p96.*

For nihilism, hedonism, egotism and other sybaritic pastimes
South Beach. It's 4am and time for another cocktail. Dance it off and then sleep on the beach before the whole vicious cycle begins again. *See p60.*

For nature that has nothing to do with the question: are they real or are they fake?
Key Biscayne, where the beaches remain (fairly) silicone-free. *See p75.*

For a real trip back in time
Little Havana, where old men still play dominoes and refer to a pre-Castro Cuba. *See p91.*

modern
and contemporary
ART

Bill Jacobson, Untitled #2943, 2000, Chromogenic print. Collection Miami Art Museum, fractional and promised gift of Charles Cowles

10 years

MAM the power of ten

Miami Art Museum

miamiartmuseum.org
305.375.3000
101 West Flagler Street

Miami by area

57th Avenue (Red Road), the Gables was one of the first planned communities in the US. Its Mediterranean architecture is immaculately maintained, and Coral Gables remains the prettiest part of urban Miami.

Coconut Grove (pp87-90/Map p277)

While some of its arty spirit has been sapped by overdevelopment, much of the Grove's wilful eccentricity still remains. It's located directly south of Little Havana and Downtown, and to the east and south-east of Coral Gables, hugging the water of Biscayne Bay.

Little Havana (pp91-95/Map p275)

Calle Ocho (SW 8th Street) is the main drag of this predominantly Latino locale, west of Brickell Avenue and Downtown and (mostly) east of Coral Gables. Its roots may have sprung from Cuban exiles who came here in the '50s and '60s, but it's now home to nearly as many Nicaraguans, Guatemalans and Puerto Ricans as Cubans.

The Design District, Wynwood & Little Haiti (pp96-100/Map p270)

The **Design District** and **Wynwood** are two up-and-came-already locales north of Downtown that are home to arts and crafts dealers and shops. Stretching roughly between NE 50th and NW 75th Streets and centred on NE 2nd Avenue, **Little Haiti**, as its name suggests, is home to many Haitian immigrants. It's a very poor and occasionally dangerous area.

North Miami & Beyond (pp101-103/Map p270)

North and west of Little Haiti, Miami opens out into a morass of suburbs, among them **Miami Springs**, largely Spanish **Hialeah**, poverty-stricken **Opa-Locka**, **North Miami Beach** (no relation to Miami Beach proper) and the swanky mall-centred suburb of **Aventura**.

South Miami & Beyond (pp104-106/Map p271)

After Coral Gables, it can seem as if all the traffic on US 1 is heading to Dadeland Mall in the southern suburb of **Kendall**. The homes are older and grounds more lush in **Cutler** and **Cutler Ridge** to the south and east, before the urban sprawl starts to let up as the road heads further south towards the farms of **Homestead**, **Florida City** and the **Redlands**.

Miami Beach (pp60-76/Map p272)

Glamour Ground Zero, Miami Beach is where you're likely to spend most of your time if you are here for pleasure rather than business. Located east of the mainland and accessible via several causeways, the Beach is divided up into a number of neighbourhoods. **South Beach** – essentially, the Miami of popular cliché – is that part of Miami Beach that sits south of Dade Boulevard. North from here to about 63rd Street is considered **Mid Beach**, and from there to 79th Street is known as **North Beach**. From 79th Street to 96th Street is **Surfside**; north of there is swanky **Bal Harbour**; and further north, until around 170th Street, is **Sunny Isles**.

Downtown (pp77-81/Map p274)

Centred on Flagler Street and bordered by NE/NW 15th Street to the north, Biscayne Bay to the east, SE 15th Road to the south and Interstate 95 to the west, Downtown proper is a combination of business district, ghetto and construction hell. Biscayne Corridor, however, which stretches along Biscayne Boulevard from 14th to 71st Streets and borders the Design District, is an up-and-coming area in which cafés, boutiques and bars are scattered in between by-the-hour motels and strip clubs.

Coral Gables (pp82-86/Map p276)

Hemmed in by SW 8th Street (aka Tamiami Trail), SW 37th Avenue (aka Douglas Road), SW 72nd Street (aka Sunset Drive) and SW

Sightseeing

The Beaches

Let's face it: it's the Big Draw.

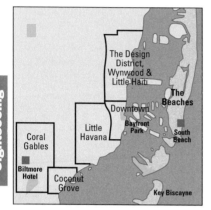

Maps p270 & p272

Miami life congregates on the shoreline, where palm trees, warm sands and balmy sea breezes dominate. But, come on, the beaches don't naturally look this good. The city's founders dredged sand and muck from the bottom of Biscayne Bay to embellish the shoreline. To this day, the coastal communities fight a never-ending battle against Mother Nature to maintain those famous sandy shores. The massive expenditure required to keep the sand attached to land is why cynics call Miami Beach the 'Billion Dollar Sandbar'.

The first thing you'll notice when you hit the tiny cluster of barrier islands making up Miami Beach is that they represent a very different world from the city of Miami itself. Separated by Biscayne Bay (which is bridged by several slender causeways; *see p74* **Islands and causeways**), Miami Beach is just three miles from the mainland but it may as well be in the next state. On this oft-photographed and highly prized sandbar sits a cluster of waterfront neighbourhoods that stretches from the sandy bacchanalia of South Beach to the forbiddingly wealthy and insulated Golden Beach to the north.

GETTING AROUND

South Beach is compact enough to get around on foot, but if you do tire there's a handy little shuttle bus called the **South Beach Local** that runs up and down Washington Avenue

every 15 minutes or so from 8am to 1am Monday to Saturday and from 10am to 1am Sunday (the route is marked on the Miami Beach map; *see p272*). The fare is just 25¢. To get up to Mid Beach and North Beach – which can be a painfully slow experience – take bus G, H, L or S from the south side of Lincoln Road; to go to Surfside, Bal Harbour or Sunny Isles, take the S.

Miami Beach

South Beach

Contemporary yet historic, tiny but diverse, South Beach commands hyperbole. It is the Miami stereotype come alive. The action centres on Ocean Drive and Collins Avenue between 5th Avenue to the south and Lincoln Road to the north. Every Miami scene ever filmed in any movie seems to have been shot here. Like wheeled Mercuries, hyper-tanned rollerbladers clad in thongs and little else, glide down Ocean Drive past whimsical, pastel-hued art deco buildings. Seven-foot, eight-stone models saunter past four-foot, ten-stone geriatrics. Eurotrash and celebs rub oiled shoulders with artists and hipsters and a sprinkling of local stock as all wander in the omnipresent sunshine past sidewalk cafés, designer boutiques, lounge bars and dusk-to-dawn clubs. Then there's the turquoise ocean, the waving palm trees and the delicious blue skies.

The whole place would be altogether too perfect were it not for the pervasive seediness that keeps South Beach from running away with its own fabulousness. The be-seen scene likes of the Nikki Beach Club and Opium Garden (for both, *see p195*) – to name but two – are neatly brought back down to earth by a scattering of wintering beach bums with possessions packed into supermarket trolleys, and by the crack-addled homeboys and skanky whores who prowl Washington Avenue after dark. Add to the mix the stubbornly egalitarian nature of good ol' redneck Florida, which leads to the startling juxtaposition of world-class hip hotels next door to grungy tattoo parlours and strip joints, and it's little wonder that the place lends itself so perfectly to lurid TV and cinema.

South of 5th Street

The lower swathe of South Beach below 5th Street (a district also known as South Pointe or, more cutely, SoFi) is in trouble or in a state of repair, depending on who you speak to. The culprit? You guessed it: development – or, as some detractors would have it – avarice. The boundaries protecting the Beach's architectural heritage stop at 5th Street and so while small-scale condos and refurbished art deco apartment buildings still fill most of the area, a growing number of mega monolith modern towers mar the overall atmosphere. The 26-storey South Pointe Tower, itself grossly out of scale with the neighbourhood, is now dwarfed by the adjacent Portofino, a controversial 44-storey condo built by controversial developer Thomas Kramer, the nemesis of local preservationists.

Still, there remains some old-school flair. You'll find one of the Beach's best restaurants here in **Joe's Stone Crab** (*see p121*), known worldwide for its succulent crab claws and key lime pie. For a cheaper bill and a dress code that leans towards sandy feet and T-shirts over wet bathing suits, head to **Big Pink** (*see p111*) for diner food, including excellent cake and pies.

A wonderful respite from urban madness is **South Pointe Park**, a verdant park on the very tip of Miami Beach. Surrounded by the Atlantic Ocean and Government Cut channel, the aquatic highway for cruise ships, it furnishes great views. Or, for a little culture, duck into the **Jewish Museum of Florida** (*see below*), which tells the story of Miami's large Hebe community. New to the local art scene and weirdness is the **World Erotic Art Museum** (1205 Washington Avenue; *see p179*), which houses a huge collection of erotic art, including sculptures, paintings, artefacts and jewellery – and penises, of course. Seeing is believing.

Jewish Museum of Florida

301 Washington Avenue, at 3rd Street (305 672 5044/www.jewishmuseum.com). South Beach Local. **Open** 10am-5pm Tue-Sun. **Admission** $6; $4 concessions. **Credit** AmEx, MC, V. **Map** p272 E3. Housed in a beautifully restored art deco former synagogue (built 1936), the museum documents the Jewish experience in Florida since 1763, and presents its own and travelling exhibitions. Its core exhibition, entitled Mosaic: Jewish Life in Florida, presents more than 500 photos and artefacts, two films and a time-line of local Jewish history.

The Deco District

A compact grid of streets easily navigable on foot, the Deco District stretches from 5th Street north to Dade Boulevard and from the Atlantic Ocean west to Biscayne Bay. Three north–south streets – Ocean Drive, Collins Avenue and Washington Avenue – are home to the highest concentration of pastel-painted, neon-lit bars, restaurants, clubs and shops. For all the self-importance, snobbishness and preening vanity, this is the beating heart of Miami Beach.

Collins Avenue. *See p63.*

Celebrity stares

While the ageing pensioners are busy miring through the sand with their metal detectors in search of lost treasures – to their dismay, they're more likely to discover faux bling and baubles and forgotten $15 flea market sunglasses than a gilded artefact from the 17th century – your time may be better spent seeking out actual celebrities, rather than their possessions. Miami Beach is a treasure trove of star spottings, and if you care about those things, we guarantee you'll strike gold.

Your best bet for a sighting of Beyoncé that doesn't require you to order overpriced bottles of booze after facing the humiliation of standing behind a velvet rope until the apathetic doorman decides to let you in after an hour or so is at South Beach's swank stay, the **Setai** (*see p37*). She and long-time lover rapper Jay Z have been rumoured to be throwing down in excess of $15 million for the hotel's posh penthouse, but in the meantime they continue to just stay there as you or I would if we were zillionaire pop stars, spending much time at one of the hotel's three pools. Bono hangs out at the Setai, too, when he's in town. He used to play at the Marlin, but then music producer Chris Blackwell sold the place and since then, they'd be lucky if they had a Spice Girl or some other has-been musician sighting. They don't.

Hotels are swarming with celebs during the daytime, and there's no exception when it comes to South Beach classics such as the **Delano** (*see p35*), **Raleigh** (*see p37*) and **Shore Club** (*see p38*). Mariah Carey holes up at the latter, where she demands her own treadmill, bottled water and that the staff call her 'Tinkerbell' (no, really). Regular folk are allowed in these places during the day, although you may be stopped at the pool and asked for your room key. You can always try the 'oops, I left it upstairs' racket, or, if you're really eager to eavesdrop on P Diddy while he raps on his cell phone, you can always attempt the 'look like you belong there' routine and walk in confidently and defiant. You may be escorted out, of course, but perhaps not before catching a glimpse of someone famous.

Less prohibitive but not always eliciting the A-list, is Lincoln Road, where the likes of local girl Gloria Estefan and an occasional B- or C-list star may be seen in shops like Victoria's Secret or Gap looking for a last-minute bargain or two. The shops on 6th Street and Collins Avenue – you know, the ones that charge $300 for a plain white T-shirt – are your better bets for spotting the Lindsay Lohans of the world, who have personal assistants sniff out their garments before buying them because God forbid they should lift a finger and break a nail. Other daytime best bets include restaurants such as **Prime 112** (*see p119*), where the haute and hungry crowd – among them OJ Simpson – hang out even during the day, not flinching at spending upwards of $400 for a quick bite of Kobe beef. Another foodie favourite, this time at night, is the **Forge** (*see p121*), on the Lincoln Road Mall, which is said to be a hangout of a certain Jenny from the block, among (many) others.

If you're looking for a Colin Farrell type, say, consider hitting Miami's landmark dive bar, **Mac's Club Deuce** (*see p134*), which is open all day and all night, serving up cheap drinks in plastic cups for, well, a pre-habbed Farrell and some other stars who just can't face the sunlight. On Ocean Drive, which once was a hotbed of celebrity activity, you're more likely to see a reality star from MTV or VH1; otherwise, the Drive's drunken mainstay **Wet Willie's** at No.760 is always a safe (sort of) bet. Britney Spears is a former **crobar** (*see p193*) regular, but possibly soured on the place since accusations that she was doing nose candy in the bathroom there; she allegedly sparred with Christina Aguilera at **Mynt Ultra Lounge** (*see p195*), where Justin Timberlake and Cameron Diaz were also (allegedly) getting jiggy.

Celebrity sightseeing on South Beach doesn't only happen in a pedestrian fashion. At any given moment you may see a $600,000 Italian sports car – only one of 400 made in the world, of course – being commandeered by, say, Queen Latifah (or, rather, her driver). Keep your eyes on the road, though, as it would financially break you to crash into one of those.

The bottom line is, if you get a kick out of seeing a pop tart or two while on holiday down here, keep your eyes on the ground, not up there on that pedestal they put themselves on.

For more on celebrity culture in Miami, *see p25* **Cel-ebb and flow**.

More than 800 buildings in the fanciful art deco style give the district its name. But the architecture not only lends its name to the area, it more or less defines it. Without the pristine glossy deco that lines almost every street, South Beach would be a shadow of itself, despite the best efforts of local hoteliers, restaurateurs and nightclub owners. Immortalised in millions of postcards, it's the one image the world outside has of Miami Beach. It's a good one to have too: without it, the Beach's tourist industry would struggle. From glamour and flash comes more glamour and flash; from Miami's architecture has, it can be argued, come its burgeoning after-dark scene. For a suggested walking tour taking in the best of South Beach deco, see p64 **Walk on**.

OCEAN DRIVE

The ten-block strip of Ocean Drive from 5th to 14th Streets is the epicentre of South Beach. On the eastern side of the street, the dunes and beach volleyball courts of **Lummus Park** front the Atlantic Ocean and the white sandy beaches that cost millions to maintain – storms regularly erode refurbishments in just a few costly hours. Six funky, campy lifeguard stands punctuate the beach: a mod antenna spikes the stand at 10th Street, while 12th Street's resembles a purple mobile home, and the one at 14th Street sports a circular roof crowned with AstroTurf.

For 11 years a fantastical sandcastle also graced the park, but the artist, Victor Leong, demolished it in winter 2003 because the local council objected to the donation buckets he had placed in front.

The western side of the street is one sidewalk café and/or bar after another, many attached to classic deco hotels. Let whim guide you or bank on the perennially popular **News Café** (see p111); occupying the corner of 8th Street and Ocean Drive, its tables are packed with sardined trendies 24 hours a day. This was the last halt on earth for Gianni Versace, who breakfasted at the café on 15 July 1997 before Andrew Cunanan followed him the three blocks to the gates of his home, and shot him dead. The scene of the crime, the **Versace Mansion** (1114 Ocean Drive, at 11th Street), aka the Amsterdam Palace, is a flashy (of course) three-storey Italianate palace built in 1930 and supposedly modelled on Christopher Columbus's home in Genoa. Since Versace's murder, the house has been sold and turned into the Casuarina Club, a members-only country club/hotel, but even with the bloodstains long gone, its front steps are still the most photographed spot in town. Next door is the sleek **Hotel Victor** (see p39).

COLLINS AVENUE

Collins is one block inland of Ocean and boasts a similar mix of deco hotels, cafés and bars – minus most of the crassness. Instead of shops selling crapulous tourist tat, Collins boasts high-end retail boutiques such as Nicole Miller, Barneys of New York and Armani. In the midst of the retail gloss is **Puerto Sagua** (see p118), a Cuban restaurant where a full meal will arrive on a plate larger than Long Island and cost less than $10.

Several blocks north, on the corner of 12th Street, is the gorgeously photogenic **Marlin** hotel (see p41); if you can't afford the room rates, at least have a drink at the bar, **Rex** (see p135), a London-style DJ bar. A couple more blocks up is **Jerry's Famous Deli** (see p111); built in 1939 as Hoffman's Cafeteria, it became a ballroom, then a nightclub and now the Taj Mahal of diners, open 24 hours for quick-fill Reubens, burgers and authentic New York cheesecake.

Above 14th Street, the building heights rise. Whereas lower Collins is all three and four storeys, suddenly we're up to ten, 15 and 20 or more floors. All of these contain beds for visitors and the neon signs these hotels carry are some of the ritziest names in town, including the **Delano** (see p35), the **Raleigh**, the **Sagamore** and the **Setai** (for all three, see p37). Each has had millions poured into renovation and restyling and, boy, it shows. Suck in your gut, put some purpose in your stride and call the doorman 'chum' as you brazen an entrance to check out the lobbies and bars. Curse the humble heritage that has bequeathed you nights at the Days Inn.

WASHINGTON AVENUE

A further block inland from Collins Avenue is Washington Avenue, where pizza-by-the-slice joints, all-night grocers and cheque cashiers intersperse with one-of-a-kind boutiques selling retro houseware, faddish clubgear and $500 sunglasses. Despite being only two blocks back from the beach, wandering homeless and some seriously substance-influenced streetfolk mean most visitors steer clear, especially after dark. Hence, the otherwise drop-dead glam art deco **Hotel Astor** (see p39) charges entirely reasonable room rates – they'd be twice as high if the hotel were located just one block east.

Diagonally across from the Astor is the **Wolfsonian-FIU** (see p69), a shamefully undervisited design museum and a place that we can't recommend highly enough. On the same block and just a few doors north is another design classic in the sleek and chrome form of the **11th Street Diner** (see p111) – beautiful to look at, and the food's not bad

Walk on Art deco

Most people go to the beach for the sun, the surf or the breeze, but arguably the best thing about South Beach is its wealth of sleek, streamlined, iridescent architecture, easily explored on foot.

Unlike the grandiose power-tripping of its distant New York or Chicago relatives, Miami Beach art deco is as giddy an assemblage of motifs and influences as any 1920s flapper decked out in beads and baubles. More than 800 buildings from the 1930s and early '40s survive in the city's historic Deco District, between 5th Street to the south and Dade Boulevard to the north. Most are modest in size, few higher than four storeys, and all were cheaply constructed. There's no single building that could be termed a masterpiece, but the impact of so many thematically harmonious structures in such a small area makes for a riotously theatrical modern streetscape, unparalleled anywhere else in the world. It's as fun as architecture gets.

It's also incredible to think that much of this was almost lost when, in the early 1970s, Ocean Drive and all that lay behind it was to be demolished and redeveloped as concrete condo canyons, similar to Mid Beach. City Hall's argument was that the land was too valuable for such small buildings. Their survival is due to the vision of a handful of activists who, in 1976, founded the Miami Design Preservation League (MDPL). Three years later, much of South Beach was listed on the National Register of Historic Places.

That the Beach has such a wealth of deco in the first place is down to two key events: the 1925 Paris Exposition Internationale des Arts Décoratifs et Industriels Modernes, and the hurricane of 1926. With most of the Beach's buildings destroyed by the latter, architects had a free hand to marry the renewed interest in decorative arts brought on by the former with the contemporary fascination for industrial design. Ship portholes, wheel crankshafts and streamlined wings were incorporated into building designs. Angular shapes and geometric patterns predominate, while whimsical decorative touches, such as bas-reliefs, incorporate tropical themes including palm trees and flamingos.

Ocean & 5th

There are examples of Miami Beach deco south of 5th Street, but the greatest haul is concentrated in the ten blocks to the north, particularly along Ocean Drive. The principal architects of deco South Beach were two relocated New Yorkers, Henry Hohauser and L Murray Dixon. The **Park Central Hotel** at 630 Ocean Drive is one of Hohauser's best efforts, while the neighbouring **Imperial** (650 Ocean Drive) is a less ostentatious design by Dixon. The former dates from 1937, the latter from '39, and both utilise the same design palette of bold vertical bands and window 'eyebrows' for shade.

The mauve, green and white colour scheme isn't, strictly speaking, authentic. The buildings of South Beach were originally painted white with subtle pastels highlighting a few details. The postcard-friendly candy colours came along in the 1980s, when Leonard Horowitz, an interior designer and MDPL preservationist, devised a palette of tones to draw attention to the architecture.

Serene as this beachfront scene is now, it's hard to imagine that in the early 1980s this area was one of the worst crime spots on the Beach – a natural choice for a scene of stomach-churning violence in the Brian DePalma movie *Scarface*, shot at 728 Ocean Drive.

The **Colony Hotel** at 736 Ocean Drive (*photo p64*) is one of Hohauser's first hotels (1935), and it's worth slipping into the lobby for a look at the original green Vitrolite fireplace with mural. A block along, at the corner with 9th Street, is the **Waldorf Towers** (860 Ocean Drive), built in 1937 and distinguished by its round observatory tower. The tower was branded unsafe by City Hall in the early 1980s and pulled down, but it has since been rebuilt by a private developer. More murals can be found at the 1939 **Breakwater Hotel** (940 Ocean Drive), which is signposted by a soaring, self-promoting pylon; the lobby paintings here were executed in the 1980s and feature a large group of politicians and preservationists turning away a wrecking ball hovering over Ocean Drive.

Appropriately enough, just over the road, the stand-alone building in the park, the former Ocean Front Auditorium, is now the **Art Deco District Welcome Center** (*see p66*) and offices of the MDPL; at the rear is a hall used for temporary exhibitions on local heritage.

When the MDPL kicked off its activities, the focus was on two blocks of Ocean Drive, from 12th to 14th Streets, and in particular the

classic deco triumvirate of the **Leslie** (1244 Ocean Drive; *photo p67 top right*), the **Carlyle** (No.1250) and the **Cardozo** (No.1300), each the work of a different architect, but all built between 1937 and 1941. Of the three, it's the Carlyle (currently undergoing major renovation that will transform it into yet another condo-hotel) that absolutely typifies Miami Beach deco: a flamboyant, flashy ensemble of striking vertical piers, bold horizontal lines, visor-like sunshades and sexily curvaceous corners. It's as camp as a building gets and a natural for the role of gay nightclub in Mike Nichols' *The Birdcage* (1996).

Collins & Española

The inspiration for the drag queen action at the Birdcage was the Warsaw, a legendary centre of homo debauchery housed in the striking **Hoffman's Cafeteria Building** (1450 Collins Avenue), a low-rise deco gem with central turret and sweeping 'angel wings' designed by Hohauser in 1939. From a cafeteria it became a ballroom, then a series of clubs, including the Warsaw; now it's the excellent Jerry's Famous Deli (*see p63; photo p67 bottom*).

Collins Avenue presents less of a unified architectural set piece than Ocean Drive, broken up as it has always been by parking lots for beach-goers. Its worth was slower to be recognised, so that as recently as 1988, developers were able to consign L Murray Dixon's splendid Senator Hotel to rubble and turn the vacant space into – what else? – a car park. Nonetheless, a handful of gems survive, notably the **Marlin**, a 1939 design by Dixon that seems to draw inspiration from the sci-fi serials of the era such as *Flash Gordon*, and a cover model of a building if ever there was one. Two blocks south of the Marlin is another beauty – Hohauser's 1938 **Essex House Hotel** (1001 Collins Avenue), where the porthole windows and smokestack-like neon tower give the building the fantastic air of a landlocked ocean liner.

Thanks to a new wave of enlightened and style-conscious South Beach hoteliers and developers – plus stringent planning regulations – these days Collins is looking better than ever, especially at dusk, as the light fades to a bruised purple and the neon is switched on.

Washington & 10th

Walk one block west and the money suddenly stops. While there are a couple of beautifully polished-up places on Washington Avenue, such as the **Hotel Chelsea** (No.944) and the neighbouring **Hotel Astor** (No.956), most of the deco back here – such as block-sharers the **Davies** (No.1020), the **Hotel Taft** (No.1044) and the **Kenmore** (No.1050) – looks like it's missed the party. One day soon their day will come around again as more people realise that you don't have to stay on the Beach to enjoy Miami. In the meantime, it's worth visiting the lobby of the Kenmore for its neon-lit staircase and seriously sensual railings. Similarly, there's a beautiful bit of gilt deco design displayed in the foyer of the **Wolfsonian-FIU** (*see p63*) across the road.

Three blocks up on the left is the **Miami Beach Post Office** (1300 Washington Avenue; *photo p67 top left*), dating from 1939 and designed in a style termed 'deco Federal'. It has a classical, central rotunda topped with a shallow dome and an ornamental lantern. The façade is virtually unadorned, while the interior features a cowboys and Indians frieze, starburst ceiling and attractive brass detailing.

Elsewhere, it's easy to miss most of Washington's deco heritage, distracted by the thrift store appearance at ground level. But just keep looking up, particularly at No.1445, the old **Cameo Theater**, now the crobar nightclub (*see p193*); above the chrome canopy and glass-block panel is a beautiful carved keystone with a flourish of palm fronds.

Taking a right on Española we're back on Collins at **Jerry's Famous Deli**, a great halt for an order of suitably retro cuisine. The architecture doesn't stop: there's more fine deco north along Collins and, for anyone with the energy for the six-block hike, a particularly impressive grouping around 21st Street.

Art Deco District Welcome Center

1001 Ocean Drive, at 10th Street (305 531 3484). Bus C, H, K, W, South Beach Local. **Open** 10am-7pm daily. **Admission** free. **Credit** AmEx, MC, V. **Map** p273 D3.
The centre offers guided deco walking tours at 10.30am Wednesday and Saturday, and 6.30pm Thursday ($15 per person; approx 90mins), or self-guided audio tours from 10am to 4pm ($10 per person). There's also a shop with books, posters and souvenirs.

South Beach – only those with great bodies (and no jobs) need apply. *See p60.*

either. There's more noteworthy architecture over the road on the corner at 13th Street with the **Miami Beach Post Office** (No.1300), which deviates from the art deco norm with nods towards the Depression Moderne style, including a rotunda with exquisite acoustics.

A couple of blocks further north is **Española Way**, a sweet – if overly contrived – block-long cluster of Spanish Mediterranea: the buildings come in peach and orange, ornamented with awnings and balconies. Originally designed in the 1930s as an artists' colony, it is now given over to twee galleries, boutiques and cafés, although **A La Folie** (see p110) adds a welcome bit of Gallic bite. The **Clay Hotel & International Hostel** (see p48), which occupies most of the south side of the street, was formerly the home of Desi '*I Love Lucy*' Arnaz. The building was also at one time the headquarters of Al Capone's gambling syndicate. On Sunday mornings, Española hosts a small but eclectic market with vintage gewgaws, ethnic handicrafts and food.

Although there are no spotlights to guide you there, if you look carefully off Española Way's historic Plaza de España, you'll see **Miami Beach Cinematheque** (512 Española Way; see p173), home to the best of indie and classic films. Come prepared for a touch of culture and class, just slightly out of place on SoBe.

Wolfsonian-FIU

1001 Washington Avenue, at 10th Street (305 531 1001/www.wolfsonian.org). Bus C, H, K, W, South Beach Local. **Open** noon-6pm Mon, Tue, Sat, Sun; noon-9pm Thur, Fri. **Admission** $7; $5 concessions. **Credit** AmEx, MC, V. **Map** p273 D2.

Housed in a finely restored 1927 storage facility, this museum and research centre founded by local millionaire Mickey Wolfson explores how design shapes and reflects the human experience. If that sounds a bit stuffy, it's not. The artefacts come from Wolfson's private collection and include some beauts – a deco post box from New York's Central Station, a stained-glass window by fey Irish illustrator Harry Clarke, and Cuban cinema posters, as well as lots of attractively displayed furniture, ceramics, metalwork, paintings and architectural drawings. The permanent exhibits are supplemented by tip-top touring exhibitions and a full programme of lectures and films. Plus there's a good little museum shop (see p155). **Photo** p72.

Lincoln Road Mall

The Lincoln Road Mall – or, in local shorthand, 'the Road' – had its heyday in the 1950s, when it was designed by iconic architectural guru Morris Lapidus (see p73 **Know your MiMo from your deco**) and dubbed the 'Fifth

Avenue of the South'. And just as Lapidus went through an unpopular period before coming back into fashion in the 1990s, so Lincoln Road waned before experiencing a resurgence as the prime South Beach spot, especially for locals jaded with the preening crowds on Ocean Drive.

Gussied up in 1997 with a $16-million facelift, the mall sits between 16th and 17th Streets and stretches from Washington Avenue to Alton Road. From one end to the other it's wall-to-wall sidewalk cafés, clubs, boutiques, high-end retail shops, restaurants, cultural venues and galleries. Once upon a time, those businesses might have qualified as legitimately avant-garde, but after the renovation, rental rates soared and today most of the shops on Lincoln Road are of the chain variety. Lincoln Road now has more Starbucks than entire cities in America's Midwest.

The Road crowd – male and female, both – typically come equipped with airdogs and wheeled feet. Busiest time is late evening, when the dozens of cafés and restaurants double their dining capacity by setting up sidewalk tables for the bridge and tunnel crowd. Choice venues include the **Van Dyke Café** (see p111), sister to Ocean Drive's News Café, and the sun-soaked outpost of pink London fave **Balans** (see p110). The Road also houses popular glam gay nightspot **Score** (see p181), which maintains foot traffic on the mall well into the early hours. Sundays are popular for the antiques and farmers' market (Oct-June, every second & fourth Sunday).

Cultural venues on Lincoln include the **Lincoln Theater** (see p187), home of the New World Symphony, and the **Colony Theatre** (see p206), a deco gem that hosts theatre, dance and music performances, and recently held screenings as part of the Miami International Film Festival (see p158). At the mall's western end is the fairly recent addition of the **Regal South Beach** cinema (see p173).

North of Lincoln Road

Immediately north of the Lincoln Road is Miami Beach's civic centre; on or just off 17th Street are **City Hall**, the super-massive **Miami Beach Convention Center**, the all-purpose **Jackie Gleason Theater** (see p186) and the Beach's most prominent place of worship, the monumental **Temple Emanu El Synagogue** (1701 Washington Avenue, 305 538 2503), which aggressively commands the junction with Washington Avenue.

West of the Convention Center is a small botanical garden where, among the fronds and flora, lurk the **Miami Beach Visitors' Center** (1920 Meridian Avenue, 305 674 1270)

Life's a beach...

... question is, which one to choose? Here's a rundown of our favourites.

Miami Beach

South Pointe Park
1 Washington Avenue, South Beach.
Map p272 F3.
Part of a 17-acre park with picnic areas, a children's playground, a fishing pier, a marked Vita course, a fitness circuit and great views of cruise ships. *See p61.*

Lummus Park Beach
Ocean Drive, between 5th & 15th Streets, South Beach. **Map** p273 C3-F2.
Volleyball, thatched huts and people-watching. There's a gay beach at 12th Street. *See p63.*

21st-35th Street Beach
Collins Avenue, Mid Beach. **Map** p272 A4/B4.
Small beaches with a boardwalk and snacks. *See p72.*

53rd-63rd Street Beach
Collins Avenue, Mid Beach. **Map** p270.
Pleasant, not-too-crowded beaches between high-rises. Very family-oriented, with a kids' playground at 53rd Street. *See p72.*

Pelican Island
Accessible on weekends by free boat taxi from the marina at 79th Street Causeway, Belle Meade (305 754 9330).
A small island reachable during the week by private boat or, on weekends, a 35-seat public boat (free). Expect barbecue grills, picnic tables, volleyball nets, horseshoe pits and – of course – pelicans.

North Shore Open Space Park
Collins Avenue, between 79th & 86th Streets, Surfside. **Map** p270.
Boardwalks, pavilions, barbecue grills and a Vita course. *See p74.*

Surfside
Collins Avenue, between 88th & 96th Streets, Surfside. **Map** p270.
There's a lifeguard station, but otherwise, facilities here are limited. *See p74.*

Bal Harbour
Beach Collins Avenue, at 96th Street, Bal Harbour. **Map** p270.
A small beach with a Vita course. *See p75.*

Haulover Beach
10600 Collins Avenue, Bal Harbour. **Map** p270.
A 12-mile stretch of white sand, open ocean surf, landscaped dunes and shaded picnic facilities. There's a nude beach (between the two northernmost parking lots) and a gay nude beach (north of the lifeguard tower), with nude volleyball. *See p75.*

Sunny Isles Beach
Collins Avenue, between 163rd & 192nd Streets, Sunny Isles. **Map** p270.
Two miles of public beaches, souvenir shops and hotels. *See p75.*

Key Biscayne & Virginia Key

Hobie Beach
Virginia Key. **Map** p271.
Windsurfing, jet-ski, sailboat and sailboard rentals. *See p75.*

Crandon Park
4000 Crandon Boulevard, Key Biscayne. **Map** p271.
Pristine sand, calm, shallow water, a winding boardwalk and convenient parking. *See p76.*

Bill Baggs Cape Florida State Recreation Area

1200 S Crandon Boulevard. **Map** p271.
A popular spot, with many activities. *See p76.*

South Miami

Matheson Hammock Park Beach

9610 Old Cutler Road, between SW 93rd & 101st Streets, South Miami. **Map** p271.
Scenic park with a man-made atoll pool that's flushed by the tidal action of Biscayne Bay.

Tips & information

Umbrellas and loungers are available at many beaches; if you don't see an attendant, claim a chair and one will soon show up to collect the fee. Topless sunbathing is permitted on Miami Beach, and there are a few places that allow nude sunbathing (notably **Haulover Beach**; *see p75*). Sun here is subtropical, and you can get burned even on overcast days. Use a sunscreen with an SPF of at least 15 (30 for children) year round, and take a hat.

Pay close attention to official warnings about beach conditions. Lifeguards post warning flags and signs by their stations. Green means it's safe to swim. 'No swimming' (red) means just that. 'Caution' (yellow) means hazardous conditions such as riptides, so your best bet is to ask the lifeguard just what dangers exist. Riptides, which occur on days with strong onshore winds, can carry even the most experienced swimmer out to sea. If it happens to you, aim to swim parallel to the shore until you're out of the rip's hold, then turn to swim towards shore. For full information on conditions or warnings, call the Miami Beach Patrol at 305 673 7714.

Watch out for Portuguese men-of-war, jellyfish-like sea creatures that look like blue bubbles floating on the water or washed up amid seaweed. Their long tentacles pack a nasty sting and occasionally cause allergic reactions. If you get stung, head for the lifeguard, who will treat the stings. You'll smart for a few hours, but that's usually all. Sea lice, or immature men-of-war, are more annoying than dangerous. They attach to your swimsuit and cause itching rather than stinging. To relieve it, shower with soap and water.

These beaches are open every day. There are public parking lots and metered street parking, but by 10am most are full.

Lummus Park.

Sightseeing

and a highly emotive **Holocaust Memorial** (305 538 1663, open 9am-9pm daily) by artist Kenneth Treister. The memorial takes the form of a 42-foot upraised beckoning hand, tattooed with an Auschwitz serial number and anchored by a writhing mass of death camp victims.

A short walk east of the convention centre, between Washington and Collins avenues, is the excellent **Bass Museum of Art** (*see below*) and the sexily curvaceous new home of the **Miami City Ballet** (*see p206*).

Bass Museum of Art

2121 Park Avenue, at Collins Avenue (305 673 7530/www.bassmuseum.org). Bus C, G, H, L, S. **Open** 10am-5pm Tue-Sat; 11am-5pm Sun. **Admission** $8; $6 concessions; free under-6s. **Credit** AmEx, MC, V. **Map** p272 B3.
The Bass is the centrepiece of Miami Beach's 'cultural campus'. A few years ago it underwent an $8-million facelift that preserved the historic architecture (the core of the building is the old Miami Beach public library built in 1930) but vastly expanded the facilities. In addition to pieces from the museum's own permanent collection (including European Old Masters, rococo court paintings, 18th-century English portraits, Flemish tapestries and Chinese woodblock prints), at any one time there will be up to three different world-class travelling exhibitions, which could be anything from folk art to photography to video installations. Exhibitions are supplemented by a programme of regular talks and workshops, and there's a good little gift shop.

Wolfsonian-FIU. *See p63.*

Mid Beach

In the 1950s the kitschy oversized hotels that sit shoulder to shoulder on mid-Miami Beach – or Mid Beach – defined the stereotypical vacation here. Grandes dames such as the **Eden Roc** and **Fontainebleau** (for both, *see p49*) went all out for a campy interpretation of glamour. These days the icons seem ironic and benign, having recently undergone substantial renovation, and catering mostly to conventioneers and Latin American visitors instead of the starlets and movie moguls who once headed here. The hotels get larger, the crowds get older and the pace gets slower as you head north out of South Beach.

West of Collins Avenue, Mid Beach is a mix of golf courses and upper-class residential, with sprawling estates fronting **Indian Creek**, a narrow waterway west of Collins where yachts bob and the University of Miami rowing club practises at dawn. If ogling grand homes intrigues, try old-money La Gorce and Pine Tree Drives on the west side of the creek for mixed imitation architecture lurking behind imposing gates. Collins is the only street of any consequence, and even it becomes more soulless up beyond 50th Street, as unremarkable beige buildings tower over both sides of the street and turn it into a condo canyon.

Ten blocks of beach behind the big hotels (36th to 46th Streets) underwent a $7-million facelift in the late 1990s to counteract erosion and give the sun-worshippers more real estate for their beach chairs. A public beach just north of the Eden Roc has ample parking, while a wooden boardwalk popular with joggers, elderly couples and orthodox Jewish families runs behind the hotels and allows visitors to peer into beachfront bars.

North Beach

North Beach is local slang; you won't find the appellation on official cartography. Extending north of the condo canyon, this working- and middle-class residential area stretches roughly from 63rd Street to 79th Street. The two smatterings of commercial activity are on 71st Street, where the JFK Causeway spans the bay, and Collins Avenue, where slightly seedy restaurants, cafés and shops intersperse with hotels that cater to budget-minded South Americans. Not as chic as South Beach nor as residential as Mid Beach, North Beach has a few hidden charms, among them the wildly popular locals **Café Prima Pasta** (*see p121*) and **Café Ragazzi** (*see p122*), where the queues outside say it all.

Know your MiMo from your Deco

'Tail-fin chic.' These days it sounds like a compliment, but for architect Morris Lapidus the label was just one of countless sneers prompted by his designs. Lapidus was the pioneer of an architectural style now dubbed 'MiMo' (Miami Modern), a style at its height during the 1950s and early '60s, which is also when it was most reviled.

Lapidus's credo was 'Less is nothing' (or, to put it another way, 'Too much is never enough' – as the title of his autobiography has it): his flagship designs, such as the 1954 Fontainebleau hotel, were sinuous celebrations of a new, optimistic post-war mindset. It was brave new architecture for the 21st century, as imagined in 1950. The sleek, functional Bauhaus-derived school of sober modernism did not find wide appeal in such a luxury-bent climate as Miami, whereas MiMo was all set to show off: 'It's the crazy hat for a woman, the bright tie for men,' Lapidus once said. The critics loved to hate his showboating curves, cheeseholes (amoeboid cutouts in walls) and woggles (his name for floating amoeboid shapes), but financially the style was a success, embodying as it did the swinging good times of high life on the Florida coast.

While art deco remains the identifying style for Miami, through the efforts of local preservationists MiMo is gradually gaining recognition throughout the US. A few years back, Miami-Dade County unveiled a photographic exhibition of MiMo architecture, which proved very popular and went on to travel to New York.

Despite its ostentatious forms, MiMo is harder to spot than the quaint, pastel-coloured art deco of South Beach, although there are occasional confusions between the two. In general, MiMo is most common in North Beach, Surfside and Bal Harbour, as well as areas of Biscayne Boulevard. High-profile examples include several hotels: Lapidus's **Fontainebleau** and the nearby **Eden Roc** (for both, *see p49; photos above*).

Not all MiMo is as visually dominating. The form is in fact immortalised in hundreds of buildings, ranging from single-family homes to apartment buildings and synagogues; not just in Miami, but also several New York buildings, including Lapidus's boomerang-shaped Americana hotel.

Although some MiMo landmarks have been demolished, Miami's more savvy politicians recognise that this extravagant take on good-time architecture may one day have the same sort of economic benefit on North Beach as art deco did on South Beach. Efforts are under way to preserve many MiMo buildings.

Lapidus died in 2001, just in time to see MiMo rediscovered. As someone who by all accounts possessed a fine sense of the absurd, he'd no doubt be very amused at the idea of his cheeseholes and woggles as a spur for regentrification.

Islands and causeways

Four causeways span the three miles of Biscayne Bay between mainland Miami and Miami Beach, while two more cross its waters further north, providing the sort of vistas that give Miami its Chamber of Commerce moniker of the Magic City.

The **MacArthur Causeway** (I-395), the busiest of the causeways, crosses just north of Downtown, spilling three lanes of traffic on to South Beach's 5th Street. On Friday and Saturday nights, traffic goes bumper to bumper as suburban club-goers make the weekend pilgrimage across the bay. Seen from MacArthur, the Downtown skyline is splendid, with 40 permanently illuminated buildings that include the NationsBank Tower, which changes colour frequently to boost sports teams and celebrate holidays.

The MacArthur also provides access to **Watson Island**, a scruffy bit of shore one mile east of Downtown. Once upon a time, there was little here but a marina, excellent fresh fish markets and a seaplane terminal. Things began to change quickly over the past few years, as first the City Commission and then voters approved a major redevelopment plan for the island. It already now includes the **Miami Children's Museum** and **Parrot Jungle Island** (for both, see p165). By late 2006 or so Watson Island will also be home to Island Gardens, a massive top-notch resort with a bay walk and nautical history museum.

Watson Island's waterside park benches are ideal for ogling the behemoth cruise ships docked across the Government Cut channel at the Port of Miami. The port itself consumes **Dodge** and **Lummus** islands, the sole working-class islands in a bay of wealth. Three small bridges lace off the MacArthur's north side to a trio of exclusive residential islands, each with its own stars: **Palm**, the former home of Al Capone; **Hibiscus**, one-time residence of author Damon Runyon; and **Star**, where you'll find the abode of Gloria Estefan.

At the Beach end of the MacArthur is the ferry dock for **Fisher Island**, a well-manicured private island clustered with Mediterranean-style condos, visible just across the channel. Originally the southernmost tip of Miami Beach, Fisher was created in 1905 when the well-named Government Cut was dredged to improve access to the port. Today the island is home to the impossibly exclusive Fisher Island Club (if you have to ask the price, you can't afford to stay here).

South is the **Rickenbacker Causeway** in the Key Biscayne area (see p75), which provides superb vantage points over the city and its waterfront.

Just over a mile north of MacArthur on the Beach side (it's considerably closer on the mainland) is the **Venetian Causeway**. The first of the water-roadways to be built, it's a slow, two-lane street that stretches from the northern edge of South Beach to Downtown. The causeway bisects several residential islands (Belle Isle, San Marino, Biscayne Isle and Dilido – signs for the latter invariably have the second 'i' painted out by local wags) and is a popular cycling and jogging trail.

North again, the **Julia Tuttle Causeway** (also known as One Ninety Five) feeds into I-95, the freeway that acts as south Florida's Main Street. On the Beach side, the Tuttle becomes 41st Street, the commercial hub of Mid Beach. At the 'Welcome to Miami Beach' sign at the foot of 41st, a dozen palms wear neon necklaces that brand the night with vibrant colours. Furthest north, the **JFK Causeway** and **Broad Causeway** form the last major physical links to the mainland, although Miami Beach will always like to believe that, in attitude at least, it's hundreds of miles from the rest of the US.

Perhaps the city's newest hotspot for café life, retail and dining is tiny **Ocean Terrace**, fronting the beach between 73rd Street and 75th Street. Proponents bill this as the next Ocean Drive, with its MiMo architecture.

The bandshell on 74th and Collins is the kind of photo background that epitomises the sun and fun of Miami Beach. Painted acqua and buttermint yellow, its rounded forms and art deco details telegraph wordlessly that, wherever you are, you ain't in Kansas any more.

Surfside to Golden Beach

Just north of North Beach, on a seedy two-block stretch of Collins Avenue, is **North Shore Open Space Park**. The park is a lovely and underused stretch of pristine beach lined with sea grape trees, sand dunes, a boardwalk, a Vita exercise course and amenities such as changing rooms, picnic tables and barbecue pits. The park forms the southern border of **Surfside**, a sleepy residential enclave, less than a mile square, clotted with two- and three-storey apartment buildings and boasting little to entice visitors save the promise of less crowded beaches.

You don't need to see a city limits sign to know you're in **Bal Harbour**, the elegant burg just north of Surfside. The landscape sports an expensive topiary manicure, luxury cars ply the streets, chauffeurs in caps keep the motor idling and the A/C on while madam shops: there's a distinct whiff of money in the air. In Bal Harbour, crime is low (the local police are notoriously zealous about dispensing speeding tickets), real-estate prices are high and the median age is at least 30 years older than on the southern half of the sandbar.

There are said to be more millionaires per capita in Bal Harbour than in any other city in the United States, and it shows. You need to be one to hang out here for long. **Bal Harbour Shops** (*see p142*) is an oppressively top-end mall where the concession list reads like a *Who's Who* of haute couture. Security guards in absurd faux-colonial uniforms and Styrofoam pith helmets prowl its parking lots in golf carts.

Haulover Beach Park, just north of Bal Harbour, scores big points as one of the area's most scenic stretches of beachfront, offering unimpeded views spanning the southern sweep of Miami Beach. Worth the drive or straightforward bus journey from South Beach (take the S from Lincoln Road), the beach is fringed with dense vegetation that blocks out the visual pollution of nearby high-rises. Known primarily for its section of nude beach, Haulover also has a 1,100-foot fishing pier, picnic tables, concession stands and a kayak rental outfit for jaunts into the nearby Oleta river, a pristine waterway that wends its way westwards through the **Oleta River State Recreation Area** (*see below*).

Beyond Haulover Beach Park lies **Sunny Isles Beach**, where architectural kitsch and older tourists once prevailed. In an effort to change its reputation forever, Sunny Isles Beach has undergone a luxury condominium building boom beachside, irritating most residents, but pleasing city fathers with the massively expanding tax base. These days Sunny Isles Beach resembles more the condo canyon of mid-Miami Beach than the low-rent beach community it was from World War II until just a handful of years ago.

One of the few redeeming features of Sunny Isles is **Wolfie Cohen's Rascal House** (*see p131*), a bustling restaurant/deli serving Jewish dishes that has been around long enough to earn the distinction of landmark status. Waitresses wear nametags and call you 'honey', and patrons kvetch in Yiddish. Not to be missed if you're in the area.

Oleta River State Recreation Area

3400 NE 163rd Street, between Biscayne Boulevard & Collins Avenue, Sunny Isles (305 919 1846). Bus E, S, V. **Open** 8am-5.30pm daily. **Admission** *Per vehicle $2-$4. On foot/bicycle* $1; free under-8s. **Credit** MC, V.

The largest urban park in the state, covering around 1,000 acres, Oleta River is another one of those splendid natural wonders that manage to exist in the shadows of condo canyons and metropolitan mayhem. Once home to the Tequesta Indians, who camped along its shores, the river is a habitat for waterbirds, manatees and dolphins. Visitors can explore the river on canoe or kayak, and there is a popular fishing pier. The park is well known for its miles of mountain bike trails, all graded at varying levels of difficulty. A concession offers kayak, canoe and bicycle rentals.

Key Biscayne

The **Rickenbacker Causeway** arcs from just south of Downtown on to two sleepy and physically striking islands: Key Biscayne and its silent partner, Virginia Key. The ratio of models to grains of sand may be considerably smaller than on Miami Beach, but what lacks in superficial beauty is compensated by a serenity and unpretentiousness that you will not find on the Beach. You can get to Key Biscayne by taking bus B from the Downtown bus terminal.

Virginia Key

Just over the causeway on Virginia Key are **Hobie Beach**, **Windsurfer Beach** and **Jet Ski Beach**, named, aptly enough, after the watersports popular on each. Rental stands for windsurfers, kayaks, sailboats and jet skis dot the white-sand shoreline down here, and the azure water of Biscayne Bay forms a wide, relatively shallow pan serviced by steady winds. If you're desperate to amuse the kids, take them to see the sad underwater creatures at the **Miami Seaquarium** (4400 Rickenbacker Causeway, 305 361 5705). But in our opinion it's a shabby affair, with forlorn-looking animals; we would advise you to go elsewhere.

On the northern side of the causeway as it hits Virginia Key sits the **Rusty Pelican**, a seafood house with a corny nautical motif, average fare and stunning views back towards the city, particularly at sunset. For better eats in funkier surroundings, duck into the **Bayside Hut** (*see p137*), which is next to the Rickenbacker Marina and the Miami Marine Stadium, an antiquated waterfront concert venue. Patrons sit outside beneath a chickee hut in shorts and T-shirts and nibble on the restaurant's signature fish dip and seafood.

The **Rickenbacker Causeway** gives great views from your car (or boat).

Further down the casual scale, and higher up the scenic pole, is **Jimbo's** (*see p137*), a slice of genuine Floridiana. The salty dive is a wooden shack-cum-menuless-restaurant tucked into Virginia Key's mangroves at the edge of Biscayne Bay. Fishermen play *bocce*, while locals buy dollar cans of beer and smoked fish. A cluster of electric-coloured façades forms a faux-Caribbean street once used as a backdrop for the TV series *Flipper*.

Key Biscayne

The Key, as locals call Key Biscayne, is the northernmost island in the Florida Keys. Its life as an exclusive resort began in the early 1900s, when sea captain William Commodore dredged the bay, zealously planted tropical foliage and built yacht basins for his moneyed pals. Locals feared the worst – the invasion of riff-raff – in the late 1940s, when flamboyant flying ace Eddie Rickenbacker opened the toll bridge; indeed, construction went into a frenzy when the condos that cluster on the western end of the island were built. Still, the Key remained an unknown, affluent burg until its most famous resident, former US president Richard Nixon, bought a home here in the 1970s.

Nixon may, in a twisted way, have helped push up property prices and put the Key on the map, but the mendacious prez did little to make the island more lively. With little in the way of nightlife, shopping or culture, the lures for visitors are purely natural: beaches, two waterfront parks, a cycling path and absurdly photographable views of Miami.

Crossing to Key Biscayne, the causeway is renamed Crandon Boulevard, and becomes the main thoroughfare. The prime attractions are **Crandon Park** on the east and **Bill Baggs Cape Florida State Recreation Area** (*see below*), the 400-acre park at the tip of the island. Palm trees line Crandon, and shallow waters, barbecues and picnic tables make it a family favourite. Bill Baggs, too, offers good swimming. The shoreline is softened by sand dunes, and boardwalks lead to the **Cape Florida Lighthouse**, built in 1825. In the distance, half a dozen houses sit in the water on wooden legs like oversized grasshoppers. The brilliantly named **Stiltsville** was built in the 1940s by fishermen who wanted to circumvent property taxes; recent laws forbid repairs, and the fate of the unusual village has been left to the vagaries of nature and an escalating legal battle.

Bill Baggs Cape Florida State Recreation Area

1200 S Crandon Boulevard (305 361 5811/ www.floridastateparks.org/capeflorida). Bus B. **Open** 8am-sundown daily. **Admission** *Per vehicle* $2-$4. *On foot/bicycle* $1. **Credit** MC, V.
Occupying the southern tip of Key Biscayne, this park's wide beaches regularly make the national top ten lists. But this is more than just a pretty place to catch some rays: there's history, wildlife and lots of activities. You can tour the Cape Florida Lighthouse, the oldest building in south Florida; explore native wildlife planted in the aftermath of 1992's Hurricane Andrew; and try your hand at shoreline fishing, ocean kayaking, windsurfing, cycling and in-line skating. Covered pavilions are available for picnicking, and the Lighthouse Café offers good cuisine.

Sightseeing

Downtown

It may have taken a while, but is the ghetto finally becoming ghetto fabulous?

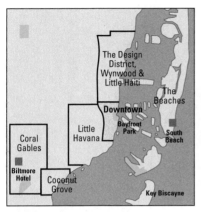

Map p274

The impact of the city's real-estate growth resonates like a sonic boom in Downtown Miami. The once-modest gathering of imperious skyscrapers is getting more imperious, and the architecture has evolved from colourful, campy '80s to post-2000 sleek. By day, big basement car parks swallow commuters, who are then whisked to their desks by elevator. Business at ground level exists largely as a motley assortment of tacky discount electronics stores, pawn shops, seedy immigration lawyers and 99-cent emporiums. By night, the few shuffling pedestrians look like extras from a George Romero movie. During the winter and spring months, turkey vultures circle.

So what's to see? In Downtown proper, not too much. There are a few interesting cultural institutions and one or two decent riverside restaurants. The most intriguing aspect of the district is perhaps its future. With the ongoing construction of the new Performing Arts Center (*see p79* **Downtown top ranking**) has come a boom in Downtown real-estate development, as wannabe Trumps race to build the most luxurious high-rises. Allegedly, once these buildings are occupied – and lately, as the real-estate market slumps downward, the question looms large if they ever will be occupied, or even built – the retail and restaurants will come.

Meantime, possibly the finest way to experience Downtown is to view it by night from either the Rickenbacker or MacArthur

Causeway. Seen from one of these vantage points, it is one of the finest illuminated skylines in the US, notable for the curved **Bank of America Tower** (200 SE 1st Avenue, at SE 2nd Street), often bathed in white light but sometimes wearing aqua and orange (the colours of the Miami Dolphins football team) or snowflakes at Christmas; the 55-storey **First Union Financial Center** (200 S Biscayne Boulevard, at SE 2nd Street); and the golden, 1925 **Freedom Tower** (*see p80*), which became a hot topic in 2005 when developer Pedro Martin wanted to tear it down in order to make way for – yep, you guessed it – more condo development.

GETTING AROUND

Buses C and K connect the Downtown bus terminal with Washington Avenue on South Beach. From the bus terminal, which is just south of W Flagler Street, Downtown is compact enough to explore on foot. Alternatively, walk one block north to Government Center station for the Metromover, a driverless elevated train that makes an inner and outer loop around the Downtown business district (*see p81*).

Around Flagler Street

Flagler Street is Downtown's main drag, lined with small shops catering mainly to South American shoppers. About the only destination outlet that does not have a sign declaring 'Todo Ten Dollars' is department store **Macy's**, which began life in 1898 as a dry goods emporium and now occupies a fine 1936 streamline Depression Moderne building at 22 E Flagler. A little way east, the **Seybold Building** (33 E Flagler Street, at N Miami Avenue) is the heart of one of the largest jewellery districts in the country; there are more than 280 jewellers here. If you need a glittery rock then this is the place for you.

Further along Flagler is Downtown's one truly outstanding building, the 1925 **Gusman Center for the Performing Arts** (*see p186*), easily recognisable by the restored marquee and the charming box office kiosk in front. Rudy Vallee and Elvis Presley played at this Mediterranean revival stunner, which features extravagant plaster details, twinkling ceiling lights and 12-foot crystal chandeliers. In 2002 the Gusman underwent a multimillion-dollar

Freedom Tower. *See p80.*

Downtown top ranking

Not many American cities harbour a downtown as anomalous and depressing as Miami's. As with many south Florida oddities, this is due to a total lack of planning in the city's heyday.

Downtown in American metropolises usually consists of a balance of office, commercial and residential components, but such a balance wasn't considered in Downtown Miami's early days. Landmark buildings were the wellspring for commercial interests and not much besides, with small retailers, discount stores and cafés servicing only local workers. Until recently, Downtown rolled up the carpet at the end of the business day, security bars were put in place and every living soul took off for the suburbs.

The authorities have finally sharpened up, however, and as this guide went to press were due to unveil a new, much-anticipated $334-million Performing Arts Center (see p207), which should bring some after-dark life into the heart of the city. Designed by Cesar Pelli, it's intended to be an architectural landmark, constructed with limestone and incorporating the existing art deco Sears Tower. Slate,

stone, stainless steel and glass embellish the exterior. The centre will be home to the city's key cultural groups (including the Florida Grand Opera, the Florida Philharmonic and the Miami City Ballet) in several auditoriums, two of them seating more than 2,000 people each. In spring 2006, plans were announced for a gala opening in October (making the project around two years behind schedule).

The centre is part of a larger regeneration scheme that includes green-site improvements along the river, and the development of an 'entertainment district'. The project is already attracting developers: at the time of writing, dozens of flashy residential developments are on the drawing board or under construction, in previously under-appreciated areas.

Like all well-laid plans, it could easily go awry; it's crucial that money isn't seen as being squandered by authorities, as it has in the past, and that poorer Downtown dwellers aren't excluded from the regeneration plans. But with some long-overdue good fortune, the redevelopment of Downtown Miami could become the story of the decade in south Florida.

renovation, restoring it to its original grandeur. If you can catch a concert here, fantastic, but if not, it's definitely worth taking a peek inside the building anyway.

Across the street, the **Alfred I DuPont Building** (169 E Flagler Street, at NE 2nd Avenue) is an elegant example of Depression Moderne style (like deco, but slightly more conservative), with ornately wrought gates and exquisite brass elevator doors. The 1927 **Ingraham Building** (25 SE 2nd Avenue, at E Flagler Street) boasts a beautifully detailed vaulted lobby ceiling. On the corner of NE 1st Avenue and NE 2nd Street lies the **Historic Gesu Church** (see below).

Although known mostly as a business district, Downtown is also home to a thriving college campus. Some 27,000 students dodge the vagrants on NE 2nd Avenue to attend **Miami-Dade College Wolfson Campus** (300 NE 2nd Avenue, at NE 3rd Street). Visitors might be more interested in the campus's third-floor **Centre Gallery** (see p80) and the fifth-floor **Frances Wolfson Art Gallery**, although the annual book fair (see p161) is a delight and draws literary names from far reaches.

One block west is the distinctive ziggurat-roofed 1928 **Miami-Dade County Courthouse** (73 W Flagler Street, at NW 1st Avenue), once

the tallest building south of Washington, DC. West again is the bunker-like **Miami-Dade Government Center** (111 NW 1st Street, at NW 1st Avenue), a modern administrative and transport hub; the severity of its architecture is only slightly mitigated by a fanciful public sculpture, *Dropped Bowl with Scattered Slices and Peels* (1990), by Claes Oldenberg and Coosje van Bruggen.

South of Government Center is the Philip Johnson-designed **Miami-Dade Cultural Center** (101 W Flagler Street, at NW 1st Avenue, 305 375 1700), a large red-brick complex that comprises the **Miami-Dade Public Library** (see p253), the **Historical Museum of Southern Florida** (see p80) and the **Miami Art Museum** (see p80).

Historic Gesu Church

118 NE 2nd Street, at NE 1st Avenue (305 379 1424). Metromover 1st Street. **Services** *English 8.30am, 11.30am Sun; phone for other times & days.* **Map** *p274 D2.*
This Venetian-style building, built in 1922, is the oldest church in Miami to remain on its original site. The main part rises to four storeys, with a belfry and a large stained-glass rose window above the main entrance, while the interior has 16 additional stained-glass windows, several large painted murals and intricately carved marble altar screens and railings.

Historical Museum of Southern Florida

101 W Flagler Street, at NW 1st Avenue (305 375 1492/www.historical-museum.org). Metromover Government Center. **Open** 10am-5pm Mon-Sat; noon-5pm Sun; 10am-9pm 3rd Thur of mth. **Admission** $5; $2 concessions; free under-6s. **Credit** AmEx, MC, V. **Map** p274 D1.

It's young, but south Florida does have a history, a fact extolled by this pleasant museum, which makes up the most visitor-friendly third of the Miami-Dade Cultural Center. Tracing the history of the region, from the early Indians to rafting Cubans, the museum succeeds in educating while entertaining, with a series of informative displays (archive photographs, reconstructions, audio presentations). The displays on the wreckers of Key West and Henry Flagler both merit an extended look, as does the section on pioneering Florida photographer Ralph Middleton Munroe. Recommended.

Miami Art Museum (MAM)

101 W Flagler Street, at NW 1st Avenue (305 375 3000/www.miamiartmuseum.org). Metromover Government Center. **Open** 10am-5pm Tue-Fri; noon-5pm Sat, Sun; 10am-9pm 3rd Thur of mth. **Admission** $5; free under-12s. **Credit** AmEx, MC, V. **Map** p274 D1.

With a collection of works from such artists as Robert Rauschenberg, James Rosenquist, Frank Stella and Ana Mendieta, not to mention some high-calibre travelling exhibitions, this relatively young museum is worth a look. Its family-friendly interactive programmes bring art home: during free Second Saturday programmes, museum teachers lead families in hands-on activities inspired by works on display, while JAM at MAM offers evenings of art and entertainment on the third Thursday of each month.

Miami-Dade College Centre Gallery

300 NE 2nd Avenue, at NE 3rd Street (305 237 3278). Metromover Government Center. **Open** 10am-4pm Mon-Wed, Fri; noon-6pm Thur. **Admission** free. **Map** p274 D3.

Of the handful of public galleries maintained by the community college, the Centre Gallery on the Downtown campus is the most frequented. Shows are invariably interesting, focusing exclusively on contemporary art by international artists and covering a broad range of timely themes, from performance art to new technological works. Exhibition openings attract large crowds of students, local artists and collectors.

Biscayne Boulevard & around

Biscayne Boulevard divides Downtown from the waterfront green space of **Mildred & Claude Pepper Bayfront Park** (301 N Biscayne Boulevard), a busy venue for concerts,

ethnic festivals and huge Independence Day, New Year's Eve and Winter Holiday celebrations. The double-helix memorial in the southwest corner, designed by Isamu Noguchi, commemorates the 1986 Challenger space shuttle disaster. North is a plaza marked by the **JFK Torch of Friendship** and adorned with statues of Christopher Columbus and Juan Ponce de León and with plaques representing Caribbean, South and Central American countries (except Cuba, naturally).

Close by is the ineffably touristy **Bayside Marketplace** (*see below*) and its often-packed marina. A pedestrian bridge is planned to cross the Port of Miami road, linking Bayside to the **AmericanAirlines Arena**, home of local basketball team Miami Heat. The arena is also a concert venue and accommodates assorted temples to consumerism (such as Gloria Estefan's **Bongos Cuban Café**; *see p188*). North of the arena is **Bicentennial Park**, once used occasionally for events but now the future site of Museum Park, a proposed grouping of city museums and other amenities intended to complete the work in progress that is the Performing Arts Center (*see p79* **Downtown top ranking**).

Bayside Marketplace

401 Biscayne Boulevard, at NE 4th Street (305 577 3344/www.baysidemarketplace.com). Metromover College/Bayside. **Open** 10am-10pm Mon-Thur; 10am-11pm Fri, Sat; 11am-8pm Sun. **Map** p274 C3.

Bayside Marketplace is held up by the local tourist industry as proof positive that Downtown is on the way up. The increased safety and accessibility of the area is apparent, but really: if Bayside represents 'up', then can someone send the elevator back down to the basement, please? It's little more than a shopping mall, and an overpriced one at that. A Hard Rock Café here, a Gap there, a food court yonder, and none of it in any way unique or appealing to any but the most easily pleased and unadventurous. Sightseeing cruises from the marina are pleasant enough, but staying on dry land will only depress. **Photo** *p81*.

North of NE 5th Street

Some of the more dodgy parts of Downtown lie north of NE 5th Street. The best way to visit may be via the Omni extension of the Metromover (see, it does have its uses after all). From the relative comfort of the train, you'll get a good look at the baroque **Freedom Tower** (600 Biscayne Boulevard, at NE 6th Street), designed in 1925 and modelled on Seville's Giralda. It was once home to the old *Miami News* but its current name came from its use in the 1960s as a processing centre for refugees. It's now being renovated as the new HQ of the Cuban American National Foundation.

To the west is the troubled district of **Overtown**, one of the earliest settlements for blacks in Miami. It's an area that has historically been plagued by poverty, drugs and, most infamously, in the 1970s and '80s, rioting. City officials had the pink **Miami Arena** built here nearly two decades ago, believing it would spur economic development. The plan failed, and with the opening of the AmericanAirlines Arena (*see p187*), the Miami Arena has become a testament to grand plans gone wrong. It costs the city a fortune to maintain, while playing host to mostly B-list events. The arena is visible from the Metromover, which is probably as close as most people need to get.

As the Metromover crosses the Miami Beach-bound MacArthur Causeway, to the right lies the bayfront **Miami Herald Building** and to the left, the construction site of the Performing Arts Center; *see p79* **Downtown top ranking**.

East of the Omni International (an old shopping mall awaiting a revival) is the neo-Romanesque **Trinity Episcopal Cathedral** (1545 N Bayshore Drive, at NE 15th Street, 305 374 3372). The current building was completed in 1924, but the church itself is the oldest in Miami, having opened a month before the city was incorporated in 1896.

It's worth strolling a couple more blocks north to lunch at the **S&S Diner** (305 373 4291, 1757 NE 2nd Avenue, at NE 17th Street), one of the city's oldest eateries. (Although at the time of writing, this art deco gem was under threat from developers.) Afterwards, press on to NE 21st Street for a look at the extraordinary Latin Moderne architecture of the **Bacardi Building**, the American headquarters of the best-known brand of rum in the world. It's actually two structures: a striking eight-storey tower (built in 1963), whose sides are adorned with ceramic-tile murals in Spanish blue and white, and a smaller square building (added in 1973) decorated with glass 'tapestries'. The larger building houses the **Bacardi Museum** (*see below*).

Bacardi Museum

2100 Biscayne Boulevard, at NE 21st Street (305 573 8511). Bus 3, 16, 36, 62, 95, T. **Open** 9am-3.30pm Mon-Fri. **Admission** free.
The museum covers corporate and Bacardi family history from 1862 through until today. It also offers regularly changing exhibitions of work by local and international artists; call for details.

South of the river

Despite its brevity, the four-mile **Miami River** is swampy south-east Florida's main stream. It was first used by a tribe of Native Americans called the Tequesta, whose village near the

Bayside Marketplace. *See p80.*

north shore was discovered by Ponce de León in 1513. It was a fateful discovery: less than 200 years on, the Tequesta were wiped out by wars and disease brought by the European explorers. The drawbridge that carries NE 2nd Avenue over the water is crowned with a bronze sculpture of a Tequesta Indian firing his arrow in the sky; it all but has an inscription that says: 'Sorry, sorry, sorry…'

The best way to visit the Miami River is by boat; the **Historical Museum of Southern Florida** (*see p80*) organises boat tours, as does the Dade Heritage Trust (*see p57*).

South of the river is an area known as **Brickell**: this is Miami's financial district, home to some of the city's 120-odd national and international banks. Miami is the financial capital of Latin America and the Caribbean, with around 60 per cent of all US trade with Central America starting here.

Conveniently enough, some of the newest and most upscale business hotels are located here, including the Marriott, the Mandarin Oriental and the towering Four Seasons, which, at 70 storeys, became the tallest building south of Atlanta when it was completed in 2002. Here, too, are many architecturally distinctive luxury condos, such as the colourful Villa Regina (1581 Brickell Avenue), the Imperial (No.1627) and the Atlantis (No.2025). Dubbed Brickell Village, the area has a lively after-hours scene, particularly around S Miami Avenue and SE 10th Street, which is home to several popular after-work hangouts like the **Gordon Biersch Brewery Restaurant** (*see p124*) and **Perricone's Marketplace & Café** (*see p123*). Also not to be missed is the **Big Fish** restaurant (*see p124*), which can be a little tricky to find, but which offers river ambience, great food and a groovy bar that's made from an actual tree.

Coral Gables

Miami's little Mediterranean sister.

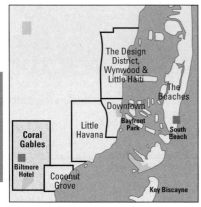

The Design District, Wynwood & Little Haiti

The Beaches

Downtown

Bayfront Park

Little Havana

Coral Gables

South Beach

Biltmore Hotel

Coconut Grove

Key Biscayne

Map p276

After taking a shrubbery shakedown from hurricanes Katrina and Wilma, vegetation is lacking in certain areas, but the self-ordained 'City Beautiful' retains much substance behind the boast. Gables residents enjoy a peachy habitat of terracotta roofs, jewel-like colours and (mostly) lush vegetation. Once a tiny Miami suburb, today the city makes a spotless home for over 175 multinational companies and a score of consulates and trade offices. There are galleries and theatres and top-notch food, with celebrity chefs like Norman Van Aken (of Norman's restaurant) and Cindy Hudson of Ortanique on the Mile (for both, *see p127*), helping it achieve the 'Fine Dining of South Florida' status. For visitors, one main attraction of Coral Gables is its beauty. But unlike many beautiful things, the Gables backs up all that beauty with substance and fun.

The district, located a few miles south-west of Downtown, was the brainchild of the quixotic developer George Merrick. The son of a prominent citrus farmer, Merrick returned to Miami from college in 1911 to find his home town in disarray, growing rapidly with no particular sense of either purpose or direction. As a man who disliked disorder, Merrick managed to convince his uncle, artist Denman Fink, and landscape architect Frank Button to help him create a newer, prettier version of the town, drawing inspiration from the Garden City and City Beautiful movements of the late 19th

and early 20th centuries and the architectural styles of 16th-century Spain and Italy.

By the mid 1920s the group had created one of the nation's first planned communities, a strange little town of tranquil loveliness, with wide streets and lush greenery, full of gabled and tiled rooftops capping dainty buildings coloured in delicate pastel shades. Its streets were even given exotic names such as Valencia and Giralda, and adorned with fountains, plazas and arched entrance gateways.

But then, in 1926, a massive hurricane slammed into the Florida coast, demolishing thousands of homes, killing dozens of people and leaving Merrick's dream in tatters. While much of the Gables stood fast in the 100 miles-per-hour winds, the economy in the Miami area was destroyed, and it was hard to convince anybody from outside the area to move to such a dangerous place. Suddenly, Merrick couldn't pay his bills; by 1928, in a final ignobility, the Coral Gables Commission removed him from the council of the community he had invented, and he slunk off into a life of anonymity.

In the modernisation movement that swept the country after World War II, much of Merrick's work was disfigured. Some of his downtown structures were demolished, while others had their original character disguised by ham-fisted renovations.

Thankfully, though, things have changed. In 1973 Coral Gables was one of the first cities in Florida to adopt a Historic Preservation Ordinance, establishing a procedure for local landmark designations. Since then, most of the district's buildings have been designated as landmarks and are protected. The current civic zeal for preserving Coral Gables' bucolic character can, in fact, border on the obsessive. A hefty list of official 'dos and don'ts' applies to everything from replacing window panes to how many guests can park their cars in front of a home for a dinner party without the host having to rent an off-duty police officer to supervise. Even the size of real-estate 'For Sale' signs is regulated by law.

GETTING AROUND

Coral Gables is an expansive 12-square-mile area bordered by SW 37th Avenue (aka Douglas Road) to the east, SW 57th Avenue (aka Red Road) to the west, SW 8th Street (aka Calle Ocho) to the north and SW 72nd Street to the south, extending down east of Old Cutler Road to Biscayne Bay. To get here by public transport, take the Metrorail from Government Center, Downtown, and get off at Douglas Road station to connect with the free Coral Gables Circulator – a small trolley bus that runs up Ponce de León Boulevard and along Miracle Mile between 7am and 7pm Monday to Friday. Alternatively, take bus 24 from the Government Center, which runs along Miracle Mile/Coral Way (SW 24th Street).

Miracle Mile & around

Coral Way – or, to give it its proper name, SW 24th Street – is the major east–west street through the Gables. The section that runs down the central business district, from SW 37th to 42nd Avenues (Douglas to Le Jeune), is known as the **Miracle Mile** – somewhat exaggeratedly, given that it's actually no more than half a mile long. Once a bustling shopping zone full of local boutiques, nowadays it's just another Disneyfied US neighbourhood with all the requisite chains: Barnes & Noble, Starbucks, Einstein Bros Bagels et al. At least the very good **Actors' Playhouse** (280 SW 24th Street; *see p204*) maintains some semblance of the creative Gables days of old.

While much of George Merrick's vision for just what a business district could be was destroyed by the very businesses he once hoped to house in beauty, a number of interesting spots have survived in the streets immediately north of Miracle Mile. One is the old John M Stabile building at 265 Aragon Avenue, now the home of **Books & Books** (*see p154*), Miami's premier independent bookstore. Built

in 1924, it was one of the area's first commercial structures. The diminutive building has a red barrel-tiled roof that is characteristic of the Mediterranean revival style, and retains its tiled floor, beamed ceilings and fireplace.

Across the street stands the **Fire House & Police Station** (285 Aragon Avenue, at SW 40th Avenue), now an office building. Combining simple Depression-era architecture with Mediterranean revival accents, it's not a Merrick building; rather, it was constructed out of coral rock by the federal Works Progress Administration (WPA) in 1939. A block north-west of the old station is the **Dream Theatre/ Consolidated Bank** (2308 Ponce de León Boulevard, at Aragon Avenue). Originally an outdoor silent-movie theatre built in 1926 and designed to emulate a Spanish bullring, it now houses the offices of Consolidated Bank. Some of the original details remain, including the tower where the film projector once stood.

Across Alhambra Circle is the tiny **Hotel Place St Michel** (162 Alcazar Avenue; *see p54*). Used as an office after it was built in 1926, in the 1960s it was converted into the Hotel Seville, which, horribly, was equipped with dropped ceilings, fluorescent lighting and Danish modern furniture. In 1979 it was extensively renovated and became the ultra-quaint Hotel Place St Michel.

Along Coral Way

Some of the Gables' most interesting residences lie on Coral Way, between Le Jeune (SW 42nd Avenue) and Granada Boulevard. The eastern end of this stretch is marked by **City Hall** (405

Sightseeing

City Hall.

Biltmore Way, at Hernando Street), a building that exemplifies Merrick's love of Spanish Renaissance style, although it was actually loosely based on the historic Philadelphia Exchange building. The stately edifice is encircled by an impressive 12 columns and topped off by a three-tiered clock tower for good measure. Inside, a number of paintings, photographs and advertisements from the town's early days are displayed.

Heading west beneath the massive banyan trees, Coral Way intersects with three other roads at **Balboa Plaza**, a typical example of a Gables plaza, featuring fountains, cisterns, gates and pergolas. South-west down DeSoto Boulevard is the **Venetian Pool** (*see p86*), while sticking with Coral Way brings you to the lovely **Pape House** (900 SW 24th Street/Coral Way, at Toledo Street). Built in 1926, it's a Mediterranean revival architectural showplace, with arched openings, exposed coral rock, French doors and a walled garden. A few doors along is one of the oldest houses in the area, **Merrick House** (*see below*), which is usually open to visitors; **Poinciana Place** (937 Coral Way/SW 24th Street, at Toledo Street) is another of the earliest buildings in the area. It was built by George Merrick for his wife, Eunice Peacock.

Two blocks further along is **Doc Dammers' House** (1141 Coral Way/SW 24th Street, at Cordova Street), constructed in 1924 by Merrick for Edward 'Doc' Dammers, the city's first mayor and Merrick's major huckster when it came to selling Gables real estate. **Casa Azul** (1254 Coral Way/SW 24th Street, at Madrid Street), as its name implies, has a striking blue element: to be specific, a blue glazed-tiled roof. Built in 1924, it was once the home of architect H George Fink, Merrick's cousin and the designer of many Gables buildings between 1921 and 1928.

Merrick House

907 Coral Way (SW 24th Street), at Toledo Street (305 460 5361). Bus 24, Coral Gables Circulator. **Open** 1-4pm Wed, Sun. *Tours* 1pm, 2pm, 3pm Wed, Sun. **Admission** $5; $1-$3 concessions; free under-5s. **No credit cards. Map** p276 C2.
The boyhood home of city founder George Merrick was designed by his mother, Althea, and built between 1900 and 1906. It offers a charming glimpse into 1920s Coral Gables, a colourful era when the City Beautiful that Merrick lovingly envisioned was starting to grow. Note the use of oolitic limestone (commonly called coral rock) quarried from the nearby Venetian Pool, the Dade County Pine and the gracious veranda. Inside, the house is filled with Merrick family artwork, photographs, furniture and memorabilia. The house is open for tours, which last about 45 minutes.

Country Club Gables

Some of the town's oldest buildings, and Merrick's masterpieces, are located in the area known as the Country Club. This is essentially the area either side of the nine-hole **Granada Golf Course**, one of the first parts of Coral Gables to be completed. The main **Country Club Building** (997 North Greenway Drive, at Cortez Street) was originally intended to house guests who came to visit the development in search of homes. It's one of the best places to check out Merrick's original architecture: the homes around here are among the finest still standing. An example of his attention to detail can be seen at 709 North Greenway Drive, while his obsession with Mediterranean revival style is on display further along the same road at Nos.737, 803 and 1251.

Along the way is the impressive **Granada Plaza** (Granada Boulevard and Alhambra Circle). Walls and pillars made of rough-cut rock, stucco and brick, plus vine-laden pergolas, complement the matching pools situated at opposite ends of the plaza. At the far end of the golf course is Alhambra Circle and its striking **Alhambra Water Tower** (Alhambra Circle and Ferdinand Street). Built in 1924, it looks like a landlocked lighthouse, but it is, in fact, nothing more than another of the mercurial Mr Merrick's fanciful ideas: a steel tank that once supplied the neighbourhood's drinking water.

One of the most beautiful elements of the Gables can be found at the far north-western end of the Country Club district, in the glorious **Country Club Prado Entrance** (SW 57th Avenue/Red Road and SW 8th Street/Calle Ocho). This elaborate gateway (one of four such fancy entrances) has 20 elliptically arranged columns, all topped with vine-covered trellises. In the centre is a Spanish-style fountain that's surrounded by a reflecting pool; you'll be lucky if you can see it at all, what with all the Miami brides posing in front for wedding portraits.

South of Coral Way

From Balboa Plaza (*see above*) on Coral Way, DeSoto Boulevard angles south-west, making a beeline for the Gables' other two golf courses, the Biltmore and the Riviera. En route is one of Miami's absolutely-not-to-be-missed sights, the **Venetian Pool** (*see p86*), a former rock quarry converted in 1924 into a freshwater pool in the style of a Venetian lagoon.

A block west of the pool is the **DeSoto Plaza** (at Sevilla Avenue, Granada and DeSoto boulevards), where three roads meet at a stepped fountain built of rough-cut rock. A column encircled by wrought-iron light

Gimme Biltmore

The Biltmore is no ordinary hotel. It blows away the average Coral Gables hotel by height, history and serious extravagance with all the ferocity of a summertime SoFla hurricane. With the exception of the Villa Vizcaya, it is arguably the most iconic historic site in Miami-Dade County.

The building was the brainchild of Coral Gables' founder George Merrick, who teamed up with hotel magnate John McEntee in 1925 to create a world-class bit of accommodation. Ten months and $10 million later, the Coral Gables Biltmore opened with national fanfare and a spectacular party that swung with jazz era zeal. It was marketed as the last word in civilised living, the acme of hostelry.

Understanding the majestic Moorish nuances of this imposing structure is perhaps easier when one considers that the designers were Schultze and Weaver, the duo behind the ritzy Waldorf-Astoria in New York. For their Coral Gables project they chose to look to an older style of architecture. More specifically, they 'borrowed' the design for the hotel's spectacular 300-foot tower from Seville's Giralda bell tower. Expense and practicality were trifling concerns. The marble came from Italy, the china from Tiffany's; chandeliers were all crystal and gold leaf on the ceiling sparkled from the light cast by fireplaces reminiscent of European estates.

During its honeymoon, the Biltmore was graced by royalty from Europe and Hollywood, Ginger Rogers, Judy Garland, Bing Crosby, Al Capone, and assorted Roosevelts and Vanderbilts. Its grand pool (the largest hotel pool in the continental US; *photo below*) was patrolled by movie-star-to-be Johnny Weissmuller, and was the setting for his first swimming world records.

In the 1940s the War Office commandeered the Biltmore as a hospital, and it remained a convalesence centre for veterans until 1968. In 1973 control passed to the City of Coral Gables but indecision over what to do with the building kept it unoccupied and derelict for a decade. Finally, in 1983, the place was restored to the tune of $55 million, reopening to paying guests on New Year's Eve, 1987.

The Biltmore is not only a National Historic Landmark, it's also a favoured site for ghost-spotters. Many long-time residents believe the hotel is haunted; at 7pm every Thursday in the lobby next to the fireplace, the Miami Storytellers Guild shares stories from the Biltmore's past, including the spectral variety.

Ghosts and grandeur aside, the hotel remains one of the architectural highlights of south Florida and hosts scores of events, including a food and wine weekend in spring. For a full listing of the hotel, *see p53*.

fixtures rises majestically from the circular pool, and a steady stream of water gurgles from four sculptured faces. From here it's a short stroll on to the astonishing Mediterranean-style **Biltmore Hotel** (*see p85* **Gimme Biltmore**) and neighbouring **Coral Gables Congregational Church** (*see below*).

To reach Coral Gables' other worthwhile sight, the **Lowe Art Museum** (*see below*), catch a southbound 52 or 56 bus from Le Jeune Road (SW 42nd Avenue).

Coral Gables Congregational Church

3010 DeSoto Boulevard, at Anastasia Avenue (305 448 7421/www.coralgablescongregational.org). Douglas Road Metrorail, then 72 bus. **Open** *Office* 8.30am-7pm Mon-Fri. *Services* 9.15am, 11am Sun. **Map** p276 C2.

The first church in Coral Gables (and today one of the most liberal), this Mediterranean revival building, with its lovely baroque belfry and sculpture over the main entrance, was designed as a replica of a church in Costa Rica and completed in 1924. In summer it hosts a popular concert series that includes well-known names in jazz, classical and folk music and even barbershop quartets; *see p186*.

Lowe Art Museum

University of Miami, 1301 Stanford Drive, at Ponce de León Boulevard (305 284 3535/ www.lowe museum.org). Bus 52, 56. **Open** 10am-5pm Tue, Wed, Fri, Sat; noon-7pm Thur; noon-5pm Sun. **Admission** $7. **Credit** (shop only) AmEx, MC, V. **Map** p276 F2.

The only area museum with a notable collection of Egyptian, Greek and Roman antiquities, the Lowe also features the Kress Collection of Renaissance and baroque art and galleries of pre-Columbian, Asian, African, Native American, European and American work. The European collection includes pieces by Picasso, Monet and Gauguin; the South-west Indian art collection contains textiles, baskets and other utilitarian objects; and the Art of Asia gallery holds objects from China, Korea, Japan and south Asia.

Venetian Pool

2701 DeSoto Boulevard, at Toledo Street (305 460 5356/www.venetianpool.com). Bus 24, 72, Coral Gables Circulator. **Open** hours vary with season; phone for details. **Admission** $9.50; $5.25 concessions; under-3s not allowed in pool. **No credit cards**. **Map** p276 C2.

This just may be the most beautiful swimming pool in the world, even if it is filled to the hilt on most sunny days. It combines an impossibly idyllic setting (tropical foliage, waterfalls, assorted Italian architectural touches) with fresh water, replenished nightly in summer months from a subterranean aquifer. Once a quarry, it was built in the 1920s as an exotic locale for swimming and entertainment, with gondolas and orchestras and movie stars such as Esther Williams and Johnny Weissmuller of *Tarzan* movie fame serenading poolside dancers. These days you might catch the filming of Spanish-language dance shows or aqua aerobics classes. Everyone wants a piece of the pool. Luckily for Joe Public, it's open to the masses seven days a week, but it is perhaps best enjoyed when not overrun with toddlers and boom-box blasts (if you want to remain sane, steer clear of weekends).

Venetian Pool.

Coconut Grove

Fair thee well, hippies! Hello yuppies!

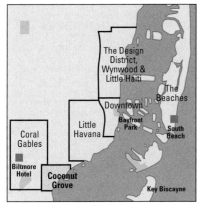

The Design District, Wynwood & Little Haiti

The Beaches

Downtown

Coral Gables

Little Havana

Bayfront Park

South Beach

Biltmore Hotel

Coconut Grove

Key Biscayne

Maps p275 & p277

Once a bastion for free-thinkin' wheeler-dealers who enjoyed its verdant landscape and serene bay setting, Coconut Grove still attracts some free spirits and creative types – only for the most part it's their press agents or marketing teams who visit. Still, the Grove, as it is known, continues to enjoy a reputation as a cultural (and cultured) enclave. The likes of Banana Republic, Hooters and Victoria's Secret reign supreme here. Beyond fancified shopping malls and boutiques, the Grove is a pretty little neighbourhood, certainly worth a half day's exploration, and there are still pockets of original appeal if you look close enough.

The area was originally settled by Bahamian seafarers and a scattering of pioneer families. One of these early residents was a man named Horace Porter. He was only around for a year (1873), but in that time he established a post office, which he named, rather lyrically, 'Cocoanut Grove'. Porter moved on, the post office closed, and that might have been the end of that.

But around the same time, an English pioneer, 'Jolly' Jack Peacock, settled in the area, and was so enamoured that he persuaded his brother Charles to join him. In one of those fortuitous moments that define south Florida's history, Commodore Ralph Munroe, visiting from New England, met the Peacocks. Munroe assured the brothers that if they built an inn, he would spread the word up north. In 1882

Charles, his wife Isabella and their three sons opened the Bay View House, later called the Peacock Inn, the first hotel in the area. On one of his many return visits, Munroe reopened the post office and repainted its sign, dropping the letter 'a' from its name.

Quirky little Coconut Grove began to flower. In 1888 Munroe moved here permanently, as did a community of sea enthusiasts, writers and intellectuals. Many migrant families from the Bahamas also arrived to work at the Peacock Inn, and so Miami's earliest black settlement was founded. With its mix of white intellectuals and poor, uneducated islanders, the Grove gained a reputation as a place of rare tolerance.

Part of the reason locals were able to avoid the kind of racial tensions that gripped the rest of the United States was that the area's residents were constantly embroiled in the unifying preoccupation of fighting exploitation by outsiders. In 1919 the Groveites incorporated, hoping to fend off annexation by the quickly growing city of Miami. They never stood a chance, and Miami consumed the Grove in 1925. Since then, independent-minded locals have banded together in repeated attempts to secede from Miami, each of which has failed. More recent attempts at secession have been hamstrung by the small matter of Miami City Hall being located in the Grove.

In the 1960s the neighbourhood was the centre of Miami's counterculture, a southern cousin to San Francisco's Haight-Ashbury and New York's Greenwich Village. In 1963 residents launched the Coconut Grove Arts Festival (*see p163*), now recognised as one of the leading arts events in the US.

Rising real estate prices in the '80s and '90s forced most of the artists out, and since that time the Grove has undergone numerous changes, much to the consternation of long-time residents. Recent squabbles between the die-hard Grovites and the newbie full-steam developers make for not-so-pleasant bedtime stories, such as when home improvement superstore Home Depot recently tried to make inroads. Still, the Grove retains a charm and tranquillity that no amount of development (or tourists) can completely displace. This may not be immediately evident, given that this is a living, working community with all the concomitant symptoms: snarled traffic,

Sightseeing

One of the Grove's more laid-back residents.

a lack of cohesion and even elements of seediness. But that's Coconut Grove, and (most of) the locals wouldn't have it any other way. Of course, Miami-based boom development has had an impact here as well, and the likes of the Ritz-Carlton and Mayfair condo/hotel projects are a testament to that boom.

GETTING AROUND

Coconut Grove sits on the shores of Biscayne Bay south of Downtown Miami, bordered by the South Dixie Highway (US 1), the Rickenbacker Causeway and the Coral Gables Waterway. To get here by public transport, take the Metrorail from Government Center, Downtown, and get off at either Coconut Grove or Douglas Road stations to connect with the free Coconut Grove Circulator, a small trolley bus that shuttles between the two stations via Grand Avenue, South Bayshore Drive and SW 27th Avenue. It runs 5am to 1.30am Monday to Saturday and 5.30am to 1.30am on Sundays.

Central Coconut Grove

The centre of activity is focused on the intersection of Grand Avenue, MacFarlane Road and Main Highway. It's an area busy with shops, offices and restaurants, and it has the blessing of being one of the best sections of Miami for walking – aside from South Beach's Lincoln Road, the Grove is just about as pedestrian-friendly as south Florida gets.

Along Grand Avenue, between Mary and Virginia Streets, is the **Streets of Mayfair** (*see p143*), once a fortress-like shopping mall, now rehabbed to be more accessible. At

Virginia Street is **CocoWalk** (*see p142*), a huge and hugely successful open-air mall that helped revitalise the Grove in the early 1990s. Shame about the chain stores.

When walking west on Grand Avenue, don't go too far inland, as beyond McDonald Street (aka SW 32nd Avenue) things can get a bit hairy. Instead, head south on vegetation-lined Main Highway. Two short blocks down, its chairs and tables crowding the junction with Commodore Plaza, is Grove's meet-central, the **Greenstreet Café** (*see p128*). A further block along, hidden behind a thicket of plants and trees, is the **Barnacle State Historic Site** (*see p89*), the pretty little original residence of Grove pioneer Ralph Munroe.

Back on Main Highway is the **Coconut Grove Playhouse** (3500 Main Highway; *see p205*). Built as a movie house in the 1920s, the Spanish-style building was converted into a theatre in the '50s. Samuel Beckett's *Waiting for Godot* had its US première here in 1956, although a third of the audience left at intermission, baffled by the metaphysical reverberations; others lined up at the box office to ask for refunds. Nowadays the Playhouse hosts mainly Broadway-wannabe productions, albeit well-received ones.

About two blocks south, on Devon Road, is the Mission-style **Plymouth Congregational Church** (3400 Devon Road, at Main Highway), which dates back to 1917, and Dade County's first public schoolhouse. Built in 1887 out of lumber salvaged from shipwrecks, the schoolhouse was originally located across from the Peacock Inn and used as a Sunday school. It was moved to its present site in 1970.

Back on Main Highway, **Bryan Memorial Church** (3713 Main Highway, at Devon Road), built in the 1920s as a memorial to orator, politician, salesman and attorney William Jennings Bryan, is an unusual Byzantine-style building. Nearby is **El Jardin at Carrollton School**, the earliest-known complete Mediterranean Revival (constructed in 1917) structure left in Miami.

Continue on Main Highway and you'll reach the end of Coconut Grove at the **Kampong** (4013 Douglas Road, at Bay Breeze Avenue), a seven-acre botanical garden that was once the home of botanist Dr David Fairchild, who went on to found the **Fairchild Tropical Garden** (*see p105*). As chief of the Seed Section of the US Department of Agriculture in the early 20th century, Fairchild travelled the world collecting plant specimens and bringing them back here. One of only two tropical plant research sites in the country, it's a stunning place, with an Indonesian-inspired house set by a lagoon. Scientists and world leaders such as Winston Churchill, Henry Ford, Thomas Edison and Dwight Eisenhower have all visited, as did Fairchild's father-in-law Alexander Graham Bell, who invented a device for extracting fresh water from sea water while staying here. To this day, botanists and horticulturists come to the Kampong, now part of the National Tropical Botanical Garden based in Hawaii, to conduct research. It's occasionally open to the public; call 305 445 8076 for details.

Barnacle State Historic Site

3485 Main Highway, at Charles Avenue (305 448 9445/www.abfla.com/parks/Barnacle/barnacle.html). Coconut Grove Circulator. **Open** 8am-4pm Mon, Fri-Sun. *Guided tours* 10am, 11.30am, 1pm, 2.30pm Mon, Fri-Sun. **Admission** $1; free under-5s. **No credit cards. Map** p277 B2.

Built in 1891 and named after the distinctive shape of its roof, Ralph Munroe's 'Barnacle' is the oldest home in Miami-Dade to remain on its original site. It was designed as a one-storey house facing Biscayne Bay. Three verandas and a skylight, which could be opened with a pulley, provided ventilation. The Munroe family continued to live at the Barnacle until 1973, when they sold the house and its furnishings to the state of Florida to be used as a museum. The pristine beauty of this bayfront pioneer home and grounds, is even more apparent now that it's been tragically sandwiched between two cramped luxury condo developments. You can tour the house and the grounds, and, if the timing is right, catch one of the regularly scheduled concerts on the lawn.

Along S Bayshore Drive

Back at Grove ground zero (that is, the intersection of Grand Avenue and Main Highway), MacFarlane Avenue slopes away south-east, down towards the waters of Biscayne Bay. Between MacFarlane and the water is **Peacock Park**, the original site of Bay View House, torn down in 1926. In the 1960s hippies hung out here, getting stoned and playing frisbee. Now a new generation does the same, albeit only on weekends. Just across the street is the **Coconut Grove Public Library** (2875 MacFarlane Road, at Peacock Park), the grounds of which contain the oldest marked grave in Dade County: that of Ralph Munroe's first wife, Eva, who died in 1882.

From MacFarlane, **S Bayshore Drive** runs north parallel to the shoreline. Just a little way along is what used to be the old Pan American seaplane base and terminal (3500 Pan American Drive, at S Bayshore Drive), the nation's busiest during World War II, when it was used as a US naval base. The building is now home to **Miami City Hall** and has been for more than 40 years.

Beyond City Hall, check out the boats docked at **Dinner Key Marina**, the city's largest. Look just past the docks towards Biscayne Bay, and you'll see still more boats at anchor, part of a controversial community known as the Anchorage that the City of Miami has been

Barnacle State Historic Site.

Sightseeing

trying to get rid of for years, without much success. If you're in the mood for a bayside frosty Margarita or Piña colada, check out **Monty's** (2560 S Bayshore Drive; *see p129*).

A little further up S Bayshore Drive, near the junction with the delightfully named Treasure Trove Lane, are the **Coral Reef Yacht Club** (No.2484) and the very exclusive **Biscayne Bay Yacht Club** (No.2540). The former is housed in a Mediterranean-style mansion built in 1923; the latter, Dade County's oldest social institution (founded by Ralph Munroe in 1887), is in a 1932 bungalow designed by prominent Miami architect Walter DeGarmo. There are more architecturally interesting historic homes just ahead (the 1600-2100 blocks), in an area known as Silver Bluff because of the large oolitic limestone formation beside the road.

Continue walking north, or hop on a 48 bus, for the swankiest historic home of them all: **Vizcaya Museum & Gardens** (*see below*). Across from Vizcaya is the **Miami Museum of Science & Planetarium** (*see below*), which has witnessed terrific expansion of its scope of exhibits, particularly since a relationship was cemented with the Smithsonian Institution.

If you want to continue walking, switch a block east to beautiful **Brickell Avenue**. This last vestige of residential bayfront property before Downtown kicks in is part of what was once known as Millionaires' Row. It's still home to loaded folks: the rich businessmen have now been joined by a smattering of celebs, although the two most famous residents – Sylvester Stallone (100 SE 32nd Road, at Brickell Avenue) and Madonna (3029 Brickell Avenue, at Alice Wainwright Park) – have both moved out.

Miami Museum of Science & Planetarium

3280 S Miami Avenue, at SW 32nd Road (305 646 4200/www.miamisci.org). Bus 48/Metrorail Vizcaya. **Open** 10am-6pm daily. **Admission** $19.95; $6 concessions; free under-3s. **Credit** AmEx, MC, V. **Map** p275 F3.

It may not be the most technologically advanced museum, but where else does a giant concrete sloth greet you? This is about as low-tech a science museum as you'll find in any major American city. The permanent exhibits are of decidedly mixed quality, while the displays compiled in association with the Smithsonian Institution are educational and occasionally fascinating. And a recent temporary exhibition about the *Titanic* featured full-size recreations of some of the ship's interior spaces, as well as hundreds of artefacts from the wreck. But the Sports Challenge section, in which visitors get to pitch a baseball and shoot an imaginary basketball, has dated about as well as a Commodore 64. The Gravity Playground is enjoyed by the under-6s, but it can seem more crèche than learning zone. The adjoining

Vizcaya Museum & Gardens.

Planetarium is similarly old school, but does at least benefit from the contagious enthusiasm of its prime mover, Jack Horkheimer, and the free observatory viewings on Fridays (8-10pm), a favourite of south Florida teens for decades.

Vizcaya Museum & Gardens

3251 S Miami Avenue, at SW 32nd Road (305 250 9133/www.vizcayamuseum.com). Bus 48/Metrorail Vizcaya. **Open** House 9.30am-4.30pm daily. *Gardens* 9.30am-5.30pm daily. **Admission** $12; $5 concessions; free under-6s. **Credit** AmEx, MC, V. **Map** p275 F3.

Incongruous, unlikely and bizarre, Vizcaya is also an utter delight. An Italian Renaissance-style villa and gardens set on Biscayne Bay, it was built by F Burrall Hoffman, Diego Suarez and Paul Chalfin for Chicagoan industrialist and committed Europhile James Deering from 1914 to 1916. It was opened as a museum in 1952, some 27 years after the death of its owner. And a wildly extravagant spot it is too. Not only architecturally: the place is crammed with European antiques and works of decorative art spanning the 16th to the 19th centuries. All the furnishings at Vizcaya are just as they were in Deering's time, including early versions of such amenities as a telephone switchboard, a central vacuum-cleaning system, elevators and fire sprinklers. The East Loggia looks out on to the bay, the exit guarded by a vast telescope. Off to the south stretch Vizcaya's idyllic gardens, with fountains, pools, greenery, a casino and a maze. Strolling here on a quiet summer's day can be magical: it's no wonder that so many couples choose the location to celebrate their weddings. Another bonus is the café, which offers above-average lunches.

Little Havana

Just like the real thing.

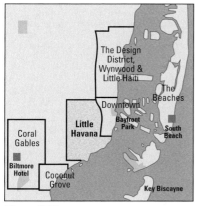

The Design District, Wynwood & Little Haiti

The Beaches

Downtown

Coral Gables

Little Havana

Bayfront Park

South Beach

Biltmore Hotel

Coconut Grove

Key Biscayne

Map p275

Miami Cubans take great pride in the Little Havana neighbourhood – even if they don't live there. SW 8th Street (commonly known as Calle Ocho) and the surrounding area are a testimony to the American dream pursued by the hundreds of thousands of Cubans who fled to Miami after Fidel Castro came to power in 1959. Ambitious émigrés from Cuba's 'society' class soon constructed businesses on Calle Ocho – many stores and restaurants were, in fact, replicas of the ones they had owned back home. Their Mediterranean-style coral rock and stucco houses, typically with cane rocking chairs placed on the ample pastel-painted front porches, continued the illusion of being at home by resembling Havana's Vedado and Miramar neighbourhoods.

Today, these houses are more likely to be inhabited by families from Central America or, more recently, by less affluent immigrants from Cuba. The early Cuban exiles have long moved to larger houses or more comfortable condos, particularly in Coral Gables, Hialeah, or further south in the suburb of Kendall. Some of their children and grandchildren, particularly those with an artistic bent, have been seduced by the faded charm and cheap costs of the Calle Ocho neighbourhood and have recently come back to live here.

City officials have also taken a renewed interest in Little Havana, and after many years of decline and decadence the neighbourhood is

making a comeback. The stretch of Calle Ocho from SW 12th to 16th Avenues is particularly vibrant, with the air of rich tobacco wafting from new cigar stores, and Cuban music coming from the open doors of Latin record stores. There are also souvenir shops and 'Anglo-friendly' restaurants where menus offer tropical-style fish and vegetables as an addition to just the standard Cuban menu, which is heavy on fried pork.

The last Friday of every month, Calle Ocho hosts a Cuban-style block party, called Cultural Fridays. This is definitely the best time to visit Little Havana. Bands play trad Cuban dance music outside **El Pub** restaurant on the corner of SW 8th Street and SW 16th Avenue. Painters exhibit and sell works depicting typical Cuban scenes, and all of the area's businesses stay open late. For further information, call 305 644 9555.

GETTING AROUND

To explore the area by car, the best bet is to park near SW 15th Avenue and meander up and down Calle Ocho on foot. Note that traffic on the eastern part of SW 8th Street is one-way only and can be reached by going west on SW 7th Street and then turning left on one of the avenues. Try to park along Calle Ocho or as close to the strip as possible. By bus, take either the No.8 or the Little Havana Circulator, both of which depart from NE 1st Street beside Government Center, Downtown, and run west along SW 7th Street, then continue on along SW 8th Street.

Alternatively, **Urban Tour Host** (305 663 4455, outside south Florida call 1-866 663 4455, or log on to www.miamiculturaltours.com) offers bus tours of Little Havana with an emphasis on its unique history. Tours are available to individuals and groups; costs vary and 'cultural' meals are sometimes included.

Memorial Boulevard

Most of the major 'sights' are in the historical district between SW 12th and SW 17th Avenues, on and off Calle Ocho. Start your tour at **Memorial Boulevard**, or SW 13th Avenue. At the entrance to the boulevard is the **Brigade 2506 Memorial**, an eternal flame that burns in memory of those killed in the disastrous Bay of Pigs invasion (*see p95*). Further down, 19th-century Cuban revolutionary heroes José Martí and Antonio Maceo are commemorated for leading the battle for Cuba's independence from Spain. Other monuments include a bronze map of Cuba and a statue of the Virgin Mary, a figure of great importance to the largely Catholic Cuban-American community.

As you walk down the boulevard, you can't miss the large ceiba tree right in the centre. Practitioners of the Santería religion consider it sacred, leaving offerings of chicken bones and cloth bundles for their deities. Santería, a syncretistic religion that originated in the Caribbean, is based on the Yoruba culture of West Africa and incorporates elements of Roman Catholicism. *Botánicas* are stores catering to its followers, selling religious articles, mystical oils and candles and offering spiritualist readings by the local *santero*. **Botánica Mística** (1512 SW 8th Street, at SW 15th Avenue, 305 631 0888) and **Botánica Negra Francisca** (1323 SW 8th Street, at SW 13th Avenue, 305 860 9328) are two of the most popular in the area. A word of advice: be respectful. This is a religion, and its followers take their beliefs very seriously.

Calle Ocho

Back on Calle Ocho, peer in the window of **Moore & Bode Cigars** (1336 SW 8th Street, at 13th Avenue, 305 649 5308) and watch tobacco workers rolling fresh cigars. Although you can't buy an authentic Cuban cigar in the US, Little Havana's tobacco factories sell hand-made cigars, many with tobacco grown from Cuban seed. **El Crédito**, which is one block back (1106 SW 8th Street, at SW 12th Avenue, 305 858 4162), takes pride in the distinguished La Gloria Cubana brand. Elsewhere, **La Tradición Cubana** (1894 SW 8th Street, at SW 19th Avenue, 305 643 4005) offers factory tours (9am-5pm Mon-Fri) and sells premium-blended tobaccos rich in flavour and aroma.

For more souvenirs, wander into **Little Havana To Go** (1442 SW 8th Street, at SW 14th Avenue, 305 857 9720) for gifts with a peculiar Miami Cuban slant. These include a Havana phone book from 1958 (listing the names of many of Miami's exile families), T-shirts with Cuban pride slogans, bright landscape paintings of Havana, and Fidel Castro playing cards (with an X through the image of *el comandante*'s face). Over the road, **Mi Tierra Antigüedades Cubana** (1333 SW 8th Street, at SW 13th Avenue, 305 648 3008) offers memorabilia and antiques from Cuba, brought from the island by exiles.

Teté Restaurant (1444 SW 8th Street, at SW 14th Avenue, 305 858 8801) is the most upscale restaurant on the street, offering 'nouvelle Cuban' dishes such as dolphin with mango sauce, and a decent wine list.

¿Hablas Spanglish?

You should be able to find someone in every Calle Ocho establishment who speaks some English (at least when pressed), but as in any foreign country, it shows good will to learn a bit of the lingua franca before you go. In this case it's Spanish, of course, but particularly the Spanglish-inflected Cuban-American dialect sometimes known as Cubonics.

Once you get past the customary *hola* (hello), or the more adventurous *buenos días* (good day), you'll have to know how to order the syrupy sweet coffee for which Calle Ocho is famous. The Cuban-American rocket fuel comes in four basic forms: the *cafecito* – a shot of black coffee in a thimble-size plastic cup; the *colada*, the black coffee in a larger Styrofoam cup, served along with a stack of the thimble-size plastic cups (Warning! This is meant for sharing, and drinking the entire *colada* yourself is comparable to mainlining speed); the *cortadito*, a *cafecito* with a little milk; and the *café con leche*, which is primarily a breakfast drink (though comforting any time), with more milk than coffee and, needless to say, lots of sugar.

Following is a brief glossary of Cuban words that could come in handy in a restaurant, shop, club, or hanging with your new Little Havana friends. *See also p253* **¿Hablas español?**

bibaporrú Vik's Vapor Rub (popular remedy among Cubans)

conflay breakfast cereal

cubanidad 'Cubaness'; the qualities that make one Cuban; Cuban pride

guajiro a peasant of people from the country; someone who's naïve

jewban a Cuban of Jewish persuasion

kenedito A traitor (ie someone who acts like John F Kennedy). The word has its origins in the Bay of Pigs invasion

kilo a penny

loca flamboyantly gay

peso a dollar

radio bemba the grapevine; the means by which gossip spreads through the Cuban community

rumba party

socio buddy, bro

tremenda rumba great party

windshiwaipers windshield wipers

yuca young upwardly mobile Cuban American

Alternatively, a more informal atmosphere recalling rural Cuba can be found at **Los Pinareños Frutería** (1334 SW 8th Street, at 13th Avenue, 305 285 1135), a lush fruit and vegetable stand where you can eat the daily lunch special at a picnic table. Try the *guarapo* – sugar-cane juice – or one of the refreshing tropical fruit juices.

At the corner of SW 14th Avenue, the combined clatter of clacking domino tiles and Spanish chatter announces **Máximo Gómez Park**. Cuban retirees have been gathering on this corner to play dominoes and drink coffee for decades; it was designated a city park in 1976 and, for obvious reasons, is popularly called Domino Park. In the late '80s, due to the presence of numerous vagrants, winos and drug dealers, the park was enclosed and membership rules were enforced. (Note that it is still closed to anyone under the age of 55; proof of age is required.)

The **Tower Theater** (1508 SW 8th Street, at SW 15th Avenue), half a block west of the park, was the only movie theatre in Miami to show English-language films with Spanish subtitles in Little Havana's heyday. These days it shows more films in Spanish (often

without English subtitles); *see p173*. Spanish-language theatre and occasional concerts are also staged here.

Next door to the theatre, stop for a super-sweet Cuban coffee at the window counter of **El Exquisito Restaurant** (1510 SW 8th Street, at SW 15th Avenue, 305 642 9942). If you're hungry, there are huge platefuls of roast pork or *palomilla* steak with rice and beans.

As you walk up and down SW 8th Street, you'll notice that the sidewalk is marked with pink marble stars, making up the **Calle Ocho Walk of Fame**. This Little Havana version of the Hollywood attraction began as a way to recognise Cuban celebrities. Mourners left flowers and notes on Celia Cruz's star after her death in 2003. Cruz was the first to be so immortalised, in 1987, and since that date singers and soap stars from all over Latin America have been honoured. It's been proven that anyone perceived to show affinity with Castro risks having their star removed.

Another Little Havana shrine can be found a few blocks north; **Casa Elián** (2319 NW 2nd Street, at SW 23rd Avenue; open 10am-6pm Sun; admission free but donations encouraged) is the house formerly belonging to the relatives of Elián González, the six-year-old boy who was rescued from a raft at sea in November 1999 and whose plight became a Cuban-exile *cause célèbre*. To the Miami Cubans' chagrin, Elián was sent back to Cuba and his father in 2000. The house is now a museum to what the exiles perceive as the child's martyred fate. Pathos-laden exhibits include Elián's toys, as well as poems dedicated to him and hundreds of collaged photographs of the boy.

For a look at another Cuban-American conflict, pay a visit to the **Bay of Pigs Museum** (*see p95*).

SON AND SHIRTS

Cubans everywhere can at least usually agree on one thing: Cuban music. Record stores on Calle Ocho stock albums by pre-revolutionary Cuban legends as well as contemporary music from the island and the latest by US-Latin pop stars. Try **Casino Records** and **Do Re Mi Music Center** (for both, *see p155*); each has a huge stock of classic and contemporary hits from Latin America and Spain. Don't be shy about asking for recommendations: staff will usually speak English even if they talk among themselves in Spanish.

Getting in gear

Nothing else says Havana (Little or otherwise) like the *guayabera*. These days, however, the ubiquitous symbol of Cubanismo worn by those old men hanging at the *cafecito* stand there in Little Havana isn't just for your *abuelo*.

No, the shirt has been caught up in the wave of Latin chic. It now shows up on revellers in Berlin nightclubs and covering the torsos of stars (and not just Marc Anthony's). The classic is white, but today a *guayabera* comes in all colours bright or cool, with extra pockets or elaborate stitching, maybe tailor made in linen, or off the rack in pure polyester.

Yet, white will always be the standard (and the favourite of tourists coming home from Miami sporting new tans – a darkened chest peeking out from a white *guayabera* is pretty

hot). The colour goes to the essence of the shirt, which is something practical yet smart that can be worn in intense tropical heat. Originally made of cotton, the shirt can be long-sleeved or short, is loose and untucked – letting air circulate – with four pockets (traditionally) on the front and vertical embroidery. It has also been noted that the design of the shirt can hide the *cerveza* belly and make any man look manly.

Like so much else involving all things Cuban, the shirt has a long and sometimes controversial history. First off, the Mexicans are known to contest the fact that this is a Cuban shirt at all. Indeed, the *guayabera* is really as much a Latin symbol as anything else – Mexicans, Panamanians and Colombians among others have all traditionally worn and crafted the shirt.

However, most agree it originated in Cuba about 200 years ago, when it was sewn, depending on which version you believe, either by a) a poor rural wife for her husband, adding extra pockets so he could carry guavas, or *guayabas* (hence *guayaberas*); or b) a rich land-owner's wife, who added extra pockets for her husband so he could carry various sundries while checking out his estate by the River Yayabo (hence, *yayabera*).

In any event, workers of the land started donning the lightweight and handy shirt, and the style spread. What is true, regardless of the confusion surrounding its origins, is that it has been seen as working man's attire and, later, as casual wear. But enough with the stuffy shirts! There are tuxedo *guayaberas*, office *guayaberas* and almost any other function *guayabera*, many of them made in Miami, which is home to numerous factories that make the shirt and shops that sell them.

Sightseeing

Cuban sartorial style really boils down to one item of clothing: the *guayabera* (*see p94* **Getting in gear**). This crisp linen or cotton button-down with four front pockets is worn loose and untucked. Plenty of places along Calle Ocho sell the shirts, but for the greatest range jump on a No.8 bus and ride way west to **La Casa de las Guayaberas** (5840 SW 8th Street, at SW 58th Avenue, 305 266 9683). In addition to classic men's styles in a variety of colours and a tailor-made service, the store makes a flattering women's version, as well as *guayabera*-style dresses.

Also out this way, a 15-minute ride from central Little Havana (take the No.8 bus), is the neighbourhood's most famous landmark, **Versailles** (3555 SW 8th Street; *see p130*). This huge mirror-lined restaurant is packed with loud families on weekends, and during the day older Cuban men hang around the coffee counter outside and talk (Cuban) politics. The food may be forgettable, but, like the rest of Little Havana, at its best this kitschy Cuban exile stalwart is truly memorable.

Bay of Pigs Museum

1821 SW 9th Street, at SW 18th Avenue (305 649 4719). Bus 8, Little Havana Circulator. **Open** 9am-5pm Mon-Sat. **Admission** free. **No credit cards.** **Map** p275 C1.

This museum has a small but interesting collection of ephemera and memorabilia relating to the failed Bay of Pigs invasion of 1961, when a small brigade of Cuban exiles in Miami was trained by the CIA as part of a covert operation to invade the island and restore US interests. But the 1,300-strong force, known as Brigade 2506, was met by the Cuban army soon after landing at the Bahía de Cochinos (Bay of Pigs). Almost 100 were killed and the rest – including the father of pop singer Gloria Estefan – were taken prisoner. Perhaps the most notable exhibit is a Brigade 2506 flag held up by President John F Kennedy during a speech at the Orange Bowl in 1962, welcoming the survivors back to Miami.

Tamiami Trail

SW 8th Street/Calle Ocho, which is Little Havana's main drag, continues arrow-straight out east of the city and all the way across southern Florida, where, as Route 41 – 'the Tamiami Trail' – it bisects the Everglades, before swinging north up the Gulf Coast. As the highway approaches the outskirts of the city, it passes by the Florida International University Park Campus, the location for the **Art Museum at FIU** (*see below*), which was in the middle of a huge expansion project as this guide went to press. While this is far from Little Havana, the campus is the terminus for the main Little Havana bus service, the No.8.

Brigade 2506 Memorial. *See p91.*

Art Museum at FIU

University Park Campus, SW 8th Street, at SW 107th Avenue (305 348 2890/www.fiu.edu. Bus 8. **Open** 10am-5pm Mon, Tue, Thur, Fri; 10am-9pm Wed; noon-4pm Sat, Sun. **Admission** free. **No credit cards.** **Map** p271.

Known for its Latin American and 20th-century American art, FIU's museum presents around six to eight exhibitions each year, exploring traditional themes from a contemporary perspective. In 2004, for instance, it presented a groundbreaking exhibit on Haitian sculpture, both folk and post-modern. Adjacent to the austere but striking concrete main building is the museum's Martin Z Margulies Sculpture Park, whose 75 works include major pieces by Anthony Caro, Jean Dubuffet, Willem de Kooning and Joan Miró; it's recognised as one of the country's most important 3D art collections. The 40,000sq ft Patricia and Phillip Frost Art Museum, complete with three-storey atrium, is scheduled to open by 2007, more than tripling the existing gallery space.

The Design District, Wynwood & Little Haiti

Shabby and chic mix to fine effect.

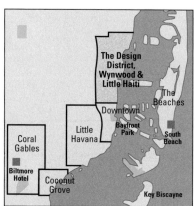

The Design District, Wynwood & Little Haiti

The Beaches

Downtown

Coral Gables

Little Havana

Bayfront Park

South Beach

Biltmore Hotel

Coconut Grove

Key Biscayne

Maps p270 & p271

People. They are just so hard to keep amused. While South Beach is still a destination with a capital D, the human appetite for new is pushing waves of tourists into previously forbidden neighbourhoods across the Julia Tuttle Causeway. Formerly best avoided, the Design District, Wynwood and Little Haiti areas are now enjoying a renaissance. In the case of the first two, reputations as bad-'hoods-made-good add edge to what are otherwise destinations for high-end boutique and gallery outings. A scattering of isolated bars and eateries represents bold ventures into untamed urban frontiers. Some 20 blocks to the north, the area known as Little Haiti is still largely a frontier too far – but give it time. It remains for the most part shabby and grittily ethnic. And not in a romantic way, either: a few bright murals do little to hide the real poverty and desperation. Intrepid explorers will encounter a strange mix of *botánicas* and Haitian bakeries co-existing with a British pub and a working farm. Leave the Armani shades at home or be prepared to lose them.

GETTING AROUND

By public transport, take the 3, 9, 10 or 16 bus from Downtown, all of which run north up either Biscayne Boulevard or NE 2nd Street.

For the Design District, hop off at NW 36th Street (by the old Police Museum, with its police car still mounted halfway up the side of the building) and walk one block west. For Little Haiti, ride up to NW 54th. For Wynwood, *see p98*.

Coming from South Beach, take the M to Mount Sinai Medical Center (which is the first stop after the bus crosses the creek) and there switch to a J; get off as the bus makes a left on to Biscayne after crossing the causeway and follow the signs for the Design District.

The Design District

This is a small place with a big impact. Vastly out of proportion with its influence on the arts and smarts scene, the Design District fills a grid a mere five streets (NE 36th to 41st) by two (NE 2nd Avenue to N Miami Avenue).

The area started out as a pineapple grove, and evolved into what then became known as Decorators' Row during the building boom of the early 1920s, when home-design stores occupied space. The neighbourhood fell on hard times in the late '80s, when crime drove many businesses north. It's still not perfectly polished, but in the last few years the area has rebounded. It is no longer as desolate and unsafe as it once was, although it's still not a place to linger at night. Currently the area attracts the type of tenants it enjoyed during its heyday: fine furnishings, kitchen- and bath-fixture showrooms.

Until recently the District catered to 'the trade', meaning it was open only to interior designers and their private clients. These days, though, establishments are open to anyone, usually from 9am to 5pm weekdays and 11am to 4pm Saturday (though some galleries are also closed on Mondays).

Antiques hunters will find tons of treasures at long-time District denizen **Evelyn S Poole Antiques** (3925 N Miami Avenue, at NE 39th Street, 305 573 7463), one of the area's last bastions of fancy old relics. Among other, pricier, showrooms are the sprawling Chicago-based **Holly Hunt** (3833 NE 2nd Avenue, at NE 38th Street, 305 571 2012), which offers deluxe contemporary furniture and interior designs by Rose Tarlow, Christian Liaigre and Wendell Castle; European kitchen cabinet maker **Bulthaup** (3841 NE 2nd Avenue, at NE 38th Street, 305 573 7771); **British Khaki** (180 NE 39th Street, at NE 2nd Avenue, 305 576 7300), home to English colonial and continental furniture made from reclaimed tropical hardwoods; **Knoll** (3930 NE 2nd Avenue, at NE 39th Street, 305 571 0900), peddling reproductions of mid-century modern classics by designers such as Harry Bertoia and Eero Saarinen; and Pacific Northwest stone and tile maven **Ann Sacks** (111 NE 40th Street, at NE 1st Avenue, 305 572 1206).

Moderately funded shoppers will be more attracted by the contemporary furniture of **Now: A Style Store** (51 NE 40th Street, at N Miami Avenue, 305 573 9988) and the whimsical plastic creations at **Kartell** (170 NE 40th Street; *see p152*). **World Resources** (45 NE 39th Street, at N Miami Avenue, 305 576 8799) sells rare Asian and African wares and furniture, but also offers mass-produced versions of its originals.

Where there's design, there's usually art, and galleries occupy many premises here. Youthful **Kevin Bruk** (3900 NE 1st Avenue, at NE 39th Street, 305 576 2000) and **Daniel Azoulay** (3900A NE 1st Avenue, at NE 39th Street) show work by locally, nationally and internationally known figures, while the **Stephen Watt Gallery** (8 NE 40th Street, at N Miami Avenue, 305 573 7020) specialises in fine art photography by Floridians, and museum-quality framing.

After moving her well-regarded gallery to various locations around the city, veteran Miami art dealer **Barbara Gillman** (2320 N Miami Avenue, at NE 23rd Street) has returned to her old stomping ground to show works by the likes of James Rosenquist, Herman Leonard and Roy Lichtenstein.

Thanks to developer/art collector Craig Robins, a pioneer on South Beach who also owns about 40 per cent of Design District property, a good deal of public art, most of it created by locals, is also on display. Rosario Marquardt and Roberto Behar's zany open-air **Living Room**, complete with couch, lamps and curtains, inhabits the corner of NE 40th Street and N Miami Avenue (*see also p176* **Public tweaking**). Antoni Miralda's giant *Gondola Shoe* sits in the middle of the Melin Building's ground floor (3930 NE 2nd Avenue, at NE 39th Street), and José Bedia's murals of mysterious dark figures facing each other amid the music made by a chirping bird and a gramophone adorn the rear of the **Buick Building** (3841 NE 2nd Avenue, at NE 38th Street).

Holly Hunt. See p96.

Complementing the art and design are food and drink. Pick of the bunch is Ethiopian restaurant **Sheba** (4029 N Miami Avenue; *see p130*), though other top choices include **Charcuterie** (3612 NE 2nd Avenue, at NE 36th Street, 305 576 7877), which dishes up appetising French cuisine, and the **Cane à Sucre** at 3535 NE 2nd Avenue, at NE 35th Street (305 572 0111), offering sandwiches and sugary delights.

There's also the **District** (35 NE 40th Street; *see p197*), which stands on the site of the former Piccadilly Garden Restaurant & Lounge. Thankfully, the new owners have kept the charming garden, with cascading waterfalls, croaking frogs and tropical bromeliads. It's a restaurant, but many people prefer to skip the food and come here for the Saturday night Poplife parties. For other restaurants and cafés in the area, *see p130*.

Although few people actually live here yet, plans for new condominiums are in place and some nightlife is subsequently trickling in. **SoHo Lounge** (175 NE 36th Street; *see p188*), on the southern edge of the District, is big on theme nights.

The word on the street. **Little Haiti**. *See p99*.

Wynwood

South of the Design District is the Wynwood neighbourhood, a large and loosely defined area (roughly bounded by NE 2nd Avenue to the east, I-95 to the west, I-395 to the south and NE 36th to the north) that runs all the way to the northern fringes of Downtown. From the Design District you can approach Wynwood by strolling south on traffic-heavy N Miami Avenue, although it might be safer to catch the bus (Nos.9 or 10) south down NE 2nd Avenue.

Wynwood is a working-class area with a big Puerto Rican population. However, in among the grit, many erstwhile factories and warehouses are now inhabited by art studios and more than 20 galleries. Quickly labelled as the Wynwood Art District, it's Miami's newest trendy enclave. The proximity of the city's new Performing Arts Center (*see p207*) and talk of New York City's Whitney Museum opening a branch locally can only hasten the art-assisted gentrification process. Area pioneers include the **Bakehouse Art Complex** (561 NW 32nd Street, at NW 5th Avenue, 305 576 2828), a former bread factory converted into low-cost studio space currently accommodating painters, sculptors and jewellers; the **Rubell Family Collection** of contemporary art (*see below*) and the **Margulies Collection at the Warehouse** (591 NW 27th Street, at NW 5th Avenue, 305 576 1051), which is home to photography, video, sculpture and installations by major artists.

The first Wynwood galleries were opened by relocated New Yorker Bernice Steinbaum, whose **Bernice Steinbaum Gallery** (3550 N Miami Avenue; *see p175*) showcases respected names such as Miriam Schapiro and Edouard Duval-Carrie; and by long-time local Brook Dorsch, whose **Dorsch Gallery** (151 NW 24th Street; *see p176*) highlights younger emerging talent. Less traditional spaces showing lowbrow and avant-garde pieces include **Locust Projects** (104 NW 23rd Street; *see p177*) and **Objex Art Space** (203 NW 36th Street, at NW 1st Avenue, 305 573 4400). Among the newer kids on the block are **Rocket Projects** (3440 N Miami Avenue; *see p177*), which boasts a strong roster of local contemporary and conceptual artists, plus a few out-of-towners, and the **Marina Kessler Gallery** (2628 NW 2nd Avenue, at NW 26th Street, 305 573 6006), displaying contemporary art by Latin Americans.

Rubell Family Collection

95 NW 29th Street, at NW 1st Avenue (305 573 6090/www.rubellfamilycollection.com). Bus 6. **Open** 10am-6pm Wed-Sun; 10am-10pm 2nd Sat of mth. **Admission** $5; $2.50 concessions. **No credit cards**. Considered one of the top private collections of contemporary art in the country, this bold, avant-garde assortment of conceptual art, photography, sculpture and painting attracts connoisseurs from all over the world. The collection is owned by brother and sister Jason and Jennifer Rubell and features important works by contemporary artists such as Jean Michel Basquiat, Keith Haring, Cindy Sherman,

Jeff Koons and Charles Ray. The works are located in a former Drug Enforcement Agency confiscation centre – something that the late Steve Rubell, founder of Manhattan's legendary Studio 54 and uncle to Jennifer and Jason – would doubtless have found hugely amusing.

Little Haiti

Twenty or so blocks north of the Design District is Little Haiti, whose official borders are between NE 55th and NE 70th Streets around NE 2nd Avenue. To get between the two neighbourhoods, ride the 9 or 10 bus on NE 2nd Avenue. The bulk of commerce and activity in Little Haiti takes place on a few busy streets, notably NE 2nd Avenue and NE 54th Street, both of which can be explored on foot. Be aware that crime is a valid concern here, so when visiting, make an effort to look as though you're not worth any mugger's time, and don't come calling after dark.

The neighbourhood's history dates back to the late 1890s, when it was the site of abundant citrus groves and strawberry fields, and known as Lemon City. Now it's home to thousands of Haitian immigrants, who first began heading here in the late 1970s, fleeing the brutal dictatorship of François 'Papa Doc' Duvalier and, later, that of his son, 'Baby Doc'.

Controversially, there exists in Miami an unspoken distinction between Cuban exiles and other immigrants. There's no question that the US government treats Haitian immigrants (who are seen as fleeing poverty) differently to their Cuban counterparts (who are seen as fleeing communism). Unlike Cuban refugees, the thousands of Haitians who packed shaky wooden boats and took to the seas in a mass exodus during the early 1980s weren't exactly welcomed to their destination with open arms. Hundreds died on their journey to freedom, and their bodies washed up on Miami's beaches. Although it took survivors years to establish a foothold, there is now a vibrant community here with a unique identity.

By day, Little Haiti bubbles over with colour, food and spirit. Bright murals depicting Caribbean landscapes, political leaders and voodoo symbols decorate storefront walls and public buildings, while street names commemorate Haitian heroes. However, there is no disguising the poverty. Little Haiti is plagued by illegal trash-dumping, crack houses and homelessness. Typical dwellings are cramped apartments and shabby wood-frame houses with chickens roaming around front yards. Inhabitants often hold two menial jobs to make ends meet for both their households, the one in Miami and the one back in Haiti.

At night, immigrants fill local school classrooms, learning to speak and write in English. Otherwise, both Creole and French are often spoken in the small independent record stores, *botánicas* (shops that supply the accoutrements of voodoo and Santeria), churches and eateries that line main NE 2nd Avenue.

'Guidebook' sights are few. Instead, satisfy appetites with dishes of *griot* (fried pork), rice, plantains and seafood at the super-cheap **Chez Le Bebe** (114 NE 54th Street, at NE 1st Court, 305 751 7639). One caveat: you get what you pay for, so expect slow service and cramped quarters. You can also sample meat-filled pastries and authentic Haitian hard-dough bread at the **New Florida Bakery** (46 NE 62nd Street, at N Miami Avenue, 305 759 1704).

Libreri Mapou (5919 NE 2nd Avenue, at NE 59th Street) carries more than 3,000 books, magazines and newspapers in Creole, French and English; records, arts and crafts also line the shelves. Owner Jan Mapou, a playwright who directs rehearsals for his Sosyete Koukouy dance and drama company on the premises (*see p208*), also sells his home-made *kremas*, a rich cream liquor made from eggs and rum. Over the way is a *botánica* selling herbs and healing oils.

A failed attempt at celebrating Haitian culture languishes next door to Mapou. The shuttered **Caribbean Marketplace** at 5927 NE 2nd Avenue, erstwhile vendor of Haitian primitive arts and crafts, opened in 1990, perhaps before its time. Inspired by Port-au-Prince's century-old Iron Market and winner of a 1991 American Institute of Architects award for its bold design and splashy bright colours, the shopping centre, located in a neighbourhood too many thought of as unsafe, failed to draw tourists. In 1997 the city foreclosed on the building. Lately, though, the City of Miami and local architects have discussed restoring the structure, giving the environs a much-needed boost. Whether the plan goes ahead remains to be seen.

Still going strong, on the other hand, is the **Earth 'n' Us Farm** (7630 NE 1st Avenue, at NE 76th Street, 305 754 0000). Founded in the late 1970s by Ray Chasser, this working farm (with goats, chickens and all the trimmings) is the last known address of a lost hippie tribe, and a purveyor of quite exceptional honey. A variety of rural-themed and New Age social and cultural activities takes place here. It isn't just the hippie nature of Ray's that is out of place here, it's the incongruously rural feel in such an intensely urban environment.

Almost as incongruous is the shabby pub at the opposite end of Little Haiti: **Churchill's Pub** (5501 NE 2nd Avenue; *see p140*), a much-loved rock venue that also serves English beer and shows UK football on satellite.

Art on the edge

Once seedier than a watermelon, the section of Miami known as the Design District is now the emerging art turf for anyone who's into the city's emerging visual wonders – and we don't mean biceps and cleavage, for once.

This new hotspot is located between NE 2nd Avenue and NE 40th Street – the grid goes like this: NE 36th Street to 41st Street and NE 2nd Avenue to N Miami Avenue. That's just five easy blocks to walk. Oil-laden canvases? Check. Botero sculptures? Check. Pig guts hanging from the rafters... come on, that was so 1998!

The explosion of the Wynwood scene is a phenomenon by any measure. In just a few short years, ever since the hip alt space Rocket Projects opened up in 2003, followed by the Dorsch Gallery and Locust Projects, the area has been transformed. While the surrounding streets were still dark and empty, these trendsetters threw cool openings and showed cool art – and it was easy to park too.

Art Basel (see p175) has also helped boost the area's profile, and by the time it rolled around in 2005, the place was packed. Many of the heavies in the local contemporary art scene, such as Fredric Snitzer Gallery, Diana Lowenstein Fine Arts, Kevin Bruk Gallery and Ingalls & Associates, had transplanted to the area, while others such as David Castillo and Edge Zones inaugurated new spaces. And the Europeans made their entrance when the Spanish Luis Adelantado and the French Emmanuel Perrotin galleries opened their first Stateside ventures. On top of that, the

Museum of Contemporary Art opened a satellite, the huge Cisneros Fontanals Art Foundation (originally from Venezuela) took over a warehouse, and the world-class collectors the Rubells unveiled their revamped two-storey space. And on it goes.

It's almost dizzying. But, fortunately, it is still alternative. Galleries continue to take the chance on strange pieces of site-specific installation (read: not very marketable), experimental music and untested artists. What this means is that there is still an abundance of affordable art set in a laid-back atmosphere (super-fashionistas have yet to arrive in this gritty neighbourhood in force).

As well as the places mentioned elsewhere in this chapter, our tips include the following. **Diaspora Vibe Gallery** (3938 N Miami Avenue, at NE 40th Street, 305 573 4046, www.diasporavibe.com) is dedicated to emerging talent from Latin America and the Caribbean, particularly young artists.

Ethnic Design (3925 NE 2nd Avenue, at NE 40th Street, 305 573 8118) keeps the soul vibe going, with rare items from around the world, such as Indonesian tropical hardwood canoes transformed into partitions.

For something mobile, visit **Miami Light Project** (3000 Biscayne Boulevard; see p205), a long-time favourite of avant-garde dance. Will it be dancers dodging cinder blocks or pirouetting prima ballerinas posing as penguins? You'll have to find out for yourself.

The prize for experimentation, surely, goes to **Enzo Enea**, with its Rainforest Garden Lounge next to the **Moore Space** (4040 NE 2nd Avenue, at NE 40th Street, 305 438 1163, www.themoorespace.org; photo above). The Moore itself also holds exhibitions including painting, sculpture, photography and performance and public art.

Finally, the **Solange Rabello Art Gallery** (180 NE 39th Street, at 40th Street, 305 571 9302) has a permanent exhibition featuring Brazilian and international artists, in all kinds of media (everything from oils to Playdoh to ant hills have all featured in the past).

If you're still hungry for art, there are cool openings on the second Saturday of every month (see p174). At other times, galleries have regular opening hours, but phone first to check if you're going out of your way. Many are closed on a Sunday and Monday. For more galleries in the area, see pp175-177.

North Miami & Beyond

Onwards and upwards.

Taking time out for a chat in **Greynolds Park**.

Map p270

Whichever direction you take out of central Miami, you enter suburbia quickly. Heading north, the somewhat dismal suburban sprawl begins to appear between I-95 and Biscayne Boulevard in the low-key neighbourhoods of Miami Shores and North Miami.

The big news is that it's getting harder to ignore North Miami. That's because, along with downtown Miami and midtown, the growth here is booming. An assortment of the chic and the slum-like, the scenic and the scary, North Miami remains a real mixed bag. It is home to Florida International University's north campus, the headquarters for the aesthetically pleasing Greater Miami Humane Society (which other shelter has the work of Romero Britto gracing the walls?), condominiums and suburbs.

The development bug has taken a large, juicy bite out of North Miami: witness the construction of the highly anticipated **Biscayne Landing**, a 200-acre behemoth community on the shores of Biscayne Bay, which includes condo towers, town homes and a town centre. If you go west on the city's main drag, NE 125th Street, you will pass through the downtown North Miami area, where trendy stores are popping up non-stop, with novelty gift shops, home stores, an upscale canine clothing boutique and – the final evidence of supreme gentrification – a new Starbucks. Art galleries are elbowing in on the action as well. Downtown North Miami even has a cute new name: the NoMi Arts District, whose boundaries include NE 125th Street between NE 6th and NE 10th Avenues, NE 6th Avenue between NE 123rd and NE 125th Streets, and West Dixie Highway from 123rd Street to NE 135th Street.

If you're looking to escape the crowds, greener pleasures are to be had in the picnickers' and ornithologists' paradise of **Greynolds Park** (17530 West Dixie Highway), north of Oleta River State Recreation Area (*see p75*).

Further north is **Aventura**, home to many a wealthy woman with a newly sculpted face and bod, multiple gold AmEx cards and a propensity to run people off the road with her big, black Caddy Escalade. Some claim that the tiny, congested but well-manicured city of Aventura (also known as 'Oyventura' due to its large New York Jewish population and 'Aventorture' by those who loathe the inevitable snowbird-related gridlock and traffic jams) is the only city in America to be named after a mall. Indeed, **Aventura Mall** (*see p142*) remains the primary attraction both to visitors and even residents.

Arch Creek Park & Museum

1855 NE 135th Street, at Biscayne Boulevard (305 944 6111). Bus 3, 28. **Open** 7am-5pm daily. **Admission** free. **No credit cards**.
Created around a natural limestone bridge formation that was once part of an important Indian trail, this small park has a museum and nature centre containing artefacts left by natives as they passed over the arched bridge. Naturalists are on hand to point out native birds, animals and insects.

Museum of Contemporary Art

770 NE 125th Street, at NE 8th Avenue (305 893 6211/www.mocanomi.org). Bus 10, 16, G. **Open** 11am-5pm Tue-Sat; noon-5pm Sun; 7-10pm last Fri of mth. **Admission** $5; free under-12s. **Credit** (over $10) AmEx, MC, V. **Map** p270.
Aiming to be a forward-thinking museum and to discover new artists, MOCA (or, even more cutely, MoCaNoMi) maintains an active schedule, presenting up to ten exhibitions each year in its Charles Gwathmey-designed structure. MOCA's permanent collection now numbers more than 350 works from artists such as John Baldessari, Louise Nevelson and Gabriel Orozco. With media coverage as far away as New York, high-profile exhibits and artists' discussions with personalities such as Yoko Ono, MOCA is firmly at the forefront of contemporary art on the East Coast. Free tours of the museum are given at 2pm every Saturday, and Jazz at MOCA, with outdoor jazz concerts and free gallery tours on the last Friday of the month from 7-10pm, is popular.

Spanish Monastery

16711 W Dixie Highway, at NE 167th Street (305 945 1461/www.spanishmonastery.com). Bus 3, V. **Open** 9am-5pm Mon-Sat; 2-5pm Sun. **Admission** $5; $2 concessions. **No credit cards**. **Map** p270.
Built in the mid 1100s near Segovia, Spain, this monastery was occupied by Cistercian monks for 700 years before it was converted to a granary and stable. In 1924 newspaper magnate William Randolph Hearst purchased the cloisters and outbuildings, and had the structure dismantled, packed into 11,000 crates and shipped to the United States. It was intended for his California coastal mansion, Xanadu, but Hearst had financial problems, so most of his collection was sold at auction, and the stones remained in a Brooklyn warehouse for 26 years before finally being purchased and reassembled at a cost of $1.5 million (an astronomical amount at the time). Today this Romanesque structure is an anomalous oasis in a noisy area. Things to look out for include a life-size statue of the Spanish king Alfonso VII (the monastery was originally constructed to commemorate one of his victories over the Moors) and a couple of attractive round stained-glass windows. The monastery is a favourite spot for weddings – so much so that it's often closed to the public, especially on Sundays; call in advance before setting out.

Miami Springs

In the 1920s Glenn Curtiss, a daredevil aviation pioneer who'd won fame by flying from Albany to New York a decade earlier, parlayed fame into fortune by using his celebrity status to attract investors to southern Florida. He and partner James Bright divided their 100,000-acre land grab into three communities:

Spanish Monastery

Hialeah, **Opa-Locka** (for both, *see below*) and Country Club Estates, now **Miami Springs**. The latter is incongruous in its location, accessible from SR 826 north-east of Miami International Airport.

While heavy industrial traffic surges past, this tiny municipality is largely untouched by the urban behemoth surrounding it. It is a quiet, scenic bedroom community most notable for its collection of homes in the style of the Pueblo Indians, and by the strong history of civic activism among its residents. However, other than for golf lovers, who may be drawn to **Miami Springs Golf** (650 Curtiss Parkway, at Pinecrest Drive), there is little of note here besides the curiosity of the municipality's ability to maintain its small-town sensibilities.

Hialeah

While Little Havana (*see pp91-95*) may be the ideological centre of Miami's Cuban-American community, Hialeah is its population centre. Bordered by the Miami Canal to the south and Le Jeune Road to the east, it's the largest of the outlying Miami communities and is less a structured city than a seemingly endless world of concrete, strip malls, neon signs and eateries. Hialeah's traffic is gridlocked, its politics are incendiary and, for some unknown reason, the district is home to a disproportunately large number of warehouses and manufacturers.

In addition, getting around Hialeah is daunting even to long-time Miami residents. How could it not be when street numbers are out of sync with the rest of the county, and, every year, more and more streets are renamed after obscure figures in Cuban and Latin American history?

That's not to say that a stroll through Hialeah can't be rewarding. Key point of interest is **Hialeah Park** (*see below*), but elsewhere, among the inexpensive cafeterias and bodegas, there are little shops specialising in authentic pre-Castro Cuban memorabilia and the ubiquitous but Miami-stylish *guayabera* (*see p94* **Getting in gear**).

Bounding the northern edge of Hialeah is **Amelia Earhart Park** (*see p165*), a family-oriented swathe of greenery with five lakes. The park is named after the famous solo flyer who, in 1937, stopped at neighbouring Opa-Locka Airport (which was then a US Navy airbase) on her ill-fated attempt to fly around the world.

Despite possible initial first impressions of foreboding, beyond the language barrier and the difficult street names, Hialeah, like Little Havana, is not legitimately intimidating at all.

Hialeah Park
2200 E 4th Avenue, at 21st Street (305 885 8000). Bus 54, L/Metrorail Hialeah. **Open** 9am-5pm Mon-Fri. **Admission** free. **Map** p270.

Part of Curtiss's development of his North Miami real estate was this horseracing track, laid out in 1925. Covering 230 acres, it was conceived as a resort facility and modelled after European racing sites such as Longchamps in France. Unfortunately, the racing stopped in 2001, although the park's owners hope it may one day resume. Even without the horse action, it's still worth a visit for the Mediterranean Revival clubhouse, the pink-and-turquoise buildings and the lush formal landscaped gardens, complete with lake, islands and flocks of pink flamingos. The park has become so famous for these birds that it has been designated an official flamingo sanctuary.

Opa-Locka

Glenn Curtiss saved travel writers everywhere much fishing around with adjectives when he completed Opa-Locka. 'The Baghdad of Dade County', he called it, a fanciful description, perhaps, but one not a million miles from the truth, at least architecturally. Curtiss had a fascination for the oriental fantasies of the tales of *The Thousand and One Nights*, and he commissioned his architect, Bernhardt Emil Muller, to build around the theme. Boy, did he ever deliver. When he set out to create his theme park with residents, Curtiss doubtless hoped it would stay fanciful and well off. It hasn't, of course. The Opa-Locka of the 21st century is economically deprived and long gone to seed, with little to offer its largely poor locals. Unsurprisingly, it's a neighbourhood blighted by crime, and real care should be taken by visitors. It goes without saying that you don't hang around after dark.

Despite the efforts of city planners to swamp Curtiss's vision, Opa-Locka retains much of the incongruous pantomime-Arab architecture for which it was initially famed. (The name comes from the Seminole Indian 'Opatishawockalocka – or 'wooded hummock' – but with the tongue-twisting 'tishawocka' removed to create something that to Curtiss looked like it might pass as Persian or Arabic.) **Opa-Locka Station** (490 Ali Baba Avenue), with its arched arcades alongside sadly silent tracks, and the **Hurt Building** (490 Opa-Locka Boulevard), are both notable surviving examples of the Curtiss-Muller style, although nothing tops the ridiculous Toytown dome-and-minaret ensemble of **Opa-Locka City Hall** (777 Sharazad Boulevard, 305 688 4611), which looks like the stage set for a low-budget production of *Aladdin*. But, these buildings aside, there is precious little reason to head this far north.

South Miami & Beyond

Where attractions stud the sprawl.

Miami Metrozoo. See p106.

Maps p212, p270 & p271

South-west of Coral Gables, South Miami is the beginning of true strip-mall suburbia, but it is also the gateway to the southern and western gems of Miami-Dade County, including the Everglades. At first sight, South Miami monuments are places like the **Dadeland Mall** and the **Shops at Sunset Place** (for both, *see p143*), the tackiness of which is at least partially countered by the charming small-town feel of Sunset Drive, with its pricey boutiques and cafés frequented by yuppies who've fled the city for the 'burbs. (These folks are not to be confused with the hipsters who may be younger and have as much moolah as the yuppies, but don't dare venture south of Coconut Grove.) The basic rule of thumb is: the further south-west you travel – either down US 1, the route to the Keys, or along the more scenic Old Cutler Road – the nicer (read: less congested, greener, friendlier) it gets. Suburbs give way to farms, and buildings to nature. By the time you reach Homestead and the agricultural Redlands (so named because of the colour of the soil), you'll be well aware

that you're in the South, a realisation that's all too easily obscured in self-consciously urban Miami.

GETTING AROUND

Going south is almost only possible by car. Other than the few exceptions noted in the listings, public transport doesn't really operate in this area. Note that distances can be quite significant; attractions such as the **Biscayne National Underwater Park** and the **Coral Castle** are way down in Homestead, which is a good 50 miles from Miami Beach and Downtown. Factor in congested traffic and you're looking at around an hour's driving time. It would make sense to schedule a visit to such places as part of an excursion to the Keys.

Biscayne National Underwater Park

9700 SW 328th Street, at SW 97th Avenue, Homestead (305 230 7275/www.nps.gov/bisc). No public transport. **Open** 8am-5pm daily. **Admission** *Park* free. *Boat tour* $24.45; $16.45 concessions. *Scuba diving* $54 (excl equipment). *Snorkelling* $35 (incl equipment).* **Credit** AmEx, DC, MC, V. **Map** p212.

Nearly all of this park's 181,500 acres are underwater, so come prepared to explore via glass-bottom boat tours (10am daily), canoe or – better yet – snorkelling or scuba diving (for more information on activities, phone 305 230 1100). Get an introduction to the park's ecosystems and wildlife at the visitors' centre, built in the style of the area's pioneer homes. Of interest are the ecologically important mangrove forest, the abundant birdlife and, of course, the dazzling coral reef filled with brilliantly coloured fish, sea turtles and other marine life. Wildlife lovers will enjoy a boat trip to the neighbouring keys, which provide homes for nesting birds, subtropical forests and nature trails. The park is located nine miles east of Homestead.

Coral Castle

28655 S Dixie Highway (US 1), at SW 288th Street, Homestead (305 248 6345/www.coralcastle.com). Metrorail Dadeland North then bus 38. **Open** 9am-8pm Mon-Thur; 9am-9pm Fri-Sun. **Admission** $9.75; $5 concessions; free under-6s. **No credit cards. Map** p212.

On the day before his wedding, Latvian Edward Leedskalnin was jilted by Agnes Scuffs on the grounds that he was too poor. Traumatised, Ed left Latvia and, after spells in California and Canada, came to Miami in 1919. It was then that he embarked on a monumental act of lovelorn folly and built this grand castle of coral. In addition to being a strange and touching testament to one man's inability to just get over it, Coral Castle is also a minor miracle of engineering. Secretive Ed built the castle himself between 1920 and 1940 using only hand tools, a feat that is mind-boggling even before you learn that Leedskalnin was just five feet tall. The mystery: how did he shift tons of rock from Florida City, where he carved it, to Homestead, where he erected it? Totally bonkers, but also quite beautiful, and certainly worth a detour for anyone driving down to the Keys.

Deering Estate

16701 SW 72nd Avenue, at SW 168th Street, South Dade (305 235 1668/http://www.deeringestate.org). No public transport. **Open** 10am-5pm daily. **Admission** $7; $5 concessions; free under-3s. **Credit** AmEx, MC, V. **Map** p271.

No, not the same Deering who built Vizcaya (*see p90*), but close. The Deering Estate was, in fact, set up and built by James's similarly well-off brother Charles, who erected his own winter retreat at about the same time that Vizcaya was constructed. The main building, the Stone House, takes a similarly revivalist tack to Vizcaya: Deering built it to remind himself of his properties in Spain. It's not as grand as his brother's place, but it's impressive nonetheless. Other buildings on site include the Richmond Cottage, built at the turn of the 19th century, and three small but delightful utilitarian buildings from 1918. The vast grounds in which the buildings are set contain all manner of nature – much of which is detailed at the visitors' centre – and canoe trips to pleasant Chicken Key are available if you book in

advance. The estate is perhaps most notable for its fossil pit of 50,000-year-old animal bones and 10,000-year-old human remains; the latter are Paleo-Indians, the first known North Americans. The admission fee includes a guided tour of the main building, its grounds and the mangrove boardwalk.

Everglades Outpost

35601 SW 192nd Avenue, S of West Palm Drive, Homestead (305 247 8000/www.everglades outpost.org). No public transport. **Admission** $7; $5 concessions. **No credit cards. Map** p212.

Lions and tigers and bears, oh my! This not-for-profit wildlife refuge in the heart of Homestead is on the way to the Keys, and less than a mile from the Everglades National Park. Home to bears, big cats and exotics of all sorts, the Outpost offers a more intimate zoo-like experience. Founded in 1993, the rehab facility is one where animals check in and then do check out. Medical care and treatment for the sick and injured are provided, and whenever possible, the animals are released back into their natural habitat. The reptile house is not to be missed.

Fairchild Tropical Garden

10901 Old Cutler Road, at SW 101st Street (305 667 1651/http://www.fairchildgarden.org). Bus 65. **Open** 9.30am-4.30pm daily. **Admission** $20; $10-$15 concessions; free under-5s. **Credit** AmEx, MC, V. **Map** p271.

One of south Florida's natural jewels, this 83-acre garden, named after renowned botanist and Miami resident David Fairchild, is filled with tropical splendour: a lush rainforest with a stream, sunken garden, dramatic vistas, an enormous vine pergola and a museum of plant exploration, to name just a few highlights. A must-see is the exquisite rare plant conservatory, a stunning showcase of palms, bromeliads, orchids and ferns. Narrated tram rides (on the hour from 10am to 3pm) give visitors a close-up look at the resident flora. The Richard H Simons Rainforest, a two-acre site dominated by a 500-ft gurgling waterfall, opened in 2001. In addition to Fairchild's well-loved annual events, among them July's International Mango Festival (*see p160*), the garden is home to occasional unplanned plant world phenomena, such as the rare blooming of the amorphophallus titan, a gigantic single bloom as large as a person, which emits the powerful stench of rotting flesh to attract insects for pollination. Fairchild recently underwent a renovation and, as a result, is grander than ever, sporting a fun gift shop and associations with well-known artists (in spring 2006, for instance, Chihuly at Fairchild featured Dale Chihuly's colourful glass sculptures throughout the garden, and drew more than 300,000 visitors.)

Fruit & Spice Park

24801 SW 187th Avenue, at SW 256th Street, Homestead (305 247 5727/www.floridaplants.com/ fruit&spice). No public transport. **Open** 10am-5pm daily. **Admission** $5; $1.50 concessions; free under-6s. **Credit** MC, V. **Map** p212.

Sightseeing

The only garden of its kind in the US, this 30-acre park, 35 miles south of Miami, exhibits more than 500 varieties of fruits, vegetables, spices, herbs, nuts and exotic edibles. An old schoolhouse and coral rock building illustrate south Florida's pioneer life, while the charming gift shop sells spices, jams and jellies, unusual seeds and aromatic teas, plus cookbooks on tropical fruits and vegetables. The park is also the site of the Redland Natural Arts Festival in January and the Asian Arts Festival in March. There are free guided tours at 11am, 1.30pm and 3pm daily.

Gold Coast Railroad Museum

12450 SW 152nd Street, at SW 124th Avenue, South Dade (305 253 0063/www.goldcoast-railroad.org). Metrorail Dadeland North then Zoobus. **Open** 10am-4pm Mon-Fri; 11am-4pm Sat, Sun. **Admission** $5; $3 concessions. *Train ride* $2. **Credit** AmEx, MC, V. **Map** p271.

Located just across from the Metrozoo (*see below*), the Gold Coast Railroad Museum suffered badly during Hurricane Andrew, but an extensive rebuilding programme is now pretty much complete, and staff are once again able to show off their collection of old and antique trains and carriages. The highlight, by some distance, is the Ferdinand Magellan, a railroad coach used by presidents Roosevelt, Truman, Eisenhower and, for one day during the 1984 election campaign, Ronald Reagan. Pretty though several of the other cars are, only enthusiasts will get the optimum benefit from them. Still, kids will enjoy rides on the Edwin Link Railroad (1pm and 3pm at weekends), and for adults, it's a nice way to spend an hour or so after a jaunt around the zoo.

Miami Art Central

5960 SW 57th Avenue, at SW 59th Street, South Miami (305 455 3333/http://www.miamiart central.org). **Open** noon-7pm Tue-Sun. **Admission** $5; free Sun. **Credit** MC, V. **Map** p271.

Founded by philanthropist Ella Cisneros, this is the best-looking museum in Miami, hands down. From the funky red and grey industrial façade to the huge exhibition space spread over two floors, it's a great place to see large, acclaimed international shows, such as an exhibition featuring the work, in various media, of South African artist William Kentridge.

Miami Metrozoo

12400 SW 152nd Street, at SW 124th Avenue, South Dade (305 251 0400/www.miamimetrozoo.com). Metrorail Dadeland North then Zoobus. **Open** 9.30am-5.30pm daily (last entry 4pm). **Admission** $11.50; $6.75 concessions; free under-2s. **Credit** AmEx, MC, V. **Map** p271.

Miracle might be too strong a word, but there's no doubt that the staff at the Metrozoo worked wonders to get the site back in decent order after the hideous destruction wrought upon it in 1992 by Hurricane Andrew. Before the storms hit, the zoo was considered one of the best in the country; if it's not quite climbed to those heights again since, it's not for want of trying, and animal lovers should put this on their agenda immediately. Originally a naval air base, it

opened in 1981 as a 'progressive' zoo: there are no cages or fences here, with animals cleverly enclosed by moat-style perimeters. And there are plenty of animals too: the site covers 940 acres, which is where the free monorail service comes in handy. It circles the zoo, which is great from a weary-legs point of view; not many animals are clearly visible from the train, but an initial lap around the site offers a nice perspective before a closer look at ground level.

Animal-wise, all the old faves are present, from elephants and rhinos to storks and flamingos, via bears, camels, kangaroos, tigers and monkeys. For kids, there's a wildlife carousel ride and Paws, a petting zoo with pony rides and meerkats, along with regular shows in the vast amphitheatre and animal feedings throughout the day. Other big draws include Dr Wilde's World, featuring a 500-gallon aquarium, and amphibians, reptiles and insects, plus what the zoo claims to be the largest open-air Asian aviary in the western hemisphere, with more than 70 bird species. **Photo** *p104*.

Pinecrest Gardens

11000 SW 57th Avenue, at SW 111th Street, Pinecrest (305 666 6942/www.pinecrest-fl.gov/ gardens). Metrorail South Miami then bus 57. **Open** 8am-sunset daily. **Admission** $5; $3 concessions; free under-3s. **No credit cards.** **Map** p271.

Parrot Jungle, which occupied this site for more than 60 years, flew the coop in 2001 to a 20-acre, $50-million complex on Watson Island (*see p74* **Islands and causeways**). Although they took their thousand-plus alligators and crocodiles, flamingos and peacocks and sundry other birdlife, they left the thousands of plants and flowers that now form the basis of this municipal park. In addition to being a place where Miamians can enjoy the great outdoors, the site contains a playground and offers classes and workshops in subjects as varied as chess and photography; it also presents monthly folk music concerts and occasional shows highlighting arts and crafts, and it plays host to chilli cook-offs and continuing education art classes.

Wings Over Miami Museum

Kendall-Tamiami Executive Airport, 14710 SW 128th Street, at SW 147th Avenue, South Dade (305 233 5197/www.wingsovermiami.com). No public transport. **Open** 10am-5pm Thur-Sun. **Admission** $9.95; $5.95 concessions; free under-6s. **Credit** AmEx, DC, MC, V.

For almost 20 years, this was known as the Weeks Air Museum until founder Kermit Weeks moved his private collection of planes to Polk City, and created Fantasy of Flight. A group of flight enthusiasts then banded together and reopened this place in 2001 under a different name. Still loaded with lots of classic and military aircraft, such as a B-26 that flew in the Bay of Pigs invasion, the site brands itself a 'living museum', in honour of aviators and veterans. (Meaning: these babies can still fly.) Every Saturday at 11am, weather permitting, you can come and watch the planes take to the sky for some formation flying.

Eat, Drink, Shop

Features

Restaurants & Cafés

This being Miami, it's all about the scene, but the food's not bad either.

Everyone's talking about Miami's burgeoning arts and culture scene, but when they're not talking about that hoity-toity stuff, they're stuffing their faces at places where art comes in an edible form. Miami has experienced its own gastronomical come-uppance, and while it's still no New York or even Las Vegas, it finally offers food snobs places where they can breathe a collective sigh of relief in between bites of foie gras and sips of Chateau Lafite Rothschild. Although at the time of writing the Ritz-Carlton in South Beach was still waiting for superchef David Bouley to set up shop, the local foodies' appetites have, in the meantime, been sated by other star chefs. Douglas Rodriguez, nouvelle Cuban cuisine creator, former head chef at South Beach's Yuca and owner of NY's über-hot Patria, missed Miami so much that he returned with a fabulous new restaurant, **Ola** (*see p118*). LA's hot, dreadlocked Swedish chef Govind Armstrong has South Beach diners on all fours begging for reservations to his sizzling **Table 8** (*see p119*). And the annual South Beach Wine & Food Festival has become an orgiastic homage to the Food Network and a nation of food lovers (*see p128* **Whining and dining**).

Not salivating news for most people, but there is an auspicious implication amid all that chatter. Because, until recently, Miami was ridiculed for its pedestrian cuisine. Especially derided was the city's most famous dining invention: the staggeringly unhip 'early bird specials', all-inclusive meal deals for diners who arrive before the sun goes down. Force-feed yourself a steak at four in the afternoon to save a couple of bucks?

Trends have moved on. These days Miami is quite taken with new world cuisine, and the naff jargon that goes with it: pity the fusion of local tropical ingredients, which has been lumbered with the tag 'Floribbean'. Could the new batch of mega chefs put an end to all that?

WHERE TO EAT

South Beach, naturally, offers a world of edible glitz and glamour – though you'll also find greasy taco and hot dog stands for the budget

> ❶ Purple numbers given in this chapter correspond to the location of each restaurant and café as marked on the street maps. *See pp272-277.*

conscious – and inebriated – club kids. But each area of Miami offers its own vibe and cuisine, and you'd do well to explore while you're here.

TIPS AND RESERVATIONS

Reservations are recommended for almost anywhere except cafés and diners. In fact, at most places they're an absolute requirement – unless you turn up before 7pm, in which case you'll probably have the place to yourself.

Miami restaurants are notorious for slow, arrogant service; by the time you finally get your cutting-edge dish of pan-roasted, pan-seared whatever, the trend that created it may well be long over. As if well aware that you might take your righteous indignation over the bad service out on the tip, many restaurants top up the bill with a 15-18 per cent gratuity 'for your convenience'. Less conveniently, of course, they often neglect to tell you they've helped in this fashion. Don't hesitate to ask if service is included, and don't be afraid to insist that the tip be adjusted down – or dropped altogether – if you see fit.

TAKE IT OUTSIDE

A law banning lighting up in any establishment whose main profit comes from serving food has forced many eateries to set up outdoor seating and smoking areas for those whose preferred *digestif* comes in a pack of 20.

South Beach

The spread of restaurants here is fairly even, although in the reverse of what you might expect, a lot of the better establishments are on gritty Washington Avenue, while the trash settles on glitzy Ocean Drive.

Asian

Blue Sea

Delano Hotel, 1685 Collins Avenue, at 17th Street (305 672 2000/www.delano-hotel.com). Bus C, G, H, L, M, S. **Open** 7pm-midnight daily. **Main courses** $14-$27. **Credit** AmEx, DC, MC, V. **Map** p273 A3 ❶
South Beach just can't get enough of sushi, which explains why the trendier-than-thou Delano hotel (*see p35*) turned its Starck-designed, eat-in lobby kitchen into a sushi bar serving spicy lobster Martinis and $18 maki rolls for hipsters who don't mind sharing a communal table and paying through the nose.

China Grill
*404 Washington Avenue, at 5th Street (305 534
2211). Bus C, H, K, W, South Beach Local.* **Open**
noon-5pm, 6pm-midnight Mon-Thur; noon-5pm,
6pm-1am Fri, Sat; 6pm-midnight Sun. **Main
courses** $18-$40. **Credit** AmEx, DC, MC, V.
Map p273 F1 ❷
The cavernous China Grill is a culinary experience
not to be missed. Provided, of course, you can land
a table – difficult if you're not a celeb (the crispy
spinach is Oprah's favourite, apparently). Tucked
away in the back of the Grill is Dragon, a private
sushi den with stellar raw stuff and some seriously
sexy cocktails, such as the lemongrass saketini.

Nemo
*100 Collins Avenue, at 1st Street (305 532 4550/
www.nemorestaurant.com). Bus H, M, W.* **Open**
noon-3pm, 7pm-midnight Mon-Fri; 7pm-midnight
Sat; 11am-3pm, 6-11pm Sun. **Main courses** $25-$38.
Credit AmEx, DC, MC, V. **Map** p272 F3 ❸
Changes in chefs at this SoFi mainstay haven't
blunted the South Beach chic elite's desire for its fine
organic, pan-Asian fare. Dishes include the likes of
wok-charred salmon with roasted pumpkin seeds,
and Nori-dusted tuna. The all-you-can-eat Sunday
brunch buffet ($29) is a blissful hangover cure.

Nobu
*Shore Club, 1901 Collins Avenue, at 20th Street
(305 695 3232/www.noburestaurants.com). Bus
C, G, H, L, M, S.* **Open** 6pm-midnight Mon-Thur,
Sun; 6pm-1am Fri, Sat. **Main courses** $10-$30.
Credit AmEx, MC, V. **Map** p272 C3 ❹
Nobu Matsuhisa is regarded as the world's greatest
sushi chef, but that's not why this place is booked
up weeks in advance. No, this outpost of the global
raw fish superpower is lodged at the Shore Club (*see
p38*) and the combination of hotelier-with-the-Midas
touch Ian Schrager and Nobu backer Robert De Niro
makes this celeb central. The likes of Madonna
and J-Lo might only drop by only once in a blue
moon, but it's the people hoping to spot them who
pack Nobu every night.

Pacific Time
*915 Lincoln Road, at Jefferson Avenue (305 534
5979/www.pacifictime.biz). Bus C, G, H, K, L, M,
S, W, South Beach Local.* **Open** 6-11pm Mon-Thur,
Sun; 6pm-midnight Fri, Sat. **Main courses** $25-$34.
Credit AmEx, DC, MC, V. **Map** p272 C2 ❺
A leader in Pacific Rim cuisine, Pacific Time has
done an impressive 13-year stint on Lincoln Road (a
lifetime in South Beach terms) and was a catalyst
for the area's 1990s rejuvenation. The kitchen is
helmed by masterchef Jonathan Eismann, who produces an ever-changing menu. Don't miss the saké-
roasted sea bass.

Shoji Sushi
*100 Collins Avenue, at 1st Street (305 532 4245/
www.shojisushi.com). Bus H, M, W.* **Open** noon-
3pm Mon-Fri; 6pm-1am daily. **Main courses** $13-
$21. **Credit** AmEx, MC, V. **Map** p272 F3 ❻

If it's eclectic sushi – spicy lobster rolls, hamachi
jalapeño or kimchi scallop – in a beautiful garden setting that you want, then take a note of the name. Shoji
uses the 'box sushi' technique, in which a wooden
box and lid compress the sushi, rice and ingredients
to form a cake, almost too pretty to eat. Some say it
beats Nobu by a long shot. Best accompanied with
one of the equally delish house cocktails.

Social Miami
*Sagamore Hotel, 1671 Collins Avenue, at 17th Street
(786 594 3344/www.sagamorehotel.com). Bus C, G,
H, L, M, S.* **Open** 7am-5pm, 6-11pm Mon-Wed, Sun;
7am-5pm, 6pm-midnight Thur-Sat. **Main courses**
$6.50-$24. **Credit** AmEx, MC, V. **Map** p273 A3 ❼
Michelle 'Michy' Bernstein, who made her name at
the Mandarin Oriental's Azul, has been all over the
world but hasn't forgotten her roots. In addition to
her eponymous eaterie on Biscayne (*see p130*), she
now has this outpost in the sleek Sagamore, where
she and executive chef Sean Mohamed, formerly
at the Blue Door (*see p115*), have created a global

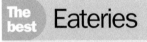

The best Eateries

For cheap eats
Versailles (*see p130*), **Lincoln Road Café**
(*see p117*), **Puerto Sagua** (*see p118*),
Dogma Grill, Andiamo! (for both, *see
p116* Fringe benefits).

For chic eats
Table 8 (*see p119*), **Social Miami** (*see
above*), **Nobu** (*see left*), **Prime 112** (*see
p119*).

For waterfront dining
Big Fish (*see p124*), **Smith & Wollensky**
(*see p119*), **Monty's** (*see p129*), **Bayside
Seafood Hut** (*see p123*), **Scotty's Landing**
(*see p129*).

For spoiling yourself on Sunday
Nemo (*see left*), **Front Porch Café** (*see
p111*), **Blue Door** (*see p115*), **Ice Box
Café** (*see p111*).

For late-night bingeing
Pizza Rustica (*see p113*), **11th Street
Diner** (*see p111*), **La Sandwicherie** (*see
p113*), **Versailles** (*see p130*), **Jerry's
Famous Deli** (*see p111*).

For the full-on Miami experience
Joe's Stone Crab (*see p121*), **Barton G
the Restaurant** (*see p114*), **Segafredo**
(*see p111*), **The Forge** (*see p121*),
News Café (*see p111*).

Eat, Drink, Shop

Social Miami – substance as well as style. *See p109.*

'small plate' menu designed to be shared like tapas. OK, as you might expect from the name, this place is a social smörgåsbord of see and be seen-dom, but in this case the food is good. There are also video art installations, a retro gaming room, and large communal areas in the gallery dining room can be curtained off to create intimate spaces.

SushiSamba Dromo

600 Lincoln Road, at Pennsylvania Avenue (305 673 5337/www.sushisamba.com). Bus C, G, H, K, L, M, S, W, South Beach Local. **Open** noon-midnight Mon-Thur, Sun; noon-2am Fri, Sat. **Main courses** $17-$35. **Credit** AmEx, MC, V. **Map** p273 A1 ❽
This hip Japanese/Brazilian/Peruvian (!) sushi parlour has a look straight out of *Wallpaper** – we adore the mother-of-pearl-speckled bar. The likes of softshell crab roll and yellowtail ceviche are as much accessories as food to the Prada-toting PYTs who convene here. Tuesday's karaoke night, Wasabi Tuesdays, attracts a beautiful crowd with, unfortunately, not-so-beautiful voices. **Photos** *p113.*

Cafés & brasseries

A La Folie

516 Española Way, at Pennsylvania Avenue (305 538 4484). Bus C, H, K, W, South Beach Local. **Open** 9am-midnight daily. **Main courses** $6-$14. **Credit** MC, V. **Map** p273 B1 ❾
Quintessentially French, *avec* the attitude to prove it, this café is run by a Parisian who decided to bring a piece of his precious city to South Beach. A decidedly Euro crowd convenes here to enjoy endless cups of café au lait (ask for small, otherwise it arrives in something the size of a soup bowl). They do a mean *croque-monsieur* and crêpes too.

Balans

1022 Lincoln Road, at Michigan Avenue (305 534 9191/www.balans.co.uk). Bus C, G, H, K, L, M, S, W, South Beach Local. **Open** 8am-midnight Mon-Thur, Sun; 8am-1am Fri, Sat. **Main courses** $8-$16. **Credit** AmEx, DC, MC, V. **Map** p272 C2 ❿
Long a fave of central London's pink brunchers, Balans' first overseas venture is here on Lincoln Road. Curiously, despite the laid-back locale, it's far more uptight than its Anglo counterparts. Wait staff want you to know that they're only doing this job until the call from their casting agent comes through. Still, the food is good (a mix of appealing Asian and Mediterranean dishes, keenly priced) and, unlike London, the umbrellas outside this Balans are there to keep the sun off, not the rain.

Café Papillon

530 Lincoln Road, at Pennsylvania Avenue (305 673 1139). Bus C, G, H, K, L, M, S, W, South Beach Local. **Open** 8.30am-midnight daily. **Main courses** $7-$14. **Credit** AmEx, DC, MC, V. **Map** p273 A2 ⓫
A Euro-style café that's known mostly for its gourmet coffees (a free biscotti with every one) and thoroughly decadent cakes (all imported from Italy). However, that's not all it does: Papillon also turns out great sandwiches, including goats' cheese, grilled aubergine and roasted peppers on focaccia. Good for a low-key meal.

Clarke's

840 1st Street, at Alton Road (305 538 9885/www.clarkesmiamibeach.com). Bus H, M, W, South Beach Local. **Open** 5pm-midnight Mon-Sat. **Main courses** $11-$27. **Credit** AmEx, MC, V. **Map** p272 F2 ⓬
An authentic Irish pub located slap bang in South Beach's swank South of Fifth (aka SoFi) area might seem like a bit of a mismatch, but it's not. The rich wood bar and warm interior separates Clarke's from the other, more down-at-heel Irish bars in the surrounding area. The food here rocks, too, with everything from authentic shepherd's pie to bangers and mash via fabulous, juicy burgers, succulent Maine scallops, and our personal fave, a big, salty New York-style pretzel served on a spike with a side of mustard. Whatever you eat, it'll wash down very nicely with a pint of Guinness – on draft, of course. *See also p134.* **Photo** *p127.*

Front Porch Café

*Penguin Hotel, 1418 Ocean Drive, at 14th Street
(305 531 8300). Bus C, H, K, W, South Beach Local.*
Open 8am-10.30pm daily. **Main courses** $5-$16.
Credit AmEx, DC, MC, V. **Map** p273 B3 ⑬
One of the quainter and less posey spots on Ocean
Drive, the Front Porch is the preferred breakfast
and lunch venue among locals looking for good
food without attitude. The fare is straightforward
American diner cuisine, and includes home-style
French toast with bananas and walnuts, fruit salads
and breakfast pancakes.

Ice Box Café

*1657 Michigan Avenue, at Lincoln Road (305 538
8448). Bus C, G, H, K, L, M, S, W, South Beach
Local.* **Open** 11am-11pm Tue-Thur, Sun; 11am-1am
Fri, Sat. **Main courses** $5-$20. **Credit** AmEx, MC,
V. **Map** p272 C2 ⑭
A few steps off the Lincoln Road Mall, the Ice Box
is a curious mix of the industrial (exposed ducting,
hard metallic surfaces), a matronly tearoom (a
counter of creamy chocolatey cakes on frilly stands)
and a gay bar (beefcake waiters, campy crowd). But
it's quite pleasant. However, lingering over coffee
and cake earns you scowls around lunchtime from
hungry shoppers queuing for table space and Med-
style cuisine ordered from a surprisingly ambitious
daily changing menu.

News Café

*800 Ocean Drive, at 8th Street (305 538 6397/
www.newscafe.com). Bus C, H, K, W, South Beach
Local.* **Open** 24hrs daily. **Main courses** $8-$17.
Credit AmEx, DC, MC, V. **Map** p273 E2 ⑮
This place practically invented the sport of South
Beach people-watching, and it remains the café king
of Ocean Drive. Wait for an outside table to fully
appreciate the experience. Service is as slow as ever,
but the menu has some good bites. International
papers and mags from the in-house shop might fill
the time until the food arrives. The café also has a
separate bar, open 24 hours daily. **Photo** *p114*.

Segafredo

*1040 Lincoln Road, at Lenox Avenue (305 673 0047).
Bus C, G, H, K, L, M, S, W, South Beach Local.*
Open 11am-1am daily. **Main courses** $6-$15.
Credit AmEx, DC, Disc, MC, V. **Map** p272 C2 ⑯
Dear 'Fredo started out as an unassuming espresso
joint but has since spiralled into *the* South Beach
hangout. It's permanently mobbed with hipsters art-
fully draped over the oversized upholstered chairs,
looking like they're the cats that got all the cream.
The menu includes sandwiches, salads, carpaccios
and desserts. Cool lounge music until the wee hours
and a full bar add to the appeal.

Van Dyke Café

*846 Lincoln Road, at Jefferson Avenue (305 534
3600/www.thevandyke.com). Bus C, G, H, K, L,
M, S, W, South Beach Local.* **Open** 8am-2am daily.
Main courses $9-$17. **Credit** AmEx, DC, MC, V.
Map p272 C3 ⑰

A two-storey offshoot of Ocean Drive's News Café (*see
above*), this place may be jazzier, but otherwise it's not
much different from the original. Just like its elder sibling, the Van Dyke is essentially a people-watching
outpost. The menus, too, are nearly identical, but a
warm, wood-floored interior, a jazz bar with nightly
live music and intense chocolate soufflés make this
the less frenzied proposition of the two. *See also p188*.

Diners, delis & cheap eats

Big Pink

*157 Collins Avenue, at 2nd Street (305 532 4700/
www.bigpinkrestaurant.com). Bus H, M, W, Electro-
wave.* **Open** 8am-midnight Mon-Wed; 8am-2am
Thur, Sun; 8am-5am Fri, Sat. **Main courses**
$8.25-$20. **Credit** AmEx, MC, V. **Map** p272 F3 ⑱
A big square room studded with big TV screens
tuned to sport and a big pink menu of home-cook-
ing favourites such as sandwiches, burgers, pasta,
pizza, all-day breakfasts and even TV dinners on a
tray. Portions are what else but big. The family-style
table arrangement promotes camaraderie, which,
late on, erupts into full-blown rowdiness. Takeouts
are delivered by a fleet of little pink VW Beetles.

Cafeteria

*546 Lincoln Road, at Pennsylvania Avenue (305 672
3663). Bus C, G, H, K, L, M, S, W, South Beach
Local.* **Open** 24hrs daily. **Main courses** $6.50-
$16.95. **Credit** AmEx, DC, MC, V. **Map** p273 A2 ⑲
This stark white New York City import draws hipsters 24/7 looking for diner fare such as macaroni
cheese, meatloaf and eggs benedict. The white decor
screams insane asylum, and indeed some say it's
insane to charge more than $2 for a plate of maca-
roni cheese as they do here. Located in a former
Cadillac dealership, this place also reeks of nostalgia, reminding you of the time in school when the
cool kids all sat together in the cafeteria.

11th Street Diner

*1065 Washington Avenue, at 11th Street (305 534
6373). Bus C, H, K, W, South Beach Local.* **Open**
24hrs daily. **Main courses** $8-$18. **Credit** AmEx,
DC, MC, V. **Map** p273 D2 ⑳
The best-looking high-carb, high-fat joint in town,
this streamlined, stainless-steel 1946 diner was
shipped in from Wilkes Barre, Pennsylvania. It's a
popular, round-the-clock spot that attracts a regular
crew of locals and club kids, plus curious tourists.
The food is above average (in terms of quality as
well as price), and there's an outdoor terrace and bar
area (until 5am only). **Photo** *p115*.

Jerry's Famous Deli

*1450 Collins Avenue, at Española Way (305 532
8030/www.jerrysfamousdeli.com). Bus C, H, K, W,
Electro-wave.* **Open** 24hrs daily. **Main courses**
$7-$15. **Credit** AmEx, MC, V. **Map** p273 B3 ㉑
At the top of the broadsheet, small print menu (allow
a good 45 minutes to read through it) is a quote:
'Some is good. More is better. Too much is just right.'

Eat, Drink, Shop

SushiSamba Dromo. *See p110.*

That about sums up the Jerry's ethos – feed 'em till they burst. Expect all the usuals: dogs, burgers, melts, reubens, platters and breakfasts, all served around the clock. The setting is a former cafeteria-turned-ballroom, with enough seating for Latvia and decor that pulls out all the stops – mirror tiles, scallops, swags and swirls. Add a disco soundtrack, a full bar and prices that would make any Jewish grandmother plotz.

Pizza Rustica
863 Washington Avenue, at 9th Street (305 674 8244). Bus C, H, K, W, South Beach Local. **Open** 11am-6am daily. **Pizza slice** $3-$4. **No credit cards. Map** p273 E2 ㉒
South Beach's refuelling pit stop par excellence, Rustica's tiny, standing-room-only space is packed through the early hours with clubbers taking time out to boost their carbs and sponge up the booze. But this Tuscan-style pizza is good enough to eat sober, with excellent toppings including spinach with blue cheese, rocket and rosemary potato, and the classic four cheeses. One slice is a meal.
Other locations: 1447 Washington Avenue, South Beach (305 538 6009); 667 Lincoln Road, South Beach (305 672 2334).

La Sandwicherie
229 14th Street, at Washington Avenue (305 532 8934). Bus C, H, K, W, South Beach Local. **Open** 9am-5am daily. **Main courses** $6-$12. **Credit** AmEx, MC, V. **Map** p273 C3 ㉓
Second only to Pizza Rustica (*see above*) for late-night/early-morning bingeing, South Beach's only gourmet sandwich bar caters to a fabulous mix of clubbers, drinkers, limo drivers and the tattoo artists who work next door, along with anyone else who appreciates a fantastically well-filled, well-made prosciutto and mozzarella, ham and turkey, or veggie sandwich on a fresh baguette. **Photo** *p118.*

European

Casa Tua
1700 James Avenue, at 17th Street (305 673 1010). Bus C, G, H, K, L, M, S, W, South Beach Local. **Open** 7pm-midnight Mon-Sat. **Main courses** $24-$42. **Credit** AmEx, DC, MC, V. **Map** p272 C3 ㉔
One of the city's finest and fussiest big-bucks restaurants, Casa Tua is a sleek and chic country Italian-style establishment set in a refurbished 1925 Mediterranean-style two-storey house. It has several dining areas, including an outdoor garden, comfy Ralph Lauren-esque living room and a communal eat-in kitchen. The lamb chops are stratospheric in price ($42), but orgasmic in taste. After dinner, head upstairs to the lounge (if they let you – they claim the place is now a members-only private club), where the beautiful convene over $15 cocktails.

Chill-out time at **News Café**. *See p111.*

Escopazzo

1311 Washington Avenue, at 13th Street (305 674 9450/www.escopazzo.com). Bus C, H, K, W, Electrowave. **Open** 6pm-midnight Tue-Thur; 6pm-1am Fri, Sat; 6-11pm Sun. **Main courses** $9-$36. **Credit** AmEx, DC, MC, V. **Map** p273 C2 ㉕

The name may mean 'crazy', but the only sign of insanity here is the fact that there are only 90 seats – nowhere near enough to accommodate the legion of diehard *escopazzosos*. Their continued loyalty is maintained by superb home-made risotto, excellent pasta, some outstanding wines and doting service. It's pricey but, we have to say, it's worth it.

Macaluso's

1747 Alton Road, at Dade Boulevard (305 604 1811). Bus M, S, W. **Open** 6pm-12.30am Tue-Sat; 6-10.30pm Sun. **Main courses** $14-$28. **Credit** MC, V. **Map** p272 C2 ㉖

Located in a strip mall away from the flashy side of South Beach, this Staten Island-style Italian restaurant is one of the best in town, with spectacular servings of pasta, meatballs and *antipasti*. Chef Michael's family recipes have snared a faithful following that includes locals and luminaries.

Osteria del Teatro

1443 Washington Avenue, at Española Way (305 538 7850). Bus C, H, K, W, South Beach Local. **Open** 6-11pm Mon-Thur; 6pm-midnight Fri, Sat. **Main courses** $13-$30. **Credit** AmEx, DC, MC, V. **Map** p273 B2 ㉗

This is the long-standing, uncrowned holder of the title of 'the Beach's best Italian' – although fans of Casa Tua, Escopazzo and Macaluso's would all beg to differ. The prices here in particular draw a lot of flak, although the north Italian specialities are tremendous and the service is exceptional. Personally, we love the view out of the big picture windows of the parade of gimps and freaks arriving at neighbouring nightclub crobar (*see p193*).

Spiga

Hotel Impala, 1228 Collins Avenue, at 12th Street (305 534 0079/www.spigarestaurant.com). Bus C, H, K, W, South Beach Local. **Open** 6-10.30pm Mon-Thur, Sun; 6pm-midnight Fri, Sat. **Main courses** $13-$26. **Credit** AmEx, DC, MC, V. **Map** p273 C2 ㉘

A quiet favourite with locals who want to enjoy a fantastic meal free from South Beach hype, Spiga is an intimate, unpretentious rustic-style Italian that concentrates on its food. The bruschetta with grilled aubergine shows Spiga's class; the mains are of a similarly superior quality.

Taverna Opa

36 Ocean Drive, at 1st Street (305 673 6730/ www.tavernaoparestaurant.com). Bus C, H, M, W. **Open** 4pm-3am daily. **Main courses** $7.50-$16. **Credit** AmEx, MC, V. **Map** p272 F3 ㉙

Top of the list for good-time dining, Opa is a big spartan barn of a place that quickly fills most nights with barely containable rafter-raising raucousness. The inspiration is festive Greek; the eats are meze, meat and grilled seafood; the plates are for smashing; and the tables are for dancing on. Order a Zorbatini – ouzo and triple sec – and let it be known: Greece is the word.

Fusion & new world cuisine

Barton G the Restaurant

1427 W Avenue, at 14th Terrace (305 672 8881/ www.bartong.com). Bus M, S, W. **Open** 6pm-midnight daily. **Main courses** $8-$30. **Credit** AmEx, DC, MC, V. **Map** p272 D2 ㉚

Owned by Barton G Weiss, an internationally renowned caterer and event planner, this unique restaurant manages to be both plush and cosy. Fabulous American cuisine is funked up with presentations that include popcorn shrimp in (you guessed it) a popcorn box, and grilled sea bass in a brown paper bag with laundry clips to keep the steam in. A phenomenal Caesar salad comes complete with mini cheese-grater and, for the grand finale, a plume of cotton candy reminiscent of Dame Edna's wig. Has to be seen and tasted to be believed.

BED

929 Washington Avenue, at 9th Street (305 532 9070/www.bedmiami.com). Bus C, H, K, W, South Beach Local. **Open** 8pm-5am Wed-Sun. **Main courses** $14-$36. **Credit** AmEx, DC, MC, V. **Map** p273 D2 ㉛

The name – it stands for 'beverage, entertainment and dining' – delivers on its suggestive title. The restaurant has no tables and chairs, just platform beds for horizontal dining. Thankfully, though, the cooking lifts the whole experience beyond a gimmick; dishes such as the intricately prepared Caribbean lobster with baked pineapple, celery and tomatoes are more than worth removing your shoes for. However, note that there's a 'strictly enforced' dress code demanding your attire be 'fashionably chic and hip'. Charming. **Photo** *p121*.

Blue Door

Delano Hotel, 1685 Collins Avenue, at 17th Street (305 672 2000/www.delano-hotel.com). Bus C, G, H, L, M, S. **Open** 11.30am-4pm, 7pm-midnight Mon-Thur, Sun; 11.30am-4pm, 7pm-1am Fri, Sat. **Main courses** $25-$46. **Credit** AmEx, DC, MC, V. **Map** Map p273 A3 ㉜

With Philippe Starck responsible for the stunning white and billowy surroundings and culinary guru Claude Troisgras in charge in the kitchen, the eyes are as well fed as the stomach. In fact, this is what it must be like to dine in heaven. Don't believe us? Try the chocopistachio dessert. Entrées are refined and French, with saucy meats and fowl, and south Florida seafood. Veranda seating and an all-you-can-eat Sunday brunch add further appeal.

Madiba Miami

1766 Bay Road, at 18th Street (305 695 1566/ www.madibamiami.com). Bus W, South Beach Local. **Open** noon-4pm, 5pm-midnight Mon-Thur; noon-4pm, 5pm-1am Fri; 10.30am-4pm, 5pm-1am Sat; 10.30am-4pm, 5pm-midnight Sun. **Credit** AmEx, MC, V. **Map** p272 C2 ㉝

Finally! A real ethnic restaurant on South Beach that's neither Italian nor Japanese, nor a combination of both. This traditional, yet modern South African restaurant/lounge/boutique/bar has been modelled after an authentic African shebeen and is a wonderful change from the usual, serving up some of Jo'burg's best wines, dishes and music. Try the prawns peri peri or the baby back ribs char-grilled with 'monkey gland sauce' – sounds hideous but it's a traditional South African gravy that has nothing to do with monkeys.

Mark's South Beach

Hotel Nash, 1120 Collins Avenue, at 11th Street (305 604 9050/www.chefmark.com/southbeach). Bus C, H, K, W, South Beach Local. **Open** noon-3pm, 7-10pm Wed, Thur; 7-11.30pm Fri, Sat. **Main courses** $26-$42. **Credit** AmEx, DC, MC, V. **Map** p273 D2 ㉞

Mark Militello hesitated to lend his name to a restaurant in a locale where restaurants are judged more by those who eat there than by what is eaten. Thank goodness he gave in: his cuisine provides strong competition to the couture-clad beauties who dine here. Stunning exotic fare includes cracked conch served ceviche-style and scorched with vanilla rum, and a $42-pistachio-crusted roasted Colorado lamb rack. Serious food with prices to match.

Fryer's delight: **11th Street Diner**. *See p111*.

Metro Kitchen & Bar

Hotel Astor, 956 Washington Avenue, at 10th Street (305 672 7217/www.metrokitchenbar.com). Bus C, H, K, W, South Beach Local. **Open** 7.30-11.30am, noon-midnight Mon-Thur, Sun; 7.30-11.30am, noon-1am Fri, Sat. **Main courses** $13-$32. **Credit** AmEx, DC, MC, V. **Map** p273 D2 ㉟

Modern American, French, Italian, whatever you want to call it, Metro Kitchen & Bar is hot – especially on Tuesday nights, when the *Who's Who* of South Beach and Hollywood society come out to toast the good life. Watch as models attempt to binge on strip steak with truffle fries, pan-cooked snapper with udon noodles, or duck breast with grilled apples and fresh spinach.

Talula

210 23rd Street, at Collins Avenue (305 672 0778). Bus M, S, C, H, G, L. **Open** noon-2.30pm, 6.30-11pm Tue-Thur; noon-2.30pm, 6.30-11.30pm Fri; 6.30-11.30pm Sat; 6-10pm Sun. **Main courses** $18-$32. **Credit** AmEx, MC, V. **Map** p272 B3 ㊱

A husband-and-wife team of chef/owners makes this one of South Beach's best restaurants – and one that's better known for its food than its fabulous clientele. Sure, celebrities hang out here, but in a very low-key, unannounced way. You won't find paparazzi hanging out in the alley garbage cans at this restaurant. Instead, you'll find a fabulous menu of seafood, steaks and signature dishes such as the grilled Sonoma foie gras with caramelised figs,

Fringe benefits

Five years ago few people would have risked walking down Biscayne Boulevard, let alone sitting at a pavement table for a pizza. This north-east corridor was one of Miami's meaner streets, filled with hookers and shady hotels.

Andiamo!

That was then, this is now. These days crime is down, prostitution is dwindling and property values are rising. Many of the fleapit hotels have either closed, been sold or are in the process of being redeveloped into more reputable businesses. My God, Biscayne's even gained a Starbucks at 69th. Whatever next?

OK, as dining destinations go, this is still no Lincoln Road, but in the last year or so a half-dozen or more restaurants, all of them offering outdoor seating, have opened along Biscayne.

It started with the 1999 debut of **Soyka** (*see p130*), a little bit of South Beach style venturing out to the badlands. Nobody razed the place, no lives were lost, and so, suitably emboldened, frontiersman Mark Soyka opened up nearby **Andiamo!** a gourmet pizza place in a former garage complete with still operational carwash.

The conquest of Biscayne appears to be gaining momentum. There's **Café 71**, where the Mediterranean fare is so much better than its not-so-cosy office lobby location suggests, and **Jimmy's Eastside Diner**, which, despite the rainbow flag flying out front, is an equal-opportunity greasy-spoon for all sexual preferences. **Dogma**, a hip little hot dog stand (motto: 'a frank philosophy') on the corner of what used to be known as Crack and Crank Boulevards,

blue corn cakes, chili syrup and candied walnuts. The all-you-can-eat Sunday brunch, with food set up directly on a counter of the open kitchen, is a fantastic way to while away the day.

Tantra

1445 Pennsylvania Avenue, at Española Way (305 672 4765/www.tantrarestaurant.com). Bus C, H, K, W, South Beach Local. **Open** 7pm-5am daily. **Main courses** $28-$94. **Credit** AmEx, DC, MC, V. **Map** p273 B2 ③

Tantra offers what it terms 'aphrodisiac cuisine'. The reality is an exorbitantly priced fusion of Middle Eastern and Indian elements. The same oriental ethic has been extended to the design, with a floor made of grass, gauzy curtained booths and a communal waterpipe. It could make for a fun evening if somebody else is paying; otherwise, the only sensual experience could be that of having your wallet felt.

Touch

910 Lincoln Road, at Jefferson Avenue (305 532 8003/www.touchrestaurant.com). Bus C, G, H, K, L, M, S, W, South Beach Local. **Open** 7pm-

midnight Mon-Thur, Sun; 7pm-2am Fri, Sat. **Main courses** $22-$75. **Credit** AmEx, DC, MC, V. **Map** p272 C2 ③

Touch boasts 'modern influenced' cuisine such as seared Sonoma Valley foie gras and crispy tobacco onions, and it's got half-naked pole dancers. So, lots of expensive food spilled down equally expensive shirt fronts, presumably. So, another restaurant-cum-club where high-falutin food is accompanied by whistles and bells – or, in this case, DJs, percussionists and fire twirlers.

1220 at the Tides

Tides Hotel, 1220 Ocean Drive, at 12th Street (305 604 5130/www.thetideshotel.com). Bus C, H, K, W, South Beach Local. **Open** 6-11pm Mon-Thur, Sun; 6pm-midnight Fri, Sat. **Main courses** $20-$40. **Credit** AmEx, DC, MC, V. **Map** p273 C3 ③

Lodged at the rather gorgeous Tides hotel (*see p38*), 1220 is lauded for its progressive American cuisine, which makes brilliant use of local produce. It's basically sexed-up seafood, and it's wonderful, as is the all-white (linen, upholstery and terrazzo floor)

manages to attract the chic elite who have no qualms sucking down a classic Chicago-style dog on the outskirts of the ghetto.

Most recently, upping the ante on the Boulevard is **Michy's** (*see p130*). What you pay for a starter here would probably see your appetite completely sated by one of the ladies for which Biscayne is better known. Pity those poor girls, facing the likelihood of being forced off their patch by the arrival of upscale pizza and hot dogs; it's either that or invest in a little Gucci to appeal to a better class of gourmet johns.

Andiamo!

5600 Biscayne Boulevard, at NE 56th Street (305 762 5751). Bus 3, 16. **Open** 11am-11pm Mon-Thur, Sun; 11am-midnight Fri, Sat. **Main courses** $5-$12. **Credit** MC, V.

Café 71

7100 Biscayne Boulevard, at NE 71st Street (305 756 7100). Bus 3, 16. **Open** 11.30am-4pm, 6-10pm Tue-Thur; 6-11pm Fri, Sat; 9am-3pm Sun. **Main courses** $6.50-$18. **Credit** MC, V.

Dogma Grill

7030 Biscayne Boulevard, at NE 70th Street (305 759 3433/www.dogmagrill.com). Bus 3, 16. **Open** 11am-9pm daily. **Main courses** $4-$5. **No credit cards.**

Jimmy's Eastside Diner

7201 Biscayne Boulevard, at NE 72nd Street (305 754 3692). Bus 3, 16. **Open** 6.30am-4pm Mon-Fri; 7am-4pm Sat, Sun. **Main courses** $5-$10. **No credit cards.**

Dogma Grill.

terrace with Atlantic views. Booze hounds also love the 1220 for the popsicle Martinis – fruity frou-frou affairs served with an icy stirrer. A blessed bit of class on the tack-fest that is Ocean Drive.

Wish

The Hotel, 801 Collins Avenue, at 8th Street (305 531 2222/www.wishrestaurant.com). Bus C, H, K, W, South Beach Local. **Open** 1-4pm, 6-11pm Tue-Thur, Sun; 1-4pm, 6pm-midnight Fri, Sat. **Main courses** $20-$33. **Credit** AmEx, DC, MC, V. **Map** p273 E2 ⑩

Chef Michael Bloise likes to call his cuisine 'unpretentious, yet artful', and we'll give him that. But it hardly describes just how good his food tastes. Don't miss the restaurant's signature dish – five-spiced pork chop with roasted beets and a spicy sweet potato and edamame hash, along with a crispy pastry cup filled with lemon goat's cheese yogurt… if you can order that without tripping over your tongue, you deserve one of the splendidly tacky signature 'electric neon' cocktails. Service is impeccable, and the alfresco dining area breathtaking.

Latin American & Caribbean

Lincoln Road Café

941 Lincoln Road, at Jefferson Avenue (305 538 8066). Bus C, G, H, K, L, M, S, W, South Beach Local. **Open** 8am-midnight daily. **Main courses** $6-$27. **Credit** AmEx, MC, V. **Map** p272 C2 ⑪

Lincoln Road Mall is getting to be known as a place where you can drop $50 on a meal and still come away hungry; the antidote is the Lincoln Road Café. A menu of budget Cuban standards (rice and beans, chicken fricassée with plantains) and dirt-cheap breakfasts (eggs and ham with coffee for a bargain $6) means that the place is perpetually packed, day and night, and more than holds its own among the surrounding trendy, gimmicky, stratospherically priced joints.

Novecento

1080 Alton Road, at 11th Street (305 531 0900/www.bistronovecento.com). Bus M, S, W. **Open** 6pm-midnight Mon-Sat; 11am-5pm Sun. **Main courses** $15-$25. **Credit** DC, MC, V. **Map** p272 D2 ⑫

Eat, Drink, Shop

La Sandwicherie – for when a cheese and pickle sarnie simply won't do. *See p113.*

If Evita was alive, we're sure she'd have approved of this elegant neighbourhood Argentinian restaurant, which hails from Buenos Aires. The kitchen specialises in a fusion of pan-Latin cuisines that's known as *nuevo bistro*, which translates into dishes prepared using exotic ingredients such as yucca, coconut and tropical fruit, as well as some serious steaks. Staff are friendly, the place has a good buzz and prices are very reasonable.

Ola

Savoy Hotel, 425 Ocean Drive, at 4th Street (305 695 9125). Bus M, W, South Beach Local. **Open** 5pm-midnight Tue-Sat. **Main courses** $12-$29. **Credit** AmEx, MC, V. **Map** p273 F2 ⁴³

Chef Douglas Rodriguez started the whole nouveau Cuban craze in Miami back in the late '80s and early '90s and then, as many predicted, he packed up and moved to Manhattan, where he became a huge star. Now Rodriguez is back with Ola, an outpost of one of his successful Big Apple eateries that, unfortunately, failed on Biscayne Boulevard but is thriving in its new South Beach digs at the Savoy hotel. Dishes like spicy clam sausage, and crackling roast pork with black beans and rice serve to remind smug foodies that Miami, not Manhattan, was first in the nouveau Latino department. Be warned: you'll need to knock back a few saffron Margaritas before dealing with the Manhattan-style bill.

Puerto Sagua

700 Collins Avenue, at 7th Street (305 673 1115). Bus C, H, K, W, South Beach Local. **Open** 7.30am-2am daily. **Main courses** $6-$24. **Credit** AmEx, MC, V. **Map** p273 E2 ⁴⁴

The best place for breakfast on Collins is this trad (as in authentically old, rather than retro) Cuban diner. Choose from a long list of set combinations, many of which give change from five bucks. Later in the day, an entertaining mix of old-time *cubanos*, hip-hop kids, beach bums and local service workers drop by for paella-style chicken and rice, ham croquettes and pork chops. On Tuesday mornings, civic activists meet here to discuss local issues, fired up by energy-boosting Cuban coffee. **Photos** *p122.*

El Rancho Grande

1626 Pennsylvania Avenue, at Lincoln Road (305 673 0480/www.elranchograndemexicanrestaurant.com). Bus C, G, H, K, L, M, S, W, South Beach Local. **Open** 11.30am-10.30pm Mon-Fri; 11.30am-11pm Sat. **Main courses** $10-$19. **Credit** AmEx, DC, MC, V. **Map** p273 A1 ⁴⁵

This former hole-in-the-wall Mexican joint was once a well-kept secret, but it was too good to remain so for long. Today the casual restaurant has added a large airy dining room to accommodate the crowds, who enjoy authentic dishes such as *enchiladas queso* in green sauce, *chile relleno* and other Mexican fare. Margaritas on the rocks are a house speciality.

Tap Tap

819 5th Street, at Meridian Avenue (305 672 2898). Bus C, K, M, S, South Beach Local. **Open** 5-11pm Mon-Thur, Sun; 5pm-1am Fri, Sat. **Main courses** $8-$20. **Credit** AmEx, MC, V. **Map** p273 F1 ⁴⁶

It looks like a shack from the outside, but that's all part of the package at this funky, arty restaurant, which pays homage to Haitian culture and cuisine. Inside, colourful murals spice up the place, and music, art exhibitions and poetry readings complement a basic menu of fish, lamb and goat, plus vegetable stews. It's like a trip to Little Haiti but with a much improved chance of finding your car where you left it at the end of the night.

El Viajante Segundo

1676 Collins Avenue, at Lincoln Road (305 534 2101). Bus C, G, H, L, M, S. **Open** 24hrs daily. **Main courses** $7-$25. **Credit** AmEx, DC, MC, V. **Map** p273 A3 ⓐ

You'd never know from the shabby frontage – a plate glass window and behind it plastic chairs, plastic table covers and laminated menus – that this is the only Cuban joint in town where Naomi Campbell will eat. However, there's a considerably more appealing, sepia-toned dining room to the rear and a bar area that time forgot with horseshoe-shaped booths. The waiters look as though they've been around since the fall of Batista. It's all enchanting in an old-world sort of way, until the deeply mediocre food (even by Cuban standards) arrives at the table.

North American

Joe Allen

1787 Purdy Avenue, at 18th Street (305 531 7007/ www.joeallenrestaurant.com). Bus A, W. **Open** 11.30am-11.30pm daily. **Main courses** $14-$24. **Credit** MC, V. **Map** p272 C2 ⓐ

Best known for its London West End and New York Broadway locations, Joe Allen makes a stylish and unpretentious departure in its Miami branch, which is buried away among the condos on the west side of the Beach, across from Island View Park. It serves as a hangout for bit players on the political and arts scenes, who network over massive salads, pasta, seafood and steaks. The Martinis are pretty good too, and the wine list has some interesting options.

Pearl

Nikki Beach Club, 1 Ocean Drive, at 1st Street (305 538 1111/www.pearlsouthbeach.com). Bus H, M, W. **Open** 7-11pm Mon-Thur; 7pm-1am Fri-Sun. **Main courses** $17-$37. **Credit** AmEx, DC, MC, V. **Map** p272 F3 ⓐ

Once just a poseur's hangout (it is, after all, attached to the Nikki Beach Club, *see p195*), this mod-squad restaurant is not just fabulous in its retro-orange glory, it's now a bona fide haute cuisinerie too. Don't be put off by the champagne and caviar bar façade because the kitchen is far better than the trendy trappings might suggest. Dishes such as orecchiette with ratatouille, celery-dusted Maine diver scallops and tandoori-grilled Atlantic salmon add genuine sheen to this Pearl.

Prime 112

112 Ocean Drive, at 1st Street (305 532 8112/ www.prime112.com). Bus M, W, South Beach Local. **Open** 11.30am-midnight Mon-Thur, Sun; 11.30am-1am Fri, Sat. **Main courses** $28-$42. **Credit** AmEx, DC, MC, V. **Map** p272 F3 ⓐ

Who in their right mind would ever pay $20 for a hot dog – OK, a Kobe beef hot dog? The people at this posh steakhouse, that's who. Command central for carnivores and those who devour a good, star-studded scene, Prime 112 ('Prime One Twelve') has been packed since the day it opened a few years back, with no signs of slowing down. The aged beef is delish, as are the sea bass and the massive salads and side dishes, but the real dish here is the crowd, a silicone and Botox-enhanced mass of glamazons and wannabes on the hunt for a man – or woman – who can afford to pay for that $20 wiener on a nightly basis. **Photo** *p126*.

Smith & Wollensky

1 Washington Avenue, at 1st Street (305 673 2800/ www.smithandwollensky.com). Bus H, M, W. **Open** noon-2am Mon-Sat; 11.30am-2am Sun. **Main courses** $11-$27. **Credit** AmEx, DC, MC, V. **Map** p272 F3 ⓐ

Nestled at the very southern tip of the Beach, overlooking Government Cut, this cavernous, 550-seat chain steakhouse, which was founded in New York in 1977, offers one of the best views in the city. And pretty good steaks too, with choice cuts of prime-grade, dry-aged beef. The waterfront location makes it a fave for Friday happy hours, Sunday brunches or for toasting passing cruise ships.

Table 8

Regent Hotel, 1458 Ocean Drive, at 15th Street (305 695 4114). Bus C, H, K, W, South Beach Local. **Open** phone for details. **Main courses** $20-$35. **Credit** AmEx, DC, Disc, MC, V. **Map** p273 B3 ⓐ

Chef Govind Armstrong is the epitome of the star chef. When word got out that he was coming to Miami to open an East Coast version of his smouldering LA restaurant, everyone in this city clamoured to be his best friend. Although its home, the swank new Regent Hotel, created a lot of buzz, the restaurant itself is what most people are talking about. Among Armstrong's signature dishes is a salt-roasted porterhouse steak that was deemed the best of the best in the (very hard-to-please) *Robb Report*. As with any haute spot, the restaurant features a private dining room for VIPs, as well as a 40-seat lounge situated beneath the hotel's stunning glass-bottom pool.

Tuscan Steak

433 Washington Avenue, at 4th Street (305 534 2233). Bus C, H, K, W, South Beach Local. **Open** 6-11pm Mon-Thur; 6pm-midnight Fri, Sat. **Main courses** $20-$40. **Credit** AmEx, DC, MC, V. **Map** p273 F2 ⓐ

Imagine Don Corleone dropping by the set of *Saturday Night Fever* and you've got Tuscan Steak. While most of the patrons resemble more a taut Travolta than an overweight Brando, the cuisine is enough to make even the frailest of waifs beef up – try T-bone steak served with garlic purée. Just like its pan-Asian cousin, China Grill (*see p109*), it's a place where everything's intended to be shared.

Time Out
Travel Guides

USA

 Boston

 California

 Chicago

Las Vegas

 Los Angeles

Miami

 New York

 San Francisco

 Washington, DC

Get into BED – literally. *See p114.*

Seafood

Joe's Stone Crab

227 Biscayne Street, at Collins Avenue (305 673 0365/www.joesstonecrab.com). Bus H, W. **Open** 5-10pm Mon-Thur; 5-11pm Fri, Sat; 4-10pm Sun. **Main courses** $8-$50. **Credit** AmEx, DC, MC, V. **Map** p272 F3 ⑤④

South Florida's most famous restaurant, Joe's (established 1913) is as much a Miami must-see as Ocean Drive. It attracts locals, tourists and celebs, serving seasonal stone crabs (October-May) with a 'secret' mustard sauce, garlic creamed spinach, fried sweet potatoes, coleslaw and hash browns. Non-seafood lovers should try the fried chicken, or the liver and onions. Joe's doesn't take reservations, so be prepared for a horrendously long wait, first to register your name, then for a table. Alternatively, if you can't face that, just go with takeouts from the adjacent shop. **Photos** *p125.*

Mid Beach

Diners, delis & cheap eats

Arnie & Richie's

525 41st Street, at Prairie Avenue (305 531 7691). Bus C, J, K, M, T. **Open** 6am-8.30pm Mon-Fri; 7am-3.30pm Sat, Sun. **Main courses** $7-$26. **Credit** AmEx, MC, V.

This traditional, New York-style deli is a refreshing alternative to the usual Miami Beach fare, with offerings such as corned beef on rye, smoked whitefish salad, chopped liver, chicken soup, cold cuts, plus a slew of other Jewish favourites. Very popular with Miami's enormous New York expat crowd.

North American

The Forge

432 41st Street, at Royal Palm Avenue (305 538 8533/www.theforge.com). Bus C, J, K, M, T. **Open** 6pm-midnight Mon-Sat; noon-3pm, 6pm-midnight Sun. **Main courses** $25-$42. **Credit** AmEx, DC, MC, V.

Local legend has it that Al Capone is alive and well and living in this steakhouse's acclaimed wine cellar. The eaterie itself is a rococo lover's fantasy: multi-chambered, ornately decorated (and priced) and completely OTT (that this is supposedly Wacko Jacko's favourite Florida restaurant should tell you all you need to know). Although the Forge stands as a monument to decadent wines, steak and fish, there is a spa menu for the calorie-conscious. You can tour and dine in the 300,000-bottle wine cellar if you so wish.

North Beach

European

Café Prima Pasta

414 71st Street, at Collins Avenue (305 867 0106/ www.primapasta.com). Bus G, L, K, R. **Open** noon-midnight Mon-Thur; noon-1am Fri; 1pm-1am Sat; 5pm-midnight Sun. **Main courses** $10-$20. **Credit** MC, V.

A bright spot on a dingy street, this café offers home-made pastas that pack 'em in, with crowds of carbo-cravers queueing up on the pavement. Rich scents of garlic and oil waft outside, making the inevitable wait almost too much to bear, but it's worth it.

Lemon Twist

908 71st Street, at Bay Drive (305 868 2075). Bus L. **Open** *5.30pm-midnight Tue-Sun.* **Main courses** *$9-$18.* **Credit** *AmEx, MC, V.*
Lemon Twist had the foresight to set up shop in the up-and-coming North Beach area well before the 'hip' whispers began. A cosy Mediterranean bistro, it offers pleasant service, a cool crowd and excellent olive oil cuisine. Expect congenial service and excellent pasta and meat dishes (try the lamb shank with caramelised garlic) at terrific prices.

Fusion & new world cuisine

Chef Allen's

19088 NE 29th Avenue, at NE 190th Street (305 935 2900/www.chefallen.com). Bus E, S, V, Biscayne Max. **Open** *6-10pm Mon-Thur, Sun; 6-11pm Fri, Sat.* **Main courses** *$22-$40.* **Credit** *AmEx, DC, MC, V.*
If anyone deserves to have a restaurant named after them, it's Allen Susser, reigning king of a new world cuisine he calls 'palm tree cuisine'. The food at his restaurant is other-worldly: fantastic fish and meat with exotic ingredients such as Key limes and

mangoes. Special tasting menus make for a great way to sample lots of different flavours. It may be way the hell up in Aventura, but it is certainly worth the long haul.

Surfside to Golden Beach

European

Café Ragazzi

9500 Harding Avenue, at 95th Street (305 866 4495). Bus H, R, S, T. **Open** *11am-3.30pm, 5-11.30pm daily.* **Main courses** *$10-$32.95.* **Credit** *MC, V.*
Size definitely doesn't matter at this tiny neigh-bourhood Italian spot, where people willingly wait out on the street for a table. The stellar cuisine includes garlicky, home-made orecchiette with broc-coli, salmon puttanesca and stuffed veal chop. Also tasty is Ragazzi's stunning male host.

Fusion & new world cuisine

Il Mulino New York

Acqualina, A Rosewood Resort, 17780 Collins Avenue, Sunny Isles (305 933 2577/www.ilmulino. com). Bus K, S. **Open** *5-10.30pm Mon-Thur; 5-11pm Fri, Sat.* **Main courses** *$45-$75.* **Credit** *AmEx, MC, V.*
An idyllic match for the elegant and Italian-inspired oceanfront resort of Acqualina (*see p50*), acclaimed

Puerto Sagua (Castro would love it). *See p118.*

Cuban meals

Like all ethnic cuisines, Cuban has its trademark dishes, most of which are calorific (the Cubans love to fry) yet wonderfully savoury. The Cuban menu is carbo-heavy, revolving around beans and rice. It's also laden with sauces, with an emphasis on plantains and meat, mostly pork and beef. Don't even think about asking for anything low fat or low calorie. There's no such thing in Cuban cuisine. The following is a list of some of the most popular Cuban delicacies. (Our favourite Cuban restaurants are listed on pp117, 118, 119 and 129-130.) So stop counting the calories and eat! ¡Buen provecho!

arroz con pollo roast chicken with saffron-seasoned yellow rice and diced vegetables.
boniato similar to a sweet potato.
café cubano strong black coffee, served in thimble-size cups with lots of sugar.
camarones shrimp.

ceviche raw fish seasoned with spice and marinated in vinegar and citrus.
churros an elongated, doughnut-like pastry.
croquetas golden-fried croquettes of ham, chicken or fish.
mojo a marinade used to spice consisting of hot olive oil, lemon juice, sliced raw onion, garlic and a touch of pepper.
moros y cristianos ubiquitous Cuban side dish of black beans and white rice.
palomilla thinly sliced beef, similar to American minute steak.
pan cubano long, white crusty Cuban bread.
picadillo a rich stew of ground meat, brown gravy, peas, pimientos, raisins and olives.
plátano macho deep-fried plantain.
pollo asado roasted chicken with onions.
ropa vieja shredded beef stew. The name literally means 'old clothes'.
sofrito a sauce made of onion, green pepper, oregano and ground pepper in olive oil.

Italian restaurant Il Mulino New York brings with it a reputation of tremendous success. It's renowned for its bustling atmosphere, market-fresh daily specials, extensive selection of fine Italian wines and impeccably polished wait staff. Sure, it comes at a price, but it's cheaper than two weeks in Tuscany.

Timo

17624 Collins Avenue, at NE 176th Street, Sunny Isles (305 936 1008/www.timorestaurant.com). Bus K, S. **Open** 11.30am-3pm, 6-10.30pm Mon-Thur, Sun; 11.30am-3pm, 6-11pm Fri, Sat. **Main courses** $11-$40. **Credit** AmEx, DC, MC, V.
Tired of taking a back seat to chef Mark Militello, the darling of Floribbean cuisine, chef Tim Andriola left Mark's South Beach (*see p115*) to make his own culinary mark on Miami with Timo. It's a fine Italian restaurant that's been the subject of tawk among the snowbirds since its opening in early 2003. The rustic chic atmosphere is abuzz with noise thanks to a top-notch menu of dishes like baby artichoke and rock shrimp gnocchi, and any one of Andriola's wood-oven pizzas. It seats 120 but, even so, good luck getting a reservation.

Key Biscayne

Seafood

Bayside Seafood Hut

3501 Rickenbacker Causeway (305 361 0808). Bus B. **Open** noon-10pm Mon-Thur, Sun; noon-11pm Fri, Sat. **Main courses** $6-$20. **Credit** AmEx, MC, V.

Locals call this place the Shack because of its ramshackle, tiki-bar atmosphere, but it's a term of endearment rather than a slur. It has been in business for around 20 years, and customers keep coming back for the laid-back vibe, along with the view across the bay to Downtown, best appreciated from the outdoor terrace, where salty beach babes and boaters snack on fresh seafood, such as conch fritters and fried fish sandwiches, all served on paper plates.

Downtown

Aside from **Los Ranchos** and the **People's Bar-B-Que**, all the decent places are on or south of the Miami River, in particular around Brickell Avenue and the business district.

European

Perricone's Marketplace & Café

15 SE 10th Street, at S Miami Avenue (305 374 9449/www.perricones.com). Metrorail Brickell. **Open** *Deli* 7am-11pm daily. *Restaurant* 11.30am-11pm Mon-Sat; 9.30am-11pm Sun. **Main courses** $10.95-$19.95. **Credit** AmEx, MC, V. **Map** p274 F2 ⑤⑤
This charming Italian restaurant and high-class food market has a woody, rustic setting – the building is actually an 18th-century barn relocated from Vermont to the middle of Miami's financial district. Attractions include excellent wines, pastas and salads, not to mention a sumptuous Sunday brunch (served 9.30am-3.30pm).

Eat, Drink, Shop

The Americas

Capital Grille

444 Brickell Avenue, at SE 4th Street (305 374 4500/www.thecapitalgrille.com). Metromover Knight Center. **Open** 11am-3pm, 5-10pm Mon-Thur, Sun; 11am-3pm, 5-11pm Fri, Sat. **Main courses** $21-$35. **Credit** AmEx, DC, MC, V. **Map** p274 E3 ⑥⑤

Located on the Capitol Hill of Miami's business movers and shakers, this is the quintessential spot for a power lunch. Like the conversation, the food here is quite heavy, with dry-aged beef sirloin, filet mignon and prime rib among the offerings. Although the Grille boasts an award-winning wine list, we recommend a trip to the clubby bar for one of the very fine pineapple-saturated Stolis.

Gordon Biersch
Brewery Restaurant

1201 Brickell Avenue, at SE 12th Street (786 425 1130/www.gordonbiersch.com). Bus 24, 48, B/ Metromover Financial District. **Open** 11.30am-midnight Mon-Thur, Sun; 11.30am-2am Fri, Sat. **Main courses** $12-$20. **Credit** AmEx, DC, MC, V.

The ideal chaser to Miami's Martini madness, this hangout is a vast homage to beer (*see p137*). But there's also an impressive gourmet menu that includes sausage gumbo and cashew chicken stir-fry, as well as pizza, burgers and salads. It's popular with young professionals during Friday happy hour, when it gets packed.

People's Bar-B-Que

360 NW 8th Street, at NW 3rd Avenue (305 373 8080). Metromover Overtown. **Open** 11.30am-11.30pm Mon-Thur; 11.30am-1am Fri, Sat; 1-9pm Sun. **Main courses** $9-$15. **Credit** AmEx, MC, V. **Map** p274 B1 ⑥⑦

Overtown is an area more associated with riots than restaurants. But when you're on I-95, you may be drawn to exit by the smell of the meat grilling down below at this cheap neighbourhood joint. Attracting the barbecue lovers are chicken and ribs and the amazing sauce with which they're served. There are also pork chops and soul-food options such as collard greens and black-eyed peas.

Los Ranchos

401 Biscayne Boulevard, at NE 4th Street (305 375 0666/www.restaurantelosranchos.com). Metromover College/Bayside. **Open** 11.30am-10.30pm Mon-Thur, Sun; noon-11pm Fri, Sat. **Main courses** $9-$29. **Credit** AmEx, DC, MC, V. **Map** p274 C4 ⑥⑧

This Nicaraguan chain is one of the best places to sink your teeth into some carcass: the menu is stacked with steak, steak and more steak. The must-try is the *churrasco* – grilled flank steak with chilli salsa, a dish famous among local carnivores. **Other locations**: 3015 Grand Avenue, Coconut Grove (305 461 8222); 8888 SW 136th Street, The Falls (305 238 6867); 2728 Ponce de León Boulevard, Coral Gables (305 446 0050); 125 SW 107th Avenue, Sweetwater (305 552 6767).

Seafood

Big Fish

55 SW Miami Avenue Road, at SW 5th Street (305 373 1770/www.thebigfishmiami.com). Bus 6, 8. **Open** noon-midnight daily. **Main courses** $15.50-$28.50. **Credit** AmEx, DC, MC, V.

Not easy to find, but worth the effort, this unassuming seafood shack on the Miami River has a corking view of the skyline and some of the freshest catches in town, including lobster, shrimp and grouper. Even if you're not into fish, grab a seat at the cosy 'bar tree' and take in the amazing view. To get here, cross Brickell Avenue Bridge heading south and take the first right (SW 5th Street); pass under a bridge and Big Fish is on the other side.

Joe's Seafood

400 NW North River Drive, at NW 4th Street (305 374 9928). Bus 11, 77. **Open** 11am-10pm Mon-Thur, Sun. **Main courses** $9-$50. **Credit** AmEx, DC, MC, V.

Not to be confused with Joe's Stone Crab (*see p121*), Joe's Seafood is a rugged, Latin-accented fish market and restaurant. With an excellent view overlooking the Miami River, this is an out-of-the-way place to stop for pleasantly laid-back service and a variety of fresh seafood dishes.

River Oyster Bar

650 S Miami Avenue, at SE 6th Street (305 530 1915/www.therivermiami.com). Metromover 5th Street. **Open** 11.30am-10.30pm Mon-Thur; 11.30am-11.30pm Fri; 6-11.30pm Sat. **Main courses** $9-$27. **Credit** AmEx, DC, Disc, MC, V. **Map** p274 F2 ⑥⑨

When it took over the space formerly occupied by the much-loved Fishbone Grill, the River Oyster Bar had a hard act to follow. But a sleekly minimalist interior, a fantastic raw bar (oysters, ceviches, clams and seafood cocktails, plus some glorious accompanying sauces) and daily fresh catches seem to have done the trick. The place is a big favourite for business lunches and after-work bingeing.

Coral Gables

You'll find a more restrained dining experience in Coral Gables, home to some of the city's most acclaimed and expensive establishments, such as **Norman's** and **Pascal's On Ponce**. They can be a bit stuffy, but that is usually an acceptable trade-off for the first-rate food.

Asian

Miss Saigon Bistro

148 Giralda Avenue, at Ponce de León Boulevard (305 446 8006/www.misssaigonbistro.com). Bus 24, 42, 72, Coral Gables Circulator. **Open** 11.30am-3pm, 5.30-10pm Mon-Thur; 11.30am-3pm, 5.30-11pm Fri; 5.30-11pm Sat; 5.30-10pm Sun. **Main courses** $8.95-$17.95. **Credit** MC, V. **Map** p276 B4 ⑥⓪

Joe's Stone Crab. *See p121.*

Get over the fact that this family-run Vietnamese bistro has been named after the cheesy musical (the soundtrack plays ad nauseam): this is a knockout. Servers are helpful, recommending dishes and even tailoring them to your taste. To get the full effect, they often suggest you order a few starters (the summer rolls are sublime), a noodle dish and a main course such as whole snapper with lemongrass and ginger, or caramelised prawns. Ric, the owner's son, may even sing an aria or two.

Other locations: 600 Brickell Avenue, Downtown (305 416 0337).

Diners, delis & cheap eats

Archie's Pizza

166 Giralda Avenue, at Ponce de León Boulevard (305 444 1557). Bus 24, 42, 72, Coral Gables Circulator. **Open** noon-11pm daily. **Main courses** $6-$15. **Credit** AmEx, MC, V. **Map** p276 B4 ⑥

Not every restaurant in Coral Gables will set you back your unborn child's college fund. Archie's is a case in point, a brick-walled gourmet pizza joint serving delicious brick-oven thin-crust pizzas to hungry crowds of business people, students and the budget-conscious. TVs – typically tuned to sport – hang over the long bar counter.

Gables Diner

2320 Galiano Street, at Aragon Avenue (305 567 0330/www.gablesdiner.com). Bus 24, 37, Coral Gables Circulator. **Open** 8am-10.30pm Mon-Thur, Sun; 8am-11.30pm Fri, Sat. **Main courses** $8-$19. **Credit** AmEx, MC, V. **Map** p276 B4 ⑥

For the times when you don't feel like partaking in haute cuisine, this is the place in which to seek comfort in a relaxed, informal setting. From meatloaf to chicken pot pie, the menu is unpretentious and the prices reasonable. There's also a good selection of imported beers, best sampled during happy hour (4-7pm).

European

Caffè Abbracci

318 Aragon Avenue, at Le Jeune Road (305 441 0700). Bus 42, 56, J, Coral Gables Circulator. **Open** 11.30am-2.30pm, 6-11pm Mon-Thur; 11.30am-2.30pm, 6pm-midnight Fri; 6pm-midnight Sat; 6-11pm Sun. **Main courses** $9-$29. **Credit** AmEx, DC, MC, V. **Map** p276 B4 ⑥

Caffè Abbracci (the name means 'hugs') embraces guests with its congenial staff, lovely atmosphere and what is perhaps the city's best Italian cuisine. Homemade black and red lobster ravioli and risotto with porcini and portobello mushrooms are irresistible.

Prime 112.
See p119.

Norman's

21 Almeria Avenue, at SW 37th Avenue (Douglas Road) (305 446 6767/www.normans.com). Bus 37.
Open 6-10.30pm Mon-Thur; 6-11pm Fri, Sat. **Main courses** $23-$39.50. **Credit** AmEx, DC, MC, V.
Map p276 C4

Gourmet magazine rates this as the best restaurant in south Florida – and some say it's the best in the US. Then again, a recent *Wall Street Journal* poll named it as one of the nation's ten most overrated kitchens. But at least everyone's talking about it and, if you're serious about food, it has to be worth a visit to make up your own mind. Celebrity chef Norman Van Aken's signature dishes include rhum- and pepper-painted grouper, seared foie gras on toasted Cuban bread, and cornbread-stuffed quail. The open kitchen setting, old colonial dining room and smart clientele make it a required, albeit pricey, experience.

Pascal's On Ponce

2611 Ponce de León Boulevard, at Valencia Avenue (305 444 2024/www.pascalmiami.com). Bus 24, 42, 72, Coral Gables Circulator. **Open** 11.30am-2.30pm, 6-10.30pm Mon-Thur; 11.30am-2.30pm, 6-11pm Fri; 6-11pm Sat. **Main courses** $18.95-$36. **Credit** AmEx, DC, MC, V. **Map** p276 C4

A former disciple of Alain Ducasse, chef Pascal Oudin brings his fussy French fare to Coral Gables, but not without a modern twist. Fusing classical French techniques with ingredients from the Americas, Oudin creates a somewhat confusing culinary collision, as seen in dishes such as sea bass with potato crust and braised leeks in a cayenne-sparked sauce. But the cooking has its fans, and Pascal's regularly tops polls of the best French restaurant in Florida.

Restaurant Place St Michel

Hotel Place St Michel, 162 Alcazar Avenue, at Ponce de León Boulevard (305 446 6572). Bus 40, 72, Coral Gables Circulator. **Open** 11am-10.30pm Mon-Thur, Sun; 11am-11.30pm Fri, Sat. **Main courses** $20-$40. **Credit** AmEx, DC, MC, V. **Map** p276 B4

For a charming old-world European restaurant, with a grand deco dining room of lovingly buffed wood, the St Michel serves up surprisingly modish cuisine. Hard to describe, it's sort of new American with a light French influence, featuring fresh local fish, prime-aged meats, game and pastas, plus excellent crêpes and great desserts.

The Americas

Chispa

225 Altara Avenue, at Ponce de León Boulevard (305 648 2600/www.chisparestaurant.com). Bus 24, 42, Coral Gables Circulator. **Open** 11.30am-3.30pm, 5.30-10.30pm Mon-Thur, Sun; 11.30am-3.30pm, 5.30-11.30pm Fri, Sat. **Main courses** $17-$36. **Credit** AmEx, DC, Disc, MC, V. **Map** p276 E4

Chispa ('spark' in Spanish) has lived up to its name, creating a real buzz among Gables foodies. What's got their tongues wagging, and glands salivating, is chef Robin Haas's nouveau Spanish cuisine – beau-

Clarke's. *See p110.*

tiful ceviches, wood-roasted shrimp with Serrano ham, garlic and capers, and some two dozen tapas dishes at prices that are surprisingly reasonable ($5-$9). The restaurant itself is a sprawling place with decor reminiscent of a loud, gaudy Wolfgang Puck eaterie in LA. The bar remains open until 12.30am, or 1.30am Fridays and Saturdays.

Christy's

3101 Ponce de León Boulevard, at Malaga Avenue (305 446 1400/www.christysrestaurant.com). Bus 24, 52, 72, Coral Gables Circulator. **Open** 11.30am-10pm Mon-Thur; 11.30am-11pm Fri; 5-11pm Sat, Sun. **Main courses** $20-$34. **Credit** AmEx, DC, MC, V. **Map** p276 C4

You can almost taste the power surging through this elegant, English-style restaurant, where the excellent food and service attract an impressive clientele. A member of the Bush family may be sitting at one table and Rod Stewart at another, but the best thing about Miami's premier steakhouse are the superlative lamb chops, steaks and prime rib.

Ortanique on the Mile

278 Miracle Mile (SW 24th Street), at Ponce de León Boulevard (305 446 7710). Bus 24, 42, 72, Coral Gables Circulator. **Open** 6-10pm Mon, Tue; 6-11pm Wed-Sat; 5.30-9.30pm Sun. **Main courses** $16-$35. **Credit** AmEx, DC, MC, V. **Map** p276 C4

Caribbean cuisine takes a creative turn at this spot named after a rare tropical fruit (an ortanique is a hybrid orange native to Jamaica – apparently). The

Whining and dining

Back in the early 1990s there was an event called the Taste of the Beach, in which a slab of South Pointe Park was transformed into a tacky, carnival-like event featuring booths hosted by the various area restaurants. Tickets had to be purchased for a small sampling of so-called haute cuisine, served on plastic plates. The event was more of a meat market than anything else and quickly faded from the radar. In 2002 Lee Brian Schrager, director of Special Events & Media Relations of Southern Wine & Spirits of America, took a big risk and decided to move his staid, one-day Florida Extravaganza food affair from the FIU campus in North Miami to the beach on Ocean Drive. Judging by the sight of things at that first event, you'd have thought people in Miami had never seen food before. The attendance was monstrous, the pricey chef dinners, parties, seminars and tastings selling out straight away. Fast forward to 2006 and the Fifth Annual fest, and you've got one of the biggest, flashiest,

splashiest – and tastiest – food events in the country. Sponsored by *Food & Wine* magazine and hosted by the *Who's Who* of the Food Network – Emeril, Tyler, Wolfgang, Nigella, Anthony, Mario, Bobby and, well, you get the idea – the **South Beach Wine & Food Festival** not only brings out the pig and lush in everyone but it also attracts the biggest and best names hailing from esteemed kitchens around the world. The 2006 event sold out in practically a week, with chi-chi events honouring Ferran Adrià, whose restaurant in Spain, El Bulli, is easily the hardest-to-get reservation in the world. Mind you, when you think about it, so are tickets to the South Beach Wine & Food Fest. Come January and the cacophony of people whining because they don't have tickets is as commonplace as the heavy bass emanating from the souped-up muscle cars cruising Ocean Drive. Book early if you can. For more information, visit www.sobewineandfood fest.com. *See also p163.*

focus here is on cuisine, not scene, and the food, created by top chef Cindy Hutson, is outstanding. Dishes such as the curried roti stuffed with potatoes, pumpkin, chickpeas and carrots are a blissful orgy of flavour. Such has been the success of Ortanique there are now branches in LA and Washington.

Coconut Grove

Collegiate Coconut Grove is far from being a gourmet destination, but the restaurants here have at least mastered the art of chicken wings, mozzarella sticks and assorted bar fare.

Asian

Anokha

3195 Commodore Plaza, at Main Highway (1-786 552 1030). Bus 42, 48, Coconut Grove Circulator. **Open** 11am-2.30pm, 6-10.30pm Tue-Thur, Sun; 11am-2.30pm, 6-11.30pm Fri, Sat. **Main courses** $10-$30. **Credit** AmEx, DC, MC, V. **Map** p277 B2 ⑳
'A guest is equal to God and should be treated as such' – that's the kind of restaurant motto we like. Anokha does a pretty good job of living up to it too. But not only is the service entirely welcoming, the Indian cuisine is also pretty special. Dishes are light and subtly flavoured, with a southern Floridian flair enlivening the usual biryanis, tandooris and curries (for example, plenty of fish and seafood, and coconutty sauces). Vegetarians get a good choice too.

Cafés

Greenstreet Café

3110 Commodore Plaza, at Main Highway (305 444 0244/www.greenstreetcafe.net). Bus 42, 48, Coconut Grove Circulator. **Open** 7.30am-11.30pm Mon-Thur, Sun; 7am-midnight Fri, Sat. **Main courses** $10-$18. **Credit** AmEx, DC, MC, V. **Map** p277 B3 ㉑
This is the Grove's command central for the socio-anthropological sport of people-watching, thanks to the Greenstreet's strategic placement on a bustling corner. To accompany this activity, management thoughtfully provides excellent salads, sandwiches, pasta and Sunday brunches. Although the kitchen is closed by midnight, the café stays open for drinks until 3am Thursday to Saturday.

European

Le Bouchon du Grove

3430 Main Highway, at Grand Avenue (305 448 6060). Bus 37, 42, Coconut Grove Circulator. **Open** 9am-3pm, 5.30-11pm Mon-Thur, Sun; 9am-midnight Fri, Sat. **Main courses** $20-$30. **Credit** AmEx, DC, MC, V. **Map** p277 B3 ㉒
Everything about this bistro screams 'France' – except the warm service, that is. The home-made duck pâté and the onion soup are especially good. In fact, the only real downside is that there's no *croque-monsieur* on the menu.

Café Tu Tu Tango
CocoWalk, 3015 Grand Avenue, at Virginia Street (305 529 2222/www.cafetutu tango.com). Bus 42, 48, Coconut Grove Circulator. **Open** 11.30am-midnight Mon-Wed, Sun; 11.30am-1am Thur; 11.30am-2am Fri, Sat. **Tapas** $5-$11. **Credit** AmEx, MC, V. **Map** p277 B3 ❼❸
While you tempt your palate with tapas, roaming artists may be dipping on to their palettes before your eyes in this restaurant-as-artist's-loft. Guests are encouraged to order and share different items, from black bean soup to spicy chicken spring rolls. The sangria is pretty good: if you drink enough, it may even help you interpret the numerous paintings that cover the interior.

Seafood

Baleen
Grove Isle Hotel & Spa, Grove Isle Drive, off S Bayshore Drive (305 858 8300/www.groveisle.com). Bus 48. **Open** 7-10pm Mon-Thur, Sun; 7-11pm Fri-Sat. **Main courses** $18-$45. **Credit** AmEx, DC, Disc, MC, V.
Baleen is different from most Miami all-style, no-substance waterfront eateries in that it provides priceless views of Biscayne Bay and pricey nouveau seafood that is actually worth every cent. The site is on an island just off Coconut Grove, while the restaurant boasts a glass-walled indoor space and an attractive classical-styled waterside courtyard. The menu is fish and shellfish, and the preparation and execution are top class.

Monty's
2550 S Bayshore Drive, at Aviation Avenue (305 858 1431/www.montysstonecrab.com). Bus 48, Coconut Grove Circulator. **Open** 11.30am-11pm Mon-Wed; 11.30am-11.30pm Thur; 11.30am-midnight Fri; noon-midnight Sat; noon-11pm Sun. **Main courses** $15-$40. **Credit** AmEx, DC, MC, V. **Map** p277 A4 ❼❷
The Disney World of waterfront dining, Monty's offers the chance to eat shrimp or stone crabs before renting a boat and heading out to sea. Though the indoor dining room overlooking the water is scenic, it's also stuffy and overpriced. The outside tiki-hut area is more popular with the happy-hour crowd for its laid-back atmosphere and seafood bar menu. *See also p140.*

Scotty's Landing
3381 Pan American Drive, off S Bayshore Drive (305 854 2626/www.sailmiami.com/scottys). Bus 48, Coconut Grove Circulator. **Open** 11am-10pm Mon-Thur; 11am-11pm Fri-Sun. **Main courses** $6-$13. **Credit** MC, V. **Map** p277 B4 ❼❺
A favourite of boaters who dock their vessels here for a beer or two, Scotty's Landing is a hidden jewel for those in the know. Seafood dishes are fresh and very reasonably priced. A beer and wine-only joint, Scotty's is a popular happy hour spot featuring live music and a decidedly Key West vibe.

Little Havana

Little Havana is Miami's gift to all who desire the tastes of Cuba. OK, so Cuban is not one of the world's greatest cuisines, but this is more than compensated for by the atmosphere. Hit **Calle Ocho** (SW 8th Street) to sample the culture's most authentic comestibles at traditional cafés and restaurants. Note that the best venues, such as **Versailles**, are miles away from the main tourist areas and you need some form of transport to get there and back.

Asian

Hy Vong
3458 Calle Ocho (SW 8th Street), at SW 34th Avenue (305 446 3674). Bus 6, 8, 37. **Open** 6-11pm Tue-Sun. **Main courses** $12-$21. **No credit cards.**
A local mainstay for 20 years, this tiny Vietnamese restaurant has only 35 seats, all constantly occupied by locals looking to fill up on expertly prepared Asian specials such as grilled lamb with curry sauce, cooked on a six-burner stove. If you arrive after 7pm, the wait for a free table can be brutal – up to two hours – but worth it.

Latin American

La Carreta
3632 Calle Ocho (SW 8th Street), at SW 36th Avenue (305 447 0184). Bus 8, 37. **Open** 24hrs daily. **Main courses** $6-$23. **Credit** AmEx, DC, MC, V.
This Cuban chain offers large doses of the usual local nostalgia for Batista-era Cuba. Still, it also has massive sugarcane plants growing on the front lawn, large portions on the plates and a backroom café for strong Cuban coffee, sweet pastries and strange sugarcane juice.

La Esquina de Tejas
101 SW 12th Avenue, at SW 1st Street (305 545 0337). Bus 12. **Open** 8am-5pm daily. **Main courses** $7-$15. **Credit** AmEx, MC, V. **Map** p275 C3 ❼❻
If it's cheap, classic Cuban food you're after, this is the place. Reagan apparently once stopped here to schmooze local Cuban-American voters, and they never forgot it. If you can forgive the political over-load, you'll enjoy outstanding Cuban-style pork, ham and cheese sandwiches.

Islas Canarias
285 NW 27th Avenue, at NW 3rd Street (305 649 0440). Bus 27. **Open** 7am-11pm daily. **Main courses** $6-$20. **Credit** MC, V.
A quarter-century old, this family-style Cuban restaurant is, as the name implies, like a tiny island, albeit one packed with hungry diners who swear by its Cuban food, as well as its Canary Islands dishes (Grandpapa García came from Tenerife), such as baked lamb and tortilla española. Reasonable prices and great specialities keep 'em coming back.

Versailles

3555 Calle Ocho (SW 8th Street), at SW 35th Avenue (305 444 0240). Bus 8, 37, 42. **Open** 8am-2.30am Mon-Thur; 8am-3.30am Fri; 8am-4.30am Sat; 9am-1am Sun. **Main courses** $5-$20. **Credit** AmEx, MC, V.

Almost as famous locally as its palatial namesake is in France, the perennially popular Versailles is a kitschy, iconoclastic, vast Cuban diner with wall-to-wall mirrors, a constant buzz and an unabridged menu featuring every dish known to the culture. Not to everybody's taste, but a local cultural tradition, and one we highly recommend. **Photo** *p131.*

The Design District, Little Haiti & around

Miami's very own version of New York's Meatpacking District, the Design District is the new place to see and be seen – not to mention enjoy a fine meal in a very cool, very anti-South Beach environment. Note, however, that the restaurants in this area are few and far between, so you'll need a car or a taxi to drop you off and pick up again later. Don't wander after dark.

Diners, delis & cheap eats

See also p116 **Fringe benefits.**

Jumbo's

7501 NW 7th Avenue, at NW 75th Street, Little Haiti (305 751 1127). **Open** 24hrs daily. **Main courses** $5-$15. **Credit** AmEx, DC, MC, V.

Family-owned for over 50 years, Jumbo's is known for its world-famous fried shrimp, fried chicken, catfish fingers and collard greens. Sure, it's located in what locals call the 'ghetto', but it's open 24/7 and it's worth it. And there's history here too: Jumbo's was the first restaurant in Miami to integrate in 1966 and the first to hire African American employees in 1967.

Fusion & new world cuisine

Food Café

130 NE 40th Street, at NE 1st Avenue, Design District (305 573 0444). Bus 9, 10. **Open** 9am-4pm Mon; 9am-10pm Tue-Fri; 6-10pm Sat. **Main courses** $7-$16. **Credit** AmEx, DC, MC, V.

Now that the Design District is hot, Food Café has decided to expand its breakfast and lunch menu to dinner and wine. A small neighbourhood affair set in an outdoor courtyard, it serves up Latin-flaired dishes such as grilled cilantro lime-charred steak and citrus-marinated grilled calamari. Cool Brazilian jazz from the house band sets off the mood perfectly.

Michy's

6927 Biscayne Boulevard, at 69th Street, Biscayne Corridor (305 759 2001). Bus 3. **Open** noon-3pm, 6-10.30pm Tue-Thur; noon-3pm, 6-11pm Fri; 6-11pm

Sat; 6-10.30pm Sun. **Main courses** $8-$25. **Credit** AmEx, DC, MC, V.

Star chef Michelle Bernstein left the Mandarin Oriental to consult on a fancy hotel restaurant in Mexico and then returned to Miami in 2006 to open this, a 100-seat neighbourhood bistro and raw bar. Bernstein partnered up with Perricone's (*see p123*) owner Steven Perricone, and the two hope to revitalise this lagging neighbourhood with some good haute Caribbean chow. Hopefully it'll work.

Sheba Ethiopian Cuisine

4029 N Miami Avenue, at 40th Street, Design District (305 573 1819). Bus 9, 10. **Open** 11.30am-11pm Mon-Thur; 11.30am-4pm-midnight Fri, Sat; 5-11pm Sun. **Main courses** $10-$23. **Credit** AmEx, MC, V.

The now-defunct Grass Restaurant & Lounge lost all its customers when the doormen started to look like something out of a B-movie. It's too bad, because the Asian fare was good. But thanks to Sheba, all sour memories of Grass have gone away and are now replaced by the savoury scents and tastes of authentic *doro wat* – Ethiopia's national dish of chicken legs and thighs marinated and seasoned in garlic, ginger and fenugreek, and stewed in a spicy *berbere* (spicy sauce with cardamom, shallots, peppercorns and fenugreek). A funky crowd of hipsters can be found at the bar, tapping their toes to the African tunes on the sound system.

Soyka

5556 Biscayne Boulevard, at NE 55th Street, Biscayne Corridor (305 759 3117). Bus 3, 16, 62. **Open** 11am-11pm Mon-Thur, Sun; 11am-midnight Fri, Sat. **Main courses** $8-$26. **Credit** AmEx, DC, MC, V.

Mark Soyka is a man who can spot a trend. He's the guy behind South Beach's News Café (*see p111*), and he was one of the first to stake a claim on Biscayne with this self-named, huge, semi-industrial styled eaterie. Very urban but also extremely comfortable, it draws mainly local professionals with unfussy dishes such as grilled chicken with tomato relish and marinated skirt steak. There's also a welcoming bar corner for potent Martinis.

North Miami & beyond

North Miami is known for shopping, not dining. You wanna eat? Well, there's the McDonald's and the Taco Bell. However, there is money up here, so happily there are a few choice spots where the server won't respond to your order with 'Would you like fries with that?'

Cafés, diners & delis

Gourmet Diner

13951 Biscayne Boulevard, at NE 139th Street (305 947 2255). Bus 3, 28. **Open** 11am-11pm Mon-Fri; 9am-11.30pm Sat; 9am-10.30pm Sun. **Main courses** $12-$24. **Credit** AmEx, MC, V.

The only 'diner' in town where you can order escargots, this is not your average greasy spoon. Creations such as the rocket and endive salad with goat's cheese lend weight to the 'gourmet' claims. Happily, prices aren't prohibitive.

Wolfie Cohen's Rascal House
17190 Collins Avenue, at 171st Street (305 947 4581). Bus E, K, S, V. **Open** 7am-1am daily. **Main courses** $8-$14. **Credit** AmEx, MC, V.
Amid the cacophony of New York, Boston and Chicago accents, take a seat in a grand 1950s vinyl booth, where a waitress pushing retirement will bring you classic corned beef, brisket or potato pancakes. Breakfast is busy, with a dollar or two buying an egg and as many breads and pastries as you can eat.

European

Oggi Café
1740 79th Street Causeway, at E Treasure Drive, North Bay Village (305 866 1238). Bus L. **Open** 11.30am-2.30pm, 6-10.30pm Mon-Thur; 11.30am-2.30pm, 6-11.30pm Fri; 6-11.30pm Sat; 5.30-10.30pm Sun. **Main courses** $13-$32. **Credit** AmEx, DC, Disc, MC, V.
Despite being tucked away in a neighbourhood strip mall, this Italian deli-style establishment – owned by a couple of Argentinians – is so hugely popular that the premises have been extended no fewer than three times. Signature dishes are freshly made pastas stuffed with fish and topped with lobster sauce, but there's also beef, poultry and fresh fish, with breads and desserts made on the premises.

North American

Shula's Steak House
7601 NW 154th Street, at Miami Lakes Drive (305 820 8102/www.donshula.com). Bus 83, E. **Open** 6.30am-11pm Mon-Sat; 6.30-11am, 5.30-10.30pm Sun. **Main courses** $14-$31. **Credit** AmEx, MC, V.
Shula's is famous not only because owner Don Shula is the much-beloved former coach of the Miami Dolphins (a bona fide hero in these parts), but also because the steaks are excellent and big enough to satisfy a linebacker. Finish one of the absolutely massive porterhouse steaks and get your name on a plaque and an autographed photo of the Don.

South Miami & beyond

Suburbia tastes good thanks to a smattering of excellent Asian eateries that for some reason decided this was the place to set up shop.

Asian

Kon Chau
8376 SW 40th Street, at SW 83rd Avenue (305 553 7799). Bus 40, 87. **Open** 11am-10pm daily. **Main courses** $5-$19. **Credit** MC, V.

France meets Cuba at **Versailles**. *See p130.*

This place isn't much of a looker, but how can you go wrong when you can eat wonderful dim sum as if it's your last meal, for under $15? Try shrimp dumplings, lotus cakes and the like by the dozen.

Siam Lotus
6388 S Dixie Highway, at SW 63rd Avenue (305 666 8134). Metrorail Dadeland North. **Open** 11am-10.30pm daily. **Main courses** $7-$17. **Credit** AmEx, MC, V.
This shack-like eyesore shouldn't be judged on looks: it serves some of the best Thai food around. Try the pad Thai and be convinced that beauty is in the mouth of the beholder.

Tropical Chinese
7991 SW 40th Street, at SW 79th Avenue (305 262 1552). Bus 40. **Open** 11.30am-10.30pm Mon-Thur; 10.30am-11pm Fri, Sat; 10.30am-10pm Sun. **Main courses** $9-$24. **Credit** AmEx, DC, MC, V.
It's hard to find decent Chinese food in this city, but follow local Chinese-American families south and you'll discover some in a nondescript strip mall. This is the place for Hong Kong-style Chinese food, not least the best dim sum in the area.

North American

Shorty's BBQ
9200 S Dixie Highway, at Dadeland Boulevard (305 670 7732). Metrorail Dadeland South. **Open** 11am-10pm Mon-Thur, Sun; 11am-11pm Fri, Sat. **Main courses** $5-$18. **Credit** MC, V.
This friendly barbecue pit is a last vestige of pre-developed, pre-trendy Miami. Barbecue chicken and ribs are served in a casual atmosphere at long picnic tables. Prissy folk need not apply here, where eating with your hands is *de rigueur* and eating with a fork is a dreadful faux pas.

Bars & Pubs

Dress up to sup up.

Drinking in Miami could be considered a sport, but it's not typically a grungy, dirty event that ends in a cleansing shower. In fact, when it comes to imbibing in this town, it's more about boozy sophistication than sloppy drunkenness. While there are a few places where such is the norm, contrary to popular belief, Miami isn't exactly a hotbed of bars and pubs. New York, San Francisco and Chicago are all much more rewarding for the casual or committed boozer (although some of us can delight in the fact that Miami has so far held off outlawing smoking in its drinking establishments). The fact is this is not a beery city. In style-conscious Miami, the notion of a bar with pool tables, rock soundtrack, football pennants and slobbish bar-stool jocks is a little beyond the pale. Put quite simply, beer isn't chic and neither is it sexy. Not to mention the havoc it can wreak on those flattened stomachs.

Instead, Miami (and if we're talking nightlife, we're talking Miami Beach) largely favours venues with a little more razzle and oodles more dazzle. Top of the list are hotel bars. Miami just loves the likes of Ian Schrager and Todd Oldham, lifestyle designers supreme, whose work oozes the kind of effortless sophistication Beach denizens consider their trademark (no sniggering, please). The studiedly cool bar counters at the likes of the **Delano** (see p35), the **Catalina** (see p41), the **Shore Club** (see p38), the **Setai** (see p37) and the **Hotel** (see p41) represent the absolute see-and-be-seen spots at which to sip. For those lacking in hauteur and poise – or who can't afford the surgery and silicone – there are other, less rarefied hotel bars that manage to encapsulate what Miami's all about without making the non-scenester feel like a thrift store-attired leper; the **Rex at the Marlin Hotel** (see p135) is as close to a London-style DJ bar as it gets, while the **Metro Bar** at the Astor (see p39) is gorgeous without it going to anybody's head. For more hotel bars, see p138 **Walk on**.

There's also the trend for restaurants to double as lounge bars. At some point in the evening, the cutlery and place settings disappear and tables become platforms to be danced on; restaurants like the **Forge** (see p121), **Social Miami** at the Sagamore hotel (see p109) and, in particular, **Taverna Opa** (see p114) are shining examples of dining-turned-disco. And that's before you get to **Stop Miami** (see p189 **The start of Stop**), a bar/restaurant/music combo that has taken its cutting-edge neighbourhood by storm since it opened in 2005.

But it's not just what you wear and where you go – and who with – but also what you consume. Miami likes its drinks to match its architecture: exotic and served up in candy colours. This is a place that sets its watch by cocktail hour. Miami Beach bar culture

The best Watering holes

For curing your ale-ments
The **Abbey**. See p133.

For channelling your best Showgirls moment
Automatic Slim's. See p134.

For meeting a mogul
The **Setai**. See p138 **Lobbying to be seen**.

For meeting a mogul in hiding
The **Room**. See p135.

For getting gritty
Ted's Hideaway. See p135.

For watery views
Shuckers Bar & Grill, Bayside Hut (for both, see p137).

For a little swank with your salsa
Bahia. See p137.

For live music
Churchill's Pub (see p140), Tobacco Road (see p139).

For sophisticated wine & cheese pairings
Vino Miami. See p135.

Eat, Drink, Shop

Mac's Club Deuce. *See p134.*

is largely fuelled by Martinis, Cosmos and Mojitos, although even these are a little tame – generally speaking, the more fruity, lurid and sickly sweet the concoction, the better. Current cocktails *du jour* are those served at the Hotel (*see p138* **Walk on**), lit with 'neon' ice cubes.

Of course, cocktail bars are not the whole story: there are sports bars, music bars, Irish bars and fishermen's bars. On Sunday afternoon at **Alabama Jack's** (*see p228*), way the hell down south past Homestead, there's even line dancing. Yeehaw!

WHERES AND WHYS

The only real concentration of bars is on South Beach. Take your pick from flash and trashy on Ocean Drive, smart and chic on Collins, and beery and rough-arse on Washington and Alton. Elsewhere – in North Beach, Coconut Grove or Coral Gables, for example – the bars are few and very far between, in most cases requiring a car or taxi to get between them. Some – and we're thinking particularly of **Jimbo's** (*see p137*) – are even worth the effort.

DOS AND DON'TS

Like most of the US, Florida has harsh under-age drinking laws. You must be 21 to purchase or consume alcohol in Florida; be prepared to

show photo ID. Authorities in Miami also take drinking and driving seriously; get busted behind the wheel of an automobile with more than the equivalent of about two drinks in your system, and you can expect to face jail time and thousands of dollars in fines. (The blood alcohol limit is 0.8 – 80mg of alcohol in 100ml of blood).

On the smoking issue, while it is permitted to light up in drinking establishments, cigarettes are banned in places where food makes up 25 per cent or more of the take at the till.

Miami Beach

In addition to the bars listed below, the **11th Street Diner**, on Washington, and **Jerry's Famous Deli**, on Collins, have separate bar areas serving until 5am and 4am respectively, while the bar at the **News Café** on Ocean Drive is open 24 hours daily. For reviews of all three, *see p111*.

South Beach

Abbey

1115 16th Street, at Alton Road (305 538 8110). Bus M, S, W. **Open** 1pm-5am daily. **Credit** AmEx, MC, V. **Map** p272 C2 ❶

Sick of candy-coloured and flavoured Martinis? Seek salvation in this hole-in-the-wall-turned-micro-brewery, which offers hard-to-find European imports as well as several own-made beers. Luckily, it didn't lose its classic dive-bar soul in the process (or the dartboard; watch out for drunken arrowists). A fine place to meet the locals.

❶ Pink numbers given in this chapter correspond to the location of each bar and pub on the street maps. *See pp272-277.*

Automatic Slim's

1216 Washington Avenue, at 12th Street (305 695 0795/www.automatic-slims.com). Bus C, H, K, W, South Beach Local. **Open** 8pm-5am Mon-Thur; 4pm-5am Fri-Sun. **Credit** AmEx, DC, Disc, MC, V. **Map** p273 C2 **②**

How can anyone resist a place whose motto is 'Where the beautiful people come to get ugly'? We couldn't have put it better when describing this wannabe dive bar, whose inspiration was *Coyote Ugly*, in which sassy shot girls stand atop the bar pouring unknown libations down guys' throats. It makes for a highly testosterone-charged environment with major fist-pumping and slack-jawed ogling. But for the very antithesis of your typical South Beach haute spot, this is the place. Ladies, beware the grimmer-than-grim toilets.

Blue

222 Española Way, at Washington Avenue (305 534 1009). Bus C, H, K, W, South Beach Local. **Open** 10pm-5am daily. **Credit** MC, V. **Map** p273 B2 **③**

So discreet that it flies below most South Beachers' radar, Blue throbs along quietly behind darkened storefront windows. It's a serenely cool haunt that manages very well, thank you, without the approval of the so-called in crowd. Rather than seeing (and being seen), the emphasis is on that other sense: hearing. Blue is all about the music: sexy, sultry and loungey, from deep house to experimental and back again. Laid-back and unpretentious, this is one of our favourite South Beach colours.

Clarke's

840 1st Street, at Alton Road (305 538 9885/ www.clarkesmiamibeach.com). Bus H, M, W, South Beach Local. **Open** 5pm-1am daily. **Credit** AmEx, MC, V. **Map** p272 F2 **④**

Although the owner's last name is Cullen – Irish, indeed – she named this brewzy South of Fifth hotspot after what is allegedly the most popular surname in Ireland. Take that, the Guinness on tap, some bangers and mash and shepherd's pie and add to it a motley crew of police chiefs, Shaquille O'Neal, moguls and barflies and what you've got is a wiggy, jiggy scene that's not quite South Beach and not exactly Dublin, but whatever it is, it's friggin' fun. *See also p110.*

Clevelander

1020 Ocean Drive, at 10th Street (305 531 3485/ www.clevelander.com). Bus C, H, K, W, South Beach Local. **Open** 11am-3am daily. **Credit** AmEx, DC, MC, V. **Map** p273 D3 **⑤**

The archetypal Ocean Drive/Miami Beach bar, the Clevelander offers a high-volume intensity of tiki stylings, pink neon and booze – it claims to sell more Bud than any other bar in the nation – all served up under open skies and illuminated palms. Nightly bands up on the back stage crank up the decibels to ensure that conversation is almost impossible, although the sickly sweet rum runners do a good job

of that on their own. On any given night, several gooning punters will try (usually in vain) not to fall into one of the several shallow pools.

Finnegan's Too

942 Lincoln Road, at Michigan Avenue (305 538 7997). Bus C, G, H, K, L, M, S, W, South Beach Local. **Open** 2pm-5am daily. **Credit** AmEx, DC, Disc, MC, V. **Map** p272 C2 **⑥**

A fairly standard bar rendered exceptional by virtue of being the only dedicated booze joint on the whole of the Lincoln Road Mall. It's big and brash, with a long bar counter but little in the way of seating. Mounted televisions are tuned constantly to sport, but any commentary is drowned out by the din of the drinkers, and, in particular, the whooping and hollering going on around the pool tables. It's nothing special, then, but if you're on the Road, it's either this or sushi. The other Finnegan's, incidentally, is a restaurant, Finnegan's Way, on Ocean Drive.

Lost Weekend

218 Española Way, at Washington Avenue (305 672 1707). Bus C, H, K, W, South Beach Local. **Open** 5pm-5am daily. **Credit** AmEx, MC, V. **Map** p273 B2 **⑦**

Part bar, part pool hall, Lost Weekend has two main points of reference: the five maroon-baize tables and the big chalkboard scrawled with the names of world beers (the bottles fill a row of meat locker-like refrigerators behind the bar). Sadly, most punters are happy to settle for whatever brand of low-grade stuff it is that's sold in cheap two-litre jugs. There's also air hockey, table football and Nirvana and Billy Idol on heavy jukebox rotation, played LOUD. We're not sure about lost weekends, but there's certainly the possibility of a few well-misspent evenings.

Mac's Club Deuce

222 14th Street, at Collins Avenue (305 531 6200). Bus C, H, K, W, South Beach Local. **Open** 8am-5am daily. **No credit cards. Map** p273 C2 **⑧**

Eclectic is too tame a word to describe the mix of South Beach denizens who gather here nightly. From transsexual hookers to nightclub glitterati and down-and-out locals to visiting slumming celebs, the Deuce attracts the motliest, coolest, scariest crowd of any bar in south Florida. We've been beaten here at pool by a go-going blonde, shared cigarettes with a real-life cowboy and traded shots of JD with a sometime writer of erotic fiction. For anyone who ever fancied a bit part in a story by Charles Bukowski, this is where you come to audition. **Photo** *p133.*

Playwright Irish Pub & Restaurant

1265 Washington Avenue, at 13th Street (305 534 0667). Bus C, H, K, W, South Beach Local. **Open** 11am-5am daily. **Credit** AmEx, DC, MC, V. **Map** p273 C2 **⑨**

A heart-warmingly inauthentic ye olde Miami pubbe, providing a welcome home from home for the Beach's expat Brits and Irish (there are more than you'd think). It's got handpumps that deliver proper draught beers, served in pints, albeit for a scary $5.50 (ouch!), and it screens Premiership footie on the telly. There are a couple of pool tables, regular evenings of live music and a kitchen that rustles up decent English-style pub food. It could be heaven, it could be hell, but it certainly ain't Miami.

Purdy Lounge
1811 Purdy Avenue, at 18th Street (305 531 4622/ www.purdylounge.com). Bus A, W. **Open** 3pm-5am Mon-Fri; 6pm-5am Sat, Sun. **Credit** AmEx, MC, V. **Map** p272 C2 ⑩
On the far west side of the Beach, near the foot of the Venetian Causeway, the Purdy has two distinct identities. During the week it acts as an unassuming and comfortable respite for locals who compete for the prime sofa seating up against the front window. On the weekend, though, it's host to a scene-conscious bridge-and-tunnel crowd (or, as they're known here, the Causeway Crowd), who are more interested in dancing and scoring than in seating and views.

Rex
Marlin Hotel, 1200 Collins Avenue, at 12th Street (305 604 5100/www.marlinhotel.com). Bus C, H, K, W, South Beach Local. **Open** 8pm-4am daily. **Credit** AmEx, MC, V. **Map** p273 C2 ⑪
Although it's no longer affiliated with former owner and Island Records mogul Chris Blackwell, and although it has been redone in a very strange, allegedly 'arty', way (graffiti carved into the bar, a quasi peep hole with a piece of art inside), the place has strong links with the music industry; it's a hangout for players (with its own in-house recording studio) and a prime DJ venue. Big names stop by to take the decks up on the mezzanine, but the Marlin's also plugged in to a more varied local underground scene and features regular sessions of jazz, soul, R&B, hip hop, reggae and dancehall.

Room
100 Collins Avenue, at 1st Street (305 531 6061). Bus H, M, W. **Open** 7pm-5am daily. **Credit** AmEx, MC, V. **Map** p272 F3 ⑫
This off-the-beaten-track bar is a xenophobe's dream come true. Hard to find and smaller than most of the walk-in closets in the ritzy South of Fifth (SoFi) area, the Room is a candle-lit beer- and wine-only bar with a CD player in lieu of a bombastic DJ. A place where most people in town go to get away from the madness, it's one of few spots on South Beach where you can actually have an audible conversation with your bar mate (although the later it gets, the more incoherent the crowd becomes). The Room also beats to a decidedly different drum, with a soundtrack that's a fusion of indie, retro and never-before-heard, ever so slyly separating itself from the hip hop-saturated scene its regulars are clearly so eager to escape.

Spy Bar
Catalina Hotel & Beach Club, 1756 Collins Avenue, at 17th Street (305 674 1160/www.catalina hotel.com). Bus C, G, H, L, M, S. **Open** 8am-2am daily. **Credit** AmEx, MC, V. **Map** p272 C3 ⑬

The **Room**, an antidote to SoFi trendiness.

Not your typical boutique hotel lobby bar, the Spy Bar at the cool-yet-down-to-earth Catalina sports a shagadelic, shabby-chic vibe thanks to, well, the red shag carpeting and Austin Powers-style mod furniture. Set to the requisite tune of lobby lounge music, it's at an ideal location across the street from all the other chi-chi hotels such as the Delano and the Shore Club, and because of that, some folks have been known to slip away from the mod squad over there for a little low-key recon here.

Ted's Hideaway
124 2nd Street, at Ocean Drive (305 532 9869). Bus H, M, W. **Open** noon-5am daily. **Credit** MC, V. **Map** p272 F3 ⑭
If Paris Hilton is your role model or you never leave home without Armani, take note: Ted's doesn't want you. Ted's people are normal people (with the exception of Bono, who frequented the dive when the U2 tour hit town), the kind who suck down Buds, take their bar snacks with a side of cheese fries and enthusiastically cheer for the Marlins on TV. When it comes to sociability versus social standing, however, the former always wins at Ted's.

Vino Miami
1601 Washington Place, between Washington Avenue & Collins Avenue (786 207 8466/www.vinomiami. com). Bus C, H, K, W. **Open** 4pm-2am Tue-Thur; 4pm-3am Fri, Sat; 6pm-2am Sun. **Credit** AmEx, MC, V. **Map** p273 A2 ⑮

Vino Miami – not a pint of lager in sight. *See p135.*

It's about time someone in Miami had the genius to open a wine bar. After all, there are only so many Mojitos and Margaritas a person can drink before tastes turn to more sophisticated fare. Vino Miami is a sleek, very modern-looking, dimly lit lounge with an impressive selection of international wines from boutique wineries, both New World and Old. There's a similarly welcome spread in the price ranges. Weekly wine tastings, Saturday night champagne soirées, and an appetising menu of cheeses (plus fondues) create further appeal for the discerning crowd. **Photos** *p136.*

North Beach

Happy's Stork Lounge

1872 North Bay Causeway (79th Street), North Bay Village (305 865 3621). Bus L. **Open** 11am-5am daily. **Credit** MC, V.

While all around Miami Beach revels in tropical glory, Happy's is determined to defy its name. It's small, dark and just a little bit seedy. Pull up a stool at the bar counter (there is no other seating) and eavesdrop on dialogue straight out of a novel by Elmore Leonard. Despite the talk of handguns, fast cars and some other things that lawyers would advise us against repeating, we've always found the folks friendly enough, although you do have to wonder about a sign on the gents that reads 'No more than two at a time'.

Shuckers Bar & Grill

1819 North Bay Causeway (79th Street), North Bay Village (305 866 1570). Bus L. **Open** 11am-2am daily. **Credit** AmEx, DC, MC, V.

It's adjacent to a prominently signed Best Western, but Shuckers has nothing of the hotel bar about it. Instead, it's a good ol' boys' hangout complete with pool, TV sport and a hard-rocking soundtrack to some serious beer drinking. What elevates the place, though, and adds a little cachet, is the location, right on Biscayne Bay. An expansive deck out back puts boozers on the bay – would-be Ahabs can even arrive by boat, neatly outmanoeuvring the eternal Miami gridlock. Additional bonuses: both the beer and the bar food are inexpensive.

Key Biscayne & Virginia Key

Bayside Hut

3501 Rickenbacker Causeway, Virginia Key (305 361 0808). Bus B. **Open** 11.30am-10pm daily. **Credit** AmEx, MC, V.

Tucked away between a boat storage yard and the decomposing hulk of the now-defunct and dodgy Miami Marine Stadium, the Bayside Hut is not, under any circumstances, to be confused with the touristic Bayside Marketplace in Downtown. Popular with insiders, it's appreciated for its waterfront setting, fresh seafood and spectacular views, especially at night, of the Miami skyline from across the waters of Biscayne Bay.

Jimbo's

Off the Rickenbacker Causeway, at Sewerline Road, Virginia Key (305 361 7026/www.jimbosplace.com). Bus B. **Open** 6am-6.30pm daily. **No credit cards.**

Owned by Jimbo Luznar, the 'friendliest man on earth', this is hands down the most difficult to find – and even more difficult to describe – watering hole in Miami. It started as a gathering spot for shrimping trawlers and has since mutated into a combination of *bocce* court, fish-smoking oven, haunt for filthy stray cats, and a dollar-a-can beer-drinking hangout. Adjacent is a tropical lagoon where *Flipper* was filmed, as well as a collection of vacant faux-Bahamian shacks that have been rented out for hundreds of photo, TV and movie shoots, from *Miami Vice* to *True Lies*. The term 'bar' doesn't begin to do this place justice. Precious few south Florida attractions can compete with the simple pleasure of sipping beer on Jimbo's dock while watching manatees loll in the lagoon. To get here, take the main road towards Key Biscayne and make a left just after the MAST Academy. **Photos** *p139.*

There's nowhere decent to get a drink in central Downtown; all of the places listed below are found south of the Miami River in the Brickell Avenue/business district area.

Bahia

Four Seasons Hotel Miami, 1435 Brickell Avenue, at SW 15th Street (305 358 3535/www.fourseasons. com/miami). Bus 24, 48, B/Metromover Financial District. **Open** 5-11pm Mon-Wed, Sun; 5pm-midnight Thur-Sat. **Credit** AmEx, DC, MC, V.

It takes something special to get the Beach crowd venturing west over the MacArthur Causeway, but since opening a few years back, Bahia has had them flocking in their hundreds to take a look. It's the open-air bar on the seventh-floor terrace of über-hotel the Four Seasons (*see p52*), and it's gorgeous. Tables, love seats and day beds are set amid immaculately manicured topiary. Off to one side is a cool expanse of blue pool, on the other is a shimmering cinema screen-sized water feature. Drinks are Latino cocktails (Caipirinhas, Margaritas, Mojitos and Piscos), complemented by a rare array of premium South American beers. There's a menu of reasonably priced tapas from 5pm to 11pm Wednesday to Saturday. Like the clown says, we're lovin' it.

Gordon Biersch Brewery Restaurant

1201 Brickell Avenue, at SE 12th Street (1-786 425 1130/www.gordonbiersch.com). Bus 24, 48, B/ Metromover Financial District. **Open** 11.30am-midnight Mon-Thur, Sun; 11.30am-1am Fri, Sat. **Credit** AmEx, DC, MC, V.

The Miami branch of this national chain is a hotspot for nine-to-fivers from Downtown and the Brickell Corridor. Gordon's 5pm happy hour attracts every lawyer, banker, power broker and dotcom-millionaire-

Walk on Lobbying to be seen

Getting people into beds is only one facet of the Miami hotel scene. Here, hotels are scored just as much on hipness as on room service. Steady bookings from overseas clientele is good, but what really counts is having the right buzz among the locals. Get the Beach scenesters on board and, fingers crossed, the fashionistas and celeb set will follow and society and gossip column inches accrue. *Condé Nast* wants to do a shoot; *CSI: Miami* wonders if it can stage a drowning in your pool.

The surest way to get that initial buzz is with a kick-ass bar and/or restaurant. At any given time, the hottest bar in town will be the one attached to the latest, high-profile, over-designed hostelry. So, it follows that if you're looking for the full-on starry Miami nights experience, lobby-hopping is the way to go.

Working from south to north, kick off at the **Royal** at the Royal Hotel (758 Washington Avenue; *see p46*), which is exactly halfway to being a great bar: a peach of a front half with crushed-velvet furniture and cigar cabinets, but the rear looks like a disused cinema foyer. The vibe is a bit seedy, but in a good way.

Heading towards the Beach, **Wish** at the Hotel (801 Collins Avenue; *see p40*) is more restaurant than bar, but a drink here is a must for the neon ice cubes ('non-toxic, FDA-approved', natch). If you prefer, high-tail it upstairs to the rooftop, where the **Spire Bar** is sure to inspire with its oceanfront views.

Heading north back on Washington, at the cute little **Metro Bar** at the Hotel Astor (No.956; *see p39*) there's room for just a few patrons at the lightbox bar counter, but plenty of spillout space courtesy of a garden terrace hung with Chinese lanterns. Très elegant.

Collins Avenue between 16th and 20th Streets is true cocktail cruising heaven. Boasting upholstered pink walls and Venetian chandeliers, the Starck-designed **Rose Bar** at the Delano (1685 Collins Avenue; *see p35*) remains the playground for all the Tinseltown types who breeze through town. Even better is the alfresco back bar area, on the terrace at the far end of the palm-fringed infinity pool.

Gorgeous as the Rose Bar is, we'd argue that the drinks are better at the dim and cosy bar at the **Raleigh** (1775 Collins Avenue; *see p37*). Visit for Miami's best Martinis, shaken or stirred, just like the crowd. Beware, though, for the Raleigh observes the first rule of Miami

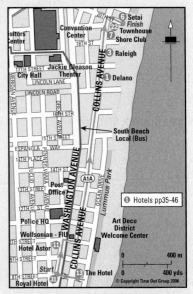

bar-keeping: namely, the cost of drinks is directly proportional to the stylishness of the venue. And this place is really, really stylish.

Just up the street, the Shore Club (1901 Collins Avenue; *see p38*) has a once super-popular nightspot in the **Sky Bar**, whose velvet-rope policy got so out of hand, people refused to go. Now anyone willing to pay the absurd prices for a cocktail is ushered in with open arms. It's worth a look, if not the money. Next, scoot round the corner to the **Bond St Lounge** at the Townhouse (150 20th Street; *see p43*), a snug, Zen-like basement eatery and bar with flattering lighting and oriental-inspired cocktails that in tandem make everyone look great. Same goes for the astronomically expensive, stylistically stunning **Setai** hotel (2001 Collins Avenue; *see p37*), whose Champagne, Crustacean and Caviar Bar is not only made of mother of pearl, but when you get the bill you may want to crawl into a shell of your own. Fabulous and fabulously expensive, the Setai and its $20-something cocktails has a captivated – if not financially-captive-for-the-rest-of-your-life-until-you-pay-off-your-credit-card-bill (if ever) – audience. And isn't that what it's all about?

turned-homeless-socialite in town, particularly on Friday, when the crowd size can reach 2,000 well-heeled people, and breathing space is at a premium. High alcohol-content beers from an impressive selection (including own-brewed bock, märzen, pilsner and dunkel) help numb the tedium of being surrounded by power suits (male and female) on the prowl for deals, contacts and flesh. *See also p124.*

M-Bar at the Mandarin Oriental

Mandarin Oriental Miami Hotel, 500 Brickell Key Drive, at Brickell Avenue (305 913 8288). No public transport. **Open** 5pm-midnight Mon-Thur, Sun; 5pm-1am Fri, Sat. **Credit** AmEx, DC, Disc, MC, V. **Map** p274 F4 ⓰

Tucked away in the corner of the lobby of one of Miami's poshest hotels (*see p53*), the M-Bar is not a Schrager-esque haute spot but, rather, a popular place for after-work types looking to impress their co-workers and clients, and well-heeled hotel guests. The seriously long Martini list earns the M its place in the little black book of any luxe lush, but make sure you steer clear of the nasty black pepper version.

Tobacco Road

626 S Miami Avenue, at SW 7th Street (305 374 1198/www.tobacco-road.com). Bus 6, 8. **Open** 11.30am-5am daily. **Credit** AmEx, DC, MC, V. **Map** p274 F2 ⓱

Al Capone once drank and gambled at the 94-year-old 'Road', which holds the oldest liquor licence in Miami-Dade County. These days it's renowned as a live music venue (*see p188*), but even when the stages are silent, the former speakeasy still qualifies as one of the grittiest yet finest drinking establishments around. The food's excellent too: stop by on Tuesday for the $13.99 lobster special. Patrons are advised to heed the management's advice and drink responsibly… using both hands.

Coral Gables

There's little nightlife in this part of town, although a smattering of chain restaurants such as Tarpon Bend and Houston's aren't far off the mark, thanks to bustling bar scenes, basketball games and beer specials. Also, the **Bar at Ponce & Giralda** (172 Giralda Avenue, at Ponce de León Boulevard, 305 442 2730) has a good boozy, rocking vibe, while **Stuart's Bar Lounge** at the Hotel Place St Michel (*see p54*) has a pleasant faux-nouveau charm.

Duffy's Tavern

2108 SW 57th Avenue (Red Road), at SW 21st Street (305 264 6580). Bus 24. **Open** 10am-1am daily. **No credit cards. Map** p276 B1 ⓲

On the far west side of the Gables, Duffy's is a favourite hangout of University of Miami football players past and present (the place prides itself on its jock-friendliness). UM boosters, who number among some of the most powerful city fathers, are also known to be frequent habitués. In recent years this humble little pub has attracted both old Anglo establishment types and the newer Latin versions simultaneously. It's nice to think that multiculturalism has got a boost from Duffy's ice-cold draught beer.

John Martin's

253 Miracle Mile (SW 24th Street), at Ponce de León Boulevard (305 445 3777/www.johnmartins.com). Bus 24, 42, Coral Gables Circulator. **Open** 11.30am-midnight Mon-Thur; 11.30am-1am Fri, Sat; 11.30am-10.30pm Sun. **Credit** AmEx, MC, V. **Map** p276 B4 ⓳

Do a little jig, make a little love, get down tonight. This landmark pub is arguably the centre for all things Irish in Miami. While that might not be a great many things, it has been enough to keep this local institution going for quite some time. In

Jimbo's. See p137.

addition to the booze and general bonhomie, there's Irish cabaret on Saturday nights and an eclectic – though, of course, Irish-tinged – open-mic night on Sunday. A popular happy hour with a decent and free buffet draws in the Gables prissies hoping to score a rough- around-the-edges Irish lad. Instead, they usually find the male version of themselves.

Coconut Grove

Another fall-back, laid-back Coconut Grove drinking haunt is **Scotty's Landing** (*see p129*) on Pan American Drive.

Flanigan's Laughing Loggerhead

2721 Bird Avenue (SW 40th Street), at SW 27th Avenue (305 446 1114). Bus 22, 27, 42. **Open** 11.30am-5am daily. **Credit** AmEx, MC, V.
A Grove institution, the Loggerhead stocks some 200 brands of bottled beer and serves an interesting menu of eats that includes a delectable sandwich of blackened dolphin (not *that* kind of dolphin), as well as splendid ribs and juicy, two-fisted burgers.

Scotty's Landing.

Naturally, a fishing motif prevails, with aged wooden walls plastered with Hemingway-esque photos of anglers and their sizeable catches. Kitschy? Yep. But it's one of the best – and only – places in these parts where you can drink until 5am.

Monty's

2550 S Bayshore Drive, at Aviation Avenue (305 858 1431/www.montysstonecrab.com). Bus 48, Coconut Grove Circulator. **Open** 10am-11pm daily. **Credit** AmEx, DC, MC, V. **Map** p277 A4 ⓴
An outdoor raw (read: seafood) bar located next to a marina, Monty's has been popular with Grove-ites for decades. Thatch-roofed, open-walled miniature tiki huts surround a stage from which reggae and calypso bands do their damnedest to persuade the diners and drinkers to dance. Those who believe young kids and alcohol don't mix should avoid it in the early evenings. However, sensible parents keep the children home on Friday, when Monty's has its über-happening happy hour, which tends to bring out the Barney (from *The Simpsons*) in everybody. *See also p129.*

Tavern in the Grove

3416 Main Highway, at Grand Avenue (305 447 3884). Bus 42, 48, Coconut Grove Circulator. **Open** 3pm-3am Mon-Fri; 1pm-3am Sat, Sun. **Credit** AmEx, MC, V. **Map** p277 B3 ⓴
Fresh-faced University of Miami co-eds frequent this no-nonsense hole-in-the-wall joint. Despite the yuppie location, the dress code here is more shorts and baseball caps than power-lunch ties and Italian shoes. Although the Tavern draws a crowd of locals every day, it's particularly raucous when UM sports are broadcast on television and, of course, at various festival times in the Grove.

The Design District & Little Haiti

Although primarily a restaurant, Biscayne Corridor's **Soyka** (*see p130*) has a good bar with lounge seating tucked into one corner.

Churchill's Pub

5501 NE 2nd Avenue, at NE 55th Street, Little Haiti (305 757 1807/www.churchillspub.com). Bus 9, 10. **Open** 11am-3am daily. **Admission** $5. **Credit** AmEx, MC, V.
The most attitudinous bar in town – mind you, it would have to be, given its location at the heart of smash-and-grab-central Little Haiti. The place is a much-loved shambolic wreck, a place that's had the shit kicked out of it so many times it wears its batterings and bruisings with pride. Most of the punters look like Kelly Osborne on a budget (and that's just the men). The beer's cheap, as is the food (good alcohol-soaking fare such as scotch eggs and anglo-curry). There are a couple of pool tables, Space Invaders and Galaxians video games and a jukebox stuffed with skatepunk. Bands of varying quality play nightly in the back room (*see p187*).

Shops & Services

The mall may rule in these parts, but there's plenty of room for some interesting independent stores too.

There's a reason why you see people scrambling to buy extra, empty suitcases in schlocky Downtown Miami shops. In the last few years the Big Orange has begun to become competitive with the Big Apple as national chains scramble to gain a foothold in the lucrative Miami market. Outposts of New York retail legends Barneys, Macy's, Bloomingdale's, Pucci and Harry Winston, as well as newer, hipper boutiques like Intermix, Leo, Jimmy Choo and Judith Ripka, have all set up shop in south Florida. Prices may be no cheaper than those up north, but local sales taxes are less.

The major retail areas (read: malls) are easy to access by bus, train or shuttle, but if you plan on buying big, it is far easier to have your own vehicle – and, of course, a few extra suitcases.

If you are taking goods out of the country, remember that you will be liable for duty and tax above a certain value (£145 in the UK).

SHOPPING AREAS
South Beach, especially Lincoln Road and along Collins Avenue between 5th and 8th Streets, is *the* area for boutiques and vintage clothing emporiums, plus plenty of chain stores. **Coral Gables** is good for posh homeware and pricey designer furniture. The **Design District** touts itself as 'one square mile of style' and features a variety of ritzy showrooms stocking furniture, plumbing fixtures, floor coverings, lighting, accessories, wall and window treatments. Nearby is Miami's burgeoning **Upper East Side**, where you'll find a newly sprouting handful of boutiques for clothes and housewares. Just south, by contrast, **Downtown** is good for nothing except discount electronics, luggage and jewellery – but remember: it's all cheap for a reason.

For one-stop shopping out of town, the easily accessible **Aventura Mall** and **Dadeland Mall** are both sprawling meccas of fashion. With every chain store imaginable, this is shopping at its safest, and most predictable. Bargain hunters should zero in on the two mega-discount malls: **Dolphin Mall** in Sweetwater and **Sawgrass Mills** in Broward County (for both, *see p146* **The mall the merrier**). Each offers more designer outlets than any sane person could possibly visit

in one day. **Bal Harbour Shops** and Coral Gables' **Village of Merrick Park** keep the rich and famous in high-priced designer duds. Gathering some top-end European names – including ones that would not normally deign to be part of mall life – these are the jewels in Miami's retail crown.

One-stop

Department stores

Bloomingdale's
The Falls, 8778 SW 136th Street, at S Dixie Highway (US 1), South Miami (305 252 6300/www.blooming dales.com). Bus 1, 52, 65. **Open** 10am-9.30pm Mon-Sat; noon-7pm Sun. **Credit** AmEx, MC, V. **Map** p271. 'Bloomies', as it's known to regulars, features classy cuts from top labels such as Donna Karan, Calvin Klein, Moschino, Chanel and Fendi, plus trendier pieces like 7 For All Mankind jeans and Diane von Furstenberg wrap dresses. Housewares, gifts, accessories and shoes also feature.
Other locations: Aventura Mall, 19501 Biscayne Boulevard, Aventura (305 792 1000).

The best Shops

For a tailored maternity tank top
Meet Me in Miami. See p149.

For a diamond cocktail ring
Judith Ripka. See p146.

For half-priced Michael Kors shoes
Shoes to You. See p150.

For anti-ageing products mixed by a Miami physician
John Martin, MD. See p151.

For hair clips that cost as much as your highlights
Scoop. See p146.

For toddler-sized designer chairs
Genius Jones. See p148.

Macy's

Aventura Mall, 19535 Biscayne Boulevard, at NE 196th Street, Aventura (305 937 5485/www.macys. com). Bus 3, 9, E, S. **Open** 10am-9.30pm Mon-Sat; 10am-6pm Sun. **Credit** AmEx, MC, V. **Map** p270.
The quintessential all-American department store, Macy's offers upscale and mid-range clothing labels, houseware, fashion accessories and cosmetics.
Other locations: The Falls, 9100 SW 136th Street, South Miami (305 278 3385); Dadeland Mall, 7303 SW 88th Street, South Miami (305 662 3400); 1675 Meridian Avenue, Miami Beach (305 674. 6300); 22 E Flagler Street, Downtown (305 835 5151).

Neiman Marcus

Bal Harbour Shops, 9700 Collins Avenue, at 96th Street, Bal Harbour (305 865 6161/www.neiman marcus.com). Bus H, K, S, T. **Open** 10am-9pm Mon-Sat; noon-7pm Sun. **Credit** AmEx, MC, V. **Map** p270.
Offering posh merchandise, Neiman Marcus is a favourite of the upper crust. But be warned: it earned the nickname 'Needless Markups' for a reason.
Other locations: Village of Merrick Park, 390 San Lorenzo Avenue, Coral Gables (786 999 1000).

Nordstrom

Village of Merrick Park, 4310 Ponce de León Boulevard, at San Lorenzo Avenue, Coral Gables (786 999 1313/www.nordstrom.com). Metrorail Douglas Road. **Open** 10am-9pm Mon-Thur; 10am-9.30pm Fri, Sat; noon-7pm Sun. **Credit** AmEx, DC, Disc, MC, V. **Map** p276 E4.
Priding itself on superior customer service and superb selection, this local outpost of the 105-year-old Seattle-based chain carries something for everyone, from designer togs to affordable middle-of-the-road fare.

Saks Fifth Avenue

Bal Harbour Shops, 9700 Collins Avenue, at 96th Street, Bal Harbour (305 865 1100/www.saksfifth avenue.com). Bus H, K, S, T. **Open** 10am-9pm Mon-

Top gear

One of Miami's best-kept shopping secrets is on the internet. Poshvintage.com (www.poshvintage.com) is the brainchild of New Yorker Patti Stoecker, who moved to Miami Beach and realised the shopping paled in comparison to her native city. After years of styling, modelling, shopping and collecting, Stoecker decided to share the wealth to those in the know – and the money. Among that wealth: one-of-a-kind Thea Porter couture, Bill Blass princess coats, brilliant nylon jersey '70s dresses and the best ever, super-soft, vintage rock 'n' roll T-shirts. The *Who's Who* of Miami shops at Posh, and now, if you can afford it, you can too.

Fri; 10am-7pm Sat; noon-7pm Sun. **Credit** AmEx, MC, V. **Map** p270.
One of the country's best-known upscale chains, Saks boasts a roster of designers that is a veritable *Who's Who* of the fashion world: Gucci, Chanel, Prada, Armani, Donna Karan, Dolce & Gabbana, Versace, Zegna, Boss and Klein. If you have to ask how much things cost, you can't afford to shop here.
Other locations: Dadeland Mall, 7687 SW 88th Street, South Miami (305 662 8655).

Malls

Aventura Mall

19501 Biscayne Boulevard, at NE 196th Street, Aventura (305 935 1110/www.shopaventuramall. com). Bus 3, 9, E, S. **Open** 10am-9.30pm Mon-Sat; noon-8pm Sun. **Map** p270.
Its inventory includes Bloomingdale's (*see p141*), Macy's (*see above*), JC Penney and Sears. In addition, there's a 24-screen cineplex (*see p171*) and restaurants such as the Cheesecake Factory and Johnny Rocket's. The mall is easy enough to get to from South Beach as several buses terminate there – it's just a hell of a long ride.

Bal Harbour Shops

9700 Collins Avenue, at 96th Street, Bal Harbour (305 866 0311/www.balharbourshops.com). Bus H, K, S, T. **Open** 10am-9pm Mon-Sat (department stores until 7pm); noon-6pm Sun. **Map** p270.
Where the ladies who lunch go with their lap dogs, and where the PYTs go with their GWMs (guys with money), the oh-so-exclusive Bal Harbour Shops has long been pinned as Miami's Rodeo Drive. In this two-storey, modernist Bali Hai, you'll find big-bucks labels, including Prada, Gucci, Tiffany & Co, Chanel, Versace and Bulgari, rubbing padded shoulders with upscale department stores Neiman Marcus and Saks Fifth Avenue (for both, *see above*). **Photo** *p143*.

Bayside Marketplace

401 Biscayne Boulevard, at NE 4th Street, Downtown (305 577 3344/www.baysidemarketplace.com). Metromover College/Bayside. **Open** 10am-10pm Mon-Fri; 10am-11pm Sat; 11am-9pm Sun. **Map** p274 C4.
Come to this bland Anytown, USA, waterside development to get your fill of touristy sightseeing tours, gambling cruises and Hard Rock Café T-shirts. The usual suspects line up for a chance at your wallet, including Bath & Body Works, Victoria's Secret, Gap, Nike and Sunglass Hut.

CocoWalk

3015 Grand Avenue, at Virginia Street, Coconut Grove (305 444 0777/www.galleryatcocowalk.com). Bus 42, 48, Coconut Grove Circulator. **Open** 11am-10pm Mon-Thur, Sun; 11am-midnight Fri, Sat. **Map** p277 B3.
Residents of this one-time boho ghetto howled at the arrival of corporate America in the form of this multi-storey semi-outdoor mall. It's everything you'd expect from a block whose residents include Gap,

Bal Harbour Shops. *See p142.*

Victoria's Secret, Banana Republic and Express. Other attractions include the Café Tu Tu Tango (*see p129*) and occasional live music, though beware the traffic snarls at weekends. There's also a 12-screen AMC movie theatre (*see p171*).

Dadeland Mall

7535 SW 88th Street, at SW 72nd Avenue, South Miami (305 665 6226). Metrorail Dadeland North/ Dadeland South. **Open** 10am-9.30pm Mon-Sat; noon-7pm Sun. **Map** p271.

This supermall fronts Florida's largest Macy's (*see p142*). Among the other 200-odd stores are Arango homeware (*see p151*), Saks Fifth Avenue (*see p142*) and a two-storey Limited Express store, the largest in the US. Dadeland is also one of the only malls easily accessible by Miami's Metrorail system.

The Falls

8888 SW 136th Street, at S Dixie Highway (US 1), South Miami (305 255 4570/www.shopthefalls.com). Bus 1, 52, 65. **Open** 10am-9.30pm Mon-Sat; noon-7pm Sun. **Map** p271.

Cashing in on the outdoor mall trend, the Falls aims to calm with its lush foliage, wooden plank walkways, waterfalls and reflecting ponds. Anchors include a United Artists megaplex, Macy's (*see p142*) and Bloomingdale's (*see p141*), though you'll also find Abercrombie & Fitch, Gap and Banana Republic for fashion, plus toiletries and make-up from Origins and Crabtree & Evelyn. There is no tacky food court here: instead, head to upscale eateries such as PF Chang's, Prezzo Italian and Seasons.

Loehmann's Fashion Island

18701 Biscayne Boulevard, at NE 187th Street, North Miami Beach (305 932 4207). Bus 3, V. **Open** 10am-9pm Mon-Sat; noon-6pm Sun. **Map** p270.

The main attraction at this open-air mall just south of Aventura Mall (*see p142*) is a sprawling Barnes & Noble bookstore (*see p154*).

Shops at Sunset Place

5701 Sunset Drive (SW 72nd Street), at US 1 & Red Road, South Miami (305 663 0873/www. simon.com). Metrorail South Miami. **Open** 11am-10pm Mon-Thur; 11am-11pm Fri, Sat; 11am-9pm Sun. **Map** p271.

With its over-the-top architecture, giant man-made banyan trees and waterfalls, this is the Disney World of malls. Stores include Armani Exchange, Bebe, Gap, Pottery Barn, Victoria's Secret, a mammoth Niketown (*see p156*) and Miami's only Virgin Megastore. A GameWorks arcade, a Vans skating ramp and a 24-screen multiplex (*see p171*) make this a hotspot for teens with time on their hands.

Streets of Mayfair

2911 Grand Avenue, at Virginia Street, Coconut Grove (305 448 1700). Bus 42, 48, Coconut Grove Circulator. **Open** hours vary. **Map** p277 B3.

Staying true to the pedestrian feel of the Grove, this mall offers sweeping expanses of wide sidewalks, balconies, pavement cafés and a broad promenade. Banana Republic, Bath & Body Works and Enzo Angiolini make it popular with kids, who cruise en masse at weekends.

Lobby labels

Gone are the days when Miami hotel shops sold just suntan oil. Today lobbies play host to some of the city's most exclusive boutiques, touting wares that mirror the vibe of the property in question. But you don't have to spend the night to browse and buy – even the swankiest welcome walk-ins. (But do remember to walk, because, in addition to top-tier prices, it sometimes costs about $20 to park a car.) The following is the cream of the beachfront crop.

Scoop at the trendy **Shore Club** (1901 Collins Avenue; *see p38*) is a hotspot for the rich and famous, selling designs from Theory, Miu Miu, Diane von Furstenberg, Missoni, Jimmy Choo and Marc Jacobs. *See also p146.*

The Signature Shop at the **Ritz-Carlton**, Key Biscayne (455 Grand Bay Drive; *see p37*) stocks piles of high-end tops, sunglasses,

sandals and jackets that go from the beach to well beyond. The shop at the sister property on South Beach, meanwhile (*see p37*), has everything from Luella Bartley handbags to some of the best handmade jewellery we've seen, as well as bathing suits and cover-ups.

The boutique at the **Setai** (2001 Collins Avenue; *see p37;* **photos** *above*) may be tiny, but it's worth a look for the one-of-a-kind eastern artefacts, art, handmade silk scarves, sarongs and jewellery you won't see anywhere else. Not that you'll be able to afford them, mind, but that's another matter.

Last but not least is the gift shop at the Todd Oldham-decorated **Hotel** (801 Collins Avenue; *see p40*). Here you'll find a limited edition of the style engineer's other creations, such as tie-dye robes, woven satin pillows and dinnerware.

Village of Merrick Park

358 San Lorenzo Avenue, at Ponce de León Boulevard, Coral Gables (305 529 0200/www.village ofmerrickpark.com). Metrorail Douglas Road. **Open** 10am-9pm Mon-Sat; noon-6pm Sun. **Map** p276 E4.
South Florida's newest upscale mall is anchored by Neiman Marcus and Nordstrom (for both, *see p142*). Three open-air storeys boast 115 shops and boutiques, including the area's only Burberry boutique, plus Gucci, Etro, Adolfo Domínguez, Jimmy Choo, Diane von Furstenburg and Sonia Rykiel. Jewellery brands include Tiffany and Swarovski. **Photo** *p156.*

Antiques

Architectural Antiques

2520 SW 28th Lane, at 27th Avenue, Coconut Grove (305 285 1330/www.miamiantique.com). Metrorail Coconut Grove. **Open** 10am-6pm daily. **Credit** MC, V.
This warehouse is filled to the gills with large-scale goodies (for example, wooden doors from a cathedral or a stone fountain from a mansion courtyard), though you'll also find smaller pieces such as lights and artworks. Bring a truck, though, just in case.

Eat, Drink, Shop

Stone Age Antiques
3236 NW S River Drive, at NW 32nd Street, North Miami (305 633 5114/www.stoneageantiques.com). Bus 32, 36, J. **Open** 9am-4.45pm Mon-Sat. **No credit cards**.
A favourite of movie prop scouts, Stone Age also sells old posters, military memorabilia, cowboy gear, primitive tribal masks, stuffed animals… You know, all the stuff you really need.

Discount

Marshalls
16800 Collins Avenue, at 170th Street, North Miami Beach (305 944 0223). Bus K, S. **Open** 9.30am-9.30pm Mon-Sat; 11am-6pm Sun. **Credit** AmEx, MC, V.
Marshalls is Miami's most popular discount shop, offering a vast selection of designer and brand-name fashions for men, women and children – as well as houseware and gifts – all at 20-60% below department store prices.
Other locations: throughout the city.

Target
8350 S Dixie Highway (US 1), at SW 83rd Street, South Miami (305 668 0262/www.target.com). Metrorail Dadeland North. **Open** 8am-10pm Mon-Sat; 8am-9pm Sun. **Credit** AmEx, MC, V.
America's coolest discount store, Target boasts a signature line of houseware and gifts by celebrated architect Michael Graves, collections of goods and clothing by Cynthia Rowley, Todd Oldham and Isaac Mizrahi, and great prices on everything including toiletries, entertainment, electronics and toys.
Other locations: 21265 Biscayne Boulevard, Aventura (305 933 4616); 14075 Biscayne Boulevard, North Miami Beach (305 944 5341); 15005 SW 88th Street, Kendall (305 386 1244).

Fashion

A/X Armani Exchange
760 Collins Avenue, at 8th Street, South Beach (305 531 5900/www.armaniexchange.com). Bus C, H, K, W, South Beach Local. **Open** 10am-9pm Mon-Wed; 10am-10pm Thur-Sat; 11am-8pm Sun. **Credit** AmEx, MC, V. **Map** p273 E2.
Smart Euro-wear for the terminally hip, with minimalist styles for men and women in subdued colour schemes, at, would you believe, not completely ridiculous prices.
Other locations: throughout the city.

Barneys New York Co-Op
832 Collins Avenue, at 8th Street, South Beach (305 421 2010/www.barneys.com). Bus C, H, K, W, South Beach Local. **Open** 11am-9pm Mon-Thur; 11am-10pm Fri, Sat; noon-7pm Sun. **Credit** AmEx, MC, V. **Map** p273 E2.
The Miami outpost of this legendary Big Apple department store features trendy designer fashions and accessories by 7 For All Mankind jeans, Daryl

K, Marc by Marc Jacobs, Diane von Furstenberg and more. Barneys 'Co-Ops' are supposed to be cut price, but that just means a T-shirt will set you back $150 instead of $300. **Photo** *p147*.

Betsey Johnson
Aventura Mall, 19501 Biscayne Boulevard, at NE 196th Street, Aventura (305 933 2621/www.betsey johnson.com). Bus 3, 9, E, S. **Open** 10am-9.30pm Mon-Sat; noon-8pm Sun. **Credit** AmEx, MC, V. **Map** p270.
For punky, flower-child rockers, no other designer ware says 'funky diva' quite like Betsey Johnson's fashion-forward collections.

Casting Paris
Suite 42, 260 Crandon Boulevard, Key Biscayne (305 365 9797). Bus B. **Open** 10am-6.30pm Mon-Sat. **Credit** AmEx, MC, V. **Map** p271.
Suntanned South American women head here to outfit themselves in 7 For All Mankind, Juicy Couture, Free People and James Perse. In step with every trend, Casting has the high-end version in stock, but get there fast because they change quickly.

Club Monaco
624 Collins Avenue, at 6th Street, South Beach (305 674 7446/www.clubmonaco.com). Bus C, H, K, W, South Beach Local. **Open** 11am-8pm Mon-Sat; noon-7pm Sun. **Credit** AmEx, DC, MC, V. **Map** p273 F2.
Still can't afford those Prada pants you've been dying for? Monaco's elite design team edits out the key pieces of each season for men and women and recreates them at prices everyone can afford.

Intermix
634 Collins Avenue, at 6th Street, South Beach (305 531 5950). Bus C, H, K, W, South Beach Local. **Open** 11am-8pm Mon-Fri; 11am-9pm Sat; 11am-7pm Sun. **Credit** AmEx, DC, MC, V. **Map** p273 F2.
Within its walls, the oh-so-trendy Intermix gathers the choicest styles by top designers such as Tocca, Kate Spade, Anna Sui, Helmut Lang and Daryl K.

Leo
640 Collins Avenue, at 6th Street, South Beach (305 531 6550/www.leomiami.com). Bus C, H, K, W. **Open** 11am-9pm Mon-Thur; 11am-10pm Fri, Sat; noon-8pm Sun. **Credit** AmEx, MC, V. **Map** p273 F2.
Style for both genders, at all price points – from $30 T-shirts to $2,600 vintage dresses. Also find souped-up classics from Nicholas K, denim from 1921 and sports jackets from Rag & Bone. Missoni shoes – loved by Kate Hudson and J-Lo – also feature.

Miss Sixty
845 Lincoln Road, at Jefferson Avenue, South Beach (305 538 3547/www.misssixty.com). Bus C, G, H, K, L, M, S, W, South Beach Local. **Open** 11am-11pm Mon-Sat; 11am-10pm Sun. **Credit** AmEx, MC, V. **Map** p272 C2.
Italian-designed stretchy blouses, T-shirts, sweaters, and the lowest of low-rider jeans are among the apparel stocked here for the young string-bean set.

Eat, Drink, Shop

The mall the merrier

When it comes to shopping in south Florida, random boutique-hopping or strolling the standard mall is strictly for amateurs. Those in search of serious bargains strap on their sneakers, get kitted up and tackle the monster that is the outlet mall. Outlet malls are vast oases of manufacturers and retailers peddling goods at cut-rate prices, with the hard sell softened by myriad food and entertainment choices. South Florida is home to two huge outlet malls, one of which, Sawgrass Mills, ranks on the list of the state's top tourist attractions.

The venerable **Sawgrass Mills** is in Broward, the next county north of Miami-Dade. It's a bit of a haul to get out there, and if you don't have a car you'll need to hire one, but it's worth it: true bargain hunters will see big returns on their investment of gas, time and money. Among the more than 400 stores enclosed in a two-mile long structure designed by noted postmodernists Arquitectonica, are Barneys, Calvin Klein, Levi's, Neiman Marcus, Off Saks Fifth Avenue and Tommy Hilfiger.

Proving that outlet popularity has reached new heights, an upscale enclave of shops, the Colonnade Outlets at Sawgrass, opened in March 2006, comprising a Burberry, Valentino, Escada and Ferragamo, among others. And valet parking, of course.

Distraction from amassing merchandise is offered by a GameWorks video-game parlour, a 23-screen cinema and the many eateries, including one run by sleb-chef Wolfgang Puck.

Also off the beaten path, in this case five miles west of Miami International Airport, is **Dolphin Mall**. When it opened in March 2001, the mall lacked the many prestigious stores found somewhere like the Sawgrass and was considered a bit of a disappointment. Over the last couple of years, though, its reputation has rebounded as it has gained more stores; the line-up now includes BCBG, Brooks Brothers, Burlington Coat Factory, Off Saks Fifth Avenue and Ralph Lauren, plus housewares by Mikasa. Dolphin also has a 19-screen movie theatre, lots of eateries and a flashy bowling alley.

Dolphin Mall

11401 NW 12th Street, at NW 114th Avenue, Sweetwater (305 365 7446/www.shopdolphin mall.com). Bus 11, 71. **Open** 10am-9.30pm Mon-Sat; 11am-7.30pm Sun. **Map** p271.

Sawgrass Mills

12801 W Sunrise Boulevard, Broward County (954 846 2300/www.sawgrassmills.com). Shuttle buses run from Miami Beach hotels Mon-Sat. **Open** 10am-9.30pm Mon-Fri; 9.30am-10pm Sat; 11am-8pm Sun.

Nicole Miller

656 Collins Avenue, at 6th Street, South Beach (305 535 2200/www.nicolemiller.com). Bus C, H, K, W, South Beach Local. **Open** 11am-8pm Mon-Sat; noon-6pm Sun. **Credit** AmEx, MC, V. **Map** p273 F2.
The best place to find that incredibly expensive but perfect little black dress, along with tropical cocktail wear and smart clothing for the modern gal.

Rebel

6669 Biscayne Boulevard, at NE 66th Street, Design District (305 758 2369/www.rebelmiami.com). Bus Metrorail Omni. **Open** 10am-6pm Mon-Sat; noon-5pm Sun. **Credit** AmEx, Disc, MC, V.
Long Island transplants flock to Rebel for top-of-the-line T-shirts with grand embellishments and price tags to match. Find the jeans of the moment and other items from Ya-Ya, Juicy Couture, Vince and Sass & Bide. It's worth going just for the sale room.

Scoop

Shore Club, 1901 Collins Avenue, at 19th Street, South Beach (305 532 5929). Bus C, G, H, L, M, S. **Open** 10am-8pm Mon-Thur; 10am-10pm Fri, Sat. **Credit** AmEx, DC, Disc, MC, V. **Map** p272 C3.

The only outpost of this starlet store outside of the north-east carries chic clothes and accessories, including its own Scoop private label wares and designer pieces by the likes of Marc Jacobs, Juicy Couture and Paul Smith. *See also p144* **Lobby labels**.

Accessories & jewellery

Judith Ripka

Bal Harbour Shops, 9700 Collins Avenue, at 96th Street, Bal Harbour (305 993 5211/www.judithripka. com). Bus H, K, S, T. **Open** 10am-9pm Mon-Fri; 10am-7pm Sat; noon-6pm Sun. **Credit** AmEx, MC, V. **Map** p270.
This jewellery maverick designs with the philosophy that her pieces should go seamlessly with anything from jeans to black tie. Topaz, sapphires and diamonds are all dripping in 18-carat gold. **Photo** *p151*.

Louis Vuitton

Bal Harbour Shops, 9700 Collins Avenue, at 96th Street, Bal Harbour (305 866 4470/www.louis vuitton.com). Bus H, K, S, T. **Open** 10am-9pm Mon-Fri; 10am-7pm Sat; noon-6pm Sun. **Credit** AmEx, DC, MC, V. **Map** p270.

For those travelling in style – or living the lives of Lord and Lady Beckham – Louis Vuitton monogrammed canvas luggage and handbags are the accepted luxury choice. **Photos** *p148*.

Mayor's Jewelers

Village of Merrick Park, 342 San Lorenzo Avenue, at Ponce de León Boulevard, Coral Gables (305 446 1233). Metrorail Douglas Road. **Open** 10am-9pm Mon-Sat; noon-6pm Sun. **Credit** AmEx, DC, MC, V. **Map** p276 E4.

Mayor's takes things decidedly upscale with brands such as Rolex, Pampaloni, David Yurman, John Atencio and Pasquale Bruni. There's also a well-rounded selection of gifts, such as glass and silver items, Limoges boxes and even estate pieces.

Me & Ro

Shore Club, 1901 Collins Avenue, at 19th Street, South Beach (305 672 3566). Bus C, G, H, L, M, S. **Open** 11am-8pm Mon-Thur; 11am-10pm Fri, Sat; 11am-7pm Sun. **Credit** AmEx, MC, V. **Map** p272 C3.

Delicately crafted silver and gold bracelets, necklaces, earrings and rings, often embellished with Tibetan, Sanskrit and Chinese characters. Favoured by the likes of Julia Roberts and Cameron Diaz.

Morays

50 NE 2nd Avenue, at E Flagler Street, Downtown (305 374 0739). Metromover 1st Street. **Open** 10.30am-5pm Mon-Fri. **Credit** AmEx, DC, MC, V. **Map** p274 D3.

Downtown's oldest jewellers (50 years young) stocks every watch brand you can think of. It's in Miami's so-called Little Switzerland (oh, please), near the Seybold Building arcade, which houses ten floors of jewellers, engravers and watchmakers. Speaking Spanish can help you get a better deal.

Tiffany & Co

Bal Harbour Shops, 9700 Collins Avenue, at 96th Street, Bal Harbour (305 864 1801/www.tiffany andco.com). Bus H, K, S, T. **Open** 10am-9pm Mon-Sat; noon-6pm Sun. **Credit** AmEx, DC, MC, V. **Map** p270.

For when you care more about the little blue box than what's in it. Still, there are excellent selections of men's and women's jewellery and gifts. **Other locations**: Village of Merrick Park, 342 San Lorenzo Avenue, Coral Gables (305 529 4390).

Beachwear

Absolutely Suitable

1560 Collins Avenue, at 15th Street, South Beach (305 604 5281). Bus C, H, K, W, South Beach Local. **Open** 10am-7pm daily. **Credit** AmEx, DC, MC, V. **Map** p273 B3.

Get suited for wet action with this upscale collection of bathing attire for both men and women by designers such as Calvin Klein, D&G, La Perla, Sauvage and Versace. Don't miss the sale rack.

Everything But Water

19501 Biscayne Boulevard, at NE 196th Street, Aventura (305 932 7207/www.everythingbut water.com). **Open** 10am-9.30pm Mon-Sat; noon-8pm Sun. **Credit** AmEx, DC, Disc, MC, V.

You never knew there were so many swimwear labels. Even so, this chain of stores went ahead and launched its own line of mix-and-match separates, just to add to the choice.

Ritchie Swimwear

160 8th Street, at Collins Avenue, South Beach (305 538 0201/www.ritchieswimwear.com). Bus C, H, K, W, South Beach Local. **Open** 10am-9pm Mon-Fri; 10am-10pm Sat; 10am-8pm Sun. **Credit** AmEx, MC, V. **Map** p273 E2.

Wild bikinidom: bright tanks, strings and one-pieces fit for a *Baywatch* babe, all made in sunny Miami. Mix-and-match tops and bottoms cost from $30. You can even choose your fabric by resort name, from Santorini to Capri, via Beverly Hills and St-Tropez. **Other locations**: 3401 Main Highway, Coconut Grove (305 443 7919).

Eat, Drink, Shop

Barneys New York Co-Op. *See p145.*

NET
TEEN IN UNIFORM

GAIL
IS A PARTY GIRL

LIVIA
DREAMS OF A DREAM DATE

ANGELA
LIKES TO GET DOWN AND DIRTY

DEBBIE
DRESSES OLDER

SAMANTHA
TAKES HER CAT EVERYWHERE

Louis Vuitton – for when only designer will do. *See p146.*

Children's

Chewing Gum Kids

548 41st Street, at Prairie Avenue, Mid Beach (305 672 3008). Bus 62, C, J, M, T. **Open** 10am-6pm Mon-Fri; 11am-4pm Sun. **Credit** AmEx, DC, Disc, MC, V.

As tiny as the customers for whom these clothes are designed, this brilliantly named shop is packed with sweats, tanks, denim and dresses, pyjamas, suits (both bathing and boys') and shoes. The barrettes and headbands are beautiful – unless you're a bargain shopper, that is.
Other locations: 3575 NE 207th Street, Aventura (305 682 9727).

Children's Exchange

1415 Sunset Drive, at SW 54th Avenue, South Miami (305 666 6235). Metrorail South Miami. **Open** 10am-7pm Mon-Thur; 10am-5pm Fri, Sat. **Credit** AmEx, DC, MC, V.

The Saks Fifth Avenue of children's used clothing has Tommy, Polo and Nautica, plus toys, small baby gear, name-brand shoes and even ski clothes.

Genius Jones

1661 Michigan Avenue, at Lincoln Road, South Beach (305 534 7622/www.geniusjones.com). Bus C, H, K, L, M, S, W, South Beach Local. **Open** 11am-7pm Tue-Thur; 11am-9pm Fri, Sat. **Credit** AmEx, DC, Disc, MC, V. **Map** p272 C2.

Design snobs for the smaller set head here. Find bold wooden children's furniture by Agatha Ruiz de la Prada and David Netto. Also, toys designed to inspire imagination without lighting up or blinking – yay!
Other locations: 49 NE 39th Street, Design District (305 571 2000).

Kidding Around

The Falls, 8888 SW 136th Street, at S Dixie Highway (US 1), South Miami (305 253 0708). Bus 1, 52, 65. **Open** 10am-9.30pm Mon-Sat; noon-7pm Sun. **Credit** AmEx, DC, MC, V. **Map** p271.

A pricey kids' boutique with quality fashion and furniture for tots and infants, plus adorable swimwear for the littlest ones.

Pottery Barn Kids

Village of Merrick Park, 350 San Lorenzo Avenue, at Ponce de León Boulevard, Coral Gables (305 446 6511/www.potterybarnkids.com). Metrorail Douglas Road. **Open** 10am-9pm Mon-Sat; noon-6pm Sun. **Credit** AmEx, DC, MC, V. **Map** p276 E4.

Bedding for cribs and for kiddie-sized beds, stuffed animals, towels, lamps, quilts and much more in cute seasonal collections.

Clubwear & street

KORE

7226 Biscayne Boulevard, at 72nd Street, Wynwood (305 759 0805). Bus 3. **Open** 10am-6pm Mon-Thur; 10am-7pm Fri, Sat. **Credit** AmEx, Disc, MC, V.

Trendy threads hang out on metal racks floating throughout the store and, perhaps because this proprietor hasn't sold his soul to sky-high mall rents, most are reasonably priced. Stock up also on bangles, baubles and belts.

Merenda

1071 NE 79th Street, at 10th Avenue, North Miami (305 754 3545). Bus 3, 16. **Open** 11am-7pm Mon-Sat. **Credit** AmEx, MC, V.
Arty apparel and accessories for the hipster from Fred Perry, Custo, Michael Stars, Adidas, Pro Keds, True Religion and Joes Jeans, plus some unique garb by local Miami talents.

Rampage

The Falls, 8888 SW 136th Street, at S Dixie Highway (US 1), South Miami (305 278 1212/ www.rampage.com). Bus 1, 52, 65. **Open** 10am-9.30pm Mon-Sat; noon-7pm Sun. **Credit** AmEx, MC, V. **Map** p271.
Skinny fly girls shop here. Expect to find American People, Girls Rule hip-hop sportswear, Converse sandals, Steve Madden heels, sexy undies, boldly patterned swimwear, trinkets and disco make-up, all at throwaway prices. The handbags and sunglasses collections are the winners, though.
Other locations: Aventura Mall, 19575 Biscayne Boulevard, Aventura (305 935 4141); Dadeland Mall, 7535 SW 88th Street, South Miami (305 661 1838).

Urban Outfitters

653 Collins Avenue, at 7th Street, South Beach (305 535 9726/www.urbanoutfitters.com). Bus C, H, K, W, South Beach Local. **Open** 10am-10pm Mon-Thur; 10am-11pm Fri, Sat; noon-9pm Sun. **Credit** AmEx, MC, V. **Map** p273 E2.
Clothing and accessories for men and women come in UO's own labels, alongside names such as Diesel, Mook, Paul Frank, Camper and Stüssy. The two-storey industrial space also has houseware for studio-dwellers, and assorted campy giftage.
Other locations: Shops at Sunset Place, 5701 Sunset Drive, South Miami (305 663 1536); Aventura Mall, 19501 Biscayne Boulevard, Aventura (305 936 8358).

Eyewear

Au Courant

Bal Harbour Shops, 9700 Collins Avenue, at 96th Street, Bal Harbour (305 866 2020). Bus H, K, S, T. **Open** 10am-9pm Mon-Sat; noon-6pm Sun. **Credit** AmEx, MC, V. **Map** p270.
Stylish specs for those who care as much about being seen as they do about seeing. Among the posh brands are Chanel, Ferragamo, Dior and Gucci.

SEE

921 Lincoln Road, at Jefferson Avenue, South Beach (305 672 6622). Bus C, G, H, K, L, M, S, W, South Beach Local. **Open** noon-10pm Mon-Thur, Sun; 11am-11pm Fri, Sat. **Credit** AmEx, MC, V. **Map** p272 C2.

For those with champagne tastes on a shandy budget, SEE offers cutting-edge styles made by the same world-class manufacturers used by designers, only at discounted prices. It's gimmick-free too.

Maternity

Meet Me in Miami

5570 NE 4th Avenue, at NE 55th Terrace, Design District (305 373 1273/www.meetmeinmiami.com). Bus 9, 10. **Open** 10am-4pm Mon-Fri by appointment only. **No credit cards.**
This warehouse is a pregnant woman's wonderland: racks and racks of stretchy, one-size-fits-all maternity wear. Find trendy halter dresses, funky sweats with matching tops, and an on-site seamstress who will make even the slightest adjustments.

Pea in the Pod

Village of Merrick Park, 350 San Lorenzo Avenue, at Ponce de León Boulevard, Coral Gables (305 648 1201). Metrorail Douglas Road. **Open** 10am-9pm Mon-Sat; noon-6pm Sun. **Credit** AmEx, DC, MC, V. **Map** p276 E4.
Proving that pregnancy does not mean foregoing jeans by 7 For All Mankind or Citizens of Humanity, the clothes here are so stylish they've even been spotted on the red carpet.

Shoes

Capretto Shoes

5822 Sunset Drive, at 58th Avenue, South Miami (305 661 7767). Metrorail South Miami. **Open** 9.30am-6pm Mon-Sat. **Credit** AmEx, MC, V.
Designer belts, handbags, jewellery, plus a discerning selection of the latest women's sandals, slingbacks, pumps, mules, boots and loafers from names such as Gucci and Prada.

Kenneth Cole

190 8th Street, at Collins Avenue, South Beach (305 673 5151/www.kennethcole.com). Bus C, H, K, W, South Beach Local. **Open** 10am-10pm Mon-Sat; 11am-8pm Sun. **Credit** AmEx, MC, V. **Map** p273 E2.
Sleek, cool and very NYC, the only free-standing Kenneth Cole boutique in town fills a beautifully designed two-storey space with modern urban clothing, footwear and bags.

Koko & Palenki Shoes

Aventura Mall, 19501 Biscayne Boulevard, at NE 196th Street, Aventura (305 792 9299/http://koko-palenki.com). Bus 3, 9, E, S. **Open** 10am-9.30pm Mon-Sat; noon-8pm Sun. **Credit** AmEx, DC, MC, V. **Map** p270.
Calling all shoe addicts: this is where to find elegant and exotic styles from D&G, Charles Jourdan, Guess, Casadei, Anne Klein and more, along with matching purses and men's shoes and belts.
Other locations: Dadeland Mall, 7535 SW 88th Street, South Miami (305 668 2233); CocoWalk, 3015 Grand Avenue, Coconut Grove (305 444 1772).

Eat, Drink, Shop

Shoes to You

4776 SW 72nd Avenue, at 47th Street, South Miami (305 667 3711). Bus 57, 65. **Open** 11am-6pm daily. **Credit** AmEx, Disc, MC, V.

A warehouse-style shoe shop with discounted Michael Kors, Anne Klein, Mystique, Kate Spade, Isabella Fiore, Diego de Lucca and more.

XOT Shoes

1423 Washington Avenue, at 14th Street, South Beach (305 532 1252). Bus C, H, K, W, South Beach Local. **Open** 10am-9pm Mon-Thur, Sun; 10am-midnight Fri, Sat. **Credit** AmEx, MC, V. **Map** p273 C2.

This store defines the concept of cheap chic with funky shoes that look fabulous but are affordable enough to ruin in a night's boogying at crobar. **Other locations:** 3448 Main Highway, Coconut Grove (305 448 0085).

Underwear

La Perla

Village of Merrick Park, 342 San Lorenzo Avenue, at Ponce de León Boulevard, Coral Gables (305 448 8805/www.laperla.com). Bus H, K, S, T. **Open** 10am-9pm Mon-Sat; noon-6pm Sun. **Credit** AmEx, MC, V. **Map** p276 E4.

Impeccably made Italian silk and lace fancies, plus stunning swimwear and accessories, all commanding a pretty penny.

Food & drink

Epicure Market

1656 Alton Road, at 16th Street, South Beach (305 672 1861). Bus M, R, W. **Open** 10am-8pm Mon-Sat; 10am-7pm Sun. **Credit** AmEx, MC, V. **Map** p272 C2.

It's pricey, but worth it, especially the kosher deli. There's also fresh fruit and veg, a fine butcher and an excellent on-premises bakery.

Fresh Market

2640 S Bayshore Drive, at 26th Avenue, Coconut Grove (305 854 7202). Bus 42, 48. **Open** 9am-9pm Mon-Sat; 9am-8pm Sun. **Credit** AmEx, MC, V.

A high-end grocery with aisles and aisles of fruits, vegetables and bulk items such as yogurt-covered pretzels. There's also a freshly prepared food section that's so big it's impossible to leave with just one container. Don't miss the seafood counter, with specialities such as crab cakes and sesame-crusted tuna.

Whole Foods Market

21105 Biscayne Boulevard, at 211th Street, Aventura (305 933 1543/www.wholefoodsmarket.com). Bus 3, 9, E, S. **Open** 7am-11pm daily. **Credit** AmEx, MC, V.

The local branch of this Austin-based organic superstore stocks all kind of organic produce, including fine meats, prepared dishes, baked goods, vitamins and toiletries. There's also a superior wine section.

Wild Oats Natural Marketplace

1020 Alton Road, at 10th Street, South Beach (305 532 1707/www.wildoats.com). Bus M, R, S, W. **Open** 7am-11pm daily. **Credit** AmEx, MC, V. **Map** p272 D2.

All the organic produce you could desire, including fresh fish and seafood, plus a deli with a to-go section of made-to-order sandwiches, salads and fruit smoothies. And the store donates 5% of its gross earnings to charity.

Other locations: 11701 S Dixie Highway (US 1), Pinecrest (305 971 0900).

Ethnic

La Brioche Dorée

4017 Prairie Avenue, at W 40th Street, Mid Beach (305 538 4770). Bus C, J, M, T. **Open** 7am-4pm Mon-Fri; 7am-2pm Sun. **No credit cards.**

Throw caution to the wind. Add ten pounds to your thighs in less than ten minutes at the best French bakery in town. Choose from delectable almond croissants, eclairs, desserts, baguettes and brioches.

Daily Bread

2400 SW 27th Street, at SW 24th Avenue, Coconut Grove (305 856 0363). Bus 17, 24. **Open** 9am-8pm Mon-Sat; 11am-5pm Sun. **Credit** AmEx, DC, MC, V.

Fab falafels and feta to go are offered at this Middle Eastern and Greek grocery store, as are pastries, cheeses and more.

Laurenzo's Italian Supermarket

16385 W Dixie Highway, at NE 164th Street, North Miami Beach (305 945 6381). Bus 3, 83, H. **Open** 8.30am-7.30pm Mon-Fri; 8am-7pm Sat; 8am-6pm Sun. **Credit** MC, V.

The largest, most extensive Italian supermarket in town, this charming place has a large selection of imported items and a separate farmer's market across the street for fresh Italian veg. If you can't find it here, you'll have to go to New York's Little Italy.

Lucky Oriental Mart

8356 SW 40th Street, at SW 84th Avenue, South Miami (305 220 2838/www.orientalfoods.net). Bus 40. **Open** 9am-8pm Mon-Sat; 10am-7pm Sun. **Credit** AmEx, MC, V.

The golden Peking ducks hanging in the window provide a glimpse of the cornucopia of ethnic edibles that lies within. Everything you need to whip up a Chinese meal and then some is here: fresh seafood, produce, canned foods, spices, snacks, sauces, wine and even frozen dim sum items. Serving pieces such as dishes, tea and saké sets are available too.

Mary Ann Bakery

1284 NE 163rd Street, at NE 12th Avenue, North Miami Beach (305 945 0333). Bus 3. **Open** 8.30am-5pm Mon, Wed-Sun. **Credit** AmEx, DC, MC, V.

The usual Chinese treats such as almond cookies can be found here, as can more unusual goodies, including curry puffs, individual chicken pies and light and airy Swiss rolls.

Judith Ripka. *See p146.*

Health & beauty

Agua Spa
Delano Hotel, 1685 Collins Avenue, at 17th Street, South Beach (305 674 6100/http://www.delano-hotel.com/delano_hotel_agua_spa.asp). Bus C, G, H, L, M, S. **Open** 9am-7pm daily for women; 7.30-11pm daily (by appointment) for men. **Credit** AmEx, MC, V. **Map** p273 A3.

This is where the celebs spa, although the Standard (*see p38*) is quickly surpassing the Delano as *the* hotel spa to be scrubbed and seen at. White-on-white Starck-ian splendour and a rooftop solarium make for a Zen-like experience, albeit a rather expensive one. Shiatsu and deep-tissue massages are offered, along with mineral treatments, facials and more.

Brownes & Co Apothecary
841 Lincoln Road, at Jefferson Avenue, South Beach (305 532 8703/www.brownesbeauty.com). Bus C, G, H, K, L, M, S, W, South Beach Local. **Open** 9.30am-9pm Mon-Fri; 9.30am-10pm Sat, Sun. **Credit** AmEx, MC, V. **Map** p272 C2.

Hard-to-get cosmetics from Trish McEvoy, Kiehl's, Aveda, Philosophy, Dr Hauschka and Geo Trumper. Get a haircut, a citrus pedicure, a facial or other spa treatments at Some Like It Hot, its full-service salon.

GBS
308 Miracle Mile (SW 24th Street), at Le Jeune Road, Coral Gables (305 446 6654). No public transport. **Open** 9am-6pm Mon-Sat; noon-6pm Sun. **Credit** AmEx, Disc, MC, V. **Map** p276 C3.

Brandless make-up that can hold its own to anything a department store puts forward – shelves of shadows, lipsticks, pencils, powders and gloss. There are also aisles and aisles of shampoos. **Other locations**: 18545 W Dixie Highway, Aventura (305 931 5291); 11297 S Dixie Highway, Pinecrest (305 254 4074).

John Martin, MD
325 Alhambra Circle, at Le Jeune Road, Coral Gables (305 444 5950). Bus J. **Open** 8.30am-6pm Mon-Fri. **Credit** AmEx, MC, V. **Map** p276 B3.

This local facial surgeon has mixed up his own line of anti-ageing potions packed with retinol, alpha-hydroxy acids and other well-tested ingredients.

MAC
650 Collins Avenue, at 6th Street, South Beach (305 604 9040/www.maccosmetics.com). Bus C, H, K, W, South Beach Local. **Open** 11am-9pm Mon-Wed; 10am-10pm Thur-Sat; noon-7pm Sun. **Credit** AmEx, MC, V. **Map** p273 F2.

RuPaul, KD Lang, Lil' Kim and Mary J Blige have all been spokesfolk for this innovative line of cosmetics. Marvellous makeovers from pros on the premises come by appointment, priced at $40 a pop (but hey, you get a free mascara).

Van Michael Aveda Concept Salon
1667 Michigan Avenue, at Lincoln Road, South Beach (305 534 6789). Bus C, G, H, K, L, M, S, W, South Beach Local. **Open** 9am-5pm Mon; 9am-9.30pm Tue; 8am-10pm Wed-Sat; 11am-7pm Sun. **Credit** AmEx, MC, V. **Map** p272 C2.

Naturally chic, this is the ultimate showcase for Aveda's flower and plant aromas, skincare, haircare, make-up and lifestyle products. It's pricey, but even walking into the store is relaxing. **Photo** *p154.*

Vidal Sassoon
660 Collins Avenue, at 6th Street, South Beach (305 672 3600). Bus C, H, K, W, South Beach Local. **Open** 10.45am-7pm Tue-Fri; 9.15am-5.30pm Sat. **Credit** AmEx, MC, V. **Map** p273 F2.

Clean, cutting-edge styles at prices in accordance with the experience of your stylist. If you don't look good, they don't look good.

Homeware & interiors

Arango
Dadeland Mall, 7519 SW 88th Street, South Miami (305 661 4229/www.arango-design.com). Metrorail Dadeland North/Dadeland South. **Open** 10am-9.30pm Mon-Sat; noon-7pm Sun. **Credit** AmEx, MC, V. **Map** p271.

This locally owned art and design shop has been around for 40 years and remains popular for sleek furnishings, accessories and gifts.

Artemide
277 Giralda Avenue, at Salzedo Street, Coral Gables (305 444 5800/www.artemide.com). Bus 24, 42, 72, Coral Gables Circulator. **Open** 10am-6pm Tue-Fri; 10am-5pm Sat. **Credit** AmEx, MC, V. **Map** p276 B4.

Shopping by area

Aventura

Beachwear Everything But Water *p147*.
Cameras & electronics Wolf Camera &
Video *p155*. **Department stores** Macy's
p142. **Fashion** Betsey Johnson *p145*. **Food
& drink** Whole Foods Market *p150*. **Malls**
Aventura Mall *p142*. **Shoes** Koko & Palenki
Shoes *p149*.

Bal Harbour

Accessories & jewellery Judith Ripka *p146*;
Louis Vuitton *p146*; Tiffany & Co *p147*.
Department stores Neiman Marcus *p142*;
Saks Fifth Avenue *p142*. **Eyewear** Au Courant
p149. **Malls** Bal Harbour Shops *p142*.

Coconut Grove

Antiques Architectural Antiques *p144*.
Food & drink Daily Bread *p150*; Fresh Market
p150. **Malls** CocoWalk *p142*; Streets of
Mayfair *p143*.

Coral Gables

Accessories & jewellery Mayor's Jewelers
p147. **Books** Books & Books *p154*.
Children's fashion Pottery Barn Kids
p148. **Department stores** Nordstrom *p142*.

Health & beauty GBS *p151*; John Martin
p151. **Homeware & interiors** Artemide *p151*;
La Cuisine Gourmet *see below*; Luminaire
see below. **Malls** Village of Merrick Park
p144. **Maternity** Pea in the Pod *p149*.
Underwear La Perla *p150*. **Video** Lion Video
p155.

The Design District & Wynwood

Clubwear & street KORE *p148*. **Fashion**
Rebel *p146*. **Homeware & interiors** Kartell
see below. **Maternity** Meet Me in Miami
p149.

Downtown

Accessories & jewellery Morays *p147*. **Malls**
Bayside Marketplace *p142*. **Specialist & gift
shops** Historical Museum of Southern Florida
Gift Shop *p155*.

Key Biscayne

Fashion Casting Paris *p145*.

Little Havana

Music Casino Records *p155*; Do Re Mi Music
Center *p155*.

Innovative stylish lamps from Italy knocked up by
an international roster of designers – everything
from Richard Sapper's classic Tizio to Ernesto
Gismondi's Duck Light.

Central Hardware

*545 Arthur Godfrey Road, at Prairie Avenue, Mid
Beach (305 531 0836/www.acehardware.com). Bus
C, M.* **Open** 9am-6pm Mon-Fri; 9am-5pm Sat;
9.30am-4pm Sun. **Credit** AmEx, MC, V.
A Beach institution, crammed to the roof with everything you could possibly need for the home and garden. Knowledgeable and friendly clerks give you
personal service, and there are useful, hand-picked
selections of small appliances, throw rugs, housewares, beach stuff and barbecue gear.

La Cuisine Gourmet

*50 Aragon Avenue, at Galiano Street, Coral Gables
(305 442 9006/www.lacuisinegourmet.com). Bus 24,
42, 72.* **Open** 10am-7pm Mon-Fri; 10am-6pm Sat.
Credit AmEx, Disc, MC, V. **Map** p276 B4.
Whether you're a professional chef or merely faking
it, the products stocked here can elevate your kitchen

to professional level, with glass-door industrial
fridges and top-of-the-line appliances. Everything is
sleek, including the utensils and sinkware.

Details

*1711 Alton Road, at 17th Street, South Beach (305
531 1325). Bus M, S, W.* **Open** 11am-9pm Mon-
Sat; noon-6pm Sun. **Credit** AmEx, MC, V. **Map**
p272 C2.
Furniture, flamboyant furnishings and oodles of
decorative knick-knacks for that perfect Miami
condo (or London flat). Great bath stuff, mirrors,
frames and lamps; all pricey, but worth it.

Kartell

*170 NE 40th Street, at NE 2nd Avenue, Design
District (305 573 4010/www.kartell.com). Bus 9, 10.*
Open 10am-6pm Mon-Fri; 11am-5pm Sat. **Credit**
AmEx, MC, V.
A fantastic plastic paradise featuring a wide variety
of pricey products created by internationally known
designers, including gnome tables by Philippe
Starck, modular bookshelves by Giulio Polvara and
cylindrical storage units by Anna Castelli Ferrieri.

Mid Beach

Children's fashion Chewing Gum Kids *p148*.
Food & drink La Brioche Dorée *p150*.
Homeware & interiors Central Hardware *p152*.

North Miami

Antiques Stone Age Antiques *p145*.
Clubwear & street Merenda *p149*.
Homeware & interiors Visiona *see below*.
Vintage & collectibles C Madeleine's *p156*.

North Miami Beach

Books Barnes & Noble *p154*. **Discount**
Marshalls *p145*. **Food & drink** Laurenzo's
Italian Supermarket *p150*; Mary Ann Bakery
p150. **Malls** Loehmann's Fashion Island *p143*.

South Beach

Accessories & jewellery Me & Ro *p147*.
Beachwear Absolutely Suitable *p147*; Ritchie
Swimwear *p147*. **Books** Kafka's Used Book
Store & Cyber Café *p154*. **Cameras** Aperture
Professional Supply *p154*; Tropicolor Photo
p155. **Children's fashion** Genius Jones *p148*.
Clubwear & street Urban Outfitters *p149*.
Eyewear SEE *p149*. **Fashion** A/X Armani
Exchange *p145*; Barneys New York Co-Op

p145; Club Monaco *p145*; Intermix *p145*; Leo
p145; Miss Sixty *p145*; Nicole Miller *p146*;
Scoop *p146*. **Food & drink** Epicure Market
p150; Wild Oats Natural Marketplace *p150*.
Health & beauty Agua Spa *p151*; Brownes &
Co Apothecary *p151*; MAC *p151*; Van Michael
Aveda Concept Salon *p151*; Vidal Sassoon
p151. **Homeware & interiors** Details *p152*;
Senzatempo *see below*; Williams-Sonoma *see
below*. **Music** Spec's Music *p155*; Uncle
Sam's Music *p155*. **Shoes** Kenneth Cole
p149; XOT Shoes *p150*. **Specialist & gift
shops** Wolfsonian-FIU Gift Shop *p155*. **Sports
& outdoors** Adidas Originals *p155*; South
Beach Dive & Surf *p156*.

South Miami

Cameras & electronics Best Buy *p154*;
CompUSA *p154*. **Children's fashion** Children's
Exchange *p148*; Kidding Around *p148*.
Clubwear & street Rampage *p149*. **Department
stores** Bloomingdale's *p141*. **Discount** Target
p145. **Food & drink** Lucky Oriental Mart *p150*.
Homeware & interiors Arango *p151*; **Malls**
Dadeland Mall *p143*; The Falls *p143*; Shops
at Sunset Place *p143*. **Music** Yesterday &
Today Records *p155*. **Shoes** Capretto Shoes
p149; Shoes to You *p150*. **Sports & outdoors**
Niketown *p156*; Sports Authority *p156*.
Vintage & collectibles Miami Twice *p156*.

Eat, Drink, Shop

Luminaire
*2331 Ponce de León Boulevard, at Aragon Avenue,
Coral Gables (305 448 7367/www.luminaire.com).
Bus 24, 42, 72, Coral Gables Circulator.* **Open**
10am-6pm Mon-Sat. **Credit** AmEx, MC, V.
Map p276 B4.
An austere glass box showroom acts as a beacon to
buyers of seriously classic modern furniture by the
likes of Le Corbusier and Arne Jacobsen, Ron Arad
and Jasper Morrison.

Williams-Sonoma
*1035 Lincoln Road, at Lenox Avenue, South Beach
(1-786 276 9945/www.williamssonoma.com). Bus C,
G, H, K, L, M, S, W, South Beach Local.* **Open**
11am-10pm Mon-Thur; 11am-11pm Fri, Sat; noon-
9pm Sun. **Credit** AmEx, MC, V. **Map** p272 C2.
Impress guests with unnecessarily nice, top-of-the-
line cookware, distinctive foods, cooking ingredients
and cookbooks. Shop here and make Martha Stewart
proud of your culinary dedication.
Other locations: Aventura Mall, 19575 Biscayne
Boulevard, Aventura (305 933 2082); The Falls, 8888
SW 136th Street, South Miami (305 256 9929).

Retro

Senzatempo
*1655 Meridian Avenue, at Lincoln Road, South
Beach (305 534 5588/www.senzatempo.com). Bus
C, G, H, K, L, S, W, South Beach Local.* **Open** 11am-
6pm Mon-Fri by appointment only. **Credit** AmEx,
MC, V. **Map** p273 A1.
More a gallery than a store, Senzatempo specialises
in 20th-century designer furniture and decorative
arts, as well as watches, clocks and other timepieces.
Designers include Alvar Aalto, Arne Jacobsen and
Charles Eames.

Visiona
*1093 NE 79th Street, at 10th Street, North Miami
(305 758 8234). Bus 3, 16.* **Open** noon-7pm daily.
Credit AmEx, MC, V.
At Visiona vintage designer pieces such as Arne
Jacobsen egg chairs, Paul McCobb china cabinets
and George Nelson clocks are paired with less
expensive but no less stylish items such as Alvar
Aalto glass vases.

Leisure

Books

Barnes & Noble

Loehmann's Fashion Island, 18711 Biscayne Boulevard, at NE 187th Street, North Miami Beach (305 935 9770/www.barnesandnoble.com). Bus 3, V. **Open** 9am-11pm daily. **Credit** AmEx, DC, MC, V. **Map** p270.

The Wal-Mart of booksellling, B&N is a monolithic clearing house for all things in print. Sales here drive the bestseller list. Lingering is encouraged.
Other locations: 7710 N Kendall Drive, Kendall (305 598 7292).

Books & Books

265 Aragon Avenue, at Ponce de León Boulevard, Coral Gables (305 442 4408/www.booksandbooks. com). Bus 24, 42, 72, Coral Gables Circulator. **Open** 9am-11pm daily. **Credit** AmEx, MC, V. **Map** p276 B4.

Absolute heaven for book lovers, B&B is a superb independent operator, well stocked with bestsellers but also lots of small publisher product. Its wooden-floored rooms include one devoted to antiquarian rarities and another to kids' books. There's a café, plus regular discussion groups and author readings.
Other locations: 933 Lincoln Road, South Beach (305 532 3222); Bal Harbour Shops, 9700 Collins Avenue, Bal Harbour (305 864 4241).

Kafka's Used Book Store & Cyber Café

1464 Washington Avenue, at 14th Street, South Beach (305 672 4526). Bus C, H, K, W, South Beach Local. **Open** 7.30am-midnight daily. **Credit** AmEx, DC, MC, V. **Map** p273 C2.

A little touch of literate angst in the middle of South Beach – it's just a pity that the selection of dog-eared airport fiction, used art books and magazines is so dismal. A bookshop for people who don't read.

Cameras & electronics

Buyer beware! The countless discount electronics stores Downtown and on Lincoln Road in South Beach are notorious. Many have a reputation for selling goods that have fallen, so to speak, from the back of a truck. Keep an eye out for missing guarantees, and never leave the store without a receipt and the name of the staffer who served you.

Aperture Professional Supply

1330 18th Street, at Bay Road, South Beach (305 673 4327/www.aperturepro.com). Bus M, S, W. **Open** 8.30am-6.30pm Mon-Fri; 8.30am-1.30pm Sat. **Credit** AmEx, MC, V. **Map** p272 C2.

This is where the pros go to get their photo essentials. As well as buying film and professional film developing, you can also rent gear – Canon, Nikon, Hasselblad – and studio space.

Best Buy

8450 S Dixie Highway (US 1), at SW 83rd Street, South Miami (305 662 7073/www.bestbuy.com). Metrorail Dadeland North. **Open** 10am-9.30pm Mon-Thur; 10am-10pm Fri, Sat; 11am-7pm Sun. **Credit** AmEx, DC, MC, V.

The proverbial candy store for grown-up gadget freaks. Mobile phones, computers, cameras, fridges, faxes, stereos: you name it, this warehouse has it. Even if the service sucks, the prices don't.
Other locations: 19191 S Dixie Highway (US 1), South Miami (305 256 9552).

CompUSA

8851 SW 136th Street, at S Dixie Highway (US 1), South Miami (305 234 5600/www.compusa.com). Bus 1, 52, 65. **Open** 10am-9pm Mon-Sat; 11am-6pm Sun. **Credit** AmEx, DC, MC, V.

This massive computer supermarket chain has everything in PC and Mac software and hardware, from games to laptops, and PDAs and digital

Van Michael Aveda Concept Salon.
See p151.

cameras, plus aisles of books, accessories and hordes of technobrats hogging the terminals.
Other locations: 900 Park Center Boulevard, North Miami (305 620 1800); 7440 SW 88th Street, Kendall (305 670 5030).

Tropicolor Photo

1442 Alton Road, at 14th Street, South Beach (305 672 3720/www.tropicolorphoto.com). Bus M, S, W.
Open 9am-8pm Mon-Fri; 10am-5pm Sat. **Credit** AmEx, MC, V. **Map** p272 D2.
This all-purpose neighbourhood photo-processing lab also provides colour photocopying and passport photo services.

Wolf Camera & Video

Aventura Mall, 19501 Biscayne Boulevard, at NE 196th Street, Aventura (305 931 5839/www.wolf camera.com). Bus 3, 9, E, S. **Open** 10am-9.30pm Mon-Sat; noon-8pm Sun. **Credit** AmEx, MC, V. **Map** p270.
Photography, video and imaging products including 35mm and 24mm APS cameras, digital cameras, video camcorders, film and accessories, plus a handy on-site, one-hour film-developing lab.
Other locations: Dadeland Mall, 7535 SW 88th Street, South Miami (305 665 3456); Kendall Mall, 8803 SW 107th Avenue, Kendall (305 270 9300); The Shoppes at Arch Creek, 13120 Biscayne Boulevard, North Miami (305 891 2120).

Music & video

Casino Records

1208 SW 8th Street, at SW 12th Avenue, Little Havana (305 856 6888/www.casinorecords miami.com). Bus 8, 12, Little Havana Circulator.
Open 9am-9pm Mon-Sat; 10am-5pm Sun. **Credit** AmEx, DC, MC, V. **Map** p275 C3.
It's said to be easier to find the hottest current Cuban records in Miami than in downtown Havana. That's certainly true in Casino, where the hottest grooves are always fresh in.

Do Re Mi Music Center

1829 SW 8th Street, at SW 18th Avenue, Little Havana (305 541 3374). Bus 8, 17, Little Havana Circulator. **Open** 10.30am-7.30pm Mon-Sat. **Credit** AmEx, MC, V. **Map** p275 C3.
From Los Van Van to Celina González, this is the house of Latin music, be it *románticos* (ballads) or salsa. With so much choice, your head will spin faster than the turntables.

Lion Video

1524 Ponce de León Boulevard, at Menores Avenue, Coral Gables (305 442 6080/www.lionvideo.com). Bus 24, 42, 72, Coral Gables Circulator. **Open** 10am-midnight Mon-Sat; 10am-10pm Sun. **Credit** AmEx, MC, V. **Map** p276 B4.
The Lion roars with more than 22,000 rare and out-of-print videos and DVDs, as well as new releases, American classics, gay/lesbian titles and an especially strong foreign film selection.

Spec's Music

501 Collins Avenue, at 5th Street, South Beach (305 534 3667). Bus C, H, K, W, South Beach Local.
Open 10am-midnight Mon-Thur; 10am-1am Fri, Sat. **Credit** AmEx, MC, V. **Map** p273 F2.
Two floors of CDs, DVDs and videos. The selection isn't great, but the store also sells used music slipped into the 'new' racks; you might find what you're looking for at a price way less than you expected.

Uncle Sam's Music

1141 Washington Avenue, at 11th Street, South Beach (305 532 0973/www.unclesamsmusic.com). Bus C, H, K, W, South Beach Local. **Open** 10am-2am Mon-Sat; 11am-2am Sun. **Credit** AmEx, DC, MC, V. **Map** p273 D2.
Dirty street kids and slick ravers mix at this store for the latest in new and used dance, trip hop, trance and house et al. It's also the spot to go for rave gear, hair dye, incense, stickers and other knick-knacks.

Yesterday & Today Records

9274 SW 40th Street (Bird Road), at 92nd Avenue, South Miami (305 554 1020/www.vintagerecords. com). Bus 40. **Open** 11am-7pm Tue-Thur; 11am-8pm Fri, Sat; noon-4.30pm Sun. **Credit** AmEx, MC, V.
This packed second-floor store features vintage vinyl. Eclectic, ever-changing stock ranges from the Beatles to Benny Goodman to Barbra Streisand.

Specialist & gift shops

Historical Museum of Southern Florida Gift Shop

101 W Flagler Street, at NW 1st Avenue, Downtown (305 375 1492/www.historical-museum.org). Metromover Government Center. **Open** 10am-4.30pm Mon-Wed, Fri, Sat; 10am-8pm Thur; noon-4.30pm Sun. **Credit** AmEx, MC, V. **Map** p274 D1.
Pure Floridiana. Here's where you buy those souvenirs for the folks back home: Southern cracker cookbooks, Seminole Indian arts and crafts, plus a wide range of local books and arts. *See also p79.*

Wolfsonian-FIU Gift Shop

1001 Washington Avenue, at 10th Street, South Beach (305 531 1001/www.wolfsonian.org). Bus C, H, K, W, South Beach Local. **Open** noon-6pm Mon, Tue, Sat, Sun; noon-9pm Tue, Fri. **Credit** AmEx, MC, V. **Map** p273 D2.
A shop devoted to beautiful design. Pieces include a colander by Starck, limited-edition pens boasting legendary designs, and reproductions of classic clocks by George Nelson. *See also p63.*

Sports & outdoors

Adidas Originals

226 8th Street, at Collins Avenue, South Beach (305 531 1240/www.adidas.com). Bus C, H, K, W, South Beach Local. **Open** 11am-8pm Mon-Thur; 11am-9pm Fri, Sat; 11am-7pm Sun. **Credit** AmEx, MC, V. **Map** p273 E2.

Eat, Drink, Shop

Village of Merrick Park – retail therapy, the Coral Gables way. *See p144.*

Everyone can have their Adidas in this popular brand's SoBe outpost filled with classic-yet-trendy sports clothing, as well as gym bags, hats and, of course, sneakers, all bearing the trio of stripes.

Niketown
Shops at Sunset Place, 5701 Sunset Drive (SW 72nd Street), at US 1 & Red Road, South Miami (305 740 0121). Metrorail South Miami. **Open** 11am-10pm Mon-Thur; 11am-11pm Fri, Sat; 11am-9pm Sun. **Credit** AmEx, MC, V. **Map** p271.
A shrine to the swoosh, this monster has interactive displays, memorabilia, a video theatre and every Nike product imaginable, from apparel to golf clubs.

South Beach Dive & Surf
850 Washington Avenue, at 8th Street, South Beach (305 673 5900/www.southbeachdivers.com). Bus C, H, K, W, South Beach Local. **Open** 9am-7pm Mon-Sat; 10am-5pm Sun. **Credit** AmEx, MC, V. **Map** p273 E2.
Surf jams, thongs, shades (Arnettes, Dragons, Black Fly, Oakleys), surfboards, boogie boards, wakeboards and skateboards. There are no surfboard rentals, though the store does have a cheap styro version (not impressive looking, but it works).

Sports Authority
8390 S Dixie Highway (US 1), at SW 83rd Street, South Miami (305 667 2280/www.thesportsauthority.com). Metrorail Dadeland North. **Open** 9.30am-9.30pm Mon-Sat; 10am-7pm Sun. **Credit** AmEx, MC, V.

A sporting goods superstore with 39,000sq ft of brand-name goods for every sport: baseball, basketball, camping, cycling, fishing, football, hockey, golf, lacrosse, yada, yada, yada.

Vintage & collectibles

C Madeleine's
13702 Biscayne Boulevard, at 137th Street, North Miami (305 945 0010/www.cmadeleines.com). Bus 3. **Open** 11am-6pm Tue, Wed, Fri, Sat; 11am-8pm Thur; noon-5pm Sun. **Credit** AmEx, MC, V.
Need a cast-iron stove from the 1940s or maybe a lava statue of a hula girl from the '70s? Find it here, along with high-necked linen and lace dresses, funky neckties, costume jewels, shoes, furs and postcards. Brands include Gucci, Pucci, Balenciaga, Chanel, Vuitton and even hard-to-find Zandra Rhodes.

Miami Twice
6562 SW 40th Street (Bird Road), at SW 65th Avenue, South Miami (305 666 0127/www.miamitwice.com). Bus 40, 73. **Open** 10am-7pm Mon-Sat; noon-6pm Sun. **Credit** AmEx, MC, V.
A retro department store, Miami Twice has an extensive Bakelite jewellery and accessories collection. It also stocks furnishings – 1950s dinettes, Fiestaware, lunchboxes – and clothes spanning the decades from flapper dresses to old leather jackets. MT wardrobes major films and the shop is apparently a huge favourite of Cameron Diaz.

Arts & Entertainment

Features

Festivals & Events

Food, drink, music and sun – Miami's non-stop calendar of activities has all the right ingredients.

Miami needs no excuse to party, that's for sure. From the traditional to the downright tacky, the city is fast on its feet when it comes to celebrations. While it's not nearly as festival-oriented as, say, Chicago or New York, it still throws its fair share of street-clogging, deafening, dazzling – and fattening – events.

Be aware that some of the bigger events – Art Deco Weekend, the Coconut Grove Arts Festival, the Miami Book Fair and the Miami International Boat Show – take place on holiday weekends and draw huge crowds. The two most popular events – Art Basel and the South Beach Wine & Food Festival – have hotels reserved for years in advance and have practically become national holidays – at least in Miami, that is. Book cars and hotel rooms well ahead, and expect traffic clogs near to the venues.

INFORMATION AND PRICES

For information on weekly events, browse the listings in the Friday *Miami Herald*. The *Miami New Times*, available free at cafés, bars, bookshops, retail stores and sidewalk dump bins, is also an outstanding source for events. Online, check out the calendar of events on www.gmcvb.com, the Greater Miami

Convention & Visitors Bureau's website. It's also worth taking a look at the websites of area attractions and museums for specific events hosted during the year.

Some of the bigger events charge admission fees. Many of the street festivals are free to attend, but keep in mind that many of these events are businesses too, and you will most likely shell out cash for food and drink.

Spring

Miami International Film Festival

Gusman Center for the Performing Arts, 174 E Flagler Street, at SE 1st Avenue, Downtown, & other locations (305 237 3456/www.miamifilmfestival.com). **Date** early Mar. **Map** p274 D3.

Now run by Miami-Dade College and under the leadership of Nicole Guillemet, formerly co-director of the Sundance Film Festival, MIFF showcases the best of world cinema. As many as 300 filmmakers and industry representatives from around the world attended the 2006 bash, including scores of Oscar winners and nominees. There is a special focus on Ibero-American cinema, and prizes are given in documentary and dramatic categories.

Ford Championship at Doral

Doral Golf Resort & Spa, 4400 NW 87th Avenue, at NW 41st Street, North-West Miami (305 447 4653/ www.fordchampionship.com). **Date** early Mar.

Four days of drive and put as top names on the PGA Tour tackle the Blue Monster Course at this swanky resort. Spectators mass on the 18th green for the free Concert on the Green and Fireworks Spectacular that kick off tournament week.

Carnaval Miami/Calle Ocho

Throughout Miami-Dade County (305 644 8888/ www.carnavalmiami.com). **Date** early Mar.

For about ten days each spring, Latino Miami struts its stuff with a full slate of beauty pageants, sports activities, food, concerts and cooking contests. The grand finale is Calle Ocho, a 23-block street festival in Little Havana that claims to be the largest block party in the world. More than a million people turn out for live entertainment on 30 stages featuring salsa, merengue and Caribbean music, plus ethnic food and drink. **Photo** *p159*.

Miami International Orchid Show

Coconut Grove Convention Center, 2700 S Bayshore Drive, at SW 27th Avenue, Coconut Grove (305 579 3310). Bus 6, 27, 48. **Date** early Mar. **Map** p277 B4.

Don't miss Festivals

South Beach Wine & Food Festival
See p163.

Art Basel Miami Beach
See p162.

Miami International Film Festival
See right.

NASDAQ-100 Open
See p159.

Carnaval Miami/Calle Ocho
See right.

Miami Book Fair International
See p161.

Arts & Entertainment

Carnaval Miami/Calle Ocho – hope that's not the queue for the loo. *See p158.*

For over 50 years this show has attracted orchid aficionados from around the world, showcasing more than half a million blooms, with plants and orchid-related items also for sale.

Winter Party Week
On the beach at Ocean Drive, at 14th Street, South Beach (305 576 6435/www.winterparty.com).
Date early Mar. **Map** p273 C3.
A benefit for the local gay community, this week-long party pulls celebrity DJs and thousands of revellers, and includes music, dance, art, film and comedy at South Beach nightclubs and hotels. It all culminates with a beach dance party. As with the White Party (*see p162*), it's all about going completely over the top. Book tickets well in advance.

Italian Renaissance Festival
Phone for details of venues (305 758 4595/ www.renaissancefestival.com). **Date** mid Mar.
This fest experienced a renaissance of its own after abandoning its long-time home at the Vizcaya Museum & Gardens for the much larger, albeit inconveniently located, Hialeah Park in the north of the city. The entertainment's still the same and should still include the popular flag-throwers from Asti and a living chess game, along with strolling minstrels, jugglers and costumed players.

Dade Heritage Days
Throughout Miami-Dade County (305 258 9572/ www.dadeheritagetrust.org). **Date** Mar-Apr.

Miami-Dade County celebrates its impressive historical, cultural and environmental heritage with six weeks of diverse events, including open houses and lectures, as well as guided walking and canoe tours of sights around town such as the Deering Estate (*see p105*), as well as off-the-beaten-track places like Boca Chita Key (*see p236*) and the Barnacle (*see p88*).

Miami-Dade County Fair & Exposition
Tamiami Park, Coral Way/SW 24th Street & SW 112th Avenue, West Dade (305 223 7060/ www.fairexpo.com). Bus 24, Coral Way MAX.
Date Mar-Apr.
One of the largest county fairs in the US, this 18-day event has rides, food, entertainment and lots of exhibits. The 100-ride midway includes a decent rollercoaster; food ranges from all-American corn on the cob and barbecue to Hispanic specialities. Exhibits include the silly (the latest miracle spot removers) to the scholarly (hundreds of haikus by elementary-school students). A must for the family.

NASDAQ-100 Open
Crandon Park Tennis Center, 7300 Crandon Boulevard, Key Biscayne (305 442 3367/www. nasdaq-100open.com). Bus B. **Date** Mar-Apr.
Your chances of seeing current stars as well as up-and-comers are excellent at this 12-day event, which is now the fifth-largest international tennis tournament in terms of players, prize money and attendance (over 270,000 people came in 2006).

Miami Book Fair International.
See p161.

Miami Spice Restaurant Month

Throughout Miami (http://www.MiamiRestaurant Month.com). **Date** Aug/Sept.

Dinner at Nobu for 30 bucks? Yup. To spice up business during the summer doldrums, many of the top Miami restaurants participate in this two-month promotion whereby you, the diner, can enjoy a classy dinner for $30 or a chic lunch for $20. There are restrictions – fixed menus, selected days and so on – but it's a splendid way to enjoy otherwise prohibitively priced meals at places such as the Blue Door at the Delano (*see p115*).

Autumn

Festival Miami

University of Miami, Gusman Concert Hall, 1314 Miller Drive, at San Amaro Drive, Coral Gables (305 284 4940/www.music.miami.edu). **Date** 4-6wks from mid Sept. **Map** p276 F1.

This festival makes for a dizzying few weeks, with concerts and musical events hosted by the University of Miami School of Music. The emphasis is on international artists; recent festivals featured musicians from China, Brazil, Cuba, Poland, Africa, England, Israel, Spain and Chile.

Hispanic Heritage Festival

Throughout Miami-Dade County (305 461 1014/ www.hispanicfestival.com). **Date** Oct.

One of the largest Hispanic festivals in the US, this month-long event commemorating the discovery of the Americas includes an outdoor music and food festival at Bayfront Park in Downtown Miami, a street fair in South Miami and a gala ball. It's all preceded, of course, by the obligatory beauty pageant.

Arts & Entertainment

Summer

Miami/Bahamas Goombay Festival

Throughout Coconut Grove (305 372 9966/www. goombayfestival.org). Bus Coconut Grove Circulator. **Date** 1st weekend June.

No need to jet over to the Bahamas – just head to this raucous three-day festival in the Grove for authentic food, music and dance. One of the largest black heritage festivals in the US, Goombay is full of dazzling costumed junkanoo groups dancing to Caribbean rhythms with rake 'n' scrape instruments and whistles, plenty of conch fritters and the like.

International Mango Festival

Fairchild Tropical Garden, 10901 Old Cutler Road, at SW 101st Street, South Miami (305 667 1651/ www.fairchildgarden.org). Bus 65. **Date** 2nd weekend July. **Map** p271.

It's mangoes agogo, with hundreds of varieties for admiring and sampling, in the form of smoothies, chutneys, candies and more. This family-friendly event includes entertainment and activities for kids, a mango-themed brunch prepared by local celeb chefs (book in advance online if you're interested; this always sells out), and a remarkably entertaining mango auction where folks have been known to bid over $100 for a plate of their favourite cultivar.

Junior Orange Bowl Festival

Throughout Miami-Dade County (305 662 1210/ www.jrorangebowl.com). **Date** Oct-Jan.

A long-running youth festival made up of sports tournaments (including tennis, soccer, swimming, golf and gymnastics) and cultural events (including creative writing, caroling and photography). The Junior Orange Bowl Parade, featuring floats, bands and huge inflatables, marches through Coral Gables between Christmas and New Year.

Columbus Day Regatta

Biscayne Bay (305 858 3320/www.columbusday regatta.net). **Date** mid Oct.

To commemorate Christopher Columbus's voyage in 1492, 200 sailboats race on Biscayne Bay, off Coconut Grove. A rowdy, clothing-optional party off Elliott Key concludes the weekend.

South Miami Art Festival

Along SW 72nd Street, off US 1, South Miami (305 661 1621). Metrorail South Miami. **Date** 1st weekend Nov.

Music, food and art from 170 juried artists around the country take over Sunset Drive (the nicest bit of South Miami) during this two-day festival.

Miami Book Fair International

Miami-Dade Community College, Wolfson Campus, 300 NE 2nd Avenue, at NE 3rd Street, Downtown (305 237 3258/www.miamibookfair.com). Metromover *Government Center.* **Date** mid Nov. **Map** p274 D3.

Miami a cultural backwater? You must be kidding. Half a million people turn out every year for this week-long literary event, which features 250 nationally and internationally renowned writers taking part in lectures and readings. An accompanying wildly popular street fair has food and entertainment and a children's alley, with a whole host of interactive diversions for kids. **Photo** *p160*.

Harvest Festival

Fair & Expo Center, Coral Way/SW 24th Street & SW 112 Avenue, Sweetwater (305 375 1492/ www.historical-museum.org). **Date** mid Nov.

Kicking off the holiday shopping season with fine crafts booths, antiques and jewellery, this benefit festival for the Historical Museum of Southern Florida (*see p79*) has homespun family activities, a giant model railroad display, vintage automobiles, historical re-enactments, live music and food.

Ford Championship Weekend – NASCAR

Homestead-Miami Speedway, 1 Speedway Boulevard, between SW 132nd & 137th Avenues, at SW 336th Street, Homestead, South Miami (305 230 7223/www.HomesteadMiamiSpeedway.com). **Date** mid Nov.

Four days of screaming cars racing around the track, plus noise, beer, excitement, beer, car-racing celebs and, well, more beer. Just don't forget the earplugs. The track hosts other events during the year.

Happy holidays

If you're visiting Miami during a national holiday, don't be just an observer – jump right in with the locals for what they like doing best: celebrating.

Independence Day (4 July)

Parades by day and firework displays at Miami Beach, Key Biscayne and Coral Gables. The biggest celebration of all is the Latin-spiced extravaganza at **Bayfront Park** (301 N Biscayne Boulevard, at NE 2nd Street, Downtown, 305 358 7550, www.bayfront parkmiami.com). There's live music, dancing, food and games for the kids, plus a laser show followed by a dazzling firework display over the bay. Best of all, it's free.

Halloween (31 Oct)

OK, not actually a public holiday, but Halloween is now an excuse for myriad horror houses populated with chainsaw-wielding maniacs and blood-splattered zombies. The biggest of them all is the **House of Terror Amusement Park** at Miami International Mall (SR 836 & NW 107th Avenue, 305 358 7550, www.houseofterror.cc), an empire of amusement rides, carnival food and games open during most of October. Local attractions dress up for Halloween too: Lincoln Road on South Beach channels the flamboyant, fabulous vibes of NYC's Greenwich Village as throngs of colourful costumers parade proudly for the unspoken title of best in show; Metrozoo (*see p106*) becomes **MetroBoo!**, with prizes and sweets for the under-12 crowd; the Miami Seaquarium (*see p75*) features **Monster**

Splash, with haunted houses and candy stations; and Parrot Jungle Island (*see p165*) turns into **Pirate Jungle Island**, with treasure hunts and pictures with spooky animals.

Christmas (25 Dec)

It might be hard to imagine, but, yes, Miamians do string up lights on their palm trees and go carol-singing in shirt sleeves. For a taste of winter wonderland, visit Downtown's **Holiday Village** (Bayfront Park, 301 N Biscayne Boulevard, at NE 2nd Street, 305 358 7550, www.holidayvillage.cc) with Christmas trees, ice skating, fairground rides, kids games and ole Saint Nick. At **Santa's Enchanted Forest** (Tropical Park, 7900 SW 40th Street (Bird Road), at SW 79th Avenue, 305 893 0090, www.santas enchantedforest.com), an impressive display of more than three million tiny lights cleverly conceals your basic carnival rides, greasy food and tacky games.

New Year's Eve (31 Dec)

Not in the mood to pay exorbitant cover charges at the clubs? Then ring in the New Year at **Bayfront Park's New Year's Eve Celebration** (301 N Biscayne Boulevard, at NE 2nd Street, Downtown, 305 358 7550, www.bayfrontparkmiami.com). It's absolutely free and includes concerts with national and local acts, a countdown with the Big Orange (Miami's equivalent of the Big Apple) and a grand display of fireworks over the bay at midnight. You'll get drenched with *cidra* (Spanish sparkling cider) and kissed by strangers – a great way to start the year!

Arts & Entertainment

Ramble, A Garden Festival

Fairchild Tropical Garden, 10901 Old Cutler Road,
at SW 101st Street, South Miami (305 667 1651/
www.fairchildgarden.org). Bus 65. **Date** Nov.
Set in the subtropical paradise that is the Fairchild
Tropical Garden (*see p105*), this is one of south
Florida's most pleasant, and venerable, events.
Stretched over two days, the festival celebrates outdoor living with plant sales and exhibits, live entertainment, garden-themed shopping, antiques and
collectible sales, plus plenty of activities for kids.

White Party

Various locations on South Beach (305 667 9296/
www.whiteparty.net). **Date** late Nov.
The crown jewel of HIV/AIDS benefits, this wee-long
non-stop string of events and parties – which draws
an estimated 10,000 people – includes the legendary
White Party itself, held at the Vizcaya Museum &
Gardens (*see p90*), and the day-long Muscle Beach
bash (dress code: swimsuits and shorts). Previous
celeb attendees include former supermodel Janice
Dickinson and *Queer Eye*'s Carson Kressley.

Art Basel Miami Beach

Miami Beach Convention Center & various venues
(305 674 1292/www.artbaselmiamibeach.com).
Date 1st wk Dec.
The high-profile, glitzy, glammy American sister
event of the well-established Art Basel in Switzerland,
Art Basel Miami Beach showcases 20th- and 21st-
century artworks by over 1,000 artists, accompanied
by special exhibitions and parties. *See also p175.*

King Mango Strut

Begins at Main Highway & Commodore Plaza,
Coconut Grove (305 401 1171/www.kingmango
strut.org). Bus Coconut Grove Circulator. **Date**
late Dec. **Map** p277 B2.
What began as a parody of the now-departed
Orange Bowl Parade continues, thankfully, to poke
tasteless and delightfully offensive fun at the year's
events and newsmakers. Perhaps the final remnant
of Coconut Grove's eccentric creativity, and the best
possible way to enter the new year laughing.

Noise in the 'hood

One of the best ways to get acquainted
with non-touristy south Florida is to visit
one of the monthly neighbourhood open-
house events. Many have free refreshments,
live entertainment and art installations.
All are a heap of fun.

Miami Beach

ArtsBeach 2nd Thursdays is the city's free
multicultural arts night, serving up a wealth of
visual and performing arts events throughout
Miami, including music, dance, theatre,
cinema, readings, art exhibits, guided
tours and storytelling. For more details,
visit www.2ndthursdays.com.

Coral Gables

On **Gallery Nights** – held from 7pm to 10pm
on the first Friday of each month – free
minibuses shuttle visitors between ten Coral
Gables galleries, an event made even more
convivial with free libations and the like. The
atmosphere is festive, and the shuttle service
is the best way to get around this parking-
challenged city.

Little Havana

If you want to take in the sights and sounds
of this distinctive Hispanic neighbourhood,
Viernes Culturales (Cultural Fridays), held
on the last Friday of each month, are just the
ticket. Restaurants, art galleries and shops

along Calle Ocho (SW 8th Street, between
14th & 17th Avenues) open their doors from
7pm to 11pm, while street entertainers and
musicians hit the high hat. At the McDonald's,
sculptors, ceramics artists and craftsmen
practise their skills. For more information,
call 305 644 9555 or log on to www.viernes
culturales.com.

North Miami

Explore the eclectic mix of restaurants, cafés
and galleries in the city's arts district on NE
125th Street (between 6th & 9th Avenues)
via **Gallery Walks**, held on the last Friday of
each month. *See also p177.*

Homestead

Get a snapshot of rural south Florida and
savour the authentic Mexican cuisine of its
migrant worker community at **Friday Fest**,
held on the first Friday of each month at
Homestead's Losner Park (Krome Avenue,
between Mowry Drive & NE 2nd Street).
Antiques and collectible shops, restored
storefronts and small-town events such as
carol contests and homespun crafts booths
may make you feel like you're in the Midwest,
not the South. It's a 45-minute drive from
Miami, so you can easily combine your trip
to Homestead with a visit to the Everglades
(*see pp221-225*) or Biscayne National
Underwater Park (*see p104*).

Arts & Entertainment

South Beach Wine & Food Food Festival.

Art Miami

Miami Beach Convention Center, 1901 Convention Center Drive, between 17th Street & Dade Boulevard, South Beach (305 573 1388/www.art-miami.com). Bus C, G, H, K, L, S, W, South Beach Local. **Date** early-mid Jan. **Map** p272 C3.

Celebrating its 17th year in 2007, this is one of south Florida's major art fairs, with more than 120 participating galleries gathered from all over Europe, Asia and the Americas. Art Miami includes young international exhibitors and a strong Spanish and Latin American contingent.

Redland Natural Arts Festival

Fruit & Spice Park, 24801 SW 187th Avenue, at SW 256th Street, Homestead, South Miami (305 247 5727/www.co.miami-dade.fl.us/parks). **Date** mid Jan.

Set in one of south Florida's most bucolic areas, this sweet local festival presents arts and crafts, old-time music, puppets, juggling and other forms of old-fashioned fun in the pretty rural setting of the Fruit & Spice Park (*see p105*). A concert kicks things off on the Friday.

Art Deco Weekend

Ocean Drive, South Beach (305 672 2014/www.mdpl.org). Bus C, H, K, W, South Beach Local. **Date** 3rd weekend Jan.

Organised by the Miami Design Preservation League (*see p64* **Walk on**), Art Deco Weekend is a hugely popular event celebrating the city's tropical art deco and Mediterranean deco heritage. Events include walking, bicycle and boat tours, plus lectures, movies, street theatre and live music on the beach.

Beaux Arts Annual Festival of Arts

University of Miami, Lowe Art Museum, 1301 Stanford Drive, at Ponce de León Boulevard, Coral Gables (305 444 2234/www.beauxartsmiami.org/events/festival.html). Bus 52, 56. **Date** 3rd weekend Jan. **Map** p276 F2.

A fine family weekend affair featuring the works of more than 300 juried artists to view and to purchase, in more then ten types of media. Doors are open 10am to 5pm both days, and admission is free.

South Beach Wine & Food Festival

Various locations in South Beach (305 460 6563/www.sobewineandfoodfest.com). **Date** late Feb.

Serious foodies and wine connoisseurs should book early for this culinary festival, which attracts superstar chefs including Alain Ducasse, Bobby Flay, Nigella Lawson, Jamie Oliver and Emeril Lagasse. In addition to tastings and culinary seminars, big-ticket events include a champagne beach barbecue on the sands of the Delano, hosted by Flay and friends. *See also p128* **Whining and dining**.

Miami International Boat Show & Strictly Sail

Miamarina at Bayside, 401 Biscayne Boulevard, Downtown (954 441 3220/www.miamiboatshow.com). **Date** 3rd wk Feb.

Here's your chance to see what a $7-million aqua juggernaut looks like. This popular event showcases the latest in powerboats, sailboats, engines, electronics and accessories. There's also a Sunset Celebration with street performers, contests and drinks specials.

Coconut Grove Arts Festival

Throughout Coconut Grove (305 447 0401/www.coconutgroveartsfest.com). Coconut Grove Circulator. **Date** 3rd weekend Feb.

This immense beer – whoops, arts – festival attracts more than 750,000 people to view the works of 300-plus artists and craftspeople. There's now a small admission fee for the arts part of the festival, but the music and culinary areas are free. Take public transport shuttles from Metrorail, or be prepared to sit in traffic for hours on end and then pay dearly for whatever parking you find.

Children

Big fun for the little ones.

My Gym. *See p166.*

Miami's main attraction for visitors of all ages is undoubtedly the beach. First the good news: the beaches here are clean and safe, with plenty of lifeguards, shelters and concession stands. Therefore, the main thing you need to worry about is the subtropical sun – plus a few pests. The strength of the sun merits vigilant adherence to basic safety rules: get the highest SPF sunblock you can find, and cover your kids from ears to toes. Repeat the process often, even if the cream is waterproof. Make sure they wear hats and that they play under beach umbrellas or covered areas whenever possible. Do this even on overcast days. And keep plenty of water on hand. Heed lifeguard warnings for riptides and warn kids about Portuguese men-of-war, jellyfish that look like purplish-blue balloons and have a vicious sting (for advice on what to do if you're stung, *see p70* **Life's a beach...**).

Note that the majority of Miami's junior-friendly attractions are inaccessible by public transport. If you don't have a rental car, you'll need to factor in some pretty expensive cab rides.

The Friday edition of the *Miami Herald* includes listings of major children's activities, as does the 'Neighbors' section on Thursdays and Sundays. The free weekly *New Times* also has comprehensive listings on local happenings, while the free monthly *South Florida Parenting* or *Miami Family* magazines, available at toy stores and bookstores, are always chock-full of child-oriented activities.

Attractions

Greater Miami has a glut of attractions ideal for keeping children amused, many of which are described and listed in other chapters of this guide. Chief among these is the delightful **Venetian Pool** (*see p84*) in Coral Gables, with its sandy beach and underwater cave, although kids under three are not admitted. **Miami Metrozoo** (*see p106*) in South Dade is a big hit with kids: in addition to the animals, the zoo has interactive exhibits and special animal-related education programmes. **Bill Baggs Cape Florida State Park** (*see p76*) on Key Biscayne is a winner for older children, with plenty of water activities to wear them out, and it can be combined with a visit to the **Miami Seaquarium** (*see p75*) on neighbouring Virginia Key for all the usual sealife.

Miami Children's Museum

980 MacArthur Causeway (305 373 5437/
www.miamichildrensmuseum.org). Bus C, K,
M, S. **Open** 10am-6pm daily. **Admission** $10;
free under-1s. **Credit** AmEx, MC, V.
Across the causeway from the Parrot Jungle Island
(*see below*), this is not a museum at all; rather it's a
highly interactive kid's playground. The fun includes
a colourful mosaic-tiled, two-storey sandcastle, a sea
room designed especially for under-fives, the world's
most cultural teddy-bear exhibit and a television studio. But what kids seem to like best are the exhibits
celebrating the mundane: the bank with teller stations and fake cheques, the supermarket with check-
out lanes, and the police motorcycle and fire truck.

Parrot Jungle Island

1111 Parrot Jungle Trail, Watson Island, MacArthur
Causeway (305 258 6453/www.parrotjungle.com).
Bus C, K, M, S. **Open** 10am-6pm daily. **Admission**
$24.95; $19.95 3-10s; free under-3s. **Credit** AmEx,
MC, V.
In 2001 this long-time attraction moved from its suburban South Miami location to the more accessible
Watson Island, bringing the same popular parrot and
wildlife shows and petting zoo. Bring loads of change
to buy seeds so that the kids can feed the parrots –
but remind them that they bite, though. **Photo** *p167.*

Parks & natural attractions

Special programmes and events at many
parks and other natural attractions can turn a
ho-hum visit into a genuine learning experience.
Places like South Miami's **Fairchild Tropical
Garden** (*see p105*) produce special activity
booklets for kids to use while exploring. At
the two national parks located in the county,
the **Everglades** (*see pp221-225*) and **Biscayne
National Underwater Park** (*see p104*), a
Junior Ranger Program lets kids earn a badge
for completing activities. Elsewhere, Miami-
Dade County Parks operates Eco-Adventure
Tours, introducing young visitors to parks
with canoe trips, bike trips, kayaking, marine
wading tours, wildlife encounters and bird
walks; for further details, visit the website
at www.co.miami-dade.fl.us/parks.

Amelia Earhart Park

401 E 65th Street, at NW 42nd Avenue/Le Jeune
Road, Hialeah, North Miami (305 769 2693).
Bus 28, 42. **Open** 9am-5pm daily. **Admission**
$3 per car. **No credit cards. Map** p270.
It's way up north of Hialeah (*see p103*), but this
park has lots of distractions for children that make
it well worth the trip, including several lakes, a
farm village with petting zoo, pony rides, a skate
park, a recreated pioneer homestead, an enormous
playground and a 'bark park' (for dogs, apparently).
It's also the venue for mountain-bike trails.

Bill Sadowski Park

17555 SW 79th Avenue, at SW 176th Street,
South Miami (305 255 4767). No public transport.
Open sunrise-sunset daily. **Admission** free.
This 30-acre park and nature centre, located half a
mile west of Old Cutler Road, has nature trails and
organises bird-watching tours. It's also an observatory site for the Southern Cross Astronomical Society,
which holds stargazing sessions from 8pm to 10pm
every Saturday night (weather permitting); call 305
661 1375 for further information.

Crandon Park

4000 Crandon Boulevard, Key Biscayne (305 361
5421). Bus B. **Open** 8am-sunset daily. **Admission**
$4 per car. **No credit cards. Map** p271.
Aside from being home to one of the best (and safest)
beaches in the county, Crandon has a family amusement centre with a restored vintage carousel, a
roller rink (bring skates) and a nature centre with
programmes that explore the seagrass and the fos-
silised mangrove reef. Best of all are the resident
iguanas and unusual reptiles. For $20 an hour, you
can rent a family-sized bike built for two peddlers
and two strapped-in seats up front. *See also p70*
Life's a beach…

Matheson Hammock Park

9610 Old Cutler Road, at SW 88th Street, South
Miami (305 665 5475). Bus B. **Open** 6am-sunset
daily. **Admission** $4 per car. **No credit cards.**
Map p271.
This picturesque park has an artificial atoll pool
that's good for safe, quiet bathing. For lunching, the
Red Fish Grill is housed in a charming coral-rock
building – and the food's not bad either. *See also*
p70 **Life's a beach…**

Pelican Harbor Seabird Rescue Station

1275 NE 79th Street, North Bay Village (305
751 9840/www.pelicanharbor.org). Bus L.
Open sunrise-sunset daily. **Admission** free
(donations appreciated).
Not strictly an attraction but a working halfway
house for seabirds rescued after being injured by
fish hooks or nets. Staff are available to show visitors around 9am-noon and 2-5pm daily, while feeding takes place at 4.15pm.

Sea Turtle Nesting & Relocation Program

Haulover Beach Park, 10800 Collins Avenue,
Miami Beach (305 947 3525); Crandon Park,
4000 Crandon Boulevard, Key Biscayne (305
365 3018).
From April to September, Florida beaches host the
largest gathering of nesting sea turtles in the United
States. Their numbers have diminished over the years
because of the demand for meat, eggs and leather, and
due to the loss of their habitat. Since 1980, thousands
of endangered sea turtles have been hatched and
released through this programme. The release takes
place in the evenings; call for specific times.

Arts & Entertainment

Fairchild Tropical Garden. *See p165.*

Museums

A lot of Miami museums have regular events aimed at the young. At the **Historical Museum of Southern Florida** (*see p79*) kids can clamber on to boats, pile into trolley cars and play with old-fashioned toys. Every second Saturday of the month there are free family fun days, with special activities. The **Lowe Art Museum** (*see p86*) lays on Art Adventures, weekend tours aimed at introducing families to the Lowe's many exhibitions that take place at 2pm Saturday and Sunday, with a different theme each month. Family Days, held twice annually, encourage kids and adults to explore art and culture through music, dance, theatre, storytelling and hands-on art activities.

Every second Saturday of the month at the **Miami Art Museum** (*see p79*), staff lead kids in an afternoon of creative projects inspired by the museum's exhibits, while the **Museum of Contemporary Art** (*see p102*) has two kids' programmes: StART Together for two- to five-year-olds and their parents (2-3pm every Sunday) and Creative Arts, for six- to 12-year-olds (2-4pm on the first Saturday of each month). Also check the website for the **Miami Museum of Science & Planetarium** (*see p90*) for events such as the annual aquarium show.

Active fun

Beginning to fear the consequences of American fast food? Then head to one of the children's gyms scattered throughout the city. Most of them offer 'open play' time slots that are a one-class commitment (handy if you're not in town for very long). True, the classes, which generally cater to under-fours, are geared for play, not sweat, but at least it gets them moving.

American Gymsters

328 Crandon Boulevard, at Sonesta Drive, Key Biscayne (305 361 7676). Bus B. **Open** 9am-5pm Mon-Fri. **Admission** prices vary. **Credit** AmEx, MC, V.

Baby Stars

3565 NE 207th Street, at NE 34th Avenue, Aventura (305 466 1886/www.baby-stars.com). Bus 3. **Open** times vary. **Admission** prices vary. **Credit** AmEx, MC, V.

Gymboree

11845 S Dixie Highway, between SW 117th Street & SW 120th Street, Pinecrest, South Miami (305 232 3399). Bus 57. **Open** times vary. **Admission** 11 classes $126; 22 classes $215; $25 membership fee. **Credit** AmEx, V.
Other locations: throughout the city.

Jungle Gym

2968 Aventura Boulevard, at NE 29th Place, Aventura (305 932 1496/www.junglegym-inc.com). Bus V. **Open** 9am-5pm Mon-Fri. **Admission** $20-$25. **Credit** AmEx, MC, V.

My Gym

2531 Coral Way, at SW 25th Avenue, Coral Gables (305 285 9440/www.my-gym.com). **Open** times vary. **Admission** 45-minute class $160; 1hr class $165; open play $6. **Credit** AmEx, MC, V.
Other locations: throughout the city.

Cultural events

As well as the theatre, dance and storytelling (the latter a regular feature at the Miami-Dade and Miami Beach libraries; call for details, *see p253*), kiddie culture often extends to sports grounds. Happily, the prices for kids' tickets for the Florida Marlins and Miami Heat sports teams' pro games (*see p199*) are reasonable – it's the peanuts and parking you'll be spending a fortune on.

Concerts for Kids

Lincoln Theater, 541 Lincoln Road, at Pennsylvania Avenue, South Beach (305 673 3330/www.nws.org). Bus C, G, H, K, L, M, S, W, South Beach Local. **Open** *Box office* 10am-5pm Mon-Fri; noon-5pm Sat on performance days. **Admission** $10. **Credit** AmEx, DC, MC, V. **Map** p273 A2.

A teaching orchestra, the New World Symphony, has an impressive range of events, including occasional Concerts for Kids on Sunday afternoons. Phone for dates and times.

Miami Children's Theater

11155 SW 112th Avenue, at SW 112th Street, Kendall (305 224 3595/www.miamichildrens theater.com). Bus 71. **Open** *Box office* 11am-6pm Mon-Fri. **Tickets** $12; $10 concessions. **Credit** Disc, MC, V.

Performances here are produced, acted and choreographed by children. The audience is also underage, but watch out for the occasional PG rating. Call or check the website for more details. **Photo** *p169.*

Miami Storytellers Guild

305 552 1675/www.miamistorytellersguild.com. **Credit** AmEx, DC, MC, V.

The guild and its members offer storytelling for kids, as well as magic shows and special party packages, ideal for birthday entertainment; call for details. At 7pm every Thursday in the upper lobby of the magnificent Biltmore hotel (*see p53 and p85* **Gimme Biltmore**), one of the guild relates spooky stories from the hotel's past – kids love it.

Musical Theatre for Young Audiences

Actors' Playhouse at the Miracle Theatre, 280 Miracle Mile (SW 24th Street), at Ponce de León Boulevard, Coral Gables (305 444 9293/www. actorsplayhouse.org). Bus 24, 72, Coral Gables Circulator. **Open** *Box office* 10am-6pm Mon-Sat. **Tickets** $9. **Credit** AmEx, MC, V. **Map** p276 C4.

The Actors' Playhouse (*see p204*) hosts an acclaimed Musical Theatre every Saturday at 2pm, which presents everything from fairytales to modern classics.

Eating out

Miami is full of kid-friendly restaurants. Cuban spots (like Puerto Sagua, *see p118,* or any of several places in Little Havana, *see pp129-130*) are a good bet, with reasonable prices and grub such as rice, beans and fried sweet plantains that should suit even the fussiest eaters.

Eateries at shopping malls and retail complexes such as CocoWalk, Bayside Marketplace, Dadeland Mall and the Shops at Sunset Place (for all, *see pp142-143*) target families and can handle requests for high chairs and booster seats. Chain restaurants such as Chili's, Denny's and TGI Friday's immediately bring kids free crayons, colouring books and children's menus; check the phone book for your nearest branch.

Alternatively, alfresco dining somewhere like Lincoln Road Mall on South Beach or along Main Highway in Coconut Grove can provide an ideal solution for noisy, restless kids.

In addition to the eateries listed below, **Taverna Opa** (*see p114*), **Archie's Pizza** (*see p126*) and **Shorty's BBQ** (*see p131*) are all very good choices if you've got kids in tow.

Bayside Hut

3501 Rickenbacker Causeway, Virginia Key (305 361 0808). Bus B. **Open** noon-10pm Mon-Thur, Sun; noon-11pm Fri, Sat. **Main courses** $6-$20. **Credit** AmEx, MC, V.

The name says it all: a laid-back atmosphere and fresh seafood in a hut beside the bay. It is, however, hard to find – take the road that parallels the old Marine Stadium and follow the signs.

Arts & Entertainment

Parrot Jungle Island. *See p165.*

Adult-sized fun

Major national productions for children always stop in Miami to perform shows that are so dazzling, with such vibrant costumes and elaborate effects, that adults are equally entertained (even if they don't always want to admit it). Check scheduling, though, as these travelling performances pop in and out of town. Most sell tickets at the box office or through Ticketmaster (305 358 5885, www.ticketmaster.com).

AmericanAirlines Arena

For listings, see p187.
This venue hosts Disney on Ice, a larger-than-life version of the movies your kids have memorised, such as *The Incredibles*. The Wiggles also tour here to mobs of screaming toddlers, while children of all ages line up for tickets to Ringling Bros and Barnum & Bailey circus.

BankUnited Center

1245 Walsh Avenue, at Dickinson Drive, Coral Gables (305 284 8686). Bus 52, 56/Metrorail University. **Open** Box office 10am-6pm Mon-Fri; 10am-4pm Sat. **Credit** AmEx, MC, V.
Sesame Street Live – featuring Muppets singing and dancing against amazing backdrops – is held at this venue, as are stage versions of other American television shows, such as *Clifford the Big Red Dog* and *Dragon Tales*.

Jackie Gleason Theater for the Performing Arts

For listings, see p186.
From traditional ballets such as *The Nutcracker* to translational cartoons like *Dora The Explorer*, this theatre often hosts shows for children. It also has the Broadway in Miami Beach series, with teen-appropriate performances that in the past have included the musicals *Mamma Mia!* and *Oliver*.

Big Pink

157 Collins Avenue, at 2nd Street, South Beach (305 532 4700/www.bigpinkrestaurant.com). Bus H, M, W, South Beach Local. **Open** 8am-midnight Mon-Wed; 8am-2am Thur, Sun; 8am-5am Fri, Sat. **Main courses** $8.25-$20. **Credit** AmEx, MC, V. **Map** p272 F3.
American comfort food, served outside. For the pick-iest little eaters, the kids' menu includes macaroni and cheese and chicken fingers. *See also p111.*

The Daily

2001 Biscayne Boulevard, at NE 19th Terrace, Downtown (305 573 4535). Bus 3. **Open** 6am-6pm Mon-Fri; 7am-5pm Sat; 8am-4pm Sun. **Main courses** $5.50-$6.95. **Credit** AmEx, Disc, MC, V.
Counter service for custom-chopped salads, hearty sandwiches, home-made soups and blended coffee drinks. But whatever you do, don't miss the banana chocolate pastry bites.

Fuddrucker's

17985 Biscayne Boulevard, at NE 179th Street, Aventura (305 933 3572/www.fuddruckers.com). Bus 3, 9, S. **Open** 11am-11pm daily. **Main courses** $7-$11. **Credit** AmEx, DC, Disc, MC, V.
Honest burgers, lots of neon and noise – you can't go wrong. Kids like the Oreo shakes and root beer floats, not to mention the sundaes and fudge brownies.

Johnny Rocket's

728 Ocean Drive, at 7th Street, South Beach (305 538 2115). Bus South Beach Local. **Open** 11am-2am Mon-Thur; 11am-3am Fri, Sat; 11am-1am Sun. **Main courses** $4-$6. **Credit** MC, V. **Map** p273 E2.
More American appeasers: burgers, fries and shakes, with a 1950s diner theme and entertaining waiters who break into song every now and then.
Other locations: 3036 Grand Avenue, Coconut Grove (305 444 1000); Aventura Mall, 19501 Biscayne Boulevard (305 682 7979); 5701 Sunset Drive, Shops at Sunset Place (305 663 1004).

Monty's

2550 S Bayshore Drive, at Aviation Avenue, Coconut Grove (305 858 1431/www.montys stonecrab.com). Bus 48, Coconut Grove Circulator. **Open** 11.30am-11pm Mon-Wed; 11.30am-11.30pm Thur; 11.30am-midnight Fri; noon-midnight Sat; noon-11pm Sun. **Main courses** $15-$40. **Credit** AmEx, DC, MC, V. **Map** p277 A4.
Skip the pricey stone crab restaurant upstairs and head directly to the casual bayside seafood house downstairs. On weekends, order a basket of fried seafood and a pitcher of beer (for you) and send the kids off to dance to the live reggae. *See also p129.*

Perricone's Marketplace & Café

15 SE 10th Street, at S Miami Avenue, Downtown (305 374 9449/www.perricones.com). Metrorail Brickell. **Open** *Deli* 7am-11pm daily. *Restaurant* 11.30am-11pm daily. **Main courses** $10.95-$19.95. **Credit** AmEx, MC, V. **Map** p274 F2.
Tucked away in Downtown Miami, Perricone's Marketplace is popular among the area's working professionals, but is also a favourite for families. In addition to a sprawling outdoor patio that can more or less handle the occasional scream, there are bibs and high-chairs. Check out the Sunday brunch buffet too. *See also p123.*

Roadhouse Grill

12599 Biscayne Boulevard, at NE 125th Street, North Miami (305 893 7433). Bus 3. **Open** 11am-11pm daily. **Main courses** $5-$16. **Credit** AmEx, MC, V.

This noisy Old West-motif chain serves basic fare such as southern fried chicken and burgers. There's a kids' menu and crayons for colouring, but what the littl'uns are more likely to remember is the free peanuts; adults will notice shells all over the floor.

Resources

Activity programmes

Many resort hotels offer special programmes for kids, typically free for hotel guests and accessible to non-guests for a fee. Ritz Kids at the **Ritz-Carlton Key Biscayne** (*see p37*) entertains kids island-style at the beachfront Ritz Kids Pavilion, with beach treasure hunts, shell expeditions, storytelling and a posh children's menu. At the **Loews Miami Beach** (*see p37*), the kids' programme includes lending game libraries, special menus, tours and welcome gifts. In Coral Gables, the **Biltmore** (*see p53 and p85* **Gimme Bilmore**) has a family values package with free kids' passes to area attractions, a free in-room movie and cookies and milk delivered to the room nightly (plus there's also the storytelling sessions on Thursday night; *see p167*).

In addition to Cookie's World, the resort's gigantic interactive water play land, the **Fontainebleau Resort** (*see p49*) has Vacation Station, a programme of family services including free toys, games and souvenirs. The **Sonesta Beach Resort** (305 361 2021) on Key Biscayne has a Family Fest programme that includes admission to the Miami Seaquarium (*see p75*), and all-you-can-eat ice-cream for kids (almost worth the cost of admission). At the **Sheraton Bal Harbour** (305 865 7511), the Harbour Kids Club has half- and full-day sessions for children aged five to 12 years old, including arts and crafts, kite flying, pool games, scavenger hunts and sandcastle building.

Babysitting

Your hotel concierge should be able to recommend babysitters. Another option is to hire a babysitter or nanny through an agency. The agencies listed below are licensed. Babysitters will come to your hotel (you may be charged a transportation and/or parking fee) and will require a four-hour minimum fee and five to 24 hours' notice. Rates vary with the number of children and the time of day. Overnight and long-term care are also available, and some agencies can also handle special-needs children.

Carestaf of Miami
305 418 4005/www.carestaf.com.
Rates $17.95 per hr for 1 or 2 children. **Credit** DC.

Nanny Poppinz
305 607 1170/www.nannypoppinz.com. **Rates** $10 per hr for 1 or 2 children, plus $1 per hr each additional child. **Credit** MC, V.

Miami Children's Theater. *See p167.*

Arts & Entertainment

Film

Festivals, arthouse and multiplexes combine for an exciting local movie scene.

Although, on the surface, Miami's cinema scene may seem like that of many other big US cities (read: full of identical-looking multiplexes), thankfully, its mega-theatres are as likely to première an indie feature from Buenos Aires as show the latest Hollywood blockbuster. South Florida's multicultural mix of high and low culture is also reflected in the vast number of films shot here (*see p261 and p172* **Reel-life fantasies**). Not only has the area's lush landscape served as the setting for numerous big-budget movies, the drop-dead gorgeous locals – comprising buff boys and cosmetically enhanced babes – have also made it a favourite location for the porn industry.

The **Miami International Film Festival** (*see p158*), these days administered by Miami-Dade College, is famous for exposing the latest Latin American and Spanish cinema, as well as showcasing international releases and new shoots from the US indie scene. The festival runs for two weeks, usually in late February or early March, and screenings are conveniently held across town, including opening and closing night at the historic Gusman Center for the Performing Arts (*see p186*). The billings include seminars with directors and screenwriters, plus gala opening- and closing-night parties.

A variety of other more specifically focused film festivals are held at other times of the year. The **Hispanic Film Festival** (305 279 1809), which runs for ten days in late March at the Regal South Beach Cinema, and the **Brazilian Film Festival** (305 899 8998, www.brazilian filmfestival.com) every May, also at the Regal South Beach, lead the pack of smaller, Latin-themed festivals, which are often sponsored by embassies to promote national film industries.

The **Miami Gay & Lesbian Film Festival** (305 534 9924, www.miamigay lesbianfilm.com) is held for a week in late April at various locations around town and features an impressive mix of independent films. The **Miami Jewish Film Festival** (305 573 7304), held each December, screens international films (many Spanish-language) with Jewish themes at the South Beach Regal and Gusman Center for the Performing Arts. October's **Miami Jazz Film Festival** (www.miamijazzfilmfestival.org), which is organised by public radio station WDNA,

serves up an excellent selection of new and historic jazz documentaries. Just north of Miami, the **Fort Lauderdale International Film Festival** (954 760 9898, www.fliff.com), held in October/November, has a bias towards US independents and Florida filmmakers. Several of its top offerings also screen at the Regal South Beach.

Cinemas

The advent of multiplexes has resulted in an explosion in the number of movie screens and a corresponding implosion in average screen size. However, the diversity of film offerings in and around the city has greatly improved over the past couple of years, even if the places in which they're screened are getting steadily more generic and uninspiring. Unfortunately,

Arts & Entertainment

visitors holed up on South Beach get very little choice – but, on the plus side, at least the popcorn's good.

TICKETS & INFORMATION

In the normal manner, you can buy tickets in cash at the box office just prior to the start of a film, but you should book for opening nights. Most cinemas offer discounts for students (with ID), and prices are reduced for afternoon shows.

Both the daily *Miami Herald* and the weekly *New Times* publish film listings. The *Herald* covers every film that opens in Miami, but its reviews – most of which run in the Friday 'Weekend' section – are substantially shorter than those in *New Times*. You can also find reviews and showtimes online at sites such as www.miami.com, or by calling 305 888 3456 for a schedule of what's playing.

First-run cinemas

AMC CocoWalk 16

3015 Grand Avenue, at Virginia Street, Coconut Grove (305 466 0450). Bus 42, 48, Coconut Grove Circulator. **Screens** 16. **Tickets** $5-$8. **Credit** AmEx, MC, V. **Map** p277 B3.

Part of the bustling CocoWalk shopping and dining complex. It typically features blockbusters and up to three non-Hollywood films at a time. Be warned: it's teen city on weekends.

AMC Sunset Place 24

Shops at Sunset Place, 5701 Sunset Drive (SW 72nd Street), at US 1 & Red Road, South Miami (305 466 0450). Metrorail South Miami. **Screens** 24. **Tickets** $6-$9. **Credit** AmEx, MC, V. South Miami's multiplex caters to suburban families and University of Miami students with the latest Hollywood fare, concentrating on action films and child-friendly movies. Host mall the Shops at Sunset Place (*see p143*) is reasonably attractive, with good post-film restaurants and cafés.

Aventura 24 Plex

Aventura Mall, 19501 Biscayne Boulevard, at NE 196th Street, Aventura (305 466 0450). Bus 3, 9, E, S. **Screens** 24. **Tickets** $6-$9. **Credit** AmEx, MC, V.
As part of the dismal mini city that is the Aventura Mall (*see p142*), even despite its staggering multiplicity of screens, this place is always busy, and weekend and first-week screenings are often sold out. All but one of its 24 screens will at any one time probably be devoted to mainstream Hollywood hits, with a token indie flick to soak up the oddballs.

Miami Beach Cinematheque. *See p173*.

Reel-life fantasies

South Florida is the kind of place where people have always come in search of their dreams. It's no surprise, then, that those in the dream business – filmmakers – often end up here. Neon glamour, quasi-tropical vistas, temperate weather – not to mention all those buff bodies and bikini babes – it's the stuff of cinematic fantasy. But long before Michael Mann highlighted Miami with his *Miami Vice* series in the 1980s, the city had already made its mark in the film world.

The motion-picture industry has been engaged in an on-again, off-again love affair with Miami almost since the advent of celluloid. In the 1920s the Miami Movie Studios in Hialeah produced a number of films, including DW Griffith's *The White Rose*. Attempts to create a Hollywood East faltered, but producers like Sam Katzman utilised the city in a number of B-movie thrillers, such as *The Miami Story* (1954) and *Miami Exposé* (1956), about gangland turf wars.

Moving into the '60s, Miami Beach's vaunted ring-a-ding nightlife cameoed in several motion pictures, including Jerry Lewis's *The Bellboy* (1960), the 1964 Bond outing *Goldfinger* and *Tony Roma* (1967) with Frank Sinatra, all of which were filmed, at least in part, on location at the Fontainebleau Hotel.

But if there's one film that has etched a lasting picture of Miami on to contemporary movie-goers' imaginations, it's Brian DePalma's overblown 1983 remake of *Scarface*. A portrait of a Cuban immigrant who rises through the ranks of the cocaine industry with the help of a shotgun, the movie was trashed by critics on release. The Cuban community was so angered by the decadent portrayal of their culture that some even suspected Fidel Castro of backing the

production. And the film didn't do much for the city's image either, portraying Miami as a hotbed of drug dealing, violence and kitsch. (Which, of course, it was.)

Despite the shaky debut, the film went on to acquire cult status on home video, to the point where many of today's gangsta rappers cite it as a major influence on their mean-mutha stylings. In Miami, street-fashion stores on Washington Avenue sell framed photos of Al Pacino as Tony 'Scarface' Montana; inset in the frame below the photo is a replica gun or a Cuban cigar. Hip hop fans lope around the city in search of the garishly decorated mansions and plentiful booty enjoyed by Montana. In fact, much of the movie was shot in LA, although everybody's favourite scene, in which Pacino's partner is carved up with a chainsaw, was shot at 728 Ocean Drive, Miami Beach, now a Johnny Rockets restaurant.

Hollywood's focus on Miami as a location surged in the 1990s, with a slew of films including the Farrelly Brothers' *There's Something About Mary* (in which Cameron Diaz unwittingly adds genetic protein to her hair at the Cardozo Hotel, 1300 Ocean Drive) and the superior adaptation of Elmore Leonard's *Out of Sight*, in which Ving Rhames and George Clooney hole up at the Adams Hotel at 2030 Park Avenue. The biggest starring role for Miami itself comes in *The Birdcage*, which is full-on flamboyant South Beach; the Birdcage club of the title was the Carlyle Hotel (1250 Ocean Drive) in drag.

And the Miami/film love affair continues. Among the films shot in and around town in the last few years are *2 Fast 2 Furious* with Vin Diesel, *Out of Time* with Denzel Washington, and *Bad Boys II*, with Martin Lawrence and Will Smith. The latter caused all amount of annoyance when the MacArthur Causeway – the main route between Downtown and Miami Beach – was shut down for four days during filming. That's not to mention CBS's big TV hit, *CSI: Miami*, which shoots on location each season, and the MTV series *8th and Ocean*, which follows the lives of South Beach models. And finally, one of the most anticipated movies in some time was released in summer 2006: the big-screen version of *Miami Vice*. It was again directed by Michael Mann, but this time starred Colin Farrell and Jamie Foxx as Crockett and Tubbs (*photo above*).

Regal South Beach Stadium 18
*1100 Lincoln Road, at Alton Road, South Beach
(305 674 6766). Bus A, M, R, S, W, South Beach
Local.* **Screens** 18. **Tickets** $6-$9. **Credit** AmEx,
MC, V. **Map** p272 C2.
With its eye-catching architecture and prime location on the corner of Lincoln Road Mall, this big,
glass-walled theatre is the hub of the South Beach
cultural scene. Tragically, most of the fare is mind-
less Hollywood pap, but there are screens to spare
for occasional independent and foreign films. On
weekdays you can have the whole theatre to yourself, but weekend screenings of blockbusters and the
critically lauded often sell out, so buy tickets early.
The second-floor café offers real-food alternatives to
the usual cinema junk.

Sunrise Cinemas Intracoastal 8
*3701 NE 163rd Street (Sunny Isles Boulevard),
Intracoastal Mall, North Miami Beach (305 949
0064/www.sunrisecinemas.com). Bus E, H, V.*
Screens 8. **Tickets** $4.50-$8. **Credit** AmEx,
MC, V.
Independent, foreign and classic films are revered
here. In addition to the latest studio releases, the
Intracoastal spotlights international film festival
favourites not shown elsewhere in Miami. It also
hosts a film club with screenings of classics introduced by local film historians.

Arthouse & repertory

Bill Cosford Cinema
*2nd Floor, Memorial Building, University of Miami,
off Campo Sano Avenue & University Drive, Coral
Gables (305 284 4861). Bus 48, 52, 56.* **Screens** 1.
Tickets $4-$6. **No credit cards.**
Named after the late *Miami Herald* film critic Bill
Cosford and completely renovated with funding from
his family, this is a gem of an independent movie
house. It's roomier and plusher than most first-run
cinemas and offers an eclectic mix of Asian, European
and arthouse fare. The downside is that it's awkward
to get to on public transport. Thankfully, it's well
worth the effort.

Louis Wolfson II Media History Center
*Miami-Dade Public Library, 101 W Flagler Street,
at NW 1st Avenue, Downtown (305 375 4527).
Metromover Government Center.* **Screens** 1.
Tickets free. **Map** p274 D1.
The Wolfson Media History Center is home to the
imaginative Cinema Vortex series, an eclectic series
of international films, held in the main auditorium
of the Downtown branch of the Miami-Dade Public
Library. The centre also screens selected historical
videos from its massive archives. If the scheduled
screenings don't tempt, nostalgia buffs, researchers
and anyone with even a passing interest in Miami's
past can still drop by the archive and check out some
of the amazing footage of the city through the years.
Just call in advance for an appointment.

Miami Beach Cinematheque
*512 Española Way, at Drexel Avenue, South Beach
(305 673 4567/www.mbcinema.com). Bus C, H, K,
W, South Beach Local.* **Screens** 1. **Tickets** $8-$10.
No credit cards. Map p273 B2.
A storefront space on Española Way is home to
Miami's only cinematheque. It's the base of the Miami
Beach Film Society, under whose aegis the cinema
screens independent and experimental movies and
film classics to a seated audience of just 50 (more
when screenings are held outside). Like every good
alt arthouse, the cinematheque is about more than
movies. Photography and painting exhibits hang on
the walls, and there may be music, a mini festival or
talks (for instance, two local drag queens recently discussed the closing of a legendary nightclub). One of
the festivals that makes an annual appearance is the
Florida Room, a series of documentaries grouped
under a theme. There's no food or drink available
at the venue itself, but the excellent little Frenchified
A La Folie (*see p110*) is just a few doors down the
street. **Photos** *p170 and p171*.

Tower Theater
*1508 Calle Ocho (SW 8th Street), at SW 15th
Avenue, Little Havana (305 649 2960). Bus 8,
17.* **Screens** 2. **Tickets** free-$2.50. **No credit
cards. Map** p275 C2.
Miami-Dade College has partnered with this historic
theatre in Little Havana to present new films from
Cuba and other Latin American countries, as well as
shorts and features by budding Miami cinéastes.
Commercially released English-language films are
also shown with Spanish subtitles at discount prices.

Wolfsonian–FIU
*1001 Washington Avenue, at 10th Street, South
Beach (305 531 1001/www.wolfsonian.fiu.edu). Bus
C, H, K, W, South Beach Local.* **Screens** 1. **Tickets**
free with museum admission ($7; $5 concessions).
Credit AmEx, MC, V. **Map** p273 D2.
South Beach's superb Wolfsonian-FIU hosts well
curated film series featuring artists' works, documentaries and other cinematic tie-ins to complement
the museum's temporary exhibitions. *See also p63.*

Other cinemas

Coral Gables
LeJeune Cinemas VI *782 Le Jeune Road (NW
42nd Avenue), at NW 7th Street (305 529 8883).*
Screens 6. **Tickets** $4.50-$7. **No credit cards.**

South Miami
AMC Kendall Town & Country 10 *Town &
Country Centre, 8400 Mills Drive, at the Florida
Turnpike Toll Road (305 466 0450).* **Screens** 10.
Tickets $5-$8. **Credit** AmEx, MC, V.
Regal Kendall 9 *1209 Kendall Drive (SW 88th
Street), at SW 123rd Avenue (305 598 5000).*
Screens 9. **Tickets** $5-$8. **No credit cards.**
South Dade 8 *18491 S Dade Highway, at Eureka
Drive (305 466 0450).* **Screens** 8. **Tickets** $5-$8.
Credit AmEx, MC, V.

Galleries

A booming new art district is helping to put the city on the international art map.

Emmanuel Perrotin Gallery. *See p176*.

Arts & Entertainment

Years ago the closest thing to art in Miami were those pesky postcard-sized club flyers promoting the hottest ladies' nights and amateur stripteases of the week. The city has also long laid claim to the title 'capital of Latin American art', a claim based quite simply on the large number of galleries here showing work by Latin American artists, particularly Cubans. But it's only quite recently that the city has earned a bright star on the map of the international art world. The sheen on that star is largely due to the annual culture-fest that is Art Basel (*see p175*), when for one week each December dealers, curators and collectors from around the world discover the pleasures of doing business by the beach.

As a result, art is now 'in' in a big way. Super-size sculptures turn heads in public spaces (check out Antoni Miralda's *Gondola Shoe* in the Design District, sized to fit the Statue of Liberty's foot; *see p97*), while newer deluxe hotels such as Downtown's Ritz-Carlton and the Four Seasons both house prestigious art collections.

Ironically, the gentrification of South Beach in the early 1990s and its subsequent ability to attract prestigious gatherings such as Art Basel have boosted rental prices and driven out the very artists who spearheaded the renewal in the first place. Only **ArtCenter South Florida** (*see p175*), a non-profit organisation that once owned valuable real estate on the Lincoln Road strip, has persevered. The art scene has been forced away to gritty mainland neighbourhoods north of Downtown, such as the Design District and adjacent Wynwood. These areas are now the venue for Miami's cutting-edge galleries showcasing young local talent.

Miami's cultural season runs from October to May, although some group shows are held in the summer months.

ART CIRCUITS

The Design District and Wynwood art district scenes are sufficiently established that they host monthly art circuits, with participating galleries debuting new exhibitions. Some galleries stay open past 10pm, free wine flows and the atmosphere is like one big block party. Most galleries throw open their doors on the nightly walk called Second Saturdays (that's the second Saturday of the month). There are also long-established art circuits/gallery walks held in Coral Gables and North Miami (for both, *see p177*). Such nights offer a good opportunity to meet artists and dealers, and to get a peek at the inside of the city's art scene.

ART MUSEUMS

Major art museums in and around Miami are reviewed in our Sightseeing chapters. For the Art Museum at FIU, *see p95*; for the Lowe Art Museum, *see p86*; for the Miami Art Museum and Miami-Dade College Centre Gallery, *see p79*; for the Museum of Contemporary Art, *see p102*; for Miami Art Central, *see p106*; for the Rubell Family Collection, *see p98*; and for the Wolfsonian-FIU, *see p63*.

South Beach

The local gallery scene has all but vanished as artists' studios now house high-rent operations such as Starbucks. Some art is still sold at the Lincoln Road Antiques Market, which is held on Sundays from October to May. South Beach is also home to the Bass Museum of Art (*see p72*), with local, national and international art.

ArtCenter South Florida

800 Lincoln Road, at Meridian Avenue (305 674 8278/www.artcentersf.org). Bus C, G, H, K, L, R, S, W, South Beach Local. **Open** 1-10pm Mon-Wed; 1-11pm Thur-Sun. **Credit** AmEx, MC, V. **Map** p273 A1.

Artists' studios and gallery space occupy the three separate structures that make up this alternative, non-profit art centre. Exhibitions reflect Miami's diverse communities and prices are affordable. Courses in various art studies are also available.

The Design District & Wynwood

Once semi-derelict areas of showrooms and warehouses from the 1920s and '30s, the Design District and neighbouring Wynwood are now meccas for the visual arts. Espresso-fuelled designers manoeuvre their portfolios past Puerto Rican crack kids to visit blue-chip interiors stores and wacky art installations. For more on the area, including details of how to get there, *see pp96-98 and p100* **Art on the edge**. Also worth a look are websites www.miamidesigndistrict.net and www.wynwoodartdistrict.com.

Bernice Steinbaum Gallery

3550 N Miami Avenue, at NE 35th Street (305 573 2700/www.bernicesteinbaumgallery.com). Bus 3, 9, 10, 16, J. **Open** 10am-6pm Mon-Sat. **Credit** AmEx, MC, V.

New Yorker Bernice Steinbaum exhibits multimedia work by an array of contemporary Americans. Cultural identity is a common theme in the work of the other artists on her books, who include Chinese

Art Basel Miami Beach

Miami Beach is better known for interminable kitsch than cutting-edge art, so it seemed odd that the organisers of Switzerland's sophisticates' annual jamboree, Art Basel, would choose Miami for its first American sortie. Many critics and commentators were highly cynical, but they came anyway when the event premièred in 2002. By 2005 there were more than 190 galleries in the main fair alone, with a myriad of side shows. Art-world delegates from as far as New York, Berlin and Tokyo soon discovered the allure of schmoozing over cocktails on the sand and alfresco power dining, not to mention a swim before the day's work began. Indeed, by the time the dealers went home, boasting not only a profit but a tan, the only unanswered question was why no one had thought of this long ago.

This being Miami, showbiz culture and celebs have also become part of the equation. Spotting designers and actors and directors buying up art, and then spotting them again

at exclusive galas thrown by other exclusive entities, seems to be as integral to the fair as getting a good deal. The South Beach clubs get in on the act by hosting art parties, and for that week in December almost everything happening attaches an Art Basel tag. Restaurants even offer Art Basel specials.

And then there is the art. Lots of it, from installations set up in cargo containers along the beach to all the satellite fairs that have sprouted on the Downtown side of the city. These side shows – such as the NADA fair in the Ice Palace, Pulse in a tent in Wynwood, and the design fair in the Design District, which in 2005 featured Zaha Hadid – have garnered as much attention recently as the main event. Local galleries and museums also host parallel exhibitions, putting their best faces forward because the art world is increasingly coming to see them.

In 2006 Art Basel will be held from 7-10 December. For more information, see www.artbaselmiamibeach.com. *See also p162.*

Public tweaking

The Argentine duo Roberto Behar and Rosario Marquardt are two of Miami's main art interventionists. And very public their interventions are too. Walk by the **Living Room** in the Design District (*see p97;* photo *below*), which takes over an entire corner on 40th Street and North Miami Avenue: the three-sided room is soaring (100 feet high), with pink wallpaper, a couch, two lamps and a window, through which you can view the changing Miami sky.

Change is the key, and part of what drew the couple to relocate to the city. 'We came to explore an unexplored land, we wanted to be part of a city in the making,' says Marquardt. Both have been schooled in architecture and are interested in helping transform the cityscape of Miami. Down the street from the Living Room, at NE 40th Street and N Miami Avenue, their two towering schoolchildren adorn the front of the city's renowned **Design & Architecture Senior High** (DASH). They are also responsible for the large red 'M' at the **Riverwalk Metromover**

Station. Moving indoors, the couple created another striking large-scale sculpture for the **Miami Art Museum** (*see p79*) in 2003, which consisted of giant playing cards and wooden scaffolding, surrounded by dolls.

The duo have exhibited across the globe, but, wherever it is shown, their art always reflects a fascination with transformation. As immigrants, they know what it's like to experience the most dramatic of changes, and have become an artistic force in a city that – whatever else one wants to say about it – is all about change.

Hung Liu, Haitian Edouard Duval-Carrie and Cuban Glexis Novoa. Monthly solo and thematic exhibitions and selections from the gallery's art roster are also on view.

David Castillo Gallery

2234 NW 2nd Avenue, at N Miami Avenue (305 573 8110/www.castilloart.com). Bus 3, 9, 10, 16, J. **Open** 10am-6pm Mon-Sat or by appointment. **Credit** AmEx, MC, V.

Formerly a private dealer, Castillo decided to enter the Wynwood world with a beautifully renovated building that exhibits not just contemporary but modern art as well, which has helped to broaden the range of offerings in the district. Expect to see some high-calibre stuff.

Dorsch Gallery

151 NW 24th Street, at N Miami Avenue (305 576 1278/www.dorschgallery.com). Bus 3, 9, 10, 16, J. **Open** 1-5pm Thur-Sat. **Credit** by appointment.

Brook Dorsch is as well known for hosting great parties as organising exhibitions. His expansive gallery hosts regular celebrations with live music and

performances, and eclectic shows by local artists. In addition, funky installations periodically take over the gallery's annexe.

Emmanuel Perrotin Gallery

194 NW 30th Street, at NW 3rd Avenue (305 573 2130/www.galerieperrotin.com). Bus 3, 9, 10, 16, J. **Open** 10am-6pm Wed-Sun. **Credit** AmEx, MC, V.

One of the most anticipated of the new galleries to move to Wynwood, this time from Paris, Perrotin opened its first American outpost in a renovated gas station in the nick of time for Art Basel 2005. The gallery represents some of Miami's big emerging artists, plus numerous international stars such as Gelatin and Takashi Murakami. **Photo** *p174.*

Fredric Snitzer Gallery

2247 NW 1st Place, at N Miami Avenue (305 448 8976/www.snitzer.com). Bus 3, 9, 10, 16, J. **Open** 11am-5pm Tue-Sat. **Credit** AmEx, MC, V.

Fredric Snitzer is more than a dealer: he has long served as a mentor to budding young Miami-based artists. His newly relocated warehouse gallery is the epicentre of the Wynwood scene, and his roster includes members of Cuba's famed '80s Generation (most notably José Bedia), as well as recent graduates of Miami's celebrated art school, the New World School of the Arts, and several of Miami's hottest stars, such as Hernan Bas.

Gary Nader Fine Arts

62 NE 27th Street, at N Miami Avenue (305 576 0256/www.garynader.com). Bus 3, 9, 10, 16, J. **Open** 10am-6pm Mon-Sat. **Credit** AmEx, DC, MC, V.
Gary Nader moved from his Coral Gables location to this huge Wynwood space in 2005. Nader is a major player on the Latin American market, organising an annual auction (December) and dealing in the re-sale of work by Latin American masters such as Wifredo Lam, Fernando Botero and Roberto Matta. Monthly exhibitions of modern artists of a similar quality are shown too.

Ingalls & Associates

125 NW 23rd Street, at N Miami Avenue (305 573 6263/www.ingallsassociates.com). Bus 3, 9, 10, 16, J. **Open** noon-5pm Wed-Sat or by appointment. **Credit** AmEx, MC, V.
In 2004 director Chris Ingalls packed up and left North Miami to be part of Wynwood, opening a space that highlights site-specific installations in the back room, with a variety of off-beat art in the front – eclectic and usually intriguing stuff.

Kevin Bruk Gallery

2249 NW 1st Place, at N Miami Avenue (305 576 2000/www.kevinbrukgallery.com). Bus 3, 9, 10, 16, J. **Open** 10am-6pm Tue-Fri; noon-5pm Sat. **Credit** AmEx, MC, V.
Kevin Bruk became one of the latest to transplant his gallery to the district, where he now shows a roster of impressive world-class artists such as Jesse Bransford, Fabian Marcaccio and Alexander Ross.

Locust Projects

105 NE 23rd Street, at N Miami Avenue (305 576 8570/www.locustprojects.org). Bus 3, 9, 10, 16, J. **Open** by appointment. **No credit cards**.
Housed in a neon lime-green warehouse, Locust Projects is a non-profit art centre that focuses on multimedia installations and experimental art projects by emerging artists. A committee of artists and art historians selects work for exhibition. Locust's fund-raising auctions (including an annual one in spring) and sales are a great opportunity to buy art at accessible prices.

Luis Adelantado Miami

98 NW 29th Street, at N Miami Avenue (305 438 0069/www.luisadelantadomiami.com). Bus 3, 9, 10, 16, J. **Open** 10am-6pm Wed-Sun; 7-10pm 2nd Sun of mth. **Credit** AmEx, MC, V.
The Spanish gallerist decided to open his first US annexe not in New York but in Miami, in a nod to the rising importance of the city's art scene, with an impressive space that will undoubtedly expose more international artists to the area.

Rocket Projects

3440 N Miami Avenue, at NE 34th Street (305 576 6082/www.rocket-projects.com). Bus 3, 9, 10, 16, J. **Open** 11am-6pm Tue-Fri; noon-5pm Sat. **No credit cards**.
Director Nick Cindric runs this storefront gallery (which also has a big backyard that's perfect for opening night parties), specialising in contemporary work by emerging Miami artists. In the Flat File Lounge, you can browse through drawers full of drawings.

Coral Gables

Like the neighbourhood they inhabit, Coral Gables' galleries are upscale and conservative. Openings are held during the Coral Gables Gallery Walk, held on the first Friday of each month. For information on getting to Coral Gables, *see p82.*

Americas Collection

2440 Ponce de León Boulevard, at Andalusia Avenue (305 446 5578/www.americascollection.com). Bus 24, 42, Coral Gables Circulator. **Open** 10.30am-5.30pm Mon-Fri; noon-5pm Sat. **Credit** AmEx, MC, V. **Map** p276 C4.
Modern and contemporary paintings, especially landscapes and portraits, are typical offerings at the Americas Collection, which caters to a wealthy but conservative clientele. The gallery, which has been running for over a decade, also features art by well-known Latin American artists.

ArtSpace/Virginia Miller Galleries

169 Madeira Avenue, at Ponce de León Boulevard, (305 444 4493/www.virginiamiller.com). Bus 24, 42, Coral Gables Circulator. **Open** 11am-6pm Mon-Fri. **Credit** AmEx, MC, V. **Map** p276 B4.
Virginia Miller opened her Miami gallery in 1974, and has since reflected art world trends by showing everything from daring installation work to photography and murals. These days the gallery showcases figurative and abstract painters from the US and Latin America. Miller also brokers masterworks from international markets.

North Miami

Galleries located near the city's Museum of Contemporary Art (*see p102*) participate with the museum in the North Miami Art Walk, held on the last Friday night of each month. Jazz and Latin bands perform free on the plaza in front of the museum.

Ambrosino Gallery

769 NE 125th Street, at NE 8th Avenue (305 891 5577/www.ambrosinogallery.com). Bus 10, 16, G. **Open** 11am-6pm Tue-Sat. **Credit** AmEx, MC, V.
Geometric abstract canvases and figurative paintings with subjects ranging from the poetic to the profane are on view at Ambrosino, one of Miami's oldest and most outstanding contemporary art galleries.

Gay & Lesbian

Working out and looking good – those are the real queer issues in Miami these days.

Thanks to the cocktail culture – as well as a newly expanded arts and culture scene – Miami has become a year-round mecca for gays. The rainbow flag waves proudly over Miami Beach, where gay pride is demonstrated not through political beliefs but the right to party.

During the day you'll find the boys working up a sweat at the gym or basting in the sun at the gay **12th Street Beach** so they can hit the clubs at night. Other alfresco action can be had at **Flamingo Park** (but be aware that it closes at midnight), and for nude swimming and sunbathing, the northern end of **Haulover Beach Park** (*see p75 and p70* **Life's a beach...**).

Miami Beach, of course, is the centre of the action. A melting pot of many cultures, and filled with a mix of beautiful people, club kids, drag queens and international travellers, its hotels, restaurants and clubs are rammed by night. If you come here and never see the light of day, that can only be a good thing – and, in any case, there's always next year.

But for those who desire a different sort of stimulation, there are also some interesting daytime activities in and around the area. Every visitor's itinerary must include a stroll along Ocean Drive, shopping on Lincoln Road, and a trip to the **World Erotic Art Museum** (*see p179*). (Note: these are probably the gay-friendliest parts of town – places you can comfortably walk hand-in-hand without drawing nasty stares; elsewhere, keep in mind that this is the Deep South, with all of the redneck intolerance that the tag implies. So keep your hands to yourselves until you reach Fort Lauderdale or Key West).

Sapphic circles in Miami are more subdued, but also more diverse. They run from Latina lesbians who still live at home to glamorous lipstick girls who run in packs to softball dykes hanging out at barbecues. One thing you're unlikely to see is hordes of lesbians going clubbing every night (unlike the men). The community is active, but more likely to come out in force for special events or fundraisers.

12th Street Beach.

World Erotic Art Museum

As if proof were needed that South Beach is the world capital of hedonism, it now boasts its own museum dedicated to erotic pleasures. The World Erotic Art Museum, a mind-boggling collection of erotica, is located on a second-floor space on the corner of Washington Avenue and 12th Street, just a block from the gay bar Twist (*see p181*), where eroticism is also worshipped nightly. Room after room of erotic art from around the world is displayed – 12,000 square feet in total (the collection is the largest of its kind in the US, and the second largest in the world). Valued at some $10 million, it spans all genres, modern and ancient, dating back as far as the Roman Empire. Expect to find examples of everything and anything, including art deco, Asian, Chinese, Victorian, ethnic, African, fetish, folk, gay, lesbian, religious satire and antique erotica. Penises of every size, shape and colour (more than you'll find at any sex shop) fill the shelves. If you're not overwhelmed by the giant penis (over six feet) then you'll be blown away (pun intended) by the giant hand-carved wooden four-poster bed, where the four posts are, you guessed it, giant penises. The art of gay icon Tom of Finland is displayed in the same room with an illustration of a homosexual orgy. While this might not be the type of museum your mother would enjoy, a visit with your boyfriend can be as stimulating as watching a porno. Not surprisingly, under-18s are not admitted.

But what is surprising, perhaps, is that the collector/owner/curator is a septuagenarian grandmother. Naomi Wilzig (aka Miss Naomi) has spent years amassing the collection, and has also written many books on the subject, such as *Forbidden Art: The World of Erotica*.

World Erotic Art Museum

1205 Washington Avenue, at 12th Street, South Beach (305 532 9336/www.weam. com). Bus C, H, K, W, South Beach Local. **Open** 11am-midnight daily. **Admission** $15. **Credit** AmEx, MC, V. **Map** p273 C2.

PRACTICALITIES

For further information on local gay and lesbian resources, including helplines and health clinics, *see pp251-252*.

Accommodation

Don't feel nervous about walking up to the reception desk of virtually any hotel in Miami Beach with your partner and asking for a queen-sized bed. Most hotels court the pink dollar and most concierges are gay friendly. The following cater primarily to a gay clientele.

European Guest House

721 Michigan Avenue, at 7th Street, South Beach (305 673 6665/www.europeanguesthouse.com). Bus M, S, W, South Beach Local. **Rates** $89-$139 single; $109-$159 double. **Credit** MC, V. **Map** p272 E2.
Promoted abroad in gay publications, the European Guest House is a quaint little getaway filled with chintz and Queen Anne furniture, plus a deck and jacuzzi. The atmosphere is friendly.

Island House

1428 Collins Avenue, at 14th Street, South Beach (reservations 1-800 382 2422/front desk 305 864 2422/www.islandhousesouthbeach.com). Bus C, H, K, W, South Beach Local. **Rates** $69-$259 single/double. **Credit** AmEx, DC, Disc, MC, V. **Map** p273 C3.
Island House is located in the heart of South Beach, within walking distance of Ocean Drive, and just steps away from the gay 12th Street beach. The guesthouse traditionally caters to gay men, although all open-minded adults are welcome. Some rooms have a kitchen with a fridge.

SoBeYou Bed & Breakfast

1018 Jefferson Avenue, at 10th Street, South Beach (305 534 5247). Bus C, H, K, W, South Beach Local. **Rates** $90-$159 single/double; $165-$205 suite. **Credit** AmEx, DC, MC, V. **Map** p272 D2.
One of the best gay and lesbian guesthouses in Miami. Located on a low-key residential block, it offers a sun deck, a spa pool, massage, a happy hour, weekend wine and cheese parties and breakfast by the pool. You'll feel like you're visiting friends.

Arts & Entertainment

Bars & clubs

Miami Beach's gay bar scene is still thriving, even if the number of venues has dwindled over the last couple of years. The truth is, most bars and clubs in the area are very gay friendly. Of the truly 'gay' establishments that remain, **Twist** remains a landmark, while the aptly named **Score** has outdoor seating for those who want to see and be seen.

Boy Bar

1220 Normandy Drive, at Rue Notre Dame, Miami Beach (305 864 2697). Bus L, M. **Open** 5pm-5am daily. **Credit** AmEx, MC, V.
Boy Bar is the only 5am full-liquor cruise bar in Miami Beach's hottest new gay neighbourhood, Normandy Isle. It's a combination of class and sleaze: the main bar has a 'clothes on' cruise area, while in the Jizz Room, anything goes. There's also an outdoor patio.

Crème Lounge

725 Lincoln Lane, at Meridian Avenue, South Beach (305 535 1163/www.cremelounge.net). Bus C, G, H, K, L, M, S, W, South Beach Local. **Open** 3pm-5am daily. **Admission** free. **Credit** AmEx, DC, MC, V. **Map** p273 A1.

This recently redecorate lounge is upstairs from Score (*see p181*). Tuesday is Latin night, Thursday is Crème & Sugar, while Saturday is women-only Siren (*see p181*).

Laundry Bar

721 Lincoln Lane, at Meridian Avenue, South Beach (305 531 7700/www.laundrybar.com). Bus C, G, H, K, L, M, S, W, South Beach Local. **Open** 7am-5am daily. **Admission** free. **Credit** MC, V. **Map** p273 A1.
In the alley behind Lincoln Road, the Laundry Bar is a full-service laundromat and bar, all in one. It's predominantly gay-oriented, with a fun, friendly atmosphere. Every night is busy, but Thursdays and Saturdays are particularly rammed, while Wednesday is karaoke night.

Loading Zone

1426A Alton Road, at 14th Street, South Beach (305 531 5623). Bus K, S, W. **Open** 7pm-5am daily. **Admission** prices vary. **No credit cards**. **Map** p272 D2.
While other clubs are populated with pretty boys, this no-frills beer-only bar, with its hard-to-find backalley entrance (oo-er!) attracts a more down-to-earth clientele, mainly from the local neighbourhood. There's a leather shop, S&M decor and video monitors that play hardcore porn, and every last Tuesday of the month is the infamous Black Out party.

Screening queens

The **Miami Gay & Lesbian Film Festival** debuted in 1999, and almost immediately became an integral part of the local cultural scene. It was headed then by Robert Rosenberg, a filmmaker from New York with a passion for celluloid and gay rights. Rosenberg gathered together a winning combination of mainstream and experimental flicks from across the globe that had queues circling around the block at the single venue, the Colony Theater in South Beach.

Nearly a decade on, the quirky little fest is fully grown, though without its founder (after a spat with the board of directors, he left in 2002). Some of the initial energy was sapped following Rosenberg's departure, but by 2005 the MGLFF was back, and it's now one of the bigger festivals of its kind. In that same year, a whopping 84 international films were showcased, reflecting the diverse world of modern gay life. In 2006 the festival kicked off with the Spanish film *Reinas* (Queens), starring one of the reigning queens of Spanish-language cinema, Carmen Maura. As always, the event included big opening and closing parties, panels and discussions,

awards ceremonies for various categories and tributes, but this time art and multimedia shows were added to the mix.

Over the years the festival's offerings have included a mixture of short and long features, documentaries and animation about gay, lesbian and transgendered adults, children and animals, with everything from docs about drag queens to movies about lesbians in Slovenia. Many movies that went on to hit the mainstream cinema unspooled here first, and some of the big early hits included British TV shows such as *Queer as Folk*, which spawned the long-running American version. And this being Miami, there are always generous helpings of film from the Latin world.

Despite this, the festival doesn't feel quite as counterculture as it used to. But that's less of a reflection of the festival itself than of the fact that gay life is less counterculture these days. Indeed, sectors of the American right fighting against gay marriage and adoption may well be dismayed by this baby's success.

Miami Gay & Lesbian Film Festival

305 534 9924/www.mglff.com. **Date** Apr.

A customer singing for his/her supper at **Palace Bar & Grill**. *See p182.*

Ozone

6620 Red Road (SW 57th Avenue), at US 1, South Miami (305 667 2888). Metrorail South Miami. **Open** 9pm-5am daily. **Admission** *Women $5-$10 daily.* **Men** *$5 Fri-Sun.*

Notable for its festive Latin nights, this massive club offers wild drag shows and an endless amount of raw machismo. If you happen to be one of the few Anglos in the crowd, expect to be the belle of the ball – these boys sure do love white meat.

Score

727 Lincoln Road, at Meridian Avenue, South Beach (305 535 1111). Bus C, G, H, K, L, M, S, W, South Beach Local. **Admission** *free.* **Credit** AmEx, DC, MC, V. **Map** p273 A1.

The name says it all. With a prime site on busy Lincoln Road Mall, this video bar/dance club is always packed with men looking for Mr Right Now. It has several bars, including one that overlooks the crowded dancefloor. The cruising starts on Lincoln Road at the outdoor café, then continues all night. For a fun night out, the mixed Saturday and Latin Tuesday nights are essential.

Twist

1057 Washington Avenue, at 10th Street, South Beach (305 538 9478/www.twistsobe.com). Bus C, H, K, W, South Beach Local. **Open** 1pm-5am daily. **Admission** *free.* **Credit** AmEx, MC, V. **Map** p273 D2.

Twist is South Beach's most infamous and longest-established gay club. Two levels and eight bars make this a must-visit for all gay tourists – you can bar hop without even leaving the premises (the two-

for-one drinks every day from 1pm to 9pm are a big plus too). Don't forget to stop at the back Bungalow Bar for the nightly dancers who dance for dollars.

Ladies only

In Miami, women who like women don't have as many places to meet as gay men do. The lesbian scene is more predominant in Fort Lauderdale than South Beach (*see p183* **Up at the Fort**), though there are a few weekly parties here too.

Cherry Pie

Club OZone, 6620 Red Road (SW 57th Avenue), at US 1, South Miami (305 667 2888). Metrorail South Miami. **Open** 9pm-5am Fri. **Admission** *$5-$10.* **No credit cards.**

Much of the Sappho set – lipstick, butch, you name it – makes the trek down to South Miami on Friday nights for Cherry Pie, a tacky-titled party featuring go-go girls, plus house, dance and salsa tunes spun by DJs Gil Rodríguez, Stingray, Shannon (one of South Beach's best) and Alex H.

Siren

Crème Lounge, 725 Lincoln Lane, at Meridian Avenue, South Beach (305 535 1163/www.icandee productions.com). Bus C, G, H, K, L, M, S, W, South Beach Local. **Open** 10pm-4am Sat. **Credit** AmEx, DC, MC, V. **Map** p273 A1.

The excellent weekly Saturday night party for women at Crème Lounge (*see p180*), upstairs at Score. Guest DJs spin a mix of lounge, house, hip hop, Latin and dance.

Restaurants & cafés

The only problem you may find when dining as a gay couple in Miami is that the waiter tries to hit on your boyfriend. The following are some of the city's best gay-friendly restaurants, but our Restaurants & Cafés chapter (*see pp108-131*) includes more, such as **Balans**, **News Café**, **Front Porch Café**, **Big Pink** and **Van Dyke**.

Da Leo

819 Lincoln Road, at Meridian Avenue, Miami Beach (305 674 0350). Bus C, G, H, K, L, M, S, W, South Beach Local. **Open** 5.30-11.30pm Mon-Sat; 11.30am-4pm Sun. **Main courses** $16-$30. **Credit** AmEx, MC, V. **Map** p273 A1.

The inside is cramped, but this value-driven trattoria features extensive outdoor seating in the middle of the Lincoln Road Mall. The menu offers a good selection of Italian cuisine, but you're best off sticking to the tried-and-tested pizzas and pastas. An innovative wine list completes the picture.

Edelweiss

2855 Biscayne Boulevard, at NE 26th Street, Wynwood (305 573 4421). Bus 3, 16. **Open** noon-10pm Tue-Sat; noon-9pm Sun. **Main courses** $6.50-$13. **Credit** AmEx, MC, V.

This gay, kitschy Bavarian *gasthaus* and restaurant dishes up some of the best German food in town. Located in a beautifully ornate house just north of Downtown, Edelweiss is very moderately priced and has an old-world atmosphere perfect for a night out with a group of friends or with that special someone.

Madame's Restaurant & Cabaret Lounge

239 Sunny Isles Boulevard, at Collins Avenue, Sunny Isles (305 945 2040/www.madamesusa.com). Bus H, K, S. **Open** *Restaurant* 6-11pm Mon, Thur-Sun. *Cabaret Lounge* 6-11pm Mon, Thur, Sun; 6pm-1am Fri, Sat. **Credit** AmEx, DC, MC, V.

Part Southern comfort eaterie, part belle époque Parisian cabaret, Madame's pleases the palate and lays on a bevy of talented drag performers to boot. If *The Birdcage* tickled your funny bone, this is your chance to relive the experience for yourself.

Magnum Lounge

709 NE 79th Street, at Biscayne Boulevard, Little Haiti (305 757 3368). Bus 3, 16. **Open** 6-11pm Tue-Sat; 5-10pm Sun. **Credit** AmEx, DC, MC, V.

Gay-owned and -operated, this romantic bistro is ideal for hand-holding and kissing over candles. The cuisine is gourmet comfort food, served by warm and generous staff. At night, diners are accompanied by live piano and singing.

Palace Bar & Grill

1200 Ocean Drive, at 12th Street, South Beach (305 531 9077). Bus C, H, K, W, South Beach Local. **Open** 10am-midnight daily. **Main courses** $9-$17. **Credit** AmEx, MC, V. **Map** p273 C3.

Comfortably positioned in view of the entrance to the gay beach, this place could serve sawdust and would still be packed. Thankfully, it doesn't: the salad and sandwich fare is basic but good. The weekly Sunday T-Dance (5pm) has revellers crowding the street, and other draws include the drag shows on a Saturday (4-6pm) and the lengthy happy hour on a Friday (5-9pm). If some deranged drag queen doesn't come up and molest you, some intoxicated shirtless muscle boy is bound to. **Photo** *p181*.

Tiramisu

721 Lincoln Road, at Meridian Avenue, Miami Beach (305 532 4538). Bus C, G, H, K, L, M, S, W, South Beach Local. **Open** noon-midnight Mon-Thur, Sun; noon-1am Fri, Sat. **Main courses** $12-$36. **Credit** AmEx, DC, MC, V. **Map** p273 A1.

Excellent Italian dining (inside and out) on the Lincoln Road Mall, with a great view of the walking parade. For dessert, don't miss – yep, you guessed it – the tiramisu.

Sport & fitness

Whether you prefer to play or watch, Greater Miami is a sports lover's paradise. Gays tend to prefer cruising sports, and rollerblading along Ocean Drive is a must (it's a great way to see and be seen). Luckily for those a little unsteady on their feet, many South Beach skate shops (*see p248*) offer classes, but the beach is filled with buff boys to grab on to if you need to stop. If you're after more serious action, read on.

The **Southeastern Great Outdoors Association** (305 667 2222; ask for Bill) puts together gay and lesbian camping trips, clothing-optional sails, and bike rides in the Everglades and local parks.

The **Atlantic Coast Dinghy Club** (ACDC) is an activity-oriented group of gay and gay-friendly sailors and boating enthusiasts. See www.atlanticcoastdinghyclub.org for details.

The **South Florida Softball League** has more than 20 teams – women's and mixed – that play each Sunday in the autumn. It's a very popular spectator sport, and most games end with an after-party at a nearby bar. Check out www.sfaaa.net for further information.

The local gay swimming club, **Nadadores of South Florida Swim Team**, works out five times a week. Guests are welcome; call Eric at 305 534 7393 or visit www.nadadores.org.

Frontrunners Miami has runs at 6.30pm on Wednesday and Saturday evenings, with several routes, each about four or five miles in length. They all start and finish in Flamingo Park on Miami Beach. For information call 305 757 5581.

The **Goffers** is a group of south Florida gay and lesbian golfers of varying abilities. They play every Wednesday and every Sunday on a local golf course. Call 954 565 8003 for details.

Up at the Fort

Miami Beach may be one of the world's biggest tourist destinations, but now Fort Lauderdale has snatched the gay crown away from it. With the demise of some of the most popular South Beach clubs such as Warsaw and Salvation, the local gay party boys have had to look elsewhere for their fun. In doing so they've discovered that while the South Beach crowd is still waiting behind the velvet ropes of the latest hot venue, Fort Lauderdale is ready for action, its clubs offering attitude-free cruising (with no VIP rooms), and there's no problem parking, either.

Whatever kind of action you're in the mood for, you'll find it here. Fort Lauderdale caters to all kinds of gay visitors – circuit boys, leather queens, drag queens – plus the old trolls looking for young dancers. Some of the city's hottest spots include dance clubs **Coliseum** (2520 S Miami Road, 954 832 0100) and the **Copa** (2800 S Federal Highway, 954 463 1507). The leather crowd, meanwhile, can find a mate in uniform, or possibly their very own cowboy, at **Cubby Hole** (823 N Federal Hwy 954 728 9001), **Dudes** (3270 NE 33rd Street 954 568 7777), **Jackhammer** (1727 N Andrews Square, 954 522 5855) and **Ramrod** (1508 NE 4th Avenue, 954 763 8219). The **Eagle** (1951 NW Powerline Road, 954 462 7224) offers 3-4-1 drinks to customers wearing jock straps or thongs (and nothing else), while the **Boardwalk** (1721 N Andrews Avenue, 954 463 6969) has occasional appearances from gay porn stars. Younger dancers congregate at **Johnny's** (1116 W Broward Blvd, 954 522 5931), where they

dance for an older crowd. And don't miss the **Club** (110 NW 5th Avenue, 954 525 3344), not a dance club at all, but one of the most popular gay bathhouses in south Florida.

Lesbians, too, have a better choice of venue in Fort Lauderdale than in Miami: here they've got **Kick's Sports Bar** (2008 Wilton Drive, Wilton Manors, 954 564 8480), where they can watch the Super Bowl over a few beers, a free buffet and a free shot for every score made in the game. At **Shero's Cabana Bar & Nite Club** (1441 S Powerline Road, Pompano Beach, 954 972 7600) punters can dance, enjoy an all-women revue, or just let it all out singing karaoke with friends.

In Fort Lauderdale the boys and girls join together in gay bars too: bars catering to both crowds include **Martini Bar** (2345 Wilton Drive, 954 563 7752), **Elements** (3073 NE 6th Avenue, 954 567 2432), and **Georgie's Alibi** (2266 Wilton Drive, 954 565 2526), where both gays and lesbians watch sports or relax outdoors on the patio.

There are also plenty of gay-owned/run eateries around town. One of the most perennially popular is **Mustard's Bar & Restaurant** (2256-60 Wilton Drive, Wilton Manors, 954 564 5116), where the boys feast on Mediterranean cuisine while being entertained by local drag queens. **Hamburger Mary's** (2449 Wilton Drive, Wilton Manors, 954 567 1320) peddles burgers, beer and general queer fun: Monday nights feature campy film classics on a big-screen TV. And then there's **Chardees** (2209 Wilton Drive, Wilton Manors, 954 563 1800), which offers Fort Lauderdale's older set (50s and upwards) a place to eat, drink and be merry.

Fort Lauderdale is also south Florida's gay guesthouse capital. One of the most luxurious is the **Royal Palms** (2901 Terramar Street, 954 564 6444), which is just steps from the beach. It's a beautiful, clothing-optional hotel with a lush garden, tasteful rooms, a heated pool and a spa. **Richard's Inn** (1025 NE 18th Avenue, 954 563 1111) has a pool, a nude sundeck, a courtyard and nicely furnished rooms. Other options include **Elysium Resort** (552 N Birch Road, 954 564 9601), the **Cabanas** (2209 NE 26th Street, 954 564 7764) and the **Flamingo Resort** (2727 Terramar Street, 954 561 4658).

For more on Fort Lauderdale, including details of how to get there, *see pp217-220.*

Arts & Entertainment

South Florida's gay soccer team, **Florida Storm Soccer**, is a non-profit organisation; membership is open to everyone – call 561 870 7135 or see www.floridastormsoccer.com.

Gay or bi dirtbike and ATV enthusiasts, meanwhile, can go online to www.gaydirt.org to find out about local events.

Gyms

Miami queens are rampant gym bunnies, and if you want to get lucky when you're in town, you'll need to look good. There's a gym or health club on practically every corner, and many hotels have one too. Below are some gay favourites (in addition, for **Crunch Fitness** and **David Barton Gym**, *see p202*).

Club Body Center

2991 Coral Way, at SW 27th Avenue, Coral Gables (305 448 2214/www.clubbodycenter.com). Bus 6, 24, 37. **Open** 24hrs daily. **Rates** $10 3mth membership. **Credit** MC, V.

This 'clothing optional' facility features free poolside buffets, safe-sex shows and an occasional porn star doing what they do best, live and uncensored. There's a gym too, but that's not why anybody's here.

Iron People Gym

715 Lincoln Lane, at Meridian Avenue, South Beach (305 532 0089/www.ironpeople.com). Bus C, G, H, K, L, S, W, South Beach Local. **Admission** $10 day pass; $26.75 3-day pass. **Credit** DC, MC, V. **Map** p273 A1.

Located on Lincoln Lane next to Laundry Bar (*see p180*) and behind Score (*see p181*), this gym is for serious bodybuilders – men are made and muscles are pumped here. See the website for details of classes, services, and even a virtual personal trainer.

Sobe Sports Club

1676 Alton Road, at 17th Street, South Beach (305 531 4743). Bus M, R, S, W. **Open** 5.30am-midnight Mon-Fri; 7am-10pm Sat; 8am-9pm Sun. **Admission** phone for details. **Credit** AmEx, MC, V. **Map** p272 C2.

A modern, popular locals' gym where the atmosphere is friendly but the workouts are serious, with top-of-the-range equipment. Classes include spinning, aerobics and yoga. Day passes are available.

Festivals & events

Miami hosts two of the US's largest events on the gay male circuit – the **White Party** (*see p162*) and **Winter Party Week** (*see p159*).

Aqua Girl Weekend

305 532 1997/www.aquagirl.org. **Date** May.

Every spring thousands of women make south Florida their destination for Aqua Girl Weekend, organised by the not-for-profit Women's Community Fund (WCF), which promotes lesbian, bisexual and transgender rights. The three days of events – which attracted more than 7,000 women in 2006 – include a raucous night of comedy, dance parties, an art exhibition, a wet and wild pool party and a jazz brunch. Great fun.

Martini Tuesdays

www.sobesocialclub.com.

The gay crowd is a notoriously fickle lot, so it's a testament to former bartender Edison Farrow that his Martini Tuesdays, a weekly cocktail party for gay professionals and their friends, is still going strong after years. Every Tuesday a group meets for drinks at a different hotel or restaurant from 9pm until midnight (past venues have included Cafeteria, the Delano and the Hotel Victor). What began as a get-together for Edison and a small group of his friends has grown so big he now has over 6,000 people on his email list, and has turned promoting parties into his full-time job. Following the success of Martini Tuesdays, Farrow has branched out to other events; his current parties are the Simple Life, at Buck 15 Lounge (707 Lincoln Lane, at Meridian Avenue, above Miss Yip Chinese Café, 305 538 3815) every Thursday night, and Euphoria Fridays, at Madiba (1766 Bay Road, at 18th Street, 305 695 1566). There's never a cover charge, and women are welcome to come along with their gay male friends. For further details, visit the website.

Buck 15 Lounge.

Music

At long last, Miami has a sound machine.

Miami's **New World Symphony Orchestra** hits all the right notes. *See p187.*

Whatever time of year you come to Miami, there will always be some music to be enjoyed. It's just a question of finding it. Offerings vary wildly from week to week, so newspaper listings are essential. Just like the city, Miami's music scene is sprawling, spontaneous and fickle. Hectic during the winter season, it's lethargic in summer.

Miami is not a big rock town – unless it's sung in Spanish, that is. But if you're a fan of Latin tunes, you're in for a treat: thanks to the city's huge immigrant population, there is a variety of live music that you'd otherwise have to travel through all of Latin America and the Caribbean to experience.

Locals love a party, and a lot of music can be found at all-day festivals on weekends. These include the **Bob Marley Festival**, the **Argentine Rock Festival** and the **Latin Rock Festival**, as well as frequent celebrations of Latin American independence days, held year-round at Bayfront Park's Amphitheater. Even in the dead of summer, you can dance all day to African, Brazilian and Latin American fusion dance bands at the

Transatlantic Festival, one of a series of hot-weather events held at the 73rd Street Band Shell (73rd Street, at Collins Avenue in Miami Beach).

Concert venues

Miami has a distinct lack of quality concert venues, although the new Performing Arts Center (*see p207*) should help remedy the situation. Most theatres, auditoriums, arenas, open-air amphitheatres and band shells are concentrated in central Miami and Miami Beach.

Tickets can usually be purchased at the venue's box office or website, or – with booking fees attached – from Ticketmaster (305 358 5885, www.ticketmaster.com).

Theatres & auditoriums

Also keep an eye out for the sporadic jazz, gospel and symphonic concerts performances held at the historic **Lyric Theater** (819 NW 2nd Avenue, at NW 8th Street, Overtown, 305 358 1146).

Rayo hope

Enter a new person to the Afro-Cuban-funk-fusion-hip-hop stage: Descemer Bueno, an early member of the now über-hip Yerba Buena group. Bueno's album, Siete Rayo, is making noises worldwide with its mix of reggaeton, cumbia and Bueno's deep Cuban roots. The album – which is also the name of Bueno's backing group – is named after a Yoruban god and means 'seven rays' – although Bueno dropped the 's' off of *rayo*, saying that playing with words is a long Afro-Cuban tradition.

Like many other musicians who grew up on the island, Bueno had classical training, which has helped bring a maturity and sophistication to the still-danceable beats. Bueno plays guitar, bass and sings, while, underneath, flamenco guitar and Chick Corea also have their say. When not touring internationally, Bueno jams around his new home of Miami. He has also found time to write the score for the film *Habana Blues*, which recently picked up a Goya (the Spanish equivalent of an Oscar). If you're lucky you'll get to hear him perform in town, perhaps along with other Cuban stars such as Orishas and Amaury Gutiérrez.

Coral Gables Congregational Church

3010 DeSoto Boulevard, at Catalonia Avenue, Coral Gables (305 448 7421/www.coralgables congregational.org). Douglas Road Metrorail then 72 bus. **Open** *Office* 8.30am-7pm Mon-Fri; from 4.30pm before performance. **Tickets** $20-$30. **Credit** MC, V. **Map** p276 C2.
A serene Mediterranean-style setting for superior jazz and world music concerts, the Congregational Church has a summer concert series that's renowned for its excellent and often unusual programme of international artists at accessible prices. These concerts sell out quickly, so buy in advance. Choral and classical concerts are offered throughout the year.

Gusman Center for the Performing Arts

174 E Flagler Street, at NE 1st Avenue, Downtown (305 374 2444/www.gusmancenter.org). Metromover Miami Avenue. **Open** *Box office* noon-2.30pm, 3-5.30pm Mon-Fri; from 2hrs before performance. **Admission** $10-$100. **Credit** MC, V. **Map** p274 D3.
Sit in one of the Gusman's velvet seats and gaze up at Shakespearean balconies and the twinkling stars that adorn the ceiling's painted night tableau. The Gusman is a fabulous fantasy, built as a silent-movie palace in 1926 during the heyday of Miami's now-decadent Downtown promenade. It makes a wonderfully enchanting venue for the occasional jazz and Latin music concerts held here during the year.

Gusman Concert Hall

University of Miami, 1314 Miller Drive, at San Amaro Drive, Coral Gables (305 284 6477/ www.music.miami.edu/facility/gusman). Bus 52, 56/ Metrorail University. **Open** *Box office* from 1hr before performance. **Admission** free unless otherwise stated. **Credit** AmEx, Disc, MC, V. **Map** p276 F1.
The University of Miami holds its Festival Miami (*see p160*) at this campus theatre in autumn, with international jazz performers and an emphasis on Latin jazz. The university's faculty orchestras and guest artists perform at other times of the year.

Jackie Gleason Theater for the Performing Arts

1700 Washington Avenue, at 17th Street, South Beach (305 673 7300/www.gleasontheater.com). Bus A, C, G, K, L, M, S, W, South Beach Local. **Open** *Box office* 10am-5.30pm Mon-Fri; from noon before performance Sat, Sun. **Admission** $10-$85. **Credit** AmEx, MC, V. **Map** p272 C3.
Comedian Jackie Gleason focused America's eyes on Miami in the 1960s, when he began taping his TV show at the Miami Auditorium, subsequently named after him. Back then Sinatra and his pack could be found in the audience. Today the crowds are as eclectic as the programme. One night it could be Elvis Costello, the next flamenco great Paco de Lucia. The Gleason also offers touring Broadway shows and was still home to the Miami City Ballet as this guide went to press, though the majority of future performances are likely to switch to the new Performing Arts Center (*see p207*).

Lincoln Theater

541 Lincoln Road, at Pennsylvania Avenue, South Beach (305 673 3331). Bus A, C, G, K, L, M, S, W, South Beach Local. **Open** *Box office* 10am-5pm Mon-Fri; from noon until intermission Sat, Sun. **Admission** prices vary. **Credit** AmEx, MC, V. **Map** p273 A2.
A perfect view from every seat, fabulous acoustics and a convenient South Beach location make this one of Miami's most outstanding concert venues. Traditionally home to the New World Symphony (though some performances are likely to move to the new Miami Performing Arts Center), the Lincoln also presents concerts by world music artists, new music ensembles and Latin outfits.

Arenas & amphitheatres

As this guide went to press, the **Miami Arena** (701 Arena Boulevard, at NW 8th Street & 1st Avenue, Downtown, 305 530 4400, www.miamiarena.com), which has recenlty been hosting some well-known rap and R&B acts, was closed for renovations.

AmericanAirlines Arena
601 Biscayne Boulevard, at NE 6th Street,
Downtown (786 777 1000/www.aaarena.com).
Metromover Freedom Tower. **Open** Box office
10am-5pm Mon-Fri; until 30mins after start of
concert performance days. **Admission** prices vary.
Credit AmEx, Disc, MC, V. **Map** p274 C3.
When not occupied by the Miami Heat basketball
team or hosting some mass-hogwash motivational
seminar, this 20,000-seat arena accommodates mega
concerts from mega mainstreamers such as Mariah
Carey and Simon & Garfunkel. Unfortunately, it has
a cold vibe and poor acoustics.

Bayfront Amphitheater
Bayfront Park, 301 N Biscayne Boulevard, at NE
3rd Street, Downtown (305 358 7550/www.bayfront
parkmiami.com). Metromover College/Bayside.
Open times vary. **Credit** AmEx, Disc, MC, V. **Map** p274 D4.
This outdoor venue is surrounded by a hilly lawn,
where food vendors set up stands during frequent
all-day shows. The Bayfront is usually booked at
weekends for Latin, reggae, rap and rock fests.

James L Knight International Center
400 SE 2nd Avenue, at SE 4th Street, Downtown
(305 372 4633/www.jlkc.com). Metromover Knight
Center. **Open** Box office 10am-5.30pm; from noon
before performance. **Admission** prices vary.
Credit AmEx, DC, Disc, MC, V. **Map** p274 E3.
The James L Knight feels suspiciously like a huge
school gym. Big-name Latin artists, from rockers to
crooners, are common fare here, but other musical
species pop up too (Sting being one example). The
programmers occasionally shoot from the hip with
unusual results (Mormon Tabernacle Choir, anyone?).

Classical & opera
As this guide went to press, one of the biggest
cultural centres in the United States was finally
due to be unveiled. The **Miami Performing
Arts Center** will become the new home of the
Concert Association of Florida organisational
body and the Florida Grand Opera, and it will
host some performances by the New World
Symphony and the Miami City Ballet (*see
p206*). It will also serve up Broadway musicals,
modern dance, world music and plain ol' big
rock concerts. For more information, *see p207*.

Florida Grand Opera
(information 305 854 7890/box office 1-800 741
1010/www.fgo.org). **Open** Box office 10am-4pm
Mon-Fri. **Admission** $20-$120. **Credit** AmEx,
Disc, MC, V.
The 60-year-old Florida Grand Opera is a respected,
if not world-renowned, company. It ended its 65th
season with *Carmen*, its final production before
moving from its Coconut Grove home to the new
Miami Performing Arts Center.

New World Symphony Orchestra
Lincoln Theater, 541 Lincoln Road, at Pennsylvania
Avenue, South Beach (305 673 3331/www.nws.org).
Bus A, C, G, K, L, M, R, S, W, South Beach Local.
Open Box office 10am-5pm Mon-Fri; from noon
until intermission Sat, Sun. **Admission** $25-$75.
Credit AmEx, MC, V. **Map** p273 A2.
Conductor Michael Tilson Thomas founded the New
World Symphony in 1988, and it has since been
Miami's cultural pride. Tilson Thomas, whose main
gig is as conductor of the San Francisco Symphony,
makes several appearances a year. Prestigious guest
conductors take the helm at other times. The symphony concerts crackle with energy, and series
devoted to student explorations in new music or
world percussion show a wilder side. Free concerts
are often offered on Mondays and Tuesdays. Some
performances will move to the new performing arts
centre (*see p207*) from autumn 2006. **Photo** *p185*.

Rock, pop, funk & electronica
Miami is frequently dismissed as a wasteland
when it comes to rock. The city has often been
excluded from tour schedules because of its
southerly location, but of late more artists are
making the effort. Some stars even live here –
you might just find yourself standing next
to Lenny Kravitz in the grocery store. Keep
the faith and watch those listings, and you
could end up at a Peaches concert in a Ukranian
dance hall, or watching Cyndi Lauper perform
as part of a cabaret.

If you're around in March, you're likely to
run into one of the world's biggest electronic
music events – and one of the biggest weeks
of partying: the **Winter Music Conference**
(*see p192* **Spin on it**). At various venues
in South Beach, internationally renowned
DJs such as Paul Oakenfold and Paul van
Dyke mind the turntables, while over on the
Downtown side of the city at Bayfront Park (*see
above*), the day-long **Ultra Music Festival**
(www.ultramusicfestival.com) delivers groups
such as the Prodigy and The Killers.

For **Stop Miami** in Wynwood, *see p189*
The start of Stop.

Churchill's Pub
5501 NE 2nd Avenue, at NE 55th Street, Little Haiti
(305 757 1807/www.churchillspub.com). Bus 9, 10.
Open 11am-3am daily. **Admission** $5. **Credit**
AmEx, V.
Often referred to as 'Miami's CBGB', Churchill's is a
beloved hole-in-the-wall venue with music every
night of the week: punk, rock, metal or rap, as long
as it's independent and loud. Local bands also regularly participate in the wonderfully monikered
Bored Shitless Fests. Churchill's is also a great
neighbourhood bar; *see p140*.

Arts & Entertainment

I/O

30 NE 14th Street, at N Miami Avenue, Downtown (305 358 8007/www.iolounge.com). Bus 10, K, M, T. **Open** 10pm-5am Mon-Sat. **Admission** $7-$15. **Credit** AmEx, MC, V. **Map** p274 A2.

From the ever-popular Cuban-funk band the Spam All Stars and touring alt Latin rocker to drum 'n' bass and DJ nights, the music here turns out a large and tightly packed crowd.

SoHo Lounge

175 NE 36th Street, Design District (305 576 1988). Bus 9, 10, J. **Open** 10pm-5am Wed-Sat. **Admission** $5-$10. **Credit** AmEx, MC, V.

Soho Lounge is a multi-level club, with enough separate spaces to have different music playing simultaneously. The Friday Britpop and retro night attracts a young, creatively dressed crowd, while DJs spin old-school hip hop and soul in one room, indie bands posture on the stage upstairs, and electronic beats reign supreme in the lounge. An intelligent alternative to South Beach clubs. *See also p98.*

Studio A

60 NE 11th Street, at N Miami Avenue, Downtown (305 358 7625/www.studioamiami.com). Bus 10, K, M, T. **Open** daily; times vary. **Admission** prices vary. **Credit** AmEx, MC, V. **Map** p274 B2.

Imagine NYC's legendary punk-rock bar CBGB with a chandelier, plush purple couches, dark teak dancefloor, house dancers and cocktails flavoured like cherry liquorice and you've got Studio A, Miami's newest homage to rock 'n' roll, albeit glam rock, featuring headliners such as Elefant, Brazilian Girls and the occasional celeb-fronted band.

Tobacco Road

626 S Miami Avenue, at SW 7th Street, Downtown (305 374 1198/www.tobacco-road.com). Bus 6, 8. **Open** 11.30am-5am daily. **Admission** $3-$5. **Credit** AmEx, DC, MC, V. **Map** p274 F2.

Blues biggies like BB King have performed here, and it's the one bar where Miami really feels – and sounds – like part of the southern United States. Acoustics predominate in the cabaret and on the cosy back patio, where you can hear blues, jazz, rock and folk seven nights a week. *See also p139.*

Jazz & world music

Arturo Sandoval Jazz Club

6701 Collins Avenue, at 67th Street, Miami Beach (305 865 5775/www.arturosandoval.com). Bus H, K, S, T. **Open** phone for details. **Admission** phone for details. **Credit** AmEx, MC, V.

Opened in April 2006 in the spectacular Miami Modern-style Deauville Beach Resort hotel, the club of the Grammy Award-winning Cuban jazz great will change the music landscape of Miami. Scheduled are national artists such as Roberta Flack and Dee Dee Bridgewater, along with local acts including Willie Chorino. And of course, the club will showcase the music of Sandoval himself, who will

be playing in a hotel that once hosted superstars such as the Beatles, Frank Sinatra and Sammy Davis Jr. The club will also open a restaurant in the future. Sets normally start at 8pm and 10.30pm.

Jazid

1342 Washington Avenue, at 13th Street, South Beach (305 673 9372/www.jazid.net). Bus C, H, K, W, South Beach Local. **Open** 9pm-5am daily. **Admission** $10 Fri, Sat. **Credit** AmEx, MC, V. **Map** p273 C2.

Jazid is a small club with a cool vibe. Local musicians perform nightly in a dimly lit setting, playing modern jazz, soul and Latin. Aficionados can get close seated at tables around the stage, or settle for a fine view from a stool at the large bar. The lounge area upstairs has a pool table, but there's no real dancefloor – customers get up and shake it where they please, thank you very much. *See also p193.*

Van Dyke Café

846 Lincoln Road, at Jefferson Avenue, South Beach (305 534 3600/www.thevandyke.com). Bus C, G, H, K, L, M, S, W, South Beach Local. **Open** 8am-2am daily. **Admission** $5 Mon-Thur, Sun; $10 Fri, Sat. **Credit** AmEx, DC, MC, V. **Map** p272 C2.

The Van Dyke Café is Miami's most serious jazz club. Chatter during sets is not viewed kindly, but then the nightly music here usually deserves full attention. The schedule features the best musos in Miami, as well as well-known players from out of town. Although he no longer plays every Thursday, watch for performances from master percussionist Sammy Figueroa, a former member of Miles Davis's band. Sets generally take place at 9pm and 11pm. *See also p111.*

Latin music

The blanket term 'Latin music' is too broad to describe the spectrum of Spanish-language grooves that set the rhythm of daily life in Miami. Most locals, be they Cuban, Argentinian, Venezuelan or Anglo-American, know their *son* from their salsa, and they sing along to their idols' pop hits in *español.*

Cuban music

Bongos Cuban Café

AmericanAirlines Arena, 601 Biscayne Boulevard, at NE 6th Street, Downtown (786 777 2100/www. bongoscubancafe.com). Metromover Freedom Tower. **Open** 5-11pm Wed, Thur; 11.30am-4am Fri-Sun. **Admission** $20 cover. **Credit** AmEx, DC, Disc, MC, V. **Map** p273 C2.

Gloria Estefan and her hubbie Emilio are the brains behind this Cuban club, which has the technicoloured feel of a Disney restaurant. Luckily, the house band that performs on Saturday nights (from 11.30pm onwards) features some of Miami's most sought-after Latin sidemen. Best accompanied with a Mojito or ten.

The start of Stop

Traditionally, some of the best places to hear music in Miami have been restaurants or small bars – no doubt something to do with the intimate setting and late-night eating habits. So when Café 190 shut up shop a couple of years ago, culturally cool Miamians lost a fave spot to run into fellow artists, writers and musicians, drink some good wine and, most of all, pull the tables to the side and dance the night – and early morning – away.

Then **Stop Miami** opened adjacent to the Design District in 2005, and there was much rejoicing. The small wine bar/impromptu jam session space quickly filled a void. It's set in an appropriately cutting-edge neighbourhood (read: still pretty grimy, and the lights from monster condominiums going up across the street give it a *Blade Runner* feel), and the crowd is racially diverse, both young and old.

Bands play on most nights. Expect lots of dreadlocks and improvisation. Sundays are for Mofungo Domingo; on Tuesdays a recently arrived Colombian band brings its style of electronica inside; Wednesdays feature the jazz experimental trio Out of the Anonymous, and Thursdays it's live from Barbados with Fitzroy and Silent Identity and their Caribbean beats. Electro-clash, Britpop, world-fusion maestro DJ Danny Ashe is at the turntables on Friday, when John Speck, with his trombone, and Buffalo Brown, with his guitar, play their excellent Latin-funk-fusion outdoors. These nights aren't set in stone, however, and other acts, such as Jesse Jackson, have been known to stop by and join in too. Come by pretty much any night and you'll catch some live music of some sort.

Away from the music, there's plenty more to admire: the walls are covered with funky local art, and at the small tables tapas and wine are consumed. But sure enough, the moment comes when it's time to push those tables to the side and do what comes naturally.

Stop Miami

3533 NE 2nd Avenue, at Federal Highway, Wynwood (305 576 0900/www.stopmiami. com). Bus 9, 10. **Open** *6pm-1am Tue-Thur; 6pm-2am Fri, Sat.* Winter *also 6pm-midnight Sun.* **Credit** AmEx, MC, V.

Café Nostalgia

3425 Collins Avenue, at 34th Street, Miami Beach (305 531 8838/http://cafenostalgia.com). Bus C, G, H, L, M, S. **Open** *8pm-5am Wed-Sun.* **Admission** $20 cover. **Credit** AmEx, MC, V. **Map** p272 A4.

By Miami standards, Café Nostalgia is an old Cuban classic – aside from the fact that it has moved three times since its founding by Pepe Horta 15 years ago. The original home on Calle Ocho (which is now another Latin club, Hoy Como Ayer; *see p190*) was a nightly tribute to old Havana, with videos and photographs from the island of the 1950s provoking much nostalgia in an already nostalgic community.

Horta transported the theme to glitzier places before winding up in 2005 in a former dive bar. But no matter the location, everyone has always come to dance to the music – *boleros*, *timba*, *son* and salsa – by local and travelling bands. For a Mojito-fuelled taste of Cuba there's no better place this side of the Florida Straits.

Club Tropigala

Fontainebleau Resort, 4441 Collins Avenue, at 44th Street, Miami Beach (305 672 7469/www.club tropigala.com). Bus G, H, L, S. **Open** *Shows* 8.30pm Tue-Thur, Sun; 8pm Fri, Sat. **Admission** $20. **Credit** AmEx, DC, MC, V.

Located in kitsch 1960s palace the Fontainebleau (*see p49*), Club Tropigala pays homage to Havana's Club Tropicana. Like the Tropicana, the Tropigala produces flamboyant floorshows with Cuban music and showgirls in sparkles and, yes, fruity headdresses. The Tropigala also presents concerts by faded singers who were stars in Cuba. Highly recommended are the club's frequent tributes to Beny Moré – the greatest Cuban singer of them all – featuring celebrated Cuban musicians now living in Miami.

Hoy Como Ayer

2212 SW 8th Street, at SW 22nd Avenue, Little Havana (305 541 2631). Bus 8, Little Havana Circulator. **Open** 9pm-4am daily (phone ahead to check). **Admission** $7-$25. **Credit** AmEx, DC, MC, V. **Map** p275 C1.

Pitch dark, and pretty ugly with its wood-panelled walls and cheap tables, this spot is not exactly style-conscious. But it is still the best place for a crash course in Cuban music. Artists perform *boleros* (ballads), *trova* (folk music), *son* (traditional Cuban dance music) and *timba* (an aggressive contemporary dance beat), every night from Wednesday to Sunday. The crowd is a raucous mix of new Cuban arrivals and second-generation Cuban-Americans.

Flamenco

Casa Panza

1620 SW 8th Street, at SW 16th Avenue, Little Havana (305 643 5343). Bus 8, Little Havana Circulator. **Open** 11am-2am Tue-Sat. **Admission** free. **Credit** AmEx, MC, V. **Map** p275 C2.

The Tuesday and Thursday fiestas at this Spanish tavern are legendary. A largely young professional crowd eats, drinks and dances around the tables until the early hours, while a guitarist plays flamenco and sings on a tiny stage, accompanied by two strutting, costumed female dancers. On Friday and Saturday the place is also bursting, but a little less *loco*, with a Spanish classical guitarist on stage.

Latin rock

Also check out **La Covacha** (*see p197*), a club where Latin rock bands play every weekend, and where young, bilingual fans turn out for concerts by South American superstars.

Macarena

1334 Washington Avenue, at 13th Street, South Beach (305 531 3440/www.macarenaweb.com). Bus C, H, K, W, South Beach Local. **Open** 7pm-midnight Mon, Tue; 7pm-3am Wed, Thur; 7pm-5am Fri, Sat. **Admission** $10-$15. **Credit** AmEx, MC, V. **Map** p273 C2.

Casa Panza.

The major Latin music labels based in South Beach often showcase their bands at Macarena. The restaurant-club hosts a popular acoustic songwriters' night on Wednesdays, when Miami-based writers of Spanish-language hits come out of the woodwork and perform their own compositions. *¡Olé!*

Salsa

Club Mystique

7250 NW 11th Street, at NW 72nd Avenue, next to Days Inn Hotel (305 262 9500). Bus 8. **Open** 7am-11pm Mon-Wed; 7am-4am Thur, Fri; 8am-4am Sat; 6pm-4am Sun. **Admission** $10. **Credit** DC, MC, V.

Miami's long-standing salsa palace may have changed venues (it's now out on the south-western edge of the airport), but it's still packed on weekends with serious dancers. You can observe some incredible moves here, and the atmosphere is something like a Latin version of the disco in *Saturday Night Fever*.

Mango's Tropical Café

900 Ocean Drive, at 9th Street, South Beach (305 673 4422/www.mangostropicalcafe.com). Bus C, H, K, W, South Beach Local. **Open** 9am-5am daily. **Admission** $5-$10. **Credit** AmEx, MC, V. **Map** p273 E2.

An infamous pick-up joint, Mango promotes an island-fever atmosphere with sweet cocktails, Jello shots and a house band playing perfunctory salsa, *merengue* and other tropical beats. Decorated with bright tropical murals, the bar opens on to the street with a nice view of the beach. The bar girls make Christina Aguilera look overdressed.

Nightclubs

The fun starts here.

Back Door Bamby at **Crobar**.
See p193.

PARIS

It's hard to have a day life in Miami without a nightlife. Whether you're a typical nine-to-fiver or a club kid who refuses to grow up despite the fact that you just celebrated your 50th birthday (at Mansion, natch), nightlife is to Miami what, say, plastic surgery is to Los Angeles – if you haven't experienced it first-hand yet, you're definitely talking about it. And, of course, a 24-hour liquor licence has made the Biscayne Boulevard area much more attractive to club owners than South Beach. While the latter is still celeb central, for those who don't find pleasure in observing 50 Cent and Paris Hilton suck down champagne, the burgeoning Downtown scene is a hip strip that's yet to be invaded by the bold-faced brigade, and the paparazzi and gossip that follow them.

Wherever you do decide to go, make sure you don't go there early: it's a die-hard no-no to be seen at a club or lounge before at least 11pm.

CLUBS WITH ATTITUDE

South Beach clubs are still sizzling, but some complain that they suffer from a Stepford-like sameness. On the other hand, a handful of

slickly original bar-clubs maintain a distinct sense of individuality and personality and draw a devoted following. The **Setai** (*see p37*), with its $1,000-a-night rooms, champagne and crustacean bar and celebrity clientele, is the haughtiest. Along with the hotel haunts, a number of restaurants moonlight as lounges. These include **Prime 112** (*see p119*), the South Beach version of a steakhouse, where silicone-injected women look to land men with meaty bank accounts; **BED** (*see p114*), in which the couture-clad crowd eats, drinks and strikes its poses lying on large beds; **Social Miami** (*see p109*), where hipsters sip $27 glasses of Lafite Rothschild while sucking on chicken-wing lollipops; **Nobu** (*see p109*), where sushi costs more than what some people make in a hard day's work, though at least it has a sleek lounge area, where it's free to gape;

▶ For **gay and lesbian clubs**, see *pp180-181*; for **Latin clubs** and **clubs with live music**, see *pp187-190*.

Arts & Entertainment

Metro Kitchen & Bar (see p115), whose Tuesday night parties are proof that models do eat; and the venerable **Forge** restaurant (see p121), whose Wednesday night scene evokes *Dynasty* reruns sliced in between clips of *Miami Vice*. Downtown's **District**, meanwhile, may serve less-than-stellar food, but at least it makes up for it with Saturday night's Poplife, an homage to Britpop that attracts the type of kids who worship Hello Kitty, Japanese animé and pretty much anything else that makes them stand apart from the ubiquitous disciples of the Gap Nation.

LICENSING LAWS & COVER CHARGES

You have to be 21 to drink alcohol in Florida. Take a photo ID even if you're very obviously older as clubs can be very paranoid. By law, clubs must stop serving alcohol at 5am, but at some places, if you're already in, you can carry on partying until 8am, when they start selling again. Most establishments stay open until 4am, sometimes 5am, at which time they're so packed you may experience the transitional shock of leaving and seeing daylight. A growing after-hours scene is also developing Downtown: the 24-hour liquor licence means you can party until the morning work commute begins.

Cover charges vary wildly. Women often get in free, while men almost always have to cough up. Quite a few places don't charge any cover, a convenient courtesy that allows you to club-hop while owners make their money jacking up the prices of drinks. In most cases, clubs run guest lists, although, contrary to popular belief, your name need not be P Diddy or Gwyneth to get on one. Many hotel concierges have access to lists, so don't hesitate to ask to be put on one (or more).

DRESS CODES

Individuality is welcomed as far as dress is concerned, but discretion is encouraged when hitting the more exclusive spots: some clubs turn away anyone not decked out in the latest couture. In general, casual dress is discouraged, but going out in a Dior ballgown is also scoffed at (unless you're coming from a black-tie gala). Generally, the freakier you're dressed (think Siouxie Sioux circa 1982), the better your chances. If all else fails, black is the universal safe bet. Shabby chic is also acceptable, though some places don't allow jeans.

DRUGS

Quite simply, drugs are forbidden. Having experienced a series of busts in the late 1980s and early 1990s, many Miami clubs are super-

Spin on it

The aural equivalent of a gathering of world leaders, the **Winter Music Conference** (1-954 563 4444, www.wmcon.com) is the most important event in many a DJ's life. For one week in March, everyone who's ever scratched the surface of vinyl, professionally or otherwise, descends on South Beach for a cacophonous confab that turns all participants into musical zombies whose badges of honour – besides the free CDs, hang tags and assorted promo items – are deep, dark circles under the eyes.

WMC is crucial in the throbbing world of dance: anyone who wants to move into the big league attends in the hope of being discovered. It's all about wheeling, dealing and, of course, spinning (music and PR). Representatives from over 50 countries flock here in the hopes of landing that elusive deal.

Perversely, though, many Miami DJs have fled the glittery Beach shores for bigger and better turntables. Victor Calderone, for instance, was discovered at now-defunct Liquid, where Madonna was so impressed she asked him to remix 'Frozen'. DJ Tracy

Young also wowed the divine Mrs Ritchie when she was spinning around town: not only was she invited to remix 'Music', but she was flown to Scotland to spin at Madonna and Guy's wedding. Neither Young nor Calderone has forgotten their roots, however, and both appear at the WMC.

For those not in the biz – and, to be frank, for most of those who are – the WMC is all about the parties. While many are closed to the general public, others are open to anyone who's willing to cough up in excess of $20 so that they can hear the next – or real – Oakenfold or Sasha. In addition to the spinsters, a virtual who's who of dance divas perform at various venues on South Beach.

And if all this inspires you to quit your day job and give DJing a try yourself, South Beach's **Scratch Academy** (642 6th Street, at Washington Avenue, 305 535 2599, www.scratch.com), a school for aspiring turntablers, is just the thing. For just $300 per 70-minute session, you, too, could be on your way to headlining at Club Space one of these days.

Arts & Entertainment

strict when it comes to narcotics, and have strategically placed narcs and cops waiting to grab the next offender.

That said, the typical drugs of choice among club kids here, as in most places, are ecstasy, cocaine and rohypnol (the so-called 'date rape drug'). Miamians never overtly bought into the heroin-chic thing, although heroin has had something of a clandestine club resurgence. One other thing: never, ever leave your cocktail unattended in the clubs. You'll be risking the possibility of someone slipping a foreign substance into it.

INFORMATION

Clubs here appear and disappear with frequency and are often closed for private parties; if you're going out of your way, call ahead or check the listings in the *Miami New Times*.

South Beach

crobar

1445 Washington Avenue, at Española Way (305 531 8225/www.crobar.com). Bus C, H, K, W, South Beach Local. **Open** 10pm-5am Mon, Thur-Sun. **Admission** $20-$25. **Credit** AmEx, DC, MC, V. **Map** p273 B2.

Storming on to South Beach by way of Chicago, this industrially chic dance club housed in a renovated deco movie theatre serves as a premier venue for superstar DJs. In addition to the impressive aural assets, crobar – which insists on spelling its name with a small 'c' – attracts a mod squad of glamazons, scenesters and serious nightlifers. Every Monday night the club goes kinky for Back Door Bamby, an anything-goes homage to racy raunch. The door policy is brutal, so dress to be noticed and, if possible, get there at the ungodly opening hour. **Photo** *p191*.

The Fifth

1045 5th Street, at Lenox Avenue (305 538 9898/ www.thefifth.com). Bus C, K, M, S, South Beach Local. **Open** 10pm-5am Fri, Sat. **Admission** prices vary. **Credit** AmEx, MC, V. **Map** p272 E2.

South Beach's latest bastion of inequity, the Fifth is an absurdly upscale lounge whose VIP rooms come complete with full-sized, fully stocked stainless-steel fridges and binoculars through which to view the haute-y hoi polloi downstairs. Great music, a sound system whose sonic boom may cause deafness and drinks at upscale prices give the A-listers reason to clamour at the gates and plead the Fifth.

Jazid

1342 Washington Avenue, at 13th Street (305 673 9372/www.jazid.net). Bus C, H, K, W, South Beach Local. **Open** 9pm-5am daily. **Admission** free; $10 after 11pm. **Credit** AmEx, DC, MC, V. **Map** p273 C2.

Smoky and sultry, illuminated by flickering candelabra, Jazid is the kind of place where you might expect to hear Sade's 'Smooth Operator' on constant rotation. While downstairs features live jazz (*see*

Snatch. *See p195.*

p188), sometimes on acid, upstairs there's a DJ spinning the very best soul and funk. A simple formula of good music and no attitude is the reason why Jazid has outlived and outlasted many a South Beach failure. Other club owners, please take note.

Mansion

1235 Washington Avenue, at 12th Street (305 532 1525/www.mansionmiami.com). Bus C, H, K, W, South Beach Local. **Open** 11pm-5am Tue-Sun. **Admission** $20-$25. **Credit** AmEx, DC, MC, V. **Map** p273 C2.

The third member of the extremely popular, nocturnally addictive Opium Group (the others are Opium Garden and its VIP bar, Privé, *see p195*), Mansion is the biggest, though not necessarily the best. Known primarily for its weekly parties hosted by B-and C-list celebrities who are flown down by liquor companies who want them to hawk their booze, Mansion does have a respectable Saturday night scene, as well as occasional live concerts by everyone from Erasure to Velvet Revolver.

NEW TIME OUT
SHORTLIST GUIDES 2007

The MOST up-to-date guides to the world's greatest cities

Mynt Ultra Lounge

*1921 Collins Avenue, at 19th Street (786 276 6132/
www.myntlounge.com). Bus C, G, H, L, M, S.* **Open**
11pm-5am Wed-Sat. **Admission** $20. **Credit** AmEx,
MC, V. **Map** p272 C3.

Ruthless door policies and hipper-than-thou staffers
only serve to make this hauter-than-hot 'in' spot
league leader on the quasi-clonish club scene. Why
this should be, we can't fathom, but maybe it has
something to do with a stellar list of celeb patrons
including Britney Spears, Christina Aguilera, Justin
Timberlake, Vin Diesel and more. Supposing you do
get inside, expect a modish mob scene of crowds at
the bar awaiting their signature Myntinis before
making ludicrous attempts to dance without tipping
their cocktail over neighbouring parties.

Nikki Beach Club

*1 Ocean Drive, at 1st Street (305 538 1111/
www.nikkibeach.com). Bus H, M, W.* **Open** 11pm-
5am Mon, Fri, Sat; 3-11pm Sun. **Admission** $10-
$20. **Credit** AmEx, DC, MC, V. **Map** p272 F3.

The quintessential beach club, this place is an outdoor fantasyland sprawling over a stretch of sand
spotted with tiki bars, lounge chairs and torches. It's
like a hybrid of the Playboy mansion and *Survivor*,
where the fittest (as in toned, firm breasts and butts)
don't just survive, they flourish. Buxom beauties
attract well-oiled, deep-pocketed sugar daddies,
and the studs also get rewarded for their packaging.
On Sundays the party gets started during daylight
hours: thongs and bikinis are de rigueur. It's an eye-
opening reminder of why you came to Miami Beach
in the first place. **Photo** *p197*.

Opium Garden

*136 Collins Avenue, at 1st Street (305 531 5535/
www.opiummiami.com). Bus H, M, W.* **Open** 11pm-
5am Thur-Sat. **Admission** $20. **Credit** AmEx, MC,
V. **Map** p272 F3.

This open-air, multi-chambered bastion of the tragically hip is habit-forming for the see-and-be-seen
set, a weekend haven of sexy house music and scant-
ily clad Barbies and Kens. The VIP area upstairs,
known as Privé, is hot on Friday nights and draws
celebs, models and the local 'in' crowd. Unless you
know someone or can convince the bouncers to part
the velvet ropes, prepare to wait. **Photo** *p196*.

Sky Bar

*Shore Club, 1901 Collins Avenue, at 19th Street
(305 695 3100). Bus C, G, H, L, M, S.* **Open**
7pm-4am daily. **Admission** free. **Credit** AmEx,
DC, MC, V. **Map** p272 C3.

A lofty place where the fabulous set still hangs out
from time to time, Sky Bar is no longer the place to
be, but it's still worth a look. Midnight in this garden is quite the scene, with beautiful people lounging on highly coveted beds lining the pool area, and
tables upstairs in the garden area and the hip hop-
heavy Red Room. Skybar is one of those places that
got too big and too hot for its britches and has sim-
mered down, which, if you ask us, is a good thing.

Snatch

*1437 Washington Avenue, at 14th Street (305 604
3644). Bus C, H, K, W, South Beach Local.* **Open**
11pm-5am Tue-Sat. **Admission** prices vary. **Credit**
AmEx, MC, V. **Map** p273 C2.

Housed in the space formerly known as Liquid, this
misnamed club – the owner claims he named it after
Guy Ritchie's flick, but we reckon it might be something more vulgar – is one of South Beach's hottest
spots. Perhaps it has something to do with the rock
'n' roll-meets-hip hop soundtrack, but we think
Snatch owes its success to the fact that it's the only
place in the city with a bona fide mechanical bull. If
that's too campy for you, go upstairs to its sister
club, Suite, where celebs like to hide out. **Photo** *p193*.

Downtown

Bongos Cuban Café

*AmericanAirlines Arena, 601 Biscayne Boulevard, at
NE 6th Street (786 777 2100/www.bongoscubancafe.
com). Metromover Freedom Tower.* **Open** 11pm-4am
Fri, Sat. **Admission** $10-$20. **Credit** AmEx, MC, V.
Map p274 C3.

Forget the fact that this massive theme restaurant
is owned by Miami's most ubiquitous celeb, Gloria
Estefan. It's a blast after 11pm on weekends, when
hordes of local Latins and salsa nuts demonstrate
the true meaning of *la vida loca* and make like dancing kings and queens until there's not a dry armpit
in the house. For claustrophobes, on the other hand,
Bongos can be hell.

Club Space

*34 NE 11th Street, at NE 1st Avenue (305 350 1956/
www.clubspace.com). Bus 6, 9, 10, K, T/Metromover
11th Street.* **Open** 10pm-10am Fri, Sat. **Admission**
$20. **Credit** AmEx, MC, V. **Map** p274 B2.

The Downtown diva of dance clubs has a penchant
for drama, to say the least. Hardly ecstatic over the
fact that Miami officials are constantly scrutinising
the place for illegal substances, the bigwigs at Club
Space, the venue of choice for superstar DJs like Paul
Oakenfold and Sasha & Digweed, among others,
once closed its doors for a bit, giving club kids the
scare of their lives. Fortunately, it was only a mild
scare, as the club reopened a few days later to the
joy of Miami's dedicated trance-heads and electronica freaks, whose loyalty shows no sign of abating.

Metropolis

*950 NE 2nd Avenue, at NE 9th Street (305 415
000). Bus 6, 9, 10, K, T/Metromover 11th Street.*
Open 10pm-9am Thur-Sat. **Admission** $20.
Credit AmEx, MC, V. **Map** p274 B3.

You haven't seen a mega club until you've got lost
in this, a 55,000sq ft monolith with five clubs within one space. It's convenient, really, because if you
like hip hop, your wife likes house and your mistress
likes world music, everyone will be happy and be
able to steer well clear of each other in their own
section of the club. Not bad if you have the energy
to keep up with it all.

Arts & Entertainment

Doing lines

Opium Garden *See p195.*

The scary truth is that it's probably easier to sneak a box cutter on to a plane than it is to get into some of Miami's hottest bars and clubs. While there are no signs as yet of racial profiling at the velvet ropes, there is evidence of an even more discriminatory selection process going on: if you ain't a famous face or at least a strikingly beautiful one, forget it. Instead, you are consigned to stand in line and patiently watch those more blessed than you waltz by and in. The hope is that perhaps, and only perhaps, after a suitable amount of time has passed, the door nazi might relent and permit you a glimpse of club heaven. Yes, it absolutely sucks, but the velvet rope is now an ingrained part of Miami nightlife. Here are some tips on how to buck the system:

● Have patience. Looking annoyed will just increase your waiting time.

● Don't touch. Tugging and pulling on the velvet ropes or, even worse, on the person guarding the door, is completely taboo. And whatever happens, do not snap your fingers at them. It's very rude.

● Don't lie. If you claim to be a close pal of the club's owner, you'd better be telling the truth. But in any case, real friends of club owners don't use the owner's name at the door for access.

● Dress to impress. The funkier the better, but don't overdo it. Nightlife is rarely a black-tie occasion: just a black one. When in doubt, go with the noir.

● Forget fashionably late. If you have doubts about your chances of getting into a club, arrive early, when the door guards are bored. A good time is usually around 10.30pm or 11pm; in other words, when the clubs first open up.

● Tipping. Some door guards are offended if you shove money in their faces unless you're prepared to part with a few hundred dollars, but trust us: no club is worth paying anyone $100 to get into. If you're planning on returning another night, though, a tip of at least $20 can help ensure you're remembered next time.

● Get guest-listed. Any concierge can help you do this, but you can also call the club yourself and add your name to the guest list, which will almost always guarantee admittance. Most guest lists are open until around 8pm or 9pm.

● Attitude. Just the right amount of attitude goes a long way. Emit an air of confidence, not cockiness, and you'll get noticed.

● Move on. If none of the above is working, get over it, move on to another club and try again elsewhere.

Nocturnal

50 NE 11th Street, at NE 1st Avenue (305 576 6996). Bus 6, 9, 10, K, T/Metromover 11th Street. **Open** 9pm-10am daily. **Admission** $20. **Credit** AmEx, MC, V. **Map** p274 B2.

If Club Space is too hardcore for you and Metropolis is just too big, Nocturnal is the happy medium, with just 20,000sq ft and three floors of techno-house-y-hip hop. Several VIP areas are swell if you want privacy, but you can't escape the music here. Nocturnal is known for its state-of-the-art sound system.

Pawn Shop Lounge

1222 NE 2nd Avenue, at NE 12th Street (305 373 3511/www.thepawnshoplounge.com). Bus 6, 9, 10, K, T/Metromover 11th Street. **Open** 10pm-5am Thur-Sat. **Admission** $20. **Credit** AmEx, MC, V. **Map** p274 B3.

Sanford and Son meets South Beach, sort of, at this tongue-in-cheek-y, cavernous former pawn shop turned hotspot. Enter at your own risk, especially on Saturday nights, when the place is filled to the brim with hipsters, and choose your spot – shall you sip your cocktails from inside the big yellow school bus or would you prefer to down your beer in the Airstream trailer-cum-VIP room? We love the jetliner fuselage, which has loads of leg room. On Friday nights the ultra-popular Revolver brings the indie kids, while Sunday's My Twisted Sister attracts the gay crowds. Saturdays are the motley-est, and when it comes to Pawn Shop, the motley-er the better.

Coconut Grove

Oxygen Lounge

Streets of Mayfair, 2911 Grand Avenue, at Virginia Street (305 476 0202/www.oxygenlounge.biz). Bus 6, 22, 27, 42, 48, Coconut Grove Circulator. **Open** 8pm-5am daily. **Admission** $5-$10. **Credit** AmEx, DC, MC, V. **Map** p277 B3.

This sprawling underground club/lounge/sushi joint is located beneath the Streets of Mayfair shopping centre. Strange bedfellows, indeed. At any rate, Oxygen is one of the only South Beach-esque spots in the entire frat-ridden Grove – as a result, it remains a breath of fresh air for those looking for a trad dance club without having to schlep over to the sandbar.

The Design District

The District

35 NE 40th Street, at N Miami Avenue (305 576 7242/www.thedistrictmiami.com). Bus 2, 36, J. **Open** 11.30am-4.30pm, 6-11pm Tue, Wed; 6pm-4am Thur-Sat. **Credit** AmEx, MC, V.

Although it's a restaurant, nobody in their right mind would eat at the District, but they will party here thanks to the fact that the owners are the founders of Saturday night's über-popular, long-running Poplife parties. Friday nights are pretty good too, especially if you're a member of the cultish indie-music community, which seems to have made the District its home away from home. *See also p98.*

South Miami & beyond

La Covacha

10730 NW 25th Street, at NW 107th Avenue (305 594 3717). No public transport. **Open** 11.30am-8pm Mon-Wed; 11.30am-midnight Thur; 11.30am-4am Fri-Sun. **Admission** $5 after 9pm Fri-Sun. **No credit cards.**

While La Covacha, located way out west near the Miami International Mall, is still one of the city's best Latin clubs, it's gone trendy and introduced a Thursday sushi and disco night that's about as un-Latin as it gets. For a less cheesy experience, try Noche Internacional on Fridays, with DJs spinning salsa, merengue and Spanish pop.

Nikki Beach Club. *See p195.*

Sport & Fitness

How else do the beautiful people stay so slim?

Blessed with beautiful weather 365 days a year, Miami is an all-round sporting destination. From competitive sunbathing to more rigorous activities like fishing, kayaking, in-line skating and boating, there is so much to do on land and on the water. Working out is a way of life here, and gyms are more social than nightclubs. But if treadmills don't turn you on, there are many sports to watch live or while downing a few beers on Ocean Drive.

Spectator sports

There are four pro sports teams in south Florida: the Dolphins (American football), Heat (basketball), Panthers (hockey) and Marlins (baseball). The Dolphins play from September to December, the Heat play November-May, the Panthers October-May and the Marlins April-October. The Panthers have struggled in recent years in the NHL, while the Heat are one of the NBA's top teams. The Dolphins are on their way back to respectability, and the Marlins – the city's last professional team to win a championship, in 2003 – remain competitive.

TICKETS AND INFORMATION
Tickets can be purchased at venue box offices or through Ticketmaster (305 358 5885 or visit www.ticketmaster.com). If you want killer seats or a game is sold out, there are plenty of ticket brokers happy to mainline your bank account; the most reputable is Todd's Tickets (305 692 8633, www.toddstickets.com).

Baseball

For years the **Florida Marlins** have been battling to get their own stadium. Until that happens, the World Series champs share the field with the footballing Dolphins at the Dolphins Stadium. Diehard fans travel to Jupiter each March for the spring training sessions.

Miami also boasts two top-level college baseball teams, the **FIU Golden Panthers** and the four-time national champs **University of Miami Hurricanes**.

FIU Golden Panthers
University Park Stadium, Florida International University, 11200 SW 8th Street, at SW 112th Avenue (305 348 4263/www.fiu.edu). Bus 8, 11. **Open** *Box office 9am-5pm Mon-Fri.* **Season** *Jan-Apr.* **Tickets** *$3-$5.* **Credit** *AmEx, MC, V.*

Florida Marlins
Dolphins Stadium, 2269 NE 199th Street, at NW 27th Avenue, North Dade (tickets 305 623 6100/information 305 626 7400/www.floridamarlins.com). Bus 27, 83. **Open** *Box office 8.30am-5.30pm Mon-Fri.* **Season** *Apr-Oct.* **Tickets** *$4-$38.* **Credit** *AmEx, MC, V.*

University of Miami Hurricanes
Mark Light Stadium, University of Miami, 6201 San Amaro Drive, at Mataro Avenue, Coral Gables (305 284 2263/www.hurricanesports.com). Bus 48, 56/Metrorail University. **Open** *Box office 9am-4pm Mon-Fri.* **Season** *Feb-May.* **Tickets** *$6-$8.* **Credit** *AmEx, MC, V.*

Basketball

The Miami Heat are sizzling right now, with players like Shaquille O'Neal and Dwayne Wade taking the team closer to the play-offs than ever before. As Downtown Miami is revitalised, basketball games are a place to see celebrities sitting courtside enjoying the amenities of the AmericanAirlines Arena. FIU's Golden Panthers and UM's Hurricanes are the city's college teams.

FIU Golden Panthers

Golden Panther Arena, SW 8th Street & 107th Avenue, Sweetwater (305 348 4263/www.fiu.edu). Bus 8, 11. **Open** *Box office* 8.30am-5pm Mon-Fri. **Season** Nov-Feb. **Tickets** $3-$5. **Credit** AmEx, MC, V.

Miami Heat

AmericanAirlines Arena, 601 Biscayne Boulevard, at NE 6th Street, Downtown (786 777 1000/ www.nba.com/heat). Metromover Freedom Tower. **Open** *Box office* 10am-5pm Mon-Fri. **Season** Nov-May. **Tickets** $10-$475. **Credit** AmEx, Disc, MC, V. **Map** p274 C3.

University of Miami Hurricanes

Convocation Center, 1245 Walsh Avenue, at George E Merrick Drive, Coral Gables (305 284 2263/ www.hurricanesports.com). **Open** *Box office* 9am-5pm Mon-Fri. **Season** Nov-Mar. **Tickets** $15-$30. **Credit** AmEx, MC, V.

Football (gridiron)

For decades football was the only sport in town, and the Miami Dolphins and Miami Hurricanes kept their fans enthralled with Super Bowl wins and National Title games. Recently, though, the Dolphins have been just good enough to raise everyone's hopes, but not quite good enough to return to the Super Bowl. The Hurricanes, on the other hand, have maintained their dominance and won 2004's Orange Bowl.

Miami Dolphins

Dolphins Stadium, 2269 NW 199th Street, at NW 27th Avenue, North Dade (1-800 462 2637/305 284 2263/www.miamidolphins.com). Bus 27, 83. **Open** *Box office* 8.30am-5.30pm Mon-Fri. **Season** Sept-Dec. **Tickets** $20-$54. **Credit** AmEx, MC, V.

University of Miami Hurricanes

Orange Bowl, 1501 NW 3rd Street, at NW 14th Avenue, Little Havana (305 643 7100/www.hurricane sports.com). Bus 7, 12, 17. **Open** *Box office* 9am-5pm Mon-Fri. **Season** Sept-Dec. **Tickets** $35-$50. **Credit** AmEx, MC, V. **Map** p275 B2.

Greyhound racing

Greyhound racing has been popular in south Florida since the '30s. Although it has lost some of its lustre, gambling enthusiasts still flock to the tracks, especially since they also offer year-round poker and simulcasts of pari-mutuels.

Flagler Dog Track

401 NW 38th Court, at NW 7th Street, nr Miami International Airport (305 649 3000/www.flagler dogs.com). **Season** early June-late Nov. **Races** 8.05pm Mon, Wed, Fri, Sun; 12.30pm, 8.05pm Tue, Thur, Sat. **Admission** free.

Hollywood Greyhound Track

831 N Federal Highway (US 1), at Pembroke Road, Hallandale (954 454 9400/www.hollywood greyhound.com). Bus Broward County Transit 1, board at Aventura Mall. **Season** Dec-May. **Races** 7.05pm Mon, Wed, Fri, Sun; 12.05pm, 7.05pm Tue, Thur, Sat. **Admission** $1-$2. **No credit cards.**

Horseracing

Horseracing in south Florida suffered a serious blow when racing stopped at **Hialeah Park** in 2001 (*see p103*). Nevertheless, the sport lives on, and both remaining facilities offer simulcasts of races from around the country.

Calder Race Course

21001 NW 27th Avenue, at NW 215th Street, North Dade (305 625 1311/www.calderracecourse.com). Bus 27, 91. **Open** from 11am daily. **Season** Apr-Dec. **Admission** $2-$5. **No credit cards.**

Gulfstream Park

901 S Federal Highway (US 1), between Hallandale Beach Boulevard & Ives Dairy Road, Hallandale Beach (954 454 7000/www.gulfstreampark.com). Bus 3. **Season** Jan-Apr. **Admission** $5-$10. **No credit cards.**

Ice hockey

The Florida Panthers are skating on thin ice with hockey fans. The team wowed the nation by making it to the Stanley Cup Finals in 1996 but ever since they have been plagued by coaching disasters and inconsistencies.

Florida Panthers

Bank Atlantic Center, 1 Panther Parkway, at Sunrise Boulevard, Sunrise (954 835 7000/www.florida panthers.com). Bus phone Broward County Transit 954 357 8400. **Open** *Box office* 10am-6pm Mon-Fri. **Season** Oct-May. **Tickets** $20-$250. **Credit** AmEx, DC, Disc, MC, V.

Jai-alai

It's known as the fastest game on earth, and for good reason. Jai-alai (pronounced 'high-aligh') was, for many years, the unofficial official game of Miami. Hailing from the Basque Country, the game has to be seen to be believed. It's played within a court with high walls,

Arts & Entertainment

similar to a large squash court, and the object is to hurl a ball, called a *pelota*, against the wall with so much speed and spin that the opposition cannot catch or return it, either on the fly or on its first bounce. It moves blindingly fast.

Dania Jai Alai

301 E Dania Beach Boulevard (A1A), at US 1, Dania Beach (954 920 1511/www.dania-jai-alai.com). Bus Broward County Transit 1, board at Aventura Mall. **Games** noon, 7pm Tue, Sat; 7pm Wed-Fri; 1pm Sun. **Admission** $1.50-$7. **No credit cards.**

Miami Jai Alai

3500 NW 37th Avenue, at NW 34th Street, nr Miami International Airport (305 633 6400/ www.fla-gaming.com/miami). Bus 36, J. **Games** noon, 7pm Mon, Fri, Sat; noon Wed, Thur; 1pm Sun. **Admission** $1. **No credit cards.**

Motor sport

If speed turns you on, then make a date with the fastest drivers in the country – just make sure to bring your earplugs too.

Hialeah Speedway

3300 W Okeechobee Road, Hialeah (305 821 6644/ www.hialeahspeedway.com). Bus 29. **Admission** $10; $3 concessions. **Credit** AmEx, MC, V.

Homestead Miami Speedway

1 Speedway Boulevard, Homestead (305 230 7223/ www.homesteadmiamispeedway.com). **Admission** $25-$200. **Credit** AmEx, MC, Disc, V.
Hosts the Toyota Indy 300 in March and the NASCAR Nextel Ford 400 and Miami 300 in November.

Active sports & fitness

To really enjoy Miami like a local, you're going to have to shake that hangover and start working up a sweat.

Bowling

Technically, it's not really exercise, but those bowling balls are heavy.

Bird Bowl

9275 Bird Road (SW 40th Street), at SW 92nd Avenue, South Miami (305 221 1221). Bus 40. **Open** 8.30am-midnight Mon-Thur, Sun; 8.30am-3am Fri, Sat. **Rates** $2.50 per person per game before 6pm; $3.50 after 6pm. *Shoe rental* $2. **Credit** MC, V.

Don Carter's Kendall Lanes

13600 N Kendall Drive (SW 88th Street), at SW 137th Avenue, Kendall (305 385 6160). Bus 88. **Open** 9am-3am daily. **Rates** $3.95 per person per game. *Shoe rental* $2.75. **Credit** AmEx, Disc, MC, V.

Lucky Strike

1691 Michigan Avenue, at Lincoln Road, Miami Beach (305 532 0307/www.bowlluckystrike.com). Bus C, H, K, W, South Beach Local. **Open** 11am-2am daily. **Rates** $4.95-$7.95 per person per game. *Shoe rental* $3.95. **Credit** AmEx, MC, V. **Map** p272 C2.

Cycling

Biking is to south Florida what walking is to Manhattan: it's just how you get around. There is no better way to enjoy some of the city's most scenic areas. For spectacular ocean views and a bit of uphill biking, try the **Rickenbacker Causeway**, an elevated bridge that links Virginia Key and Key Biscayne to the mainland. For shady comfort, **Coconut Grove** and **Coral Gables** offer some of the leafiest roads. Just make sure you have an excellent lock, as bikes have a way of disappearing in Miami. For bicycle rentals, *see p248.*

Fishing

Despite all evidence to the contrary, south Florida's pristine Atlantic waters are not merely a gigantic swimming pool designed by nature. As anyone who has ever been stung by a jellyfish will tell you, the waves are also home to abundant sealife. At-one-with-nature line casting is available all around, with Florida Bay, Biscayne Bay, the Intracoastal Waterway, the Gulf Stream and the Everglades all providing plenty of options.

The waters of south Florida are home to everything from freshwater bream to sailfish and sharks. For sport fishing, try a local charter service: it'll take you to a fish-rich spot where you can drift or anchor off a reef and see what's biting. **Mark the Shark** offers half-day and full-day deep-sea fishing trips for groups of up to ten; fishing for sailfish and marlin is done from the boat **Therapy IV** at Haulover Marina; **Reel Time Charter** specialises in sailfish, wahoo and dolphin; and **L&H** offers sailfishing and dolphin fishing (that's dolphin the fish, not the mammal).

Charter boats are pricey, but there is always the option of party boats. These 60- to 90-footers carry up to 100 people and provide tackle, bait and instruction. The downside is that they often tend to be crowded with boozed-up families from the Midwest. If that's fine with you, the **Kelley Fleet** has two 65-footers and an 85-footer, and the **Reward** fleet has the 70-foot *Reward* and the 60-foot *Reward Won*.

If money is really tight, join the locals in fishing from the many bridges that connect the islands of Miami Beach to the mainland.

Beach bodies

There are countless activities you can do at the beach that will provide you with health benefits, and they won't seem like exercise at all – well, most of them, anyway.

If you want something low key, grab a paddleball set or frisbee at any store up and down South Beach, join a game of soccer or round up a team for volleyball (8th-9th Street Volleyball Courts in Lummus Park).

Or perhaps you live for the thrill of riding a wave, or have always wanted to learn how. Hiring an instructor is the perfect way to get up on that board (we recommend Florida Surf Lessons, 561 625 5375, http://www.florida surflessons.com).

Kick it up a couple of notches with South Beach Bootcamp, where personal trainer Lisa Gaylord puts you through a rigorous training programme. The classes take place at 6.15pm on Mondays, Wednesdays and Fridays at the playground at 13th Street and Ocean Drive (305 531 4314, www.lisagaylord.com, $15).

If that seems too intense, a sunset yoga class will put you on cloud nine. Synergy Yoga provides sunrise and sunset classes on South Beach at 7am and 5pm daily (305 538 7073, $5 donation; *photo below*).

Although, remember, you are here on holiday, so building a sand castle may be the only kind of workout you want.

You don't need a saltwater fishing licence if you fish from a charter boat, but you do if you are renting your own boat. Neither do you need a saltwater licence if fishing from land or a structure tied to land. Freshwater and saltwater licences for non-residents cost $6.50 for three days, $16.50 for seven days and $31.50 for a year. To buy a fishing licence, call 1-888 486 8356 or visit www.floridaconservation.org. Tackle shops, such as **Crook & Crook**, also sell them.

Crook & Crook

2795 SW 27th Avenue, at US 1, Coconut Grove (305 854 0005/www.crookandcrook.com). Bus 27. **Open** 7am-8pm Mon-Fri; 6am-8pm Sat; 6am-3pm Sun. **Credit** AmEx, DC, Disc, MC, V.

Kelley Fleet

Haulover Marina, 10800 Collins Avenue, at 108th Street, Bal Harbour (305 945 3801/www.miamibeach fishing.com). Bus H, K, S, T. **Rates** $29 per half day; $43 per day. **Credit** AmEx, Disc, MC, V.

L&H

Crandon Marina, 4000 Crandon Boulevard, Key Biscayne (305 361 9318/www.landhsportfishing.com). Bus B. **Rates** $550 per half day; $800 per day. **Credit** AmEx.

Mark the Shark

Biscayne Bay Marriott Marina, 1633 N Bayshore Drive, at Venetian Causeway, Downtown (305 759 5297/www.marktheshark.com). Bus 48. **Rates** $650 per half day; $1,050 per day. **Credit** AmEx, DC, MC, V.

Arts & Entertainment

Reel Time Charter

2560 S Bayshore Drive, at Aviation Avenue, Coconut Grove (305 856 5605/www.fishmiami.com). Bus 48. **Rates** $500 per half day; $750 per day. **Credit** AmEx, DC, MC, V. **Map** p277 A4.

Reward/Reward Won

Dock A, Miami Beach Marina, 300 Alton Road, at 3rd Street, South Beach (305 372 9470/www.fishingmiami.com). Bus H, M, W. **Trip times** 9am-1pm, 1.45-5pm, 8pm-12.30am daily. **Rates** $35 per half day. **Credit** AmEx, MC, V. **Map** p272 E2.

Therapy IV

Haulover Marina, 10800 Collins Avenue, at 108th Street, Bal Harbour (305 945 1578/www.therapy4.com). Bus H, K, S, T. **Trip times** 8am-noon, 1-5pm daily. **Rates** $500 per half day; $800 per day; or $85 per person. **Credit** AmEx, DC, MC, V.

Golf

Not only is golf a serious sport in these parts, it's also a great networking tool and a pleasant way to unwind.

Biltmore Golf Course

1210 Anastasia Avenue, at Granada Boulevard, Coral Gables (305 445 8066/www.biltmorehotel.com). Bus 52, 72. **Open** 7am-6.30pm daily. **Rates** $37-$46. **Credit** AmEx, MC, V. **Map** p276 D2.
Located at the magnificent Biltmore Hotel (*see p53 and p85* **Gimme Biltmore**), this historic 18-hole course was built in 1925.

Crandon Golf Course

6700 Crandon Boulevard, Key Biscayne (305 361 9129). Bus B. **Open** 7am-6.30pm daily. **Rates** $149.65; $28 after 4pm. **Credit** AmEx, MC, V.
Crandon Golf Course features the world's largest tee, seven saltwater lakes and many holes overlooking Biscayne Bay.

Doral Golf Resort

4400 NW 87th Avenue, at NW 41st Street, Doral (305 592 2000/www.doralgolf.com/golf). Bus 36, 87. **Open** 6am-6.30pm daily. **Rates** $95-$195. **Credit** AmEx, DC, Disc, MC, V.
One of the top courses in south Florida, the Doral is home to the PGA Ford Championship, held in March. For civilians, it's nearly impossible to get a tee time, so book way in advance.

Gyms

In Miami, people are obsessed with looking good and seem to spend every spare minute at the gym. To blend in, you're going to have to make a bit of an effort. For gyms that cater largely to a gay clientele, *see p184*.

Crunch Fitness

1259 Washington Avenue, at 12th Street, South Beach (305 674 8222/www.crunch.com). Bus C, H, K, W, South Beach Local. **Open** 6am-midnight Mon-Fri; 8am-9pm Sat; 9am-8pm Sun. **Rates** *Day membership* $21. **Credit** AmEx, DC, Disc, MC, V. **Map** p273 C2.
Crunch attracts the best-looking men and women in town. Not only is it currently *the* sweat-soaked Beach hotspot – and particularly popular with the gay crowd, though not exclusively so – but the classes are cutting edge too.

David Barton Gym

Delano, 1685 Collins Avenue, at 16th Street, South Beach (305 674 5757/www.davidbartongym.com). Bus C, G, H, L, M, S, South Beach Local. **Open** 6am-midnight Mon-Fri; 8am-9pm Sat, Sun. **Rates** *Day membership* $25; $20 Delano guests. **Credit** AmEx, DC, Disc, MC, V.
Located in the hyper-trendy Delano Hotel, the David Barton Gym is for people who want to be seen. So, throw on your most stylish workout ensemble and try to glow rather than sweat.

Fitness Company

200 S Biscayne Boulevard, at SE 3rd Street, Downtown (305 358 9988). Bus 3, 16, 48, C, S. **Open** 6am-10pm Mon-Thur; 6am-9pm Fri; 8.30am-4.30pm Sat. **Rates** *Day membership* $20. **Credit** AmEx, DC, Disc, MC, V.
This is the place to go if you are looking to meet a banker, lawyer or business executive. The gym also includes two racquetball courts, a basketball court, sauna and whirlpools.

Gold's Gym

1400 Alton Road, at 14th Street, South Beach (305 538 4653/www.goldsgym.com). Bus M, S, R, W, South Beach Local. **Open** 6am-11pm Mon-Fri; 8am-10pm Sat; 9am-9pm Sun. **Rates** *Day membership* $20. **Credit** AmEx, DC, Disc, MC, V.
A no-frills chain but with state-of-the-art machines. Classes range from Boot Camp and Awesome Abs to belly dancing and Pilates Plus.

In-line skating

The in-line fervour has died down some, but it's still a preferred mode of transport, particularly along Ocean Drive and on Lincoln Road, where most stores, bars and restaurants are so used to skaters that they don't even ask them to remove their wheels before they enter. For skate rentals, *see p248*.

Pool & billiards

Pool purists disdain the lone table in the back of a bar. Instead, they prefer to patronise true pool halls like **Felt Billiards** (1242 Washington Avenue, South Beach, 305 531 2114), **Jillian's Billiard Club** (12070 SW 88th Street, Kendall, 305 595 0070) and **New Wave Billiards** (1403 SW 107th Avenue, Kendall, 305 220 4790). Tables cost about $8 to $13 an hour, depending on the time of day.

Swimming & water sports

Everything in south Florida revolves around
Biscayne Bay or the ocean – from swimming
and sailing to scuba diving and kayaking. You
can pick a relaxing day at sea or spend your
holiday getting a great watery workout.

CANOEING, KAYAKING AND ROWING

For rentals, accessories and guided expeditions
(you must provide your own group; ask about
minimum requirements), try **Urban Trails
Kayak Rentals** (3400 NE 163rd Street, North
Miami, 305 947 0302). Its guided expeditions
of the Everglades and Oleta River Park are
excellent. For rowing, try the **Miami Beach
Rowing Club** (6500 Indian Creek Drive, Miami
Beach, 305 861 8876), which meets regularly
and offers sculling (two oars per person) and
sweeping (one oar each) classes.

SAILING

The joys of sailing are too numerous to
describe, so you'll just have to rent a sailboat
and find out for yourself.

Sailboats of Key Biscayne

*Crandon Marina, 4000 Crandon Boulevard, Key
Biscayne (305 361 0328). Bus B.* **Open** 10am-6pm
daily. **Rates** *Boat rental* $35 per hr; $110 per half
day; $170 per day. **Credit** MC, V.

SCUBA DIVING

Some of south Florida's best treasures are
underwater, from shipwrecks to sunken
museums, which is why so many people – locals
and tourists alike – are diving into the Atlantic
Ocean. Be warned, however: the rules are strict,
and if you're a beginner, you'll be required to
take lessons and get certified. Happily, most dive
shops offer lessons as well as equipment rental.
By far the most amazing dives in the region are
down in Key Largo at the **John Pennekamp
Coral Reef State Park** (*see p228*).

Austin's Diving Center

*10525 S Dixie Highway (US 1), at SW 105th
Terrace, Kendall (305 665 0636/www.austins.com).
Bus 104.* **Open** 9am-7pm Mon-Sat. **Rates** prices
vary. **Credit** AmEx, DC, Disc, MC, V.

Divers Den

*12614 N Kendall Drive (SW 88th Street), at SW
126th Avenue, Kendall (305 595 2010). Bus 88.*
Open 10am-8pm Mon-Fri; 9am-6pm Sat. **Rates**
prices vary. **Credit** AmEx, Disc, MC, V.

Divers Paradise

*Crandon Marina, 4000 Crandon Boulevard, Key
Biscayne (305 361 3483/www.keydivers.com). Bus
B.* **Open** 10am-5pm Mon-Fri; 8am-5pm Sat, Sun.
Rates $375-$450 for certification classes. **Credit**
AmEx, DC, Disc, MC, V.

SWIMMING

For information on beaches and swimming in
the Atlantic, *see p70* **Life's a beach...** If your
hotel doesn't have a pool, it's worth the trek to
the **Venetian Pool** (*see p84*). For other public
pools, contact the Miami-Dade Park and
Recreation Department on 305 755 7800 or go to
www.miamidade.gov/parks/swimming.htm.

WAVE RUNNERS

The fastest way to get around on the water is
on the back of a wave runner, the loudest and
most fun aquatic toy on the market. They can
be dangerous, though, especially with all of the
boat traffic in Miami. Always wear your life
jacket and ask the rental agency for safety tips,
like how to get back on if you've fallen off.
(It's not as easy as it looks.)

Fantasy Water Sports

*100 Sunny Isles Boulevard, at 163rd Street, Sunny
Isles (305 940 2628/www.fantasywatersports.com).
Bus E, H, V.* **Open** 10am-5pm Mon-Fri; 9am-5pm
Sat, Sun. **Rates** $85 per hr. **Credit** AmEx, Disc,
MC, V.
This facility rents wave runners only for use on the
Intracoastal Waterway. Riders must be at least 21
years old and possess a major credit card.

Key Biscayne Boat Rentals

*3301 Rickenbacker Causeway, Virginia Key (305 361
7368). Bus B.* **Open** 9am-5pm Tue-Sun. **Rates** $45
per half hr; $80 per hr. **Credit** AmEx, Disc, MC, V.

Tennis & racquetball

Miami is home to one of the tennis world's
biggest non-Grand Slam tournaments, the
NASDAQ-100 Open (*see p159*). Tennis is big
with the locals, so there are some wonderful
private and public courts. For information
about public courts, call the Miami-Dade Park
and Recreation Department at 305 755 7800 or
go to www.miamidade.gov/parks/tennis.htm.

Crandon Park Tennis Center

*7300 Crandon Boulevard, Key Biscayne (305 365
2300). Bus B.* **Open** 8am-10pm daily. **Rates** $3-$5
per person per hr. **No credit cards.**
Seventeen Laykold hard courts, four European red
clay, four American green clay courts and two grass
courts. Six of the hard courts are lit for night play.

Salvadore Park Tennis Center

*1120 Andalusia Avenue, at Columbus Boulevard,
Coral Gables (305 460 5333). Bus 24.* **Open** 7am-
9pm Mon-Fri; 7am-8pm Sat, Sun. **Rates** $4.50-$6
per person per hr. **No credit cards. Map** p276 C2.

Tropical Park Tennis Center

*7900 SW 40th Street, at SW 79th Avenue, South
Miami (305 223 8710). Bus 40.* **Open** 9am-8pm
daily. **Rates** $2-$2.50 per person per hr. **No credit
cards.**

Theatre & Dance

Miami's theatre scene is no longer a tragicomedy.

Fort Lauderdale's **Broward Center of Performing Arts**. *See p205.*

Long gone are the days when the only productions and drama in Miami were either political or pathetic, third-rate nursing home productions of *Annie* and *Cats*. Miami theatre audiences have grown over the past few years, and every season seems to top the last. The new **Miami Performing Arts Center** (*see p207*) – the third-largest performing arts centre in the country – will be the icing on the cake, placing the city firmly on the culture map. Assuming it opens, that is: numerous delays have beset the multi-million-dollar project, but as this guide went to press all the signs were that it would open as scheduled in early October 2006.

This new behemoth aside, every season brings a new crop of blockbusters, often straight from Broadway runs, such as *Movin' Out, Hairspray* and *Mamma Mia!* Add to this the many local productions and national tours and you have a scene that's looking pretty healthy these days.

Information & tickets

For performance information, call the venues or dance companies directly or pick up a copy of the weekly *New Times* (complete listings are also online at www.miaminewtimes.com). The Weekend section of the *Miami Herald*'s Friday edition is also a useful guide. For dance news check out the bi-monthly *Florida Dance Calendar*, published by the Florida Dance Association (305 867 7111). Tickets for major companies and venues can be bought from Ticketmaster (305 358 5885). Discount theatre tickets to some shows can be purchased from Ticket Madness (1 800 249 2787) or by visiting www.culturalconnection.org.

Theatre

Major venues

Actors' Playhouse
280 Miracle Mile (SW 24th Street), at Ponce de León Boulevard, Coral Gables (305 444 9293/www.actors playhouse.org). Bus 24, 72, Coral Gables Circulator. **Open** *Box office* 10am-6pm Mon-Sat. *Performances* 8pm Wed-Sat; 2pm Sat. **Tickets** $30-$35. **Credit** AmEx, MC, V. **Map** p276 C4.
A prime location on Miracle Mile makes this a great locale for theatre-goers who can enjoy a meal and shopping before the show. This non-profit theatre presents a full season of theatrical productions for adults, a children's theatre series, extensive educational programming and a wide array of community services.

Broward Center of Performing Arts

201 SW 5th Avenue, Fort Lauderdale (954 462 0222/www.browardcenter.org). **Open** *Box office* 10am-5pm Mon-Fri; noon-5pm Sat, Sun. **Credit** AmEx, MC, V.

This $52 million theatrical complex consists of the 2,700-seat Au-Rene Theater and the intimate 590-seat Amaturo Theater, which offers a wide range of performances from Broadway musical to serious drama, modern dance or ballet, classical music and award-winning pop concerts, comedy and a delightful season of children's theatre. OK, Fort Lauderdale is a bit of a trek from Miami for a show, but it's well worth it, and the centre is situated in the middle of the city's Riverwalk Arts & Entertainment District (*see p217*), with restaurants and cafés for pre- or post-theatre refreshment. **Photo** *p204.*

Coconut Grove Playhouse

3500 Main Highway, at Charles Avenue, Coconut Grove (305 442 4000/www.cgplayhouse.com). Bus 6, 52, Coconut Grove Circulator. **Open** *Box office* 10am-5pm Mon, Sun; 10am-8pm Tue-Sat. *Performances* 8pm Tue-Fri; 2pm, 8pm Sat. **Tickets** $25-$45. **Credit** AmEx, MC, V. **Map** p277 B2.

Coconut Grove Playhouse celebrates its 50th year of delighting audiences with quality regional theatre, often with stars like Theodore Bikel, Dixie Carter, Hal Holbrook and Lucie Arnaz, and cementing its reputation as Broadway by the Bay.

Smaller venues

GableStage

Biltmore Hotel, 1200 Anastasia Avenue, at Granada Boulevard, Coral Gables (305 445 1119/www.gable stage.org). Bus 52, 56, 72. **Open** *Box office* noon-5pm Mon-Sat; also 1hr before performance. *Performances* 8pm Tue-Sat; 2pm Sun. **Tickets** $7-$40. **Credit** AmEx, MC, V. **Map** p276 D2.

Offering an eclectic season of contemporary drama and comedy, with the occasional classic sprinkled in, GableStage productions are hand-picked by artistic director Joe Adler, who travels regularly to London and New York in search of the latest hits. This house is by far Miami's most reliable in turning out shows with solid production values and excellent acting. Rumour has it that GableStage was in search of new digs, but it looks like it'll remain at the Biltmore for the next few years at least.

New Theatre

4120 Laguna Street, at SW 40th Street, Coral Gables (305 443 5909/www.new-theatre.org). Bus 40, 42, J/Metrorail Douglas Road. **Open** *Box office* 2-8pm Wed-Sat; noon-2pm Sun. *Performances* 8pm Wed-Sat; 2pm Sun. **Tickets** $25-$30. **Credit** AmEx, MC, V. **Map** p276 D4.

While the quality of theatre is sometimes uneven, the mission is clear: a careful blend of modern classics and new, occasionally controversial, pieces by up-and-coming playwrights. In 2003 New Theatre put Miami on the map when it produced the world debut of Cuban-born, Miami-bred playwright Nilo Cruz's *Anna in the Tropics*, which received a Pulitzer Prize in 2003.

Other companies & series

For the **Jackie Gleason Theater for the Performing Arts**, *see p186.*

City Theatre

Office: Suite 229, 444 Brickell Avenue (305 365 5400/www.citytheatre.com). **Open** *Box office* 11am-5pm Mon-Fri; noon-3pm Sat, Sun. *Performances* times vary. **Tickets** $20-$25. **Credit** AmEx, MC, V.

From an edgy short by Neil LaBute to a poignant piece by Shell Silverstein, City Theatre's Summer Shorts is an annual marathon of one-act plays. The festival selects from hundreds of national submissions, and also showcases the finest local talent. The festival takes place in June at the University of Miami's Jerry Herman Ring Theatre at 1312 Miller Drive in Coral Gables (305 284 3355).

Cultura del Lobo

Miami-Dade Community College, Wolfson Campus, 300 NE 2nd Avenue, at NE 3rd Street, Downtown (305 237 3010/www.culture.mdc.edu). Metromover College/Bayside. **Open** *Office* Oct-June 9am-5pm Mon-Fri. Closed July-Sept. *Performances* times vary. **Tickets** free-$26. **No credit cards. Map** p274 D3.

Founded in 1990 by Miami-Dade College, this series brings some of the most innovative contemporary dance, music and performance to Miami. In one season, it's not unusual to see masters such as Indian vocalist Lakshmi Shankar and rising stars like world music diva Lila Downs.

M Ensemble Theater Company

12320 W Dixie Highway, at NE 123rd Street, North Miami (305 895 8955). Bus 9, 10, 75, G. **Open** *Box office* 4-10pm Thur-Sat; 2-6pm Sun. *Performances* 8pm Thur-Sat; 3pm Sun. **Tickets** $10-$20. **Credit** AmEx, MC, V.

M Ensemble's primary goal is to revive classics by African-American playwrights, such as August Wilson's *The Piano Lesson*, and to venerate black icons, as seen in Bill Harris's *Robert Johnson: Trick the Devil*, a tribute to the legendary bluesman. Founded in 1971, this is Florida's oldest-established black theatre company and the only one in Miami-Dade County with a regular season.

Miami Light Project

3000 Biscayne Boulevard, at NE 30th Street, Wynwood (305 576 4350/www.miamilightproject. com). Bus 3, 16, T. **Open** *Office* 10am-5pm Mon-Fri. **Tickets** $12-$28. **Credit** AmEx, MC, V.

MLP is known for bringing both avant-garde and stalwart performers to Miami. Past visitors have included Laurie Anderson, Los Muñequitos de Matanzas and Danny Hoch. Annual favourites are the gay/lesbian comedy series (June-July) and the Here & Now Festival (March) showcasing cutting-edge works-in-progress by local performers.

PS 742

1165 SW 6th Street, at SW 12th Avenue, Little Havana (305 324 0585/www.ps742.org). Bus 6, 11, 17. **Open** *times vary.* **Tickets** *prices vary.* **No credit cards. Map** p275 C3.

PS 742 is an alternative, shopfront black box theatre located in the heart of Little Havana. It's one of the best places to see diverse, cutting-edge performance in an intimate setting. It's located in the 6th Street arts complex, which also includes artist studios and the 6th Street Dance Studio.

Hispanic theatre

Updated weekly, www.teatroenmiami.com is an outstandingly comprehensive website dedicated to Spanish-language theatre. The website's creator, Cuban-born composer and writer Ernesto García, culls articles (mostly in Spanish, though some are in English) from Miami, New York, Latin America and Europe and posts them on the website, along with original articles and interviews. If there's something interesting going on in Miami's Hispanic theatre scene (and there usually is), you'll find it on this website.

International Hispanic Theater Festival

Teatro Avante, 235 Alcazar Avenue, at Ponce de León Boulevard, Coral Gables (305 445 8877/ 305 446 7144/www.teatroavante.com). Bus 42, 52, Coral Gables Circulator. **Open** *9am-9pm Mon-Fri; 2-8.30pm Sat, Sun.* **Tickets** $16-$25. **Credit** AmEx. **Map** p276 B4.

Held during the first two weeks of June, this is the largest Hispanic theatre festival in the US and one of the most important Hispanic theatre events in the world. Classical, contemporary and experimental works are performed in Spanish, Portuguese and English by companies from across the globe. The main venue/base is Teatro Avante, but shows take place all over town, as do lectures and workshops.

Dance

Miami offers audiences a vast variety of dance, from ballet to flamenco and from jazz to modern, representing a broad range of styles and cultures. The city has an impressive grouping of home-grown dance companies, including the **Miami City Ballet**, **Ballet Gamonet Maximum Dance** and the **Momentum Dance Company**. Many local companies have dedicated studio space, and all of them hold performances elsewhere in rented venues, as well as at the **Colony Theatre** and the **New World School of the Arts Theater**. Plenty of touring companies also make an appearance in town, so you may well catch something good while you're here.

Venues

Colony Theatre

1040 Lincoln Road, at Lenox Avenue, South Beach (305 674 1040). Bus C, G, H, K, L, M, S, W, South Beach Local. **Open** *Box office noon-5pm Tue-Sat & 1hr before performances. Office 10am-5pm Tue-Sat. Performances times vary.* **Tickets** *prices vary.* **No credit cards. Map** p272 C2.

New World School of the Arts Theater

25 NE 2nd Street, at N Miami Avenue, Downtown (305 237 7020/3541). Metrorail Government Center. **Open** *Box office 10am-4pm; reservations only. Performances times vary.* **Tickets** $1-$10. **No credit cards. Map** p274 D2.

Ballet

Ballet Gamonet Maximum Dance

Gusman Center for the Performing Arts, 174 E Flagler Street, at NE 1st Avenue, Downtown (305 259 9775/www.maximumcompany.com). **Open** *Box office 9am-5pm Mon-Fri. Performances times vary.* **Tickets** *prices vary.* **Credit** AmEx, MC, V. **Map** p274 D3.

Maximum Dance Company was founded in 1997 and quickly brought south Florida audiences the best in contemporary ballet from around the world. In 2005 the company merged with Ballet Gamonet, but the intention remains the same, and you can expect a programme of international choreographers and award-winning performances. In addition, Ballet Gamonet Maximum Dance's community programmes reach over 10,000 children annually, and the company provides neighbourhood performances throughout Miami-Dade County. **Photo** *p209.*

Miami City Ballet

2200 Liberty Avenue, at 22nd Street, South Beach (305 929 7000/www.miamicityballet.org). Bus C, G, H, L, M, S. **Open** *Box office 10am-5pm Mon-Fri. Performances times vary.* **Tickets** $18-$60. **Credit** AmEx, MC, V. **Map** p272 C3.

MCB is one of the largest classical ballet companies in the United States, with 40 dancers and a $10 million annual budget. Former New York City Ballet principal Edward Villella founded the company more than two decades ago, in 1985; in more recent times he has moved beyond Balanchine classics to show off his own choreographic skills, with excellent results. In future, some productions are likely to take place at the city's brand-new Performing Arts Center (*see p207*).

Modern

Black Door Dance Ensemble

Information: 305 380 6233.

Combining classical ballet with jazz, blues, R&B and traditional African music, this company usually takes on one full production a year. Cast members

Miami Performing Arts Center

After much anticipation Miami will soon have one of the largest performing arts centres in the country. Designed by world-renowned architect Cesar Pelli, the Miami Performing Arts Center (MPAC; *photos below*) may be 20 months late and more than $100 million over budget, but it seems like the wait will be worth it. The huge complex, slap bang in Downtown, will include three state-of-the-art theatres, an education centre, an expansive outdoor plaza and even an art deco tower.

The opening of MPAC is set to shake up the city's art scene dramatically, with various long-standing companies moving here from their traditional homes. The 2,400-seat Sanford and Dolores Ziff Ballet Opera House and the 2,200-seat Carnival Concert Hall will stage productions by local favourites such as the Florida Grand Opera (*see p187*), Miami City Ballet (*see p206*) and New World Symphony (*see p187*). But there's much, much more – the programme will also feature a wide array of national, and international performances, from Broadway musicals and visiting classical artists to world and urban music. The more intimate 200-seat Studio Theater will stage cutting-edge and experimental performances by up-and-coming organisations. The Peacock Education Center, meanwhile, will hold acting and dancing courses for the public. Finally, the huge central Plaza for the Arts, will be a dramatic setting for outdoor entertainment

and informal gatherings. The complex also includes a restored octagonal art deco tower, the remains of the first art deco building in Miami-Dade County, dating from 1929.

Amazingly, while close to $450 million was spent on the centre itself, no funds were allotted for parking until July 2005, when plans were announced to allocate 2,500 valet and self-park spaces in the area around the centre.

Despite the fact that the MPAC went over schedule, all the signs were that the Grand Opening Weekend would take place as scheduled (5-8 October 2006), with four days of performances and free entertainment. The première season promises some interesting productions, among them *Alice* by Whoopi Goldberg, Yin Mei Dance from China, Bobby McFerrin, Burt Bacharach and Lily Tomlin. The 2007/08 Broadway Across America season features some stunners too, including *Dirty Rotten Scoundrels*, *Wicked* and *Twelve Angry Men*. In addition, the world-renowned Cleveland Orchestra will perform for three weeks a year in the Carnival Concert Hall.

Miami Performing Arts Center

1300 Biscayne Boulevard, between 13th & 14th Streets, Downtown (information 305 372 7611/box office 305 949 6722/ www.miamipac.org). Bus 3, 16, 32, 36, 48, 62, 95, A, C, K, M, S, T. **Open** *Box office phone for details.* **Map** p274 A3.

are recruited from Miami's Haitian, Caribbean and Cuban populations, with soloists from the Dance Theatre of Harlem.

Giovanni Luquini & Dancers

Information: 305 604 9765.
Luquini is a Brazilian who skilfully incorporates DJs, video images and even skateboarding into his choreography, along with elements of Afro-Brazilian culture and religion. Luquini maintains a core company of dancers who have been integral to the troupe's evolving aesthetic.

Karen Peterson & Dancers Inc

Information: 305 378 6626/www.karenpeterson dancers.org.
South Florida's only self-proclaimed 'mixed-ability' dance company, this unique troupe features a mix of able-bodied dancers and dancers in wheelchairs. It also has its own black box performance space.

Miami Contemporary Dance Co

Information: 305 365 7900/www.miamicontemporary dance.org.
This company emerged on the modern dance scene in 2000 and has been producing provocative work ever since. Artistic director Ray Sullivan integrates

Colony Theatre. *See p206.*

traditional forms such as tango into his modern choreography. He often veers towards the political, as seen in the recent exploration of human rights, *If You Were in My Shoes, What Color Would They Be?* Well worth a look.

Momentum Dance Company

Information: 305 858 7002/www.momentum dance.com.
Momentum performs works by local choreographers, as well as by pioneers such as Isadora Duncan. This is also one of the few dance companies in town offering extensive programming for children; each show is followed by a workshop.

World dance

Duende Ballet Español

Office: Suite 1402, 12209 SW 14th Lane (305 225 4275/www.duendeballet.org).
This company has only been around for a few years, but is already building a solid reputation in the dance community. Artistic director Rosa Mercedes also runs flamenco classes, at the Conchita Espinosa Academy, 12975 SW 6th Street, for various levels of ability (phone for details).

Flamenco Theatre La Rosa

13126 West Dixie Highway, at NE 131st Street, North Miami (305 899 7729/www.larosaflamenco theatre.com). **Open** 10am-7.30pm Mon-Thur. **Tickets** $8-$20. **No credit cards.**
This is one of Miami's oldest flamenco dance companies. Founded by Ilisa Rosal, it has earned a reputation for melding flamenco with other music and dance styles such as Middle Eastern, Indian and tap. Rosal and company also offer daily classes in dance, music and theatre.

Ifé-Ilé Afro-Cuban Music & Dance Ensemble

Office: Suite 13, 4545 NW 7th Street (305 476 0388/www.ife-ile.org). **Open** 9am-9pm Mon-Fri; 11am-3pm Sat. **Tickets** prices vary. **Credit** AmEx, MC, V.
The Ifé-Ilé troupe is best known for its dances of the Yoruba, Congo and Bantu forms. It also performs modern dance and popular Latin moves such as rumba, salsa and mambo. Founder Neri Torres danced with the National Ballet of Cuba, before defecting in 1991.

Sosyete Koukouy

Libreri Mapou, 5919 NE 2nd Avenue, at NE 59th Street, Little Haiti (305 757 9922). Bus 9, 10. **Open** 10.30am-7pm Mon-Sat; 11am-5pm Sun. **Tickets** prices vary. **No credit cards.**
This dance and drama company, founded in Miami by Haitian arts advocate and bookstore-owner Jan Mapou (*see p99*) in 1985, is exotic from top to bottom. Its name is Haitian for 'Firefly Society', and it regularly performs traditional Haitian dances, combined with live music and original plays.

Dance series & festivals

Baila USA Annual Dance & Cultural Arts Festival
Information: 305 476 0388/www.bailausa.com.
Date Feb.
Dance, drumming and performance workshops on Afro-Cuban, Brazilian and African-American dance forms. Five years old, the festival is gaining a reputation for its combination of engaging lectures and dynamic performances.

Caribbean Dance Celebration
Information: 305 757 9922. **Date** Apr.
This annual celebration is a tumble of performances and workshops by African, Caribbean, Haitian and African-American groups. At the time of publication, CDC was still in the early stages of planning; call for information.

Florida Dance Festival
Information: 305 867 7111/www.fldance.org.
Date late June-early July.
A quarter century old and by far the most important contemporary dance festival in Miami. Spanning two weeks, it offers extensive workshops, master classes and, of course, plentiful performances by a roster of international artists.

Dance classes

Miamians don't have much time to look down on bad dancers – they're too busy looking for admiring glances. Still, there can be no harm in brushing up on a few tidy moves, with the aid of a professional.

The Best of Dance
6255 SW 8th Street, at 62nd Avenue, Little Havana (305 266 1897/www.bestofdance.com).
Bus 8. **Open** 1-10pm daily. **Rates** $10 per group class. **No credit cards**.
Advanced and beginner classes, with belly dancing, flamenco, salsa and ballroom, as well as Argentinian tango, hustle and swing.

Kendall Dance Studio
8838 SW 129th Street, off SW 87th Avenue, Kendall (305 233 8700/www.kendalldance.com).
No public transport. **Open** 9am-9pm Mon-Sat.
Rates prices vary. **No credit cards**.
Advanced and beginner classes for every type of dancing imaginable, including ballroom, formation, foxtrot, jitterbug, waltz, bolero and salsa.

Lorraine Florido Dance Academy
15507 Bullrun Road, off N Main Street, Miami Lakes (305 824 9465/www.weteachdance.com).
Bus E. **Open** 5.30-7.30pm Mon-Fri; 10.30am-1.30pm Sat. **Rates** prices vary. **No credit cards**.
Advanced and beginner classes, including hip hop, jazz, ballet, tap and modern.

Ballet Gamonet Maximum Dance. *See p206.*

Miami Beach Dance Festival
Byron Carlye Theatre, 500 71st Street, at SW 5th Street, Miami Beach (305 867 4194/www.momentumdance.com). **Date** Mar & Apr.
Dance performances, events and classes. The Byron Carlyle is the main venue, but others are involved too. For information and tickets, call 305 858 7002.

Mid-Eastern Dance Exchange
350 Lincoln Road, at Washington Avenue, South Beach (305 538 1608/www.emerald-dreams.com).
Bus C, G, H, K, L, M, S, W, South Beach Local.
Open 11am-9.30pm Mon-Sat. **Rates** $12 per class.
Credit AmEx, MC, V. **Map** p273 A2.
All levels of belly dancing. Dancers are available for both instruction and performances.

OUR CLIMATE NEEDS
A HELPING HAND TODAY

Be a smart traveller. Help to offset your carbon emissions
from your trip by pledging Carbon Trees with Trees for Cities.

All the Carbon Trees that you donate through Trees for Cities
are genuinely planted as additional trees in our projects.

Trees for Cities is an independent charity working with local
communities on tree planting projects.

www.treesforcities.org   Tel 020 7587 1320

Trees for Cities
Charity registration number 1032154

Trips Out of Town

Features

Maps

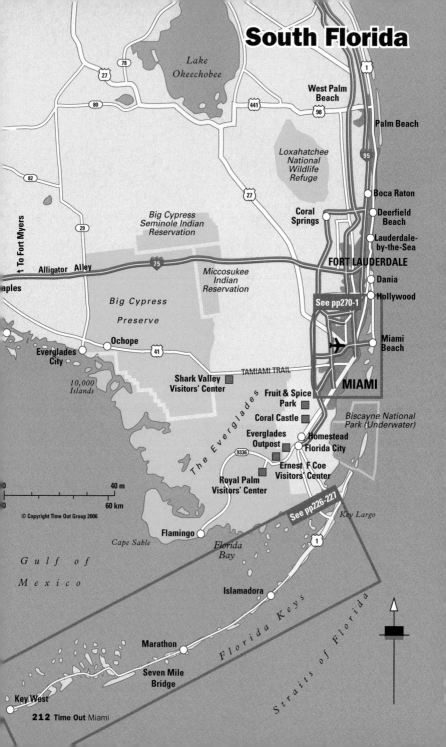

South Florida

Lake Okeechobee

West Palm Beach

Palm Beach

Loxahatchee National Wildlife Refuge

Boca Raton

Coral Springs

Deerfield Beach

Lauderdale-by-the-Sea

Big Cypress Seminole Indian Reservation

FORT LAUDERDALE

Dania

Alligator Alley

Miccosukee Indian Reservation

See pp270-1

Hollywood

aples

Big Cypress Preserve

Miami Beach

Everglades City

Ochope

MIAMI

10,000 Islands

TAMIAMI TRAIL

Shark Valley Visitors' Center

Fruit & Spice Park

Coral Castle

Biscayne National Park (Underwater)

The Everglades

Everglades Outpost

Homestead

Florida City

Ernest F Coe Visitors' Center

40 m

© Copyright Time Out Group 2006

60 km

Royal Palm Visitors' Center

See pp226-227

Key Largo

Flamingo

Cape Sable

Florida Bay

Gulf of Mexico

Islamadora

Florida Keys

Marathon

Straits of Florida

Seven Mile Bridge

Key West

Getting Started

Tripping out of town – no acid required.

The trips you make out of Miami may well turn out to be the highlight of your visit. For the locals, heading out of town on a regular basis is the only way to keep sane. While the Gold Coast resorts to the north, including Fort Lauderdale and Palm Beach, offer more of the same – but with less of an ethnic element and far greater wealth – somewhere like the Everglades is simply unlike anywhere else on earth (except possibly subtropical Queensland in Australia). You can visit for half a day or lodge in the national park and spend days hiking, kayaking or boating.

Likewise, driving down through the Florida Keys is a unique and awesome (in the true, non-dude-speak sense of the word) experience. To motor over Seven Mile Bridge with nothing in sight except a thin sliver of silvery road bisecting a vast and alarmingly infinite canvas of blue is nothing short of trippy. But remember to keep your eyes on the road!

Beyond the trips described in this chapter, there are several other worthwhile destinations outside the scope of this book but still visitable from Miami. Chief among these are the sleepy towns and resorts of the **Gulf Coast**. Just a further half-hour's drive beyond Everglades City (*see p223*), **Naples** is the west coast version of Palm Beach, a ritzy resort of trendy boutiques and gourmet restaurants with 41 miles of public beach. It's a far cry from the razzle and dazzle of Miami, but if you're looking for powdery sand and to be in bed by 10pm, when most bars are closed, this is the place for you. A short drive north is **Fort Myers** and neighbouring **Fort Myers Beach** on Estero Island, which is like a downmarket version of Miami/Miami Beach. We recommend keeping the foot on the gas and pushing on to the nearby island of **Sanibel** and its northern extension, **Captiva**. Sparsely populated but with miles of compacted seashell beaches, they are that rarity – beauty spots in which carefully controlled human intervention has permitted wildlife to flourish. To reach the islands from Miami is about a three-hour drive along US 75. Accommodation is plentiful, and there's a tourist information office right at the entrance to Sanibel to help with bookings.

TIMING YOUR TRIP
As temperatures in Florida soar, the cost of a holiday plunges. From late April and early May, when the weather is usually gorgeous,

hotel, car rental and other prices dip. As summer progresses, vacation deals become vacation steals. Of course, you do have to consider your tolerance for steamy humid weather, as well as your enthusiasm for hurricanes, as the annual hurricane season runs from June to the end of November.

Information

Tourist information

Check local papers. One of the best sources can be found in the Sunday *Miami Herald*, which features an impressive and useful travel section.

Visit Florida

US: Suite 300, 661 E Jefferson Street, Tallahassee, FL 32301 (1-850 488 5607/1-888 735 2872/ www.flausa.com).
UK: 0870 770 1177/www.visitflorida.com/UK.
A useful holiday pack containing a vacation guide, maps and other information that can be downloaded from these websites or mailed by calling the above numbers. Both websites also contain information on restaurants, accommodation, activities and more.

Camping & outdoors

Florida Association of RV Parks & Campgrounds (FARVC)
1340 Vickers Drive, Tallahassee, FL 32303 (1-850 562 7151/www.floridacamping.com). **Open** 8.30am-5pm Mon-Fri.
Call or write for a *Florida Camping Directory*.

Florida Department of Environmental Protection

Division of Recreation & Parks, MS 535, 3900 Commonwealth Boulevard, Tallahassee, FL 32399 (1-850 245 2118/www.dep.state.fl.us). **Open** 8am-5pm Mon-Fri.

Contact the Department to request a free copy of the comprehensive *Guide to Florida State Parks*.

Transport

Further transport information is given in individual Trips Out of Town chapters.

Air

It's easiest to book any internal US flights through an agent in your home country, or as part of your international ticket. However, this is not always the cheapest way. Do your research by calling around local travel agents. Reduced-rate return fares are usually cheapest on weekdays, and often require seven-day advance booking and a Saturday stopover. Flights from Fort Lauderdale are often cheaper than those from Miami.

Airlines running regular flights from Miami to various points in Florida include **American Eagle** (American Airlines' regional affiliate; 1-800 433 7300, www.aa.com), **Continental** (1-800 525 0280, www.continental.com), **Delta** (1-800 221 1212, www.delta.com), **United** (1-800 241 6522, www.united.com) and **US Airways** (1-800 428 4322, www.usairways.com).

Bus

Greyhound

1-800 229 9424/www.greyhound.com. 4111 NW 27th Street, at 41st Avenue, nr Miami International Airport (305 871 1810). Bus 7, 37, 42, J. **Open** *Ticketing office* 24hrs daily. **Credit** AmEx, Disc, MC, V.

The national long-distance bus service. Travel is cheaper Monday to Thursday, and buying a return ticket at the time of departure will save 5-15%.

Car

For driving tips and car rental companies, *see pp247-248*. The best Florida maps for drivers are from the Triple A or Rand McNally, and the official Florida Transportation Map. For the Keys, we recommend UniversalMAP.

American Automobile Association (AAA/Triple A)

1-800 596 2228/www.aaa.com. **Open** 24hrs daily. *Florida Division: 1000 AAA Drive, Member Services Department 68, Heathrow, FL 32746 (407 444 4240).* **Open** 8.30am-5.30pm Mon-Fri.

South Miami office: 6101 Sunset Drive (SW 72nd Street), at SW 61st Avenue, Miami 33143 (661 6131/fax 669 3614). Bus 37, 48, 72/Metrorail South Miami. **Open** 8.30am-5.30pm Mon-Fri.

The Triple A is the US road emergency and information company. It provides excellent – and free – maps, guidebooks, specific travel routes (TripTiks) and towing services to its members and to members of affiliated organisations (such as the British AA). You can fax specific requests to 1-800 350 7437: include your membership number, a daytime telephone number and date of departure.

Rail

Amtrak

1-800 872 7245/www.amtrak.com. Station: 8303 NW 37th Avenue, at NW 79th Street, nr Hialeah (305 835 1221). Bus 32, 42, L/Metrorail Tri-Rail.

Long-distance train service. You can travel from New York to points on the east coast of Florida, including Miami. The connecting bus service (available only to rail passengers) provides a service to Orlando, Tampa, Key West, West Palm Beach and other points. Its bus service between Orlando and Fort Myers can be accessed by any traveller. If you travel by Amtrak, it's worth planning ahead, since return tickets are cheaper than two one-ways.

Tri-Rail

1-800 874 7245/www.tri-rail.com.

A commuter rail line that runs the 70-plus miles between Miami and Fort Lauderdale and the Palm Beaches. It links with Miami's rapid transit system Metrorail and various Miami bus routes (for further details of city public transport, *see p246*). Fares vary by zones. Flat-fare, all-day tickets offering unlimited travel are available on weekends for $4 (adults) or $2 (concessions).

Sea

The **Port of Miami** (305 371 7678) is one of the busiest passenger and freight ports in the world, with millions of cruise-ship passengers passing through each year. As this guide went to press, there was talk of expanding the existing 12 passenger terminals with up to four more, all to be located on the Downtown waterfront.

You can book cruises to points as geographically and culturally diverse as the east and west coasts of Mexico, Puerto Rico, France, Haiti, St Thomas, Jamaica, Key West, Colombia, the Panama Canal and most of the Caribbean island paradises. Try **Carnival Cruise Lines** (1-800 327 9501), **Discovery Cruise Line** (1-800 937 4477), **Norwegian Cruise Line** (305 327 7030) or **Royal Caribbean Cruise Lines** (1-800 255 4373).

Fort Lauderdale & Palm Beach

Home of the real Florida – but get here soon before it changes.

It's tough being a lifeguard at the **International Swimming Hall of Fame**. *See p217.*

Although they are all part of what's called the Gold Coast – the stretch of sandy-fringed real estate running north of Miami – places like Palm Beach, Boca Raton and Delray Beach nonetheless retain a certain individuality. The further north you travel, the less urban clutter there is, the more pristine the beaches, the more neatly trimmed the lawns and the more sedate the pace. Of course, the population is also more homogeneous (which is to say, white) – and less interesting for it – made up in large part by communities of spring-stepped retirees.

For anyone in search of 'old Florida', then, this is the place – for now. Affordable, decidedly un-chic 1950s beachfront hotels still exist in places like Delray Beach and Hollywood, along the old Dixie Highway, serving up top-notch service and a relaxing atmosphere, although probably not for long. A spate of real-estate development has resulted in some of these kitschy mom-and-pop spots

selling out for the big money. Palm Beach, a world of its own, remains the ideal place for a luxurious escape. Fort Lauderdale has become the favoured destination for travellers in search of groomed beaches, well-manicured golfing greens and plushly carpeted high-end shops.

Hallandale, Hollywood & Dania

Skip **Hallandale**, which is full of condos for retirees, unless, that is, you want to play the horses at **Gulfstream Park**, south Florida's recently renovated top thoroughbred horse track (*see p199*). The park markets itself as a family attraction, with activities for the kids and weekend concerts by name performers. If you prefer old-fashioned pari-mutuels, **Hollywood Greyhound Track** (*see p199*) has dog racing from December through to May.

Hollywood's main draw is **Hollywood Beach**, which has been undergoing a renaissance of sorts, making it a quirky, if low-key, destination. Long popular with French Canadian snowbirds (winter residents), its downtown has quietly developed into a lively area of boutiques, cafés and even clubs. Regular events such as Hollywood Nights, held on two Fridays a month, and Saturday antiques and collectible markets on Harrison Street, keep things buzzing – or at least try to.

Despite efforts to attract trendier crowds with festivals and special events, the beachfront **Broadwalk**, a two-mile promenade for pedestrians and cyclists, retains a slightly seedy old-time charm. Small family-owned hotels are easy to find.

Not far from the urban hubbub is the **Anne Kolb Nature Center** (*see below*), a 1,500-acre mangrove estuary and habitat for wading birds that you can explore on foot or by boat, kayak or canoe.

Quiet **Dania Beach's** claim to fame is its antiques shops, lining several blocks on US 1, and Dania Beach Boulevard. There's also the dubious appeal of jai-alai, reputedly the fastest game in the world. Games are held at **Dania Jai-Alai** (*see p200*). The city's beaches are clean and accessible, with a long fishing pier where you can rent gear and buy bait.

Dania's newer attractions are just off I-95, between the Stirling and Griffin Road exits. On the west side is the International Game Fish Association's **International Fishing Hall of Fame & Museum** (*see below*), a massive facility housing galleries, virtual reality fishing and an outdoor marina. Next door is **Bass Pro Shops Outdoor World** (*see below*), a superstore for outdoorsy types with a huge aquarium and, surely most impressive of all, three full aisles of worms.

Across the interstate is **Boomers** (*see below*), with go-karts, video games, mini-golf and the **Dania Beach Hurricane**, one of the world's tallest wooden rollercoasters.

Anne Kolb Nature Center

West Lake Park, 751 Sheridan Street, Hollywood (954 926 2480/www.broward.org/parks). **Open** May-Sept 8am-7.30pm daily. Oct-Apr 8am-6pm daily. **Admission** $1; free under-5s. **No credit cards.**

Bass Pro Shops Outdoor World

220 Gulf Stream Way, Dania Beach (954 929 7710/ www.outdoorworld.com). **Open** 9am-10pm Mon-Sat; 10am-7pm Sun. **Credit** AmEx, Disc, MC, V.

Boomers

1801 NW 1st Street, Dania Beach (954 921 1411/ www.boomersparks.com). **Open** 10am-2am Mon-Thur, Sun; 10am-4am Fri, Sat. **Rides** *Dania Beach Hurricane* $6; other rides vary. **Credit** MC, V.

International Fishing Hall of Fame & Museum

300 Gulf Stream Way, Dania Beach (954 922 4212/ www.igfa.org). **Open** 10am-6pm daily. **Admission** $4.99; $3.99 concessions; free under-4s. **Credit** MC, V.

Where to eat

For table dancing, plus good Greek food, head for **Taverna Opa** (twin to the restaurant on South Beach, *see p114*), which is on the Intracoastal Waterway. The laid-back **Le Tub**, also on the water, is popular with locals for decent seafood, burgers, gumbo and chilli at equally good prices. The **Rustic Inn Crabhouse** is renowned for garlic crabs served on newspaper-covered tables (and whacking the crustaceans with mallets is great fun for kids), while **Jaxson's Ice Cream Parlor** is quintessential Americana, serving up gaudy ice-cream concoctions, plus hot dogs, burgers and steaks.

Jaxson's Ice Cream Parlor

128 S Federal Highway, Dania (954 923 4445/ www.jaxsonsicecream.com). **Open** 11.30am-11pm Mon-Thur, Sun; 11.30am-midnight Fri, Sat. **Main courses** $8-$11. **Credit** AmEx, Disc, MC, V.

Rustic Inn Crabhouse

4331 Ravenswood Road (Anglers Avenue), Dania Beach (954 584 1637). **Open** 11.30am-10.45pm Mon-Sat; 2-9.45pm Sun. **Main courses** $16-$33. **Credit** AmEx, Disc, MC, V.

Taverna Opa

410 N Ocean Drive, at Hollywood Boulevard, Hollywood Beach (954 929 4010). **Open** 4pm-2am Mon-Thur, Sun; 4pm-3am Fri, Sat. **Main courses** $7-$19. **Credit** AmEx, Disc, MC, V.

Le Tub

1100 N Ocean Drive, Hollywood Beach (954 921 9425). **Open** 11am-4am daily. **Main courses** $7-$25. **No credit cards.**

Where to stay

Greenbriar Beach Club

1900 S Surf Road, Hollywood (954 922 2606/ www.greenbriarbc.com). **Rates** $89-$209. **Credit** AmEx, Disc, MC, V.
An oceanfront, all-suites hotel with a good swimming pool and lovely gardens.

Westin Diplomat Hotel

3555 S Ocean Drive, Hollywood (954 602 6000/ www.diplomatresort.com). **Rates** $189-$400. **Credit** AmEx, Disc, MC, V.
A behemoth structure that hovers over the ocean like a big bully, the Diplomat is a top-notch, luxe oceanfront resort with pool, beach, restaurants, bars and the occasional celebrity sighting.

Fort Lauderdale

Neat, clean and well-tended, Lauderdale has, for the most part, managed to shed its long-standing image as a haven for bacchanalian college Spring Breakers. Some strict public ordinances have caused the party crowds to move on upstate to Panama City Beach or south of the border to Cancún. In their absence, Fort Lauderdale has become an upscale destination for fine dining, nightlife and culture (and also something of a gay hotspot; *see p183* **Up at the Fort**).

Everything in this so-called 'Venice of America' revolves around the water. There are more than 300 miles of inland waterways, from the New River that runs through the heart of Downtown to the yacht-lined canals and excellent ocean beaches, with their distinctive stucco wave walls.

Fittingly, there are many water-based ways of seeing the city. One option is the **Water Taxi** (954 467 6677, www.watertaxi.com), which scoots along the Intracoastal Waterway and the New River, serving both as public transport and tour vessel. There are 21 stops, and an all-day pass costs just $7. Sightseeing cruises are also offered on two Mississippi-style paddle wheelers: the **Jungle Queen Riverboat**, operating from the Bahia Mar Yacht Center (954 462 5596, www.junglequeen.com), and the **Carrie B**, which sails from just off Las Olas on SE 5th Avenue (954 768 9920, www.carriebcruises.com). Sightseeing trips on either cost around $14; evening cruises with dinner and show on the Jungle Queen are $32 per person.

Fort Lauderdale Beach is a wide and handsome sandy strip with a brick promenade for skaters, joggers and cyclists. Postcard-perfect, it comes complete with bronzed lifeguards, coconut palms and cruise ships in the distance. The nearby **Elbo Room** (*see below*), the bar made famous in the 1960s teen-lust classic *Where the Boys Are*, is a lone remnant of formerly giddy times. Today's less hormonally driven beach-goers head to **Beach Place**, located on A1A just north of Las Olas Boulevard, a shopping, dining and entertainment emporium. Other nearby attractions include the **International Swimming Hall of Fame** (*see below*), with two 50-metre pools and a theatre that screens the films of Esther Williams and Johnny Weissmuller, and **Bonnet House Museum & Gardens** (*see below*), a 35-acre subtropical oasis and historical house. Another big patch of green (linked to the beach via a tunnel) is the **Hugh Taylor Birch State Park** (*see below*), with nature trails, wildlife watching, canoe rentals and other recreational activities.

It's also worth strolling the **Riverwalk**, a mile-long waterside promenade that leads to the Riverwalk Arts & Entertainment District, a 22-block area that's home to the **Museum of Art**, the **Fort Lauderdale Historical Museum**, historic **Stranahan House**, the city's oldest structure (1901), and the interactive **Museum of Discovery & Science**, with IMAX theatre attached (for all, *see below*). There's also the excellent **Broward Center of Performing Arts** (*see p205*). If you're staying in town for a while, buy a Riverwalk Arts & Entertainment Passport, which gives discounts on attractions.

Thrifty shoppers, meanwhile, might like to check out the **Fort Lauderdale Swap Shop** (3291 W Sunrise Boulevard, 954 791 7927, www.floridaswapshop.com), home to cheap designer gear, accessories and perfume. There are even free circus performances every day.

Bonnet House Museum & Gardens
900 N Birch Road (954 563 5393/www.bonnet house.org). Open *May-Nov* 10am-3pm Tue-Sat; noon-4pm Sun. *Dec-Apr* 10am-4pm Tue-Sat; noon-4pm Sun. **Admission** $15; free under-6s. **Credit** AmEx, Disc, MC, V.

Elbo Room
241 S Fort Lauderdale Beach Boulevard (954 463 4615/www.elboroom.com). Open 10am-2am Mon-Thur, Sun; 11am-3am Fri, Sat. **Credit** AmEx, Disc, MC, V.

Fort Lauderdale Historical Museum
219 SW 2nd Avenue (954 463 4431/www.oldfort lauderdale.org). Open 11am-5pm Tue-Fri; noon-5pm Sat, Sun. **Admission** $5; free under-6s. *Tours* $8. **Credit** AmEx, MC, V.

Hugh Taylor Birch State Park
3109 E Sunrise Boulevard, at A1A (954 564 4521/ www.floridastateparks.org). Open 8am-sunset daily. **Admission** $4 per car. **No credit cards**.

International Swimming Hall of Fame
501 Seabreeze Boulevard (954 462 6536/ www.ishof.org). Open 9am-7pm Mon-Fri; 9am-5pm Sat, Sun. **Admission** $5. **Credit** AmEx, MC, V.

Museum of Art
1 E Las Olas Boulevard (954 763 6464/www. moafl.org). Open 11am-7pm Mon, Wed, Fri-Sun; 11am-9pm Thur. **Admission** $25-$30; free under-6s. **Credit** AmEx, Disc, MC, V.

Museum of Discovery & Science
401 SW 2nd Street (954 467 6637/www.mods.org). Open 10am-5pm Mon-Sat; noon-6pm Sun. **Admission** $14; $12 concessions. **Credit** AmEx, MC, V.

Stranahan House
335 SE 6th Avenue (954 524 4736). Open 10am-3pm Wed-Sat; 1-3pm Sun. **Admission** $6; $3 concessions. **No credit cards**.

Trips Out of Town

Where to eat

The fresh seafood is a standout at the **Blue Moon Fish Company**, while Mark Militello's **Mark's Las Olas** (sibling venue to Mark's South Beach, *see p115*) is worth a splurge for its innovative cuisine. Dinner at **Mai Kai** comes complete with Polynesian revue – pure kitsch, of course, but hugely entertaining all the same. The Himmarshee Village district, in the heart of Downtown's Arts & Entertainment district, also has plenty of lively bars and restaurants to choose from.

Blue Moon Fish Company

4403 W Tradewinds Avenue (954 267 9888). **Open** 11.30am-3pm, 6-10pm Mon-Thur, Sun; 11.30am-3pm, 6-11pm Fri, Sat. **Main courses** $20-$30. **Credit** MC, V.

Mai Kai

3599 N Federal Highway (954 563 3272/www. maikai.com). **Open** 5-10.30pm Mon-Thur, Sun; 5-11.30pm Fri, Sat. **Main courses** $15-$33. **Credit** AmEx, MC, V.

Mark's Las Olas

1032 E Las Olas Boulevard (954 463 1000/www. chefmark.com). **Open** 6-10pm Mon-Thur, Sun; 6pm-midnight Fri, Sat. **Main courses** $18-$42. **Credit** AmEx, MC, V.

Where to stay

In addition to major beachfront resorts, Fort Lauderdale has plenty of smaller places to stay along A1A or nearby.

Green Island Inn

3300 NE 27th Street (954 566 8951). **Rates** $50-$99. **Credit** AmEx, MC, V.
A small, family-owned property that offers some very competitive room rates.

Lago Mar Resort & Club

1700 S Ocean Lane (954 523 6511/www.lagomar. com). **Rates** $160-$570. **Credit** AmEx, DC, Disc, MC, V.
An award-winning family-owned resort landmark, with a huge spa and upscale Italian restaurant.

Pillars

111 N Birch Road (954 467 9639/www.pillars hotel.com). **Rates** $129-$499. **Credit** AmEx, DC, Disc, MC, V.
A member of the Small Luxury Hotel group, Pillars offers a good location and top-flight service.

Riverside Hotel

620 E Las Olas Boulevard (954 467 0671/www.river sidehotel.com). **Rates** $139-$369. **Credit** AmEx, DC, Disc, MC, V.
A beautifully renovated hotel in the heart of tony Las Olas Boulevard.

Tourist information

Pick up the free *New Times* or *City Link* weeklies, or check out the Friday *Sun-Sentinel* for the latest entertainment and dining listings.

Greater Fort Lauderdale Convention & Visitors Bureau

Suite 200, 100 E Broward Boulevard (954 765 4466/www.sunny.org). **Open** 8.30am-5pm Mon-Fri.

Boca Raton & Delray Beach

The largest county south-east of the Mississippi River, Palm Beach County encompasses a huge national wildlife refuge and the northern reaches of the Everglades, as well as part of Lake Okeechobee, the second-largest freshwater lake in the country. But it's the string of beach towns on the coast that has traditionally attracted visitors, from Spanish explorers in the 1500s to entrepreneurs in the late 1800s and the current crop of retirees and general sun-seekers.

The southernmost city is **Boca Raton**, a sterile-looking enclave of gated communities housing nouveau-riche residents. There is some history here, visible in the exquisite **Boca Raton Resort & Club**, which began life as the Cloister Inn in 1926. Designed by visionary Addison Mizner, the fanciful property was at the time the most expensive 100-room hotel ever built, furnished with his private collection of rare antiques. Though the land boom soon collapsed, stifling many of Mizner's grand plans for developing Boca Raton, his architectural style continues to influence the city. Boca's shopping and cultural district, **Mizner Park** (built in 1991), is home to the **Boca Raton Museum of Art** (*see p219*), along with the usual upscale mall shops and restaurants.

If you want to stop between Fort Lauderdale and Palm Beach, make it at **Delray Beach**, an intimate little town with an artistic bent, wide beaches, navigable traffic, plenty of young people and arts festivals, trolley tours and year-round special events. There's a burgeoning cultural scene here; a 1.3-mile walking trail downtown connects the museums, galleries and historic sites that are part of this diverse community. One treasure worth visiting (or staying at, if you want to splurge) is **Sundy House** (*see p219*), a splendid old inn with lush tropical gardens and, in De La Tierra (*see p219*), an outstanding restaurant. Also in Delray, west of I-95, is **Morikami Museum & Japanese Gardens** (*see p219*), which tells the story of the Japanese agricultural workers who came to Florida in the early 1900s; there's also a café and nature trails along the extensive lake and serene gardens.

De La Tierra

Sundy House, 106 S Swinton Avenue, Delray Beach (877 439 9601). **Open** 11.30am-2.30pm, 6-10pm Tue-Thur; 5-11pm Fri, Sat; 10.30am-2.30pm, 6-10pm Sun. **Main courses** $22-$35. **Credit** AmEx, Disc, MC, V.

Where to stay

Boca Raton Resort & Club

501 E Camino Real, Boca Raton (888 491 2622/www.bocaresort.com). **Rates** $190-$760. **Credit** AmEx, DC, Disc, MC, V.

Sundy House

106 S Swinton Avenue, Delray Beach (877 439 9601/www.sundyhouse.com). **Rates** $175-$680. **Credit** AmEx, Disc, MC, V.

Tourist information

Greater Delray Beach Chamber of Commerce

64A SE 5th Avenue, Delray Beach (561 278 0424/ www.delraybeach.com). **Open** 9am-5pm Mon-Fri.

Fort Lauderdale Beach. See p217.

Boca Raton Museum of Art

Mizner Park, 501 Plaza Real, Boca Raton (561 392 2500/www.bocamuseum.org). **Open** 10am-5pm Tue, Thur, Fri; 10am-9pm Wed; noon-5pm Sat, Sun. **Admission** $8; free under-12s. **Credit** AmEx, Disc, MC, V.

Morikami Museum & Japanese Gardens

4000 Morikami Park Road, Delray Beach (561 495 0233/www.morikami.org). **Open** 10am-5pm Tue-Sun. **Admission** $10; $6 concessions. **Credit** AmEx, Disc, MC, V.

Where to eat & drink

Get an outside table at **De La Tierra** for splendid garden views while you enjoy seasonal fare from its own gardens. For homesick Brits and Anglophiles, there's the **Blue Anchor Pub**. The owners, former editors of the *Daily Mirror* newspaper, were regulars at the old Blue Anchor on London's Chancery Lane. When the pub was demolished they bought its façade and had it shipped over here and reassembled.

Blue Anchor Pub

804 E Atlantic Avenue, Delray Beach (561 272 7272). **Open** 11.30am-2am daily. **Main courses** $8-$21. **Credit** AmEx, DC, Disc, MC, V.

Palm Beach & West Palm Beach

Unlike most of Florida, the city of Palm Beach does little to openly encourage tourists. The only visitors this island town wants are those they already know: people who would rather pick up a bauble from Tiffany's than a seashell from the beach. Palm Beach is still the winter playground of corporate heirs, obscure royalty and American bluebloods, a place where the rest of the world must content itself with admiring exteriors and window-shopping. Public beaches are all but non-existent; those that are open might as well be private due to the strategic lack of parking. There's little reason to stay overnight: lodge elsewhere and make Palm Beach a day trip.

Worth glancing at while you're around is the **Henry Morrison Flagler Museum** (*see p220*), housed in Whitehall, the former luxury home of the railway magnate. Take a guided tour, which will give you an overview of Palm Beach history and explain how this oil tycoon was the catalyst for Florida's development. **The Breakers**, Flagler's sublime oceanfront hotel, rises above the palms and still serves as the town's charity ball central. Even if you're not staying here, take a walk inside the Florentine lobby, splurge on afternoon tea or try Sunday brunch.

Well-named **Worth Avenue** is the town's main shopping street, and it is worth a look just for the Mediterranean architecture, tranquil

Trips Out of Town

courtyards and crassly displayed wealth. There's nothing nouveau or cutting edge here, however. This is where Palm Beach style was born: conservative and slightly aquatic.

Mansion-spotting is tricky: most places are surrounded by tall stucco walls covered with vegetation and guarded by retired CIA agents. Most impressive is **Mar-a-Lago** (Southern Boulevard & S Ocean Boulevard), sometime home to Donald and Melania Trump. Being the attention hog that he is, the Donald has turned part of it into an absurdly lavish private club.

Henry Flagler persuaded the black labourers who had helped build Palm Beach to remove themselves from his paradise by offering them free land on the mainland. He also left them little choice in the matter by torching their houses on the island. Thus, the town of **West Palm Beach** was born. It has since eclipsed its affluent neighbour in population and diversity and serves as the county seat.

Downtown's main **Clematis Street** begins at the waterfront with a public library and a fun fountain, and continues westwards with an array of theatres, bistros, clubs and boutiques. Nearby is **CityPlace** (*see below*), one of the country's biggest shopping/dining/residential conglomerations, with fountains, cobbled streets, jazz brunches and other predictable entertainments. A free trolley connects CityPlace and Clematis. Neighbourhood cultural attractions include the highly regarded **Norton Museum of Art** (*see below*), with its 19th- and 20th-century art and photography collections, including pieces by Miró, Picasso and Brancusi, as well as temporary exhibitions.

CityPlace

700 Rosemary Avenue, at Okeechobee Boulevard, West Palm Beach (561 366 1000/www.cityplace.com). **Open** 11am-10pm Mon-Sat; noon-6pm Sun.

Henry Morrison Flagler Museum

1 Whitehall Way, Palm Beach (561 655 2833/www.flagler.org). **Open** 10am-5pm Tue-Sat; noon-5pm Sun. **Admission** $10; $3 concessions. **Credit** AmEx, DC, MC, V.

Norton Museum of Art

1451 S Olive Avenue, West Palm Beach (561 832 5196/www.norton.org). **Open** 10am-5pm Tue-Sat; 1-5pm Sun. **Admission** $8; $3 concessions; free under-12s. **Credit** AmEx, DC, Disc, MC, V.

Where to stay

The Breakers

1 South County Road, Palm Beach (561 655 6611/www.thebreakers.com). **Rates** $270-$3,000. **Credit** AmEx, DC, MC, V.

If you've got the bucks, this palatial residence, set in 140 acres overlooking the sea, is the place to spend them. Ask about special deals, especially off season.

Tourist information

Chamber of Commerce of the Palm Beaches

401 N Flagler Drive, West Palm Beach (561 833 3711). **Open** 8.30am-5pm Mon-Fri.

Palm Beach County Convention & Visitors Bureau

Suite 800, 1555 Palm Beach Lakes Boulevard, West Palm Beach (561 233 3000). **Open** 8.30am-5.30pm Mon-Fri.

Getting there & around

Train and bus services are generally inconvenient because of far-flung stations and infrequent schedules. The exception is the Tri-Rail service to West Palm Beach, where the station is within walking distance of many attractions.

By car

From Miami, head north on I-95, the main freeway, or US 1 (Federal Highway). For Hollywood, exit at Hollywood Boulevard east. For Fort Lauderdale (about 30mins from Miami), from I-95 take I-595 east and follow signs for 'Fort Lauderdale US 1 North'; once on US 1, turn right on 17th Street. This leads to the beach and major hotels. From Fort Lauderdale to Delray Beach, the fastest route is via I-95; the most scenic is via A1A (Ocean Drive). Exit at Atlantic Avenue east (take care not to confuse this with the Atlantic Avenue exit in Pompano Beach). For both West Palm Beach and Palm Beach (a 90min drive from Miami), exit I-95 at Okeechobee Boulevard east.

By train

Tri-Rail (1-800 874 7245, www.tri-rail.com) operates an infrequent service between Miami and the Gold Coast. From Miami International Airport, 14 trains depart daily (13mins past the hour from 4.13am to 11.13am, then 29mins past the hour from 1.29pm to 7.29pm) to points north, including Hollywood, Fort Lauderdale (journey time 40mins) and Palm Beach (just under two hours). Miami–Fort Lauderdale return is $6.75, while Fort Lauderdale–Palm Beach return tickets cost $7.75.

By bus

Greyhound (1-800 231 2222, www.greyhound.com) runs 21 buses daily from its Miami terminal (4111 NW 27th Street, near Miami International Airport) to Fort Lauderdale (515 NE 3rd Street); the return fare is $10.50 and the journey takes an hour. From Fort Lauderdale, 14 buses daily run up to West Palm Beach for a return fare of around $10.

The Everglades

Don't forget the mossie spray!

Commonly and inaccurately thought of as swamp, the Everglades is actually more a shallow, bankless river; 'a river of grass', as iconic Florida environmentalist Marjory Stoneman Douglas termed it in her famous book of the same name, first published in 1947. The Everglades occupies the southernmost 80 miles or so of the state of Florida, of which the Everglades National Park at the tip, on which this chapter focuses, is just a part.

The natural course of the river flows the 100 miles from Lake Okeechobee to the Florida Bay at a rate of 100 feet per day, with the water's depth varying from as much as three feet to as little as three inches.

The national park is the only one in the US to be recognised by the United Nations as both an International Biosphere Reserve and World Heritage Site, and is home to plant and animal life found both in the West Indian tropics and in more temperate northern zones. Nowhere is the idea of south Florida as a meeting point of north and south more true than here.

'River of grass' is actually far too limiting a definition for the variety of plant life within the Everglades: saw palmetto (commonly called sawgrass) may be dominant overall, but there are more than 1,000 kinds of seed-bearing plants and 120 types of trees. Mangrove and various hardwood-tree hammocks (islands of land) dot the expanses of sawgrass, and, during the summer, flowering plants add splashes of colour to the green canvas.

Laid-back **Everglades City**. *See p223.*

WILD WILDLIFE

The park also teems with animal life. Deer wander, and the area is the only place in the world where alligators and crocodiles co-habit. The alligators (flat nose, raised nostrils) are far more abundant, with the more aggressive crocodiles (tapered snout, visible teeth) keeping to the saltier waters nearer the coast. During a walk along one of the park's trails, expect to see the aforementioned reptiles (don't get too close and *do not feed them*), as well as snakes (some are poisonous), turtles and frogs, and less ugly stuff like rabbits, butterflies and some of the 350 species of birds that either reside in the park or make it a migratory rest stop.

As full of wildlife as the Everglades may seem, it is, in fact, a troubled sanctuary of last resort for many species. The number of wading birds in the southern area has plummeted in the last half-century, as has its population of Florida panthers. Similarly, although the Everglades has never had a large population of black bears, they're more reluctant than ever to show themselves to visitors.

Although it is the country's second-largest national park, the Everglades (founded in 1947) is not as obviously stunning as some of its more mountainous western cousins. As such, its beauty cannot be appreciated from the windows of a camper speeding down the road from one rest stop to the next. Even exploring the area on a noisy airboat climaxes when the driver turns off the engine and leaves you floating silently in endless sawgrass.

PLANNING YOUR TRIP

In terms of access, the park can be divided into two main areas: the northern section, reached via the Tamiami Trail (aka SW 8th Street, aka US 41) and accessed by Shark Valley and Everglades City; and the southern section,

Feeding time for the alligators: **Coopertown Airboat Rides**. *See p223*.

accessed via Homestead and Florida City on US 1. Of the two access points, Shark Valley is the closer to central Miami; it's a journey of about 70 to 90 minutes. Getting down to the Ernest F Coe Visitors' Center, which marks the entrance to the southern part of the national park, can take closer to two hours. However, there is accommodation down here (at the Flamingo Lodge; *see p225*), whereas there's nowhere to stay at Shark Valley.

Unfortunately, there is no public transport into either area, and renting a car is really the only option.

It is advisable year-round to bring suntan lotion, a hat and sunglasses. During the wet season – June to October – mosquito repellent is *absolutely essential*, and it's not a bad idea even in the dryer months, when there are still enough of the pests around to be a nuisance to anyone with sensitive skin. Mosquitoes are only half the problem; dawn and dusk in summer brings out the 'no-see-ums', tiny, near-invisible insects with a ferocious bite. Wet season also brings heavy rains that raise the water levels causing wildlife to disperse, with the result that animal sightings are less frequent. Parts of the Everglades can also flood, including the Shark Valley Trail.

Regardless of which access point you use, entrance to the park costs $10 per vehicle for a seven-day pass, or $25 for a year's access.

Northern Access

Twenty-five miles west of the Florida Turnpike (SR 821), Shark Valley is the most accessible part of the Everglades from Miami and makes for a perfect half- or full-day outing. The **Tamiami Trail** (US 41), which leads here, is the old, two-lane road across the southern part of the state, along the park's northern boundary. It's named after its two end points, Tampa and Miami. Recent plans have called for the park's boundaries to be stretched to protect against encroaching development. To accomplish this would involve the government buying out the tourist businesses that line the edge of the park, most of which are relics of a simpler, albeit tackier, era.

Beyond Shark Valley, the Tamiami Trail continues west, making a beeline for the Gulf Coast. Before then, turn south on SR 29 for Everglades City and the Gulf Coast Visitors' Center (about a two-and-a-half hour drive from Miami).

Airboat operators, tours of **Miccosukee Indian Village** (*see p223*) and alligator wrestling shows along the Tamiami Trail are pleasantly worn at the edges, though for the most part lacklustre. It's only marginally impressive to watch a grown man wrestle a 'gator that looks more interested in being left alone than in fighting; and, in truth, it's far less representative of traditional Indian culture than it is of Florida's myriad ways of luring dollars out of tourists.

At tiny **Coopertown**, airboat tours have been running for close to 60 years. The guides are knowledgeable, and this may be the best of several places to take a ride, if only so you can have a beer before or after in the **Coopertown Restaurant** (*see below*), where the walls are covered with decades' worth of Everglades memorabilia. Given the rarity of tourists lingering here, it's a good idea to indulge in only a quick snack with that beer.

Coopertown Airboat Rides & Restaurant

Tamiami Trail/US 41, Miami (305 226 6048/ www.coopertownairboats.com). **Open** 8am-6pm daily. **Main courses** $9-$22. **Credit** AmEx, DC, MC, V.
Airboats are flat-bottomed skiffs powered by a great big fan at the back. They are loud and environmentally dubious but a heap of fun. Rides depart every 20 minutes throughout the day, last around 40 minutes and cost $18 per person or $9 for children under 12. Under-6s go for free. **Photo** *p222*.

Miccosukee Indian Village

500 SW 177th Avenue, off the Tamiami Trail/US 41, Miami (305 223 8380/www.miccosukeetribe. com). **Open** *Museum* 9am-5pm daily. *Restaurant* 8am-4pm daily. **Admission** *Museum* $5; $3.50 concessions; free under-4s. **Credit** (restaurant only) AmEx, MC, V.
A bridge between old and new lifestyles, the Village presents Miccosukee arts and crafts (patchwork sewing, doll making, basket weaving), a museum of Indian heritage, airboat tours, alligator wrestling and a bloody great ultra-modern casino.

Shark Valley

Shark Valley features a 15-mile paved road leading to an observation tower overlooking the heart of the Everglades. You can walk it or cycle it (bikes are rented at the park entrance at $5.25 per hour; the last rental is at 3pm). Alternatively, the **Visitors' Center** (*see below*) offers two-hour ranger-guided tram tours, though you might need to book up to three weeks in advance (call 305 221 8455 for reservations). There are also briefer trails, including the third-of-a-mile **Bobcat Boardwalk** and the slightly longer **Otter Cave Trail**. Even these walks are likely to bring encounters with the park's inhabitants, including many alligators, which delight in napping on the road with near (if not absolute) indifference to visitors. Remember, though: this isn't Disney World, so keep your wits about you and be careful where you tread.

Shark Valley Visitors' Center

36000 SW 8th Street (Tamiami Trail/US 41), Miami (305 221 8776/www.nps.gov/ever). **Open** 8.30am-6pm daily. **Tram tours** $12.75; $7.75 concessions. **No credit cards.**
Tram tours run on the hour 9am-4pm December to April, and at 9.30am, 11am, 1pm and 3pm from May to November. They last around 90 minutes.

Where to stay

There is no accommodation at Shark Valley. Neither is camping permitted. The closest accommodation options are in Everglades City, about 40 miles further west.

To Everglades City

After Shark Valley, less than ten miles west along the Tamiami Trail the road passes through **Big Cypress National Preserve**, with its tracts of cypress and pine trees growing amid the swampy terrain. The main access point is the **Big Cypress Visitors' Center** (*see p224*), starting point for a couple of trails and scenic drives. Some 20 miles further on the Tamiami, the tiny town of **Ochope** boasts the smallest post office in the US, which measures a little more than seven by eight feet. The 'panther crossing next five miles' sign is worth a snapshot, but don't wait around for a sight of the rare big cats: there aren't too many left.

South of SR 29 from the Tamiami Trail is **Everglades City**, the gateway to the **Ten Thousand Islands**. This is where the Glades meets the Gulf of Mexico, and the coastline fractures into thousands of islands, many thick with mangroves. The town itself is not much to write home about, although it has a remote, quaint feel and a handful of colourful shops aimed at visitors. Outside, of course, Mother Nature's version of reality may not be air-conditioned, but the environment is incredibly lush and rich in wildlife. For information, as well as permits for camping within the park, visit the **Gulf Coast Visitors' Center** (*see p224*), which is three miles south of the Tamiami Trail on SR 29.

Porpoises and some of Florida's remaining 1,200 manatees can be found here, as can the noble American bald eagle. The easiest way to get on the water is with **Everglades National Park Boat Tours** (*see p224*). Ninety-minute tours of the nearby islands and an overview of the area's ecology start at 9am and leave every half-hour until 4.30pm. A number of local concerns rent canoes and kayaks by the hour or day, as well as rentals for overnight camping trips along the Wilderness Waterway trail leading south to the Flamingo Visitors' Center.

Big Cypress Visitors' Centre

HCR 61, Tamiami Trail/US 41, Miami (239 695 1201/www.nps.gov/bicy). **Open** 8.30am-4.30pm daily. **Admission** free.

Everglades National Park Boat Tours

Gulf Coast Ranger Station, SR 29, Everglades City (within Florida 1-800 445 7724/outside Florida 1-239 695 2591/www.nps.gov/ever). **Open** 9am-5pm daily. **Rates** *Canoes* $24 per day 8.30am-5pm; $48 overnight. *Boat tours* $16; $8 concessions. **Credit** AmEx, MC, V.

Gulf Coast Visitors' Center

SR 29, Everglades City (239 695 3311/www.nps. gov/ever). **Open** 8am-4.30pm daily.

Where to stay

In Everglades City, around the Gulf Coast Visitors' Center, there are a limited number of hotels. Local recreational vehicle (RV) sites permit camping, but they're not really designed to make you feel at one with nature. Along the Wilderness Waterway are a number of chickees – covered wooden platforms elevated above the open water – that also offer camping. During the winter, campsites ($14) on the islands and chickees must be reserved in person at the Gulf Coast Visitors' Center (*see above*).

Captain's Table

102 E Broadway, Everglades City (239 695 4211/ www.captainstablehotel.com). **Rates** $50-$80 standard; $120-$170 deluxe. **Credit** Disc, MC, V.
All rooms at this English-owned hotel have private bathrooms. There's also an Olympic-sized pool, heated in the winter.

Everglades Spa & Lodge

201 W Broadway, Everglades City (239 695 3151/ www.banksoftheeverglades.com). **Rates** $100-$135. **Credit** AmEx, DC, MC, V.
Set in a former bank, this B&B has four rooms with shared bathrooms and five apartments with kitchen and private bathrooms (you can choose your room by its old function, such as Mutual Funds Department). Breakfast is served in the old walk-in vault. The on-site spa offers massages, facials and other pampering treats.

Ivey House

107 Camellia Street, Everglades City (239 695 3299/ www.iveyhouse.com). Closed May-Oct. **Rates** $50-$105 lodge; $75-$200 inn; $100-$200 cottage. **Credit** MC, V.
This family-run accommodation includes an inn, cottage and lodge, which dates from the 1920s. When the weather getsa bit steamy, guests can retreat to the shared swimming pool, complete with waterfall. The owners also run North American Canoe Tours, offering rentals of canoes etc, as well as eco tours.

Rod & Gun Club Lodge

200 Riverside Drive, Everglades City (239 695 2101). **Rates** *Nov-May* $110. *June-Oct* $85. **No credit cards**.
An erstwhile hunting club, this charming lodge is now a small hotel. It has always attracted an august crowd: past guests have included no fewer than five US presidents (Roosevelt, Truman, Eisenhower, Hoover and Nixon) and assorted other notables from Ernest Hemingway to Mick Jagger.

Southern access

Ernest F Coe, Royal Palm & Flamingo visitors' centers

The main southern access point to the park is just south-east of Homestead and Florida City off SR 9336 (*see p225* **Getting there**). It's here that you find the main **Ernest F Coe Visitors' Center** (*see p225*), which was built and expanded after the original buildings were damaged by Hurricane Andrew in 1992. It now houses educational exhibits, a small cinema screening orientation films, and a bookshop. No trails start from the Coe, but four miles inside the park is the **Royal Palm Visitors' Center** (*see p225*), a sub-centre serving as the head of both the Gumbo Limbo and the Anhinga walking trails, which encompass the abundant wildlife within Taylor Slough, the smaller of the two main sloughs, or marshy bogs, within the park (the other is Shark River Slough in the centre of the park). The animals and birds here are well known for their ease around humans, and the Royal Palm area presents some of the best wildlife photo opportunities in the whole park.

Except for the swampy terrain of the Slough, the Everglades here is more wooded than it is in the northern part of the park. At **Long Pine Key** there are picnic areas within the slash pine forests and on the banks of numerous small lakes. Just under 13 miles west of the Coe Center is **Pa-hay-okee Overlook** (Pa-hay-okee is the Indian name for the Everglades; it means 'Big Water'); a quarter-mile boardwalk leads to an observation tower where you can watch some of the park's larger birds, typically including vultures and hawks, fly over their domain.

The road dips south from here, first passing some small hammocks of stately mahogany trees, then on to the mangrove forests that signal the approaching shoreline of Florida Bay. Around 38 miles from the park entrance is **Mrazek Pond**, noted as a prime viewing spot for some of the park's more exotic waterfowl.

Just beyond Mrazek, at the very end of SR 9336, is **Flamingo**, site of a small (and, to be honest, not particularly good) visitors' centre, a busy marina and a commodious lodge. This is very much the jewel of the Everglades. The scenery is straight out of Robinson Crusoe, with walking and canoe trails wandering off through dense mangrove forests and along the calm, island-filled waters of Florida Bay. Flamingo is also the gateway for water trips to campsites up and down the coast and unspoiled beaches like Cape Sable. Local concessions rent canoes, kayaks, motorboats and even houseboats, and there are daily sightseeing cruises; *see below*. Fishing is permitted, but check with the ranger's office for licensing requirements and restrictions, which are seasonal and fluctuating.

Ernest F Coe Visitors' Center

40001 SR 9336, Homestead (305 242 7700/www.nps. gov/ever). **Open** 8am-5pm daily. **Credit** MC, V.

Flamingo Marina

1 Flamingo Lodge Highway (239 695 3101/www. flamingolodge.com). **Open** *Rental desk* 7am-6.30pm daily; last rental 4pm. **Rates** *Bicycles* $3 per hr; $8 per half-day; $14 per day. *Canoes* $8-$12 per hr; $22-$30 per half-day; $32-$40 per day. *Kayaks* $11-$16 per hr; $27-$38 per half-day; $43-$54 per day. **Credit** AmEx, DC, MC, V.

A Backcountry Cruise aboard the *Pelican* departs at 10am, 1pm and 3.30pm daily; the round trip takes two hours and costs $18, or $10 for children. The Florida Bay Cruise aboard the *Bald Eagle* departs at 11am, 1.30pm and 4.30pm daily, and takes 90 minutes; it costs $12, or $7 for kids.

Royal Palm Visitors' Center

40001 SR 9336, Homestead (305 242 7700/www.nps. gov/ever). **Open** 8am-4.15pm daily. **Credit** MC, V.

Getting there

From Miami, head west on I-395 to SR 821 south, aka the Florida Turnpike. The Turnpike ends in Florida City, where you take the first right turn through the centre of town and follow the signs to the park entrance on SR 9336; take a left turn when you come to **Robert Is Here** (19200 SW 344th Street, Homestead, 305 246 1592), a near-legendary fruit stand that also does great juices and a fine Key lime pie. It's open 8am to 7pm daily but closed July to September.

Where to stay

Outside the park, there are numerous motels and hotels in Homestead and Florida City, although these are both fairly grim, highway-side developments lacking in any charm. Inside the park, the only place to stay is the **Flamingo Lodge** (*see below*), at the end of the road on the

park's southernmost tip. There are managed campsites at Long Pine Key, Flamingo and Chekika; during the winter, though, you must book primitive campsites ($10) in person at the Flamingo Visitors' Center.

Best Western: Gateway to the Keys

411 South Krome Avenue, Florida City (305 246 5100/www.bestwestern.com). **Rates** *Jan-Apr* $135-$150. *May-Dec* $109-$124. **Credit** AmEx, DC, MC, V.

Clean, simple rooms, though there's often a minimum stay (usually three nights) at peak season.

Days Inn of Homestead

51 S Homestead Boulevard (US 1), Homestead (305 245 1260/www.daysinn.com). **Rates** $40-$99. **Credit** AmEx, DC, MC, V.

A pretty standard Days Inn with 100 rooms and one suite. It's about 15 miles from the Everglades.

Flamingo Lodge

1 Flamingo Lodge Highway, Flamingo (239 695 3101/www.flamingolodge.com). **Rates** $79-$95. **Credit** AmEx, DC, MC, V.

Basic accommodation but in a gorgeous setting, with all rooms overlooking Florida Bay. There's a swimming pool, a restaurant and a shop, while adjacent are the Flamingo Visitors' Center and the Flamingo Marina (*see above*) for rentals and boat trips. A few minutes' walk beyond the lodge is the Eco Pond, where, at sunset, hundreds of ibis and other birds seek out treetop perches for the night: a spectacular sight.

Shark Valley. See p223.

Trips Out of Town

The Florida Keys

Have fun in the sun, or take it nice and easy – you decide.

Just as any Floridian will tell you that their state is unlike the rest of the US, inhabitants of the Keys are proud to claim the Keys are unlike the rest of Florida. And they're right. This group of 45 islands south of Miami trails the rounded mainland coast like a procession of tadpoles. A 113-mile roadway links the Keys (from the Spanish 'cayo', meaning small island) to the bottom of the mainland, but that's where any ties with the frenetic Miami pace ends. The isles, flanked by the Atlantic Ocean to the south and the Gulf of Mexico to the north and shadowed on both sides by the Florida Reef, a vast strip of living coral a few miles off the coast, are rich in marine, bird and plant life. Some of the islands are monstrously overpopulated and lure tourists with vulgar neon and nasty T-shirts. But the further south-west you travel, the more peaceful the backdrop.

It's not clear when the islands were first inhabited, but it's believed Native American Indians made their home here long before white settlers staked their claim in the 19th century. At first, farming communities made a living with fruit orchards, and on Big Pine Key a thriving shark processing factory was established butchering up to a hundred of the creatures a day for their hides and oil-rich livers. Cubans, who only had to sail 90 miles from Havana, soon joined the white Americans. Today, their influence is still apparent across the islands, albeit less so than in Miami.

Tourism struck in the early 1900s, when Henry Flagler built his ambitious railway to Key West. Pinned as 'Flagler's Folly', the mammoth project was originally designed to open up trade routes. But the 1935 Labor Day Hurricane put an end to Flagler's 20-year vision when 40 miles of line washed out to sea. Just three years later, though, the first Overseas Highway (US 1) was completed, linking the islands to the mainland forever. Parts of Flagler's Folly became fodder for Hollywood when they were blown up for scenes in several movies such as the Sylvester Stallone, er, bomb, *The Specialist*.

Many visitors choose to head straight to Key West, skipping the islands en route. Aside from the fact that the touristy vibe that permeates Key West is not to everyone's taste, it's a little foolhardy to drive straight through the rest of the Keys. Some hold more-than-worthwhile attractions, others offer unique natural beauty, while others still are just wonderfully peaceful.

For the purposes of this guide, we've split the Keys into four sections: the Upper Keys, including Key Largo and Islamorada; the

Middle Keys, from Long Key to Marathon; the Lower Keys, which run from the south-west end of the Seven Mile Bridge all the way to the edge of Key West; and Key West itself. We've listed a selection of hotels and motels for each, but for more options in the Keys, contact the various chambers of commerce (*see below*).

Useful information

Key West is the driest city in Florida and sunny nearly all year. Temperatures during summer can reach the mid 30°s (Centigrade), but cool winds sweep across the Atlantic to the Gulf and keep the heat down. In December temperatures can drop to the low teens. Throughout the year, afternoon showers are possible and will soak you to the skin in minutes, but they rarely last more than a couple of hours. Mosquitoes are no more of a problem here than in Miami. A 24-hour hotline (1-305 229 4522) gives a pre-recorded Florida weather report, as well as tide times.

Bicycle theft excepted, crime is almost non-existent in Key West. Walking around Key West at night is far safer than in many areas of the US, but it is advisable to stay clear of the area around Bahama Village after dark. The further north-east you travel, the more alert you should be; in Key Largo, revert to savvy traveller mode.

At peak season – January to April, especially at weekends – the Keys get extremely busy. Prices rise in hotels, and availability plummets: the Keys, and Key West in particular, are even more lacking in affordable accommodation than is Miami. Though you'll usually be able to find somewhere, it may not be easy, and it may not be in Key West. In other words, book early.

Florida Keys & Key West Tourist Development Council

Visitors' Bureau, PO Box 1146, Key West, FL 33041 (1-800 527 8539/1-305 296 1552/www.fla-keys.com). Call 1-800 771 5397 for the problem-solving operator.

Islamorada Chamber of Commerce

MM 82.5. Postal address: PO Box 915, Islamorada, FL 33036 (1-800 322 5397/1-305 664 4503). **Open** 9am-5pm Mon-Fri.

Key Largo Chamber of Commerce

MM 106. Postal address: 10600 Overseas Highway, Key Largo, FL 33037 (1-800 822 1088/1-305 451 1414). **Open** 9am-6pm daily.

Key West Chamber of Commerce

402 Wall Street, Key West, FL 33040 (1-305 294 2587/www.keywestchamber.org). **Open** 8.30am-6.30pm Mon-Fri; 9am-5pm Sat, Sun.

Lower Keys Chamber of Commerce

MM 31. Postal address: PO Box 430511, Eight Pine Key, FL 33043 (1-800 872 3722/1-305 872 2411). **Open** 9am-5pm Mon-Fri; 9am-3pm Sat.

Marathon Chamber of Commerce

MM 122. Postal address: 12222 Overseas Highway, Marathon, FL 33050 (1-800 842 9580/1-305 743 5417). **Open** 9am-5.30pm Mon-Fri.

Phone codes

Note that, although the telephone area code for the Keys is the same as for Miami – 305 – if you are phoning from Miami or anywhere else outside the Keys, the call does not count as local and you must prefix all numbers with 1 plus the area code. If you are phoning from anywhere within the Keys, you don't need to use the code.

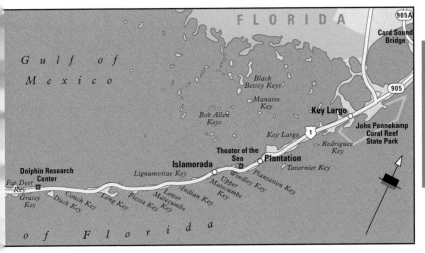

By car

The simplest way to get to the Keys is to head south on I-95, which leads into US 1 (aka Overseas Highway), and just keep going straight. However, a more pleasant detour can be had by ducking off US 1 a little south of Homestead and taking a left on to **Card Sound Road** (SR 905-A). It's worth the detour for three reasons. One, you'll avoid most of the tourist traffic. Two, you get to ride over the **Card Sound Bridge**, which soars a stunning 65 feet over Barnes Sound. And three, you get to stop by **Alabama Jack's** (58000 Card Sound Road, 1-305 248 8741), a wonderful bar and eaterie built on a couple of barges and frequented by a glorious mix of boaters, boozers, bikers, downhome country folk and vaguely boho Keysians. It's only open during the day, but try and stop by on Sunday afternoons, when the Card Sound Machine chivvy along proceedings with some fine country and bluegrass music.

The journey from Miami to Key West takes three to four hours, more if it's a holiday weekend. When you reach the Keys, US 1 becomes a narrow, two-lane highway with a speed limit of 55mph, often less. **Mile Markers** (MM), small green signs beside the road, start in south Miami at MM 126 and end at Key West with MM 0. Addresses en route are followed by – or, in some cases, consist solely of – their mile marker location. Look closely, as the signs are not always easy to spot.

In places, the Florida Keys make for a gloriously scenic drive. The **Seven Mile Bridge** (MM 40-47), in particular, offers the terrifically weird illusion of driving on water as it soars endlessly into the distance. But several other stretches, while not as spectacular, are no less lovely. It's worth buying a detailed Keys map that shows which side roads are worth a detour; UniversalMAP does a good one.

By bus

The **Keys Shuttle** (1-888 765 9997 or 305 289 9997) is a door-to-door service from Fort Lauderdale and Miami International Airports to Key Largo and other points in the Keys. Call 24hrs ahead to make reservations. **Greyhound** (*see p214*) operates three buses a day to Key West – four on Fridays and Sundays – from Miami International Airport and Downtown Miami. There are several scheduled stops along the Keys, but you can flag down the bus at any point. The journey from Miami to Key West takes four to five hours and costs $32-$34 one-way, $62-$66 return.

By air

There are a number of daily services to Marathon and Key West airports from Miami and Fort Lauderdale. Prices start at $120 for a one-way trip. Contact **Cape Air** (1-800 352 0714), **US Air** (1-800 428 4322) or **American Airlines** (1-800 433 7300).

The Upper Keys

Entering the Keys by road is an underwhelming experience. None of the Keys' famed character is at all visible, with US 1 lined on either side by faded T-shirt shops, seen-better-days motels, raggedy billboards and almost no scenery. Don't be too disheartened. It gets better…

… but before it gets better, you'll have to get through **Key Largo**, which couldn't be less like the film of the same name if it tried. Where the film reeked of glamour, exoticism and intrigue, Key Largo just reeks. It's the longest, largest and easternmost of the Keys islands (the name comes from the Spanish for 'Long Island'), and every other building seems to be a cheap motel, a sandal retailer or a T-shirt shop. Indeed, on this evidence, you'd be forgiven for thinking that the population of the Keys can be split into two groups: those who sell T-shirts and those who buy them.

That said, tucked away here is one of the Keys' treasures in the form of the mostly underwater **John Pennekamp Coral Reef State Park** (*see p230*), which takes in a mammoth 54,000 acres, stretching into the Atlantic and encompassing vast tracts of coral reef. **Dolphin Cove** (*see below*) and **Dolphins Plus** (MM 99.5, 1-305 451 1993, www.pennekamppark.com) both offer sea mammal interaction, including recreational dolphin encounters. Dolphins Plus also specialises in therapeutic dolphin swimming.

South of Key Largo, at MM 93, is **Tavernier**, a small town that's notable chiefly for its protected strip of architecturally intriguing wooden buildings from the turn of the century – that and the very worthwhile **Florida Keys Wild Bird Rehabilitation Center** (*see below*).

Dolphin Cove

MM 101.9, Key Largo (1-305 451 4060/www. dolphinscove.com). **Open** times vary. **Admission** prices vary. **Credit** AmEx, MC, V.
One of many watery attractions in the Keys, Dolphin Cove is set in a natural lagoon and offers a mix of entertaining and educational programmes and activities, among them ecology and kayak tours around the Florida Bay, snorkel trips and swimming with dolphins (book ahead). Phone for opening times.

Florida Keys Wild Bird Rehabilitation Center

MM 93.6, Tavernier (1-305 852 4486/www.fkwbc. org). **Open** 8am-6.30pm daily. **Admission** by donation. **No credit cards**.

Bahia Honda State Park. *See p235.*

Bogie and Key Largo

In terms of the Humphrey Bogart pantheon it's no *Casablanca*, but John Huston's adaptation of the Maxwell Anderson play *Key Largo* is a fine claustrophobic drama with Edward G Robinson as a truculent gangster, Bogart as an embittered ex-army officer and Lauren Bacall as the girl who loves him. Most of it was shot on sound stages in California, but Huston filmed several brief scenes for the movie at the Caribbean Club in Rock Harbor, a small settlement on the island of Key Largo. When the film was released in 1948, local businessmen saw dollar signs, and out went the name Rock Harbor to be replaced with the newly adopted moniker Key Largo. Bogey himself never came to Key Largo neé Rock Harbor, so, in the absence of the man himself, local entrepreneurs went and bought his boat. The *African Queen*, the vessel occupied by Bogart and his co-star Katherine Hepburn in the film of the same name is displayed at the Key Largo Holiday Inn (MM 100, 1-305 451 4655). Its steam-driven engine is still in working order, and the old Queen's for hire for parties, weddings and attacking German gunboats.

A heart-warming, not-for-profit spot whose role in helping preserve bird life on the Keys shouldn't be underestimated, this centre is not an attraction as such, but does welcome both visitors and donations.

John Pennekamp Coral Reef State Park

MM 102.5, Key Largo (1-305 451 1621/www. pennekamppark.com). **Open** 8am-sunset daily. *Boat tours* 9.15am, 12.15pm, 3pm daily. **Admission** *By car* $3.50 per person; 50¢ each additional person over 2. *Boat tours* $22; $15 concessions. **Credit** Disc, MC, V.

The terrestrial portion of this vast park is pleasant, encompassing hammock trails and beachy areas, but the main reason to head here is the underwater area, which contains a vast, accessible swathe of the living coral reef that runs the length of the Keys. No array of colour pictures or brochure flim-flam can really prepare you for the beauty of the coral reef, which can be seen from inside a glass-bottomed boat (tours last two and a half hours). Garish fish and exotic sea creatures glide around, and can be viewed close up by snorkelling and diving (tours also available, along with equipment rental). The much-photographed Christ of the Abyss statue is within the boundaries of the park, submerged in 25ft of water six miles east-north-east of Key Largo's South Cut.

Where to eat

Unfortunately, dining in Key Largo suffers from its proximity to Islamorada (*see p231*), where the eating options are better and more varied. However, the seafood and vast beer selection at the **Crack'd Conch** (MM 105.5, 1-305 451 0732), the sangria and imaginative seafood dishes at **Calypso's Seafood Grill** (MM 99.5, 1-305 451 0600) and the home-style cooking at **Mrs Mac's Kitchen** (MM 99.4, 1-305 451 3722) all manage to hit some of the right spots.

Where to stay

There are plenty of independent motels in and around Key Largo, many of them pretty much of a muchness. Among the chains around these parts are **Ramada** (MM 100, 1-305 451 3939), **Holiday Inn** (MM 99.7, 1-305 451 2121), **Howard Johnson** (MM 102, 1-305 451 1400) and **Best Western** (MM 100, 1-305 451 5081), along with large and pricey **Marriott** (MM 103, 1-305 453 0000) and **Westin** (MM 97, 1-305 852 5553) resorts. There's also camping at the **John Pennekamp Coral Reef State Park**, with 47 campsites for tents or RVs costing $26 per night (for reservations call 1-800 326 3521; for more on the park, *see above*).

Bay Harbor Lodge

97702 Overseas Highway (MM 97.7), Key Largo (1-305 852 5695/www.thefloridakeys.com/bayharbor lodge). **Rates** $65-$135 room; $95-$155 efficiency; $115-$195 cottage. **Credit** AmEx, MC, V.
One of the nicer budget spots on Key Largo, with a 40ft-long heated pool.

Jules' Undersea Lodge

51 Shoreland Drive (MM 103.2), Key Largo (1-305 451 2353/www.jul.com). **Rates** $295-$395 per person. **Credit** AmEx, Disc, MC, V.
A unique and understandably pricey underwater hotel that sleeps six people 30ft below the water. Surprisingly, it has mod cons such as air-conditioning, and further bonuses include unlimited diving.

Kona Kai Resort

97802 Overseas Highway (MM 97.8), Key Largo (1-800 365 7829/1-305 852 7200/www.konakai resort.com). **Rates** $176-$331 room; $235-$937 suite. **Credit** AmEx, Disc, MC, V.
An impressive, cosy, independent resort with more amenities and attractions than you'd expect of an 11-unit operation, including an art gallery and hundreds of species of orchid.

Islamorada

The name prepares you for a reality that's possibly more idyllic than the one you'll find. That said, the group of islands known as **Islamorada** – Plantation, Windley, Upper Matecumbe, Shell Lignumvitae, Indian and Lower Matecumbe Keys, running from MM 90 to MM 74 – does offer a bunch of pretty spots. Whereas Key Largo is a dive centre, here it's fishing that dominates – or, as the T-shirts put it, 'Islamorada, a quaint little drinking town with a fishing problem'. Islamorada (the name comes from the Spanish for 'Purple Isles' – why purple, nobody knows) also offers the first glimpses of a quieter, more traditional Keys existence.

Classic sights along this 16-mile stretch are few, with the **Theater of the Sea** (*see below*) the main attraction. However, the **Lignumvitae Key State Botanical Site** and the **Indian Key State Historic Site** (for both, *see below*) are both nice diversions, while the small but splendid beaches that sit by the roadside offer the first validation of the Keys' reputation as an idyllic, restful stop. The Chamber of Commerce at MM 82.5 (*see p227*) has a wealth of local information.

Indian Key State Historic Site

Postal address: PO Box 1052, Islamorada, FL 33036. Accessible from MM 79.5 (1-305 664 4815/tour boat 1-305 664 9814). **Open** *Ranger tours* 9am, 1pm Mon, Thur-Sun. *Tour boats* 8.30am, 12.30pm Mon, Thur-Sun. **Admission** *Ranger tours* $1. *Tour boats* $15; $10 concessions. **Credit** AmEx, DC, Disc, MC, V.

An island with a rich history (the Indian tribe that once lived here was booted out by fishermen from the Bahamas, and then by wreckers), Indian Key is now uninhabited. The tours are worth taking, though you'll have to go by boat from Robbie's Marina at MM 77.5; booking is recommended, especially as, at the time of writing, public access to the island was limited due to severe damage sustained during the ruthless 2005 hurricane season.

Lignumvitae Key State Botanical Site

Accessible from MM 79.5 (1-305 664 4815/tour boat 1-305 664 9814). **Open** *Ranger tours* 10am, 2pm Mon, Thur-Sun. *Boat tours* 9.30am, 1.30pm Mon, Thur-Sun. **Admission** *Ranger tours* $1. *Boat tours* $15; $10 concessions. **Credit** AmEx, DC, Disc, MC, V.

As with the Indian Key State Historic Site, tours to this untarnished preserve of tropical forests and rare-ish birds can be taken from Robbie's Marina (*see above*), but you'll need to book ahead. As always in this neck of the woods, don't forget to bring the insect repellent – and proper walking shoes for the walking tours.

Theater of the Sea

84721 Overseas Highway (MM 84.5) (1-305 664 2431/www.theaterofthesea.com). **Open** 9.30am-4pm daily. **Admission** $24; $16 concessions. **Credit** MC, V.

If Miami's Seaquarium is a poor imitation of SeaWorld in Orlando, then the Theater of the Sea is a poor imitation of the Seaquarium. A little harsh, perhaps, but as you'd expect for an attraction that's getting on for 60 years old, it's lacking a little lustre. That said, kids will enjoy the performing animal shows, and, if you book ahead, swimming with dolphins, sea lions and giant rays.

Where to eat

Perhaps the second best of all the Keys in terms of dining options, Upper Matecumbe Key crams several fine eateries into its four or so miles. The **Green Turtle Inn** (MM 81.5, 1-305 664 9031) has been offering fine seafood (including turtle soup) at fine prices since the 1920s, although you might want to avoid Friday and Saturday nights, when everything comes with cheese, courtesy of the cabaret acts. Another old stager is the **Islamorada Fish Company** (MM 81.5, 1-305 664 9271), which has a nice bayside deck for consumption of fish sandwiches. Keep your eyes peeled for manatees, which are aplenty here. **Marker 88** (MM 88, 1-305 852 9315) is a pricey gourmet option with fans and detractors in about equal numbers; it's open evenings only and closed Monday. **Papa Joe's** (MM 79.9, 1-305 664 8109) is pure Keys, a restaurant with a free-standing terrace bar surrounded by boats and water; it's perfect for a po' boy sandwich and a beer. Alternatively, the **Tiki Bar** (MM 84, 1-305 664 2321) is a very tacky (ie fun) frozen drink outpost on the water, where getting drunk is a requirement, or there's **Woody's** (MM 82, 1-305 664 4335), a strip club-cum-hard rock joint – not for anyone who shies away from audience participation – where the house band is the delightfully named Big Dick and the Extenders.

Where to stay

There are branches of **Days Inn** (MM 82.5, Upper Matecumbe Key, 1-305 664 3681), **Hampton Inn** (MM 80, Upper Matecumbe Key, 1-305 664 0073) and **Howard Johnson** (MM 84, Windley Key, 1-305 664 2321).

Cheeca Lodge

MM 82, Upper Matecumbe Key (1-305 664 4651/www.cheeca.rockresorts.com). **Rates** $249-$599 room; $359-$1,500 suite. **Credit** AmEx, DC, Disc, MC, V.

A huge, popular and pricey resort set on 30 acres of waterfront property with practice links, tennis courts, a heliport and a 5,000sq ft spa. George Bush Snr comes so often there's a suite named after him.

Trips Out of Town

Laid-back **Key West**.
See p236.

ICE CREAM LOVER PARKING
← ONLY →
ALL OTHERS WILL SPLIT

Holiday Isle Resort

MM 84 (1-800 327 7070/1-305 664 2321/www. holidayisle.com). **Rates** $115-$199 room; $245-$485 suite. **Credit** AmEx, Disc, MC, V.

A vast four-resort complex of 176 rooms, efficiencies, cottages and suites, infinitely less smart (and so less wallet-sapping) than Cheeca Lodge, but still with plenty of amenities, fine beaches and even better booze spots.

The Middle Keys

Long Key

The original Spanish name was Cayo Vivora, or Rattlesnake Key – not because the island was particularly snake infested but because its sinuous shape reminded early settlers of a striking rattler. It's now largely taken up by the 965-acre state recreation area *(see below).*

Long Key State Recreation Area

MM 67.5 (1-305 664 4815). **Open** 8am-sunset daily. **Admission** $3.50 per car. **No credit cards.**

There's some beautiful nature to be enjoyed around here, including mangroves that harbour a variety of water birds. The water is very shallow, and from the beach you can safely wade way, way out into the Atlantic: it's great for kids. You can also go snorkelling or canoeing.

Conch Key to Fat Deer Key

There are few points of interest on the short drive from Long Key to Marathon, through Conch Key, Grassy Key and the assorted smaller Keys. Some keys are home to fishermen, especially at **Tom's Harbor Cut**, while others offer super-swanky resorts: Duck Key, reached via bridge at MM 61, is where you'll find the Morris Lapidus-designed **Hawk's Cay Resort** (1-305 743 7000). The high point for visitors is undoubtedly the **Dolphin Research Center** *(see below),* but aside from that, you're best off pushing on to Marathon.

Dolphin Research Center

MM 59, Grassy Key (1-305 289 1121/reservations 1-305 289 0002/www.dolphins.org). **Open** 9am-5pm daily. **Admission** $19.50; $13.50 concessions. *Dolphin encounters* $155. **Credit** AmEx, Disc, MC, V.

This non-profit spot is part research facility, part education organisation and part tourist attraction, and it fulfils all three of its roles with aplomb. Those expecting – and hoping for – a standard cutesy dolphin show will be disappointed, but that's not really the point: staff here are more concerned with the benefits of dolphin-related therapy on handicapped kids, although anyone can swim with the dolphins

by booking in advance. The tours are illuminating and interesting. The giant statue of a bottlenose dolphin out in front of the centre is of Mitzi, the star of the original movie *Flipper*.

Key Vaca & Marathon

Marathon, on the island of **Key Vaca** (named after the manatees, or sea cows, that once thrived in these waters) is the last major settlement before Key West. It's an odd mix of delicious beaches (the lively **Sombrero Beach**, off Sombrero Road at the south side), subtropical forests (**Crane Point**; *see below*), cheap motels, variable restaurants and seamy bars. The town seems unable to settle on its own character, so it picks and chooses bits and pieces from other Keys. The result is an indelicate mish-mash of a place, neither natural nor urban, neither quiet nor loud, neither great nor lousy. Appropriate, then, that it should sit at the halfway mark between Key Largo and Key West.

Most of the locals who work here (as opposed to the many who have retired down here) are fishermen or tourist industry operatives. At times, it seems everyone who isn't running a motel is out fishing, and those who aren't doing either are out on a boat taking those who are staying in the motels out to watch the fishermen.

Crane Point

5550 Overseas Highway (MM 50.5), Marathon (1-305 753 9100/www.cranepoint.org). **Open** 9am-5pm Mon-Sat; noon-5pm Sun. **Admission** $10; $5 concessions. **Credit** AmEx, Disc, MC, V.

This extraordinary 63.5-acre subtropical forest, the last remaining virgin palm hammock in the US, is named after philanthropists Francis and Mary Crane, who lived here for years. The property includes the Museum of Natural History of the Florida Keys and the compact Florida Keys Children's Museum, which will keep young ones occupied at least for a short spell. The Adderley House, built by a Bahamanian immigrant in 1904, offers a glimpse into how things used to be. But the real attraction is undoubtedly the steamy nature trail, leading to the water. All in all, this is a splendid, undervalued spot, and a lovely way to pass a few hours.

Where to eat

Crocodiles on the Water (MM 48, 1-305 743 9018) offers fare that's pricey for these parts, **Shuckers Raw Bar & Grill** (MM 50.5, 1-305 743 8686) does all right with its seafood, the **Cracked Conch Café** (MM 49.5, 1-305 743 2233) is half-bar, half-grill, and the **Wooden Spoon** (MM 50.5, 1-305 743 7469) offers no-frills breakfasts and terrific Key lime pie. Most

Trips Out of Town

of the bars are seedy spots with 'entertainment' from dreadful bands keen to submit audiences to death by cover version. You're best off sticking to **Gary's Pub & Billiards** (MM 50, 1-305 743 0622), a good-size pool hall and bar.

Where to stay

Chain-wise, try the **Wellesley Inn** (MM 54, Marathon, 1-305 743 8550). Most other options are cheap 'n' cheerful motels.

Conch Key Cottages

62250 Overseas Highway (MM 62.3), Conch Key, Walkers Island (1-800 330 1577/1-305 289 1377/www.conchkeycottages.com). **Rates** $74-$122 efficiency; $120-$288 1-bed cottage. **Credit** AmEx, Disc, MC, V.

If you want to stay in a luridly coloured efficiency or pleasant cottage on your own island with your own private beach, head here. No smoking.

Pigeon Key was once home to the labourers on Flagler's railroad. These days it's all but deserted, although it merits a visit for the tranquillity, for its informative museum and for the chance to ride by train on the old **Seven Mile Bridge**. The island is accessible only by train, bike or on foot. Head to the **Visitors' Centre** (located, appropriately, in a red railway carriage at MM 47, right before the bridge, 1-305 289 0025), where you can leave your car.

Right by the visitors' centre begins the Seven Mile Bridge (which is actually only 6.7 miles long), a soaring structure opened in 1982 replacing the original, built 70 years earlier. When the original was completed back in 1912 newspapers proclaimed it the Eighth Wonder of the World; now it's the world's longest guano-spattered fishing pier. Thinking about the construction of it boggles the mind. Instead, just thrill to the most spectacular part of the drive down the Keys.

The Lower Keys

By the time they've crossed the Seven Mile Bridge and realised their ultimate destination is only 35 or so miles away, many visitors hurry through the Lower Keys and head straight for Key West. But though traditional Keys sights and activities – read: T-shirt shops and glass-bottom boat tours – are few and far between, the Lower Keys offer some lovely scenery, and a couple of the Keys' most effortlessly enchanting stops.

On and around Key West's **Mallory Square**. *See p236.*

Bahia Honda & Big Pine Keys

Bahia Honda is home to the uniquely beautiful and tranquil **Bahia Honda State Park** (*see below*). More typical signs of life arrive in **Big Pine Key**, the Keys' second-largest island after Key Largo. Traffic can snarl up going through here, especially around the island's small and – given what's gone before – perversely normal strip of shops. For visitors, though, the attraction is more special: the presence on the island of Key deer. There are fewer than 300 of these pint-size deer left on the island, and those that remain are protected by the 2,251-acre **National Key Deer Refuge**, set up in the 1950s. Don't expect to just be able to drive up and pet them, mind: they're reclusive creatures, and only really come out around dawn and dusk. However, look out while you're driving through too: upwards of 50 deer are killed each year by careless drivers. (Other endangered species in the area include the Lower Keys marsh rabbit and silver rice rabbit). For more information, stop by the **National Key Deer Refuge Headquarters** (*see below*); to get to the refuge, turn west off the highway just south of MM 31 on to Key Deer Boulevard (940), from where signs point the

way to the headquarters. A right turn off Key Deer Boulevard on to Watson Boulevard leads to a concrete bridge across Bogie Channel and on to **No Name Key**, a tiny cul-de-sac of an island that once hosted a clandestine training base for anti-Castro Cuban guerrillas.

Bahia Honda State Park

MM 37, Bahia Honda Key (1-305 872 2353/ www.bahiahondapark.com). **Open** 8am-sunset daily. **Admission** $5 per car. *Kayak rentals* single $10 per hr; double $18 per hr. **Credit** AmEx, Disc, MC, V.

Perhaps the prettiest of all the parks in the Keys, Bahia Honda offers the proverbial something for everyone: nature trails for the exploratory-minded, diving and snorkelling for the adventurous (equipment rental is available at the marina), camping for real outdoor types (and cabins for real indoor types), and the loveliest white sand beaches in the Keys. It's the perfect way to get some R&R before or after a Key West binge. **Photo** *p229.*

National Key Deer Refuge Headquarters

Winn Dixie Shopping Plaza (MM 31), Big Pine Key (1-305 872 0774). **Open** 8am-5pm Mon-Fri. This is the place to come for information about the Key Deer that roam around these parts, and where best to see them. Staff are helpful and can provide maps and other literature.

The Torch Keys to Boca Chica Key

For visitors, after Big Pine the rest of the Keys serve as the home-straight run into Key West. However, there are a few stops you can make. The **Torch Keys** – Little, Big and Middle – which are named after the sappy torchwood trees found around here, are missable, unless that is, you have the cash for **Little Palm Island Resort & Spa** (*see below*) on Little Torch Key, a luxury retreat whose restaurant is consistently rated as the best dining spot on the Keys outside of Key West. Otherwise, at MM 17 on **Sugarloaf Key** is what appears to be a sailless windmill: this is **Perky's Bat Tower**. In the 1920s, a man named Richter C Perky, a real-estate developer from Miami, had plans to turn the Key into a private vacation and fishing retreat. Before he could do that he needed to clear the area of pests, in particular the viciously bloodthirsty local mosquitoes. Perky read that bats could help rid places of the insects, so he built this 35-foot tower in a bid to lure bats. But the bats never showed up, the mosquitoes stayed, and Perky went bust, leaving the tower as a monument to his entrepreneurial dreams.

Little Palm Island Resort & Spa

28500 Overseas Highway (accessible from MM 28.5), Little Torch Key (1-305 872 2524/www. littlepalmisland.com). **Rates** $695-$950 bungalow suite; $1,195-$1,695 deluxe suite. **Credit** AmEx, Disc, MC, V.

As exclusive as the Keys get, private Little Palm Island is accessible only by boat or seaplane. Accommodation is in beachfront bungalows set among the palms. There are endless activities – but, blissfully for some, no phones, TVs or alarm clocks – above and below water and a world-class spa. Like an R-rated fantasy, children under 16 are not allowed.

Key West

Settlers came to Key West in the early 1800s, a mix of farmers, wreckers and opportunists. Later, others just happened to chance upon the island. And today, many will admit they never intended to live here, but somehow could not bear to return across the bridge to the mainland. As one local said: 'In the 1970s came the hippies, followed by the gays, and in the 1990s the cruise ship brigade.'

Key West was once Florida's wealthiest city, but suffered a slump in the 1940s, several years after the wrecking, sponge and cigar industries collapsed or departed and the 1935 hurricane destroyed the bridge that linked it to the mainland. It took a while for the island to recover its economic footing, but recover it has.

Key West is a strange place. But it's not, you feel, as strange as the locals like to think it is. The island is the last of the Keys – it's geographically closer to Havana than Miami – and is home to a mere 30,000, but it is visited by thousands more tourists each year, drawn by thoughts of eccentric charm, lively nightlife and quirky individuality. All those characteristics still exist, but they've been overwhelmed by the chase for the tourist dollar.

There's no doubt that the town badly needed regenerating a few decades ago, and that the tourist industry was a worthwhile buck to pursue. Still, the pursuit has gone too far, and much of the spirit that gave Key West its reputation has vanished. It's been replaced by a weird kind of good-time hippy theme park in and around **Old Town**, the westernmost area of Key West, and the centre of the action. Worse, the locals, while keen to play up their quirks and mannerisms – they once tried to secede from the US and rename Key West the Conch Republic – and happy to take the money, can also be outwardly disparaging about the tourists that make them their living. Walking down main Duval Street, you can't help but feel like the joke's on you.

That said, there is some of the old Key West left: you just have to look beyond Old Town to find it. The architecture here is pretty – a collection of Caribbean and New England-style homes along narrow streets – and some of the attractions genuinely attractive. A couple of good beaches – at **Fort Taylor** and the artificial and rocky **Smathers Beach** – allow chill-out time, while snorkellers and fishermen dive in along the coast.

Old Town

Waterfront **Mallory Square** is where in 1822 American sailors raised the US flag to mark the purchase of Florida from Spain. Boy, what did they start – it's now the crassest place in the Keys, particularly in the hour or two before sunset, when the plaza fills with godawful street entertainers and expensive food stands taking advantage of the hundreds who gather each evening to watch the big orange ball dip below the horizon. However, Mallory Square is an obvious place to begin exploring, not least because just off it is the **Key West Chamber of Commerce** (*see p227*), distributor of free tourist information, maps and brochures. The building that houses the chamber was owned in the 1800s by one of the town's wealthiest citizens, wrecking master Asa Tift; his story, and the background to the business that made

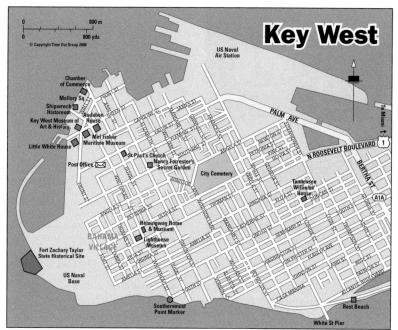

Key West rich – wrecking – is told in the **Key West Shipwreck Historeum** (*see p239*), which is one block west of the chamber.

West of the Historeum, at the end of Wall Street, is the old red-brick Custom House, now serving as the **Key West Museum of Art & History** (*see p238*). The well-tended triangular park in front of the Custom House is Clinton Square, with a monument to the Union soldiers and sailors who lost their lives here during the Civil War (taken by yellow fever; no shots were fired down here). South of Union Square is the very worthwhile **Mel Fisher Maritime Heritage Museum** (*see p239*); if you are only going to visit a couple of Key West attractions, this should be one of them.

WHITEHEAD STREET

Running south from Union Square is Whitehead Street, and at No.205 is **Audubon House** (*see p238*). Across the street is an old Navy cistern, one of several on the island that were at one time used to collect rainwater for drinking supplies (Key West only got running water in 1942). Beyond the cistern are the Presidential Gates, originally designed to be opened for US presidents only. The last sitting president to pass through was JFK, who came here in 1962 during the Cuban Missile Crisis. The gates now give public access to the **Little White House**

(*see p239*). Back across Whitehead Street, what is now **Kelly's Caribbean Bar, Grill & Brewery** (*see p240*) was formerly the first home of PanAm Airlines; the first round-trip ticket to Havana was sold here in 1927. Three blocks down, on the corner with Southard, is the **Green Parrot** (*see p240*), Key West's best bar, and one of the few in town not connected to the island's best-known boozer, who's commemorated a further three blocks up the street at the **Hemingway Home & Museum** (*see p238 and p241* **Hemingway or the highway**). Opposite is the eminently missable **Lighthouse Museum** (*see p239*) – although at one time the lighthouse keeper must have enjoyed incomparable views into Ernest's bathroom.

Whitehead ends at the **Southernmost Point of the USA**, marked by a great big red-and-black striped bottle-recycling bin. This is Key West's prime 'I was here' photo op. But beware of the men who offer to take your picture and then demand a tip.

DUVAL STREET

Key West's main street boasts more souvenir outlets than DisneyWorld, alongside a bar scene unrivalled in its hideousness. But it's not all bad. The southern end is the nicer part. At the junction with United Street, one of a row of pleasingly dilapidated wooden residences

Duval Street.
See p237

and fire stations. Just to prove that Miami doesn't have the monopoly on official corruption, in 1976 the fire chief, with the bizarre but true name of Bum Farto, was charged with the sale and delivery of cocaine but disappeared before sentencing, leaving behind a wife, and has never been heard of since. In 1984 the assistant police chief was charged with delivering cocaine in fried chicken boxes.

Two blocks further east (passing en route No.608 Angela Street, where Elizabeth Taylor was a frequent visitor to the house of her father-in-law, Shakespearean scholar Philip Burton), at the junction of Margaret and Angela, is the small but neatly kept **City Cemetery**, with its collection of strange and witty gravestones (most famously, 'I told you I was sick'). Tours are offered by the Historic Florida Keys Foundation (1-305 292 6718) every Tuesday and Thursday, leaving at 9.30am from the main gate. A donation of $10 is requested; reservations are not required.

houses the thoroughly batty **Chicken Store** (1229 Duval Street, 1-305 294 0070), a refuge for injured hens and roosters, of whom hundreds roam the island's streets and gardens wild. Get your raunchy/humorous Key West chicken-themed memorabilia here. Another of the buildings is home to the splendid **Banana Café** (*see p239*).

Literary types intrigued by the sign for **Naked Lunch** (4 Charles Street), which is arrowed down a side alley off Duval, should be aware that this is nothing to do with William Burroughs or the Beats; rather, it is instead exactly what it says, a place to do lunch naked. It's south Florida's first naturist restaurant – and those with weak stomachs who can't handle the sight of the unsightly should avoid it at all costs. Signs warn 'No Dogs. No Glass. No Photography' and in the toilets, 'No sex'.

Hemingway's old drinking haunt **Sloppy Joe's** (*see p240*) is on Duval at the corner with Greene Street, but the coach-party atmosphere makes boozing here these days a thoroughly depressing experience.

EAST OF DUVAL

One block east of Duval is Simonton Street; at No.314 is the **Casa Antigua Apartments**, Hemingway's first lodgings when he arrived in Key West in 1928. The **William Kerr House** at No.410 is particularly gorgeous, executed in 1880 in a style known locally as 'carpenters' Gothic'. In the middle of the 500 block is a small alley leading to the utterly charming **Nancy Forrester's Secret Garden** (*see p239*). On the corner of Simonton and Angela is Key West City Hall, which also houses the police

Audubon House & Tropical Gardens

205 Whitehead Street, at Greene Street (1-305 294 2116/www.audubonhouse.com). **Open** 9.30am-5pm daily. **Admission** $10; $5 concessions. **Credit** AmEx, MC, V.

John James Audubon, pioneering ornithologist and painter of *Birds of America*, never lived in this house; it merely commemorates his visit here. The self-guided audio tours preserve the tranquillity of the lovely building, while the rare Audubon prints and the calming gardens are attractive.

Hemingway Home & Museum

907 Whitehead Street, at Olivia Street (1-305 294 1575/www.hemingwayhome.com). **Open** 9am-5pm daily. **Admission** $10; $6 concessions. **Credit** (shop only) MC, V.

Relentlessly hyped – especially when you consider that Ernest only lived here for eight years – and often extremely busy, but this is one of Key West's most appealing sights. It is definitely worth tagging along to listen to the stories related by the bunch of laconic guides (they set off every 15 minutes or so), which have the effect of really bringing the house to life. And it's an absolute must for fans of six-toed cats named after celebrities.

Key West Museum of Art & History

281 Front Street, at Greene Street (1-305 295 6616). **Open** 10am-3pm Mon-Fri; 9am-5pm Sat, Sun. **Admission** $10; $5 concessions. **No credit cards**.

A grand old building housing a miscellany of art-works by local painters, old PanAm memorabilia, painted woodcarvings by local luminary Mario Sanchez, as well as exhibits on pirates and young Ernest Hemingway. A real mixed bag, but there's bound to be something to interest.

Key West Shipwreck Historeum

*1 Whitehead Street, at Front Street (1-305 292 8990/
www.historictours.com).* **Open** *Shows* every 30mins
9.45am-4.45pm Mon, Wed-Sun; 9.45am-6.45pm Tue.
Admission $10; $5 concessions. **Credit** AmEx,
Disc, MC, V.

A lively actor-led presentation on the wreck of the
Isaac Allerton, told from the perspective of wrecker
Asa Tift. Good, knockabout fun, and a decent companion to the Mel Fisher Museum (*see below*).

Lighthouse Museum

*938 Whitehead Street, at Truman Street (1-305
295 6616).* **Open** 9.30am-5pm daily. **Admission**
$10; $5 concessions. **Credit** AmEx, Disc, MC, V.

A small lighthouse museum is only half the attraction here: if you can be bothered to walk 88 steps to
the balcony, you get spectacular views of the island.

Little White House

*111 Front Street, at Caroline Street (1-305 294 9911/
www.historictours.com).* **Open** *Tours* 9am-4.30pm
daily. **Admission** $11; $5 concessions. **Credit**
AmEx, Disc, MC, V.

The building to which President Harry Truman, a big
fan of the Keys, retreated for rest and recreation after
World War II is now a nice little museum. If you don't
fancy a full tour, a small section is open at no cost.

Mel Fisher Maritime Heritage Museum

200 Greene Street, at Front Street (1-305 294 2633).
Open 9.30am-5pm daily. **Admission** $11; $4.50
concessions. **Credit** AmEx, MC, V.

An assortment of impressive and rare artefacts at
this museum commemorates the work of Mel Fisher,
an old-school salvager with new-school technology
who unearthed a whopping $400 million of treasure
from wrecks in 1985.

Nancy Forrester's Secret Garden

*1 Free School Lane, at Simonton Street (1-305 294
0015/www.nfsgarden.com).* **Open** *Winter* 10am-5pm
daily. *Summer* phone for details. **Admission** $6.
Credit AmEx, Disc, MC, V.

This 25-year labour of love for Nancy and her partner Elliot Wright contains a unique collection of
botanical plants. Nancy is a licensed pastor and also
conducts weddings in the enchanted jungle.

Where to eat & drink

The Key lime, a small yellow fruit resembling
a roundish lemon, is sold on every corner in a
variety of guises. No visitor can leave without
trying conch (pronounced 'conk'), a shellfish;
it's best deep-fried and sampled as a fritter.

Restaurants & cafés

Banana Café

*1211 Duval Street, at Catherine Street (1-305 294
7227).* **Open** 8am-3pm, 7-11pm Mon, Wed-Sun.
Main courses $4.25-$10.50. **Credit** AmEx, DC.

A gorgeous little place down at the southern end of
Duval, the Banana is the place for breakfast. Join the
queue waiting for a table in the varnished hardwood
interior or, better still, out on the deck. The menu is
brief – sweet and savoury crêpes, omelettes, salads
and sandwiches – but it's all excellent stuff.

She's made it to the **Southernmost Point of the USA**, but does she care? *See p237.*

Blue Heaven

729 Thomas Street, at Angela Street (1-305 296 8666). **Open** 8am-3pm, 6-10.30pm daily. **Main courses** $17-$34. **Credit** Disc, MC, V.

A perennial favourite, BH, a former bordello, serves truly excellent Caribbean cuisine (BBQ shrimp, jerk chicken, surf 'n' turf) in laid-back surroundings. Note the slate billiard table bases inset into the sandy floor of the rear yard, where Hemingway used to attend cockfights. There's a fine little beach bar to patronise while you wait (make sure you try the locally brewed Sunset Ale).

El Siboney

900 Catherine Street, at Margaret Street (1-305 296 4184). **Open** 11am-9.30pm Mon-Sat. **Main courses** $5-$13. **No credit cards**.

Off the beaten track – but then the best eateries usually are – El Siboney is an unpretentious single-storey, red-brick shack offering the finest Cuban food in town. It's also really cheap.

Half Shell Raw Bar

231 Margaret Street, at Caroline Street (1-305 294 7496). **Open** 11am-10.30pm daily. **Main courses** $6-$34. **Credit** AmEx, Disc, MC, V.

The Half Shell is right on the wharf, so if you are lucky enough to get one of the tables at the edge of the room beside the water, you can throw bread and watch as the surface is churned up by shoals of hungry big fish. Avoid the conch fritters, which are too doughy, and instead go for one of the excellent po' boy shrimp or oyster sandwiches.

Kelly's Caribbean Bar, Grill & Brewery

301 Whitehead Street, at Caroline Street (1-305 293 8484/www.kellyskeywest.com). **Open** noon-10pm daily. **Main courses** $11.95-$24.95. **Credit** AmEx, DC, Disc, MC, V.

The 'Kelly' in question being *Top Gun* actress Kelly McGillis (no, we don't know what happened to her, either). The food is surprisingly decent, if not especially Caribbean. Fans claim they do the best conch fritters here – and they're certainly big and meaty. There's also an attached microbrewery. But Kelly dear, please do something about those grubby bathrooms.

Louie's Backyard

700 Waddell Street, at Vernon Street (1-305 294 1061/www.louiesbackyard.com). **Open** 11.30am-3pm, 6-10.30pm daily. **Main courses** $45-$50. **Credit** AmEx, DC, MC, V.

The Floribbean cuisine here is outstanding, but the real winner is the setting – smack on a prime slab of the Gulf. Reservations are hard to come by, but there's always the outdoor bar, where you can drift away on pina coladas and an Eden-istic ambience.

Muriel's Café

703 Duval Street, at Southard Street (1-305 295 6411). **Open** 8.30am-5pm daily. **Main courses** $6.95-$10.95. **Credit** AmEx, DC, Disc, MC, V.

A homely little café, peachy toned with fresh flowers on the table, serving up home-cooked breakfasts, wraps, sandwiches and burgers. It's all way superior to anything else down at this end of Duval.

Pepe's

806 Caroline Street, at William Street (1-305 294 7192). **Open** 6.30am-11pm daily. **Main courses** $12-$20. **Credit** Disc, MC, V.

Opened in 1909 Pepe's is a ramshackle shack, but that doesn't stop the throngs of people waiting in line to dive into Apalachicola Bay oysters and chipped beef on toast at low prices.

Bars

As with the food culture, the epicentre of drinking culture on Key West is Duval Street, which at night turns into a heaving, wretched mass of lairy, boozed-up fun-seekers. If you can still walk in a straight line after a night out, you should get as far away as possible, and as quickly as you can.

Captain Tony's Saloon

428 Greene Street, at Whitehead Street (1-305 294 1838/capttonyssaloon.com). **Open** 10am-2am Mon-Sat; noon-2am Sun. **Credit** MC, V.

The oldest bar in Florida™. This was the original Sloppy Joe's (*see below*) before a rent hike caused Joe and his patrons to pack up all the furnishings and ship out to these nearby premises. The walls are papered with yellowing business cards, the ceiling beams are hung with yellowing brassieres, and the tourists are in heaven.

Green Parrot

601 Whitehead Street, at Southard Street (1-305 294 6133/www.greenparrot.com). **Open** 10am-4am Mon-Sat; noon-4am Sun. **No credit cards**.

The Parrot, here since 1890, can get as loud and lairy as some of the Duval Street spots, but at least it's mostly locals doing the shouting. It's got a great divey atmosphere and a decent range of beers (about ten of them on draught).

PT's Late Night Bar & Grill

920 Caroline Street, at Margaret Street (1-305 296 4245). **Open** 11am-4am daily. **Credit** DC, MC, V.

A popular sports bar with the added bonuses of food served late and pool tables. An excellent alternative to the crush on Duval Street.

Sloppy Joe's

201 Duval Street, at Greene Street (1-305 294 5717/ www.sloppyjoes.com). **Open** 9am-4am Mon-Sat; noon-4am Sun. **Credit** Disc, MC, V.

The most famous bar in south Florida, and all the worse for it. If you really must, go during the day, before the dreadful live music starts and everyone gets hammered on the slush puppy-style house cocktails. One thing's for sure: if Hemingway were alive today he would not be drinking here.

Hemingway or the highway

Ernest Hemingway arrived in Key West in April 1928. He brought with him a wife, Pauline – his second – whose rich Uncle Gus in 1931 provided the couple with the grand home that continues to draw the tourists on Whitehead Street (*see p238; photos below*). Hemingway had a fine old time here – mornings he worked on his novels, including *A Farewell to Arms*, which was written during this period, and in the afternoons he went deep-sea fishing and hung with the boys at Sloppy Joe's (*see p240*), where he ran a monthly tab on his whisky and sodas. One day in 1936 a journalist called Martha Gelhorn walked into the bar on assignment to interview the writer. Almost immediately, the two began an affair that ended his marriage in 1939 when,

almost eight years to the day that he'd moved into Whitehead Street, Hemingway packed his clothes and moved out. The following year, 13 days after divorcing Pauline in Miami, he married Martha (wife three of four), and they moved to Havana. The discarded Pauline stayed on in Key West, running an interior design shop on the corner of Caroline and Ann Streets and occupying the Whitehead Street house until her death in 1951.

For all the time he spent here, Key West only made it into one of Hemingway's novels, the indifferent *To Have and Have Not*. Howard Hawks used the tale as source material for the far superior movie starring Humphrey Bogart and Lauren Bacall, in which he transferred all the action to Martinique.

Shopping

Key West is a town with a classy literary pedigree. It has acted as a retreat, haven or hideaway not just for Hemingway but also John Dos Passos in the 1920s, poet Robert Frost, who spent 16 winters here from 1934, and Tennessee Williams, who arrived in 1941 and stayed because he 'liked to swim'. More recently, the island has harboured James Leo Herlihy, author

of *Midnight Cowboy*, Pulitzer Prize-winning novelist Alison Lurie and sexologist Nancy Friday. Pick up their work at **Blue Heron Books** (826 Duval Street, 1-305 296 3508) or at the superb **Key West Island Books** at 513 Fleming Street (1-305 294 2904), just off Duval.

Otherwise, everything in Key West is expensive, and decent shops are few and far between (T-shirt shops breed far more successfully than the beleaguered manatee).

Trips Out of Town

Queer as Keys

Although the place has the ugliest drag queens alive, Key West is a gay mecca where rainbow flags used to designate gay-friendly businesses are wholly unnecessary. Indeed, the gay spots, where boozing is the universal language, can be some of Key West's most entertaining. Two popular venues are the **801 Bourbon Bar/Number One Saloon** (801 Duval Street & 514 Petronia Street, 305 294 9349 for both), featuring ugly but entertaining drag and deafening disco. A mostly male clientele frequents this hotspot from 9pm until 4am. Another Duval Street favourite is **Aqua**, at No.711 (1-305 292 8500), where you might catch those same ugly drag queens belting out torch songs, or clueless Midwesterners participating in wet-skivvies contests.

Sunday nights are fun at two places in particular. **Tea by the Sea**, on the pier at the Atlantic Shores Motel (510 South Street, 1-800 520 3559), attracts a faithful following of shirtless regulars and visitors. The clothing-optional pool is either an attraction or a turn-off, depending on who's disrobing there. Show up after 7.30pm. Better known around town as **La-Te-Da**, La Terraza de Martí (1125 Duval Street, 1-305 296 6706), the former Key West home of Cuban exile José Martí, is a great spot to gather poolside for the best Martini in town – but don't bother with the food. Upstairs is the **Crystal Room** (1-305 296 6706), where life is, indeed, a cabaret – much like life in general in Key West.

There are some unusual shops worth checking out. At the **Cuban Leaf Cigar Factory** (310 Duval Street, 1-305 295 9283), you can watch cigars being made before buying them. **Capricorn Jewelry** (706B Duval Street, 1-305 292 9338) has a good selection of Native American jewellery. The **Key West Kite Company** (409 Greene Street, 1-305 296 2535) is worth a visit to see all the colourful designs, while **Glass Reunions** (825 Duval Street, 1-305 294 1720) sells locally made, hand-blown art and household items that'll never make it home in one piece.

If you're in self-catering accommodation, don't shop at the small supermarkets along the main strips, where tourists are charged more than natives. **Key Plaza** and **Searstown**, both on N Roosevelt Boulevard, have decent stores. If you get the munchies at night, head for the 24-hour **Sunbeam Groceries & Deli** (500 White Street, 1-305 294 8993). Otherwise, best food shopping of all is at **Fausto's Food Palace** (522 Fleming Street, 1-305 296 5663), a superb deli-cum-supermarket; it's open 8am-8pm six days a week, 8am-7pm Sunday.

Where to stay

During the high season in Key West (November to April), accommodation prices soar, and booking is advised. Both the **Hilton** (245 Front Street, 1-305 294 4000) and the **Wyndham** (1435 Simonton Street, 1-305 296 5000) have big resorts right in Key West. However, most of the chains are clustered on N Roosevelt Boulevard, away from the Old Town. They include:

Best Western (No.3755, 1-305 296 3500)
Comfort Inn (No.3824, 1-305 294 3773)
Days Inn (No.3852, 1-305 294 3742)
Holiday Inn (No.3841, 1-800 695 8284)
Quality Inn (No.3850, 1-305 294 6681)

Off-season, you can find good deals at the numerous guesthouses and B&Bs, which can be really cost-effective if four people share a room with two beds. Budget accommodation can be found at the youth hostel near the centre of town or at the chain motels. Alternatively, stay in one of the old gingerbread-style family homes. Prices start at $40 per night off-season and run to $200-plus.

Duval Gardens

1012 Duval Street, at Truman Street (1-800 867 1234/1-305 292 3379/www.duvalgardens.com). **Rates** *June-late Dec* $89-$169. *Late Dec-May* $119-$229. **Credit** AmEx, Disc, MC, V.
A mid-priced, family-run B&B up at the quieter end of Duval, with a small pool and free off-street parking. Rooms are small but comfortable.

Island City House

411 William Street, at Eaton Street (1-305 294 5702/www.islandcityhouse.com). **Rates** $120-$210. **Credit** AmEx, Disc, MC, V.
The oldest guesthouse on the island consists of three lovely lacy-balconied houses ranged around a semi-tropical courtyard, with 12 luxurious suites of colonial-style furnishings and hardwood floors. There's a large pool and four cats, two of which has six toes.

Key West International Youth Hostel

718 South Street, at Elizabeth Street (1-800 748 2238/1-305 292 7918/www.keywesthostel.com). **Rates** $28-$31 per person. **Credit** MC, V.
Cheap dorm rooms down near the Southernmost Point, a five-minute walk from central Old Town. There are full kitchen facilities, bike rentals, free

parking, a pool table, a picnic area, and complimentary wireless internet access. Another bonus is the 24-hour access. Booking is essential in winter.

Marquesa Hotel

600 Fleming Street, at Simonton Street (1-800 869 4631/1-305 292 1919/www.marquesa.com). **Rates** *June-Oct* $175-$205 standard; $225-$255 deluxe. *Nov-May* $235-$285 standard; $275-$335 deluxe. **Credit** AmEx, DC, MC, V.

Key West's – and, some say, one of the country's – finest old hotel is a small complex of four historic buildings set around a lush garden with two pools. The place has won countless awards, and it's not hard to see why.

Southernmost Point Guest House

1327 Duval Street, at United Street (1-305 294 0715/www.southernmostpoint.com). **Rates** *May-late Dec* $75-$120. *Late Dec-Apr* $115-$185. **Credit** AmEx, MC, V.

This family-run establishment is a rambling old colonial villa in lush gardens down at the classier end of Duval. It has gorgeous hardwood verandas with wicker chairs and ferns and a small pool.

Getting around

Key West's streets are narrow, and the island is small, so don't plan on using a car while here. However, if you do have one, you're best off parking it at the garage on the corner of Caroline and Grinnell Streets. Walking is the most sensible way to get around, although bikes, mopeds and scooters can be hired for between $7 and $30 a day; most firms insist on a credit card for vehicle rentals. Shop around for the best deal. Large rental firms include the **Bicycle Centre** (523 Truman Avenue, 1-305 294 4556), the **Bike Shop** (1110 Truman Avenue, 1-305 294 1073) and **Adventure Bicycle & Scooter Rentals** (locations including 601 Front Street at the Hyatt Hotel, 1-305 293 9944). Many firms that rent scooters offer one- or two-seater vehicles. Try **Pirate Scooter** (401 Southard Street, 1-305 295 0000) or **Paradise Rentals** (112 Fitzpatrick Street, 1-305 292 6441 or 430 Duval Street, 1-305 293 1112).

Tours & excursions

Most popular among tourists are the 90-minute **Conch Tour Train** (1-305 294 5161) and the **Old Town Trolley** (1-305 296 6688), which give similar – they're owned by the same firm – guided commentaries on the town's main attractions. Both run 9am-4.30pm daily and both yield intriguing nuggets of information, but at a price: about $20 per person. Pick-up points and ticket offices are at the junction of Duval and Wall Streets and over at Flagler Station at the northern end of Margaret Street.

For twilight touring, try **Original Ghost Tours** (1-305 294 9255, www.hauntedtours.com) or **Ghosts & Legends of Key West** (1-305 294 1713, www.keywestghosts.com), both of which lead nightly excursions costing $15 per person; call to make reservations.

There are numerous sunset cruises, tours to the coral reefs and glass-bottom boat trips, all touted at numerous booths along Duval Street.

The Dry Tortugas

Contrary to popular tourist belief, the Dry Tortugas are not a Tex-Mex snack, but a group of islands 70 miles off the coast of Key West ('tortuga' means turtle in Spanish). The **Dry Tortugas National Park** (PO Box 6208, Key West, FL 33041, 1-305-242-7700, www.nps. gov/drto) is home to the Civil War monument **Fort Jefferson** and a wildlife sanctuary. The park makes a perfect day trip from the bustle of Key West and is excellent for snorkelling and fishing. Visitors must bring all food, water and supplies. Free camping is allowed at ten sites. You can get to the park via the **Yankee Freedom** ferry service (1-305 294 7009), **Sunny Days Catamaran** (1-305 296 5556), **Tortugas Ferry** (1-305 294 7009) and **Fort Jefferson Catamaran** (1-305 292 6100). All services run daily.

City Cemetery. See p238.

Trips Out of Town

timeout.com

Over 50 of the world's greatest
cities reviewed in one site.

Directory

Features

Directory

Getting Around

By air

Miami International Airport (MIA)

305 876 7000/www.miami-airport.com. **Maps** p271 & p277.
MIA is north-west of Downtown Miami. Unless you're planning to rent a car, the easiest and cheapest way to get from the airport is the **SuperShuttle**, a shared-ride van service. You'll find dispatchers waiting on the kerb wherever you exit on the lower level of the arrivals building. Fares are $19 ($8 additional passengers) to a South Beach hotel or private residence; and $17 to Coral Gables or Coconut Grove. You can arrange for the SuperShuttle to take you back to MIA by calling 305 871 2000, 24 hours in advance.

You'll find taxis waiting outside MIA's arrival terminals. There is a $32 flat rate to South Beach – be sure to ask for it. The fare to Coral Gables is about $21-$24 and to Coconut Grove $17-$23, both without tip.

You can take the J bus from MIA to Miami Beach; it goes to 41st Street (aka Arthur Godfrey Road) and then turns north on Collins Avenue, ending at 72nd Street. If you're going to South Beach, you'll have to change to the C or H bus at 41st Street. Buses stop outside the lower level of the arrivals building at concourse E. There's a computerised information kiosk in the bus waiting room.

The Triangle, the area of MIA containing over two dozen car rental agencies, is an incredibly confusing place where many tourists get lost. Make sure you get good directions before heading out there. It's now a legal requirement that the rental agency gives you a map, and most provide a sheet of directions out of the labyrinthine parking lots. Note that there are several gas stations along Le Jeune Road (NW 42nd Avenue) that are handy for pre-return refills. For a map of the Triangle, *see p277.*

Fort Lauderdale-Hollywood International Airport

954 359 1200/www.broward.org/airport.

From Fort Lauderdale Airport you have several options on how to make the 30-mile trip to Miami. The best is to rent a car at the airport and drive south on either I-95 or the Florida Turnpike. Alternatively, take a shuttle bus from the lower level at the eastern end of Terminals 1 and 3 to the airport's Tri-Rail station and then take a commuter train south to Miami. Note, however, that the **Tri-Rail** schedule is very limited, running hourly or every two hours during the week, less frequently at the weekend.

There is also a shared-ride van service, **Bahama Link**, which will take you to your hotel in Miami or Miami Beach ($45 for 1-2 people to South Beach; $60 for 1-2 to Coconut Grove or Coral Gables; $12 per person for groups of ten). Book 24 hours in advance on 954 779 7600.

When it comes time to return to Fort Lauderdale Airport, there is another, cheaper option: you can book the **SuperShuttle** (305 871 2000) 24 hours in advance for $28 ($12 additional passengers) from South Beach, $33.50 from Coconut Grove and Coral Gables. Unfortunately, it doesn't pick up from the airport.

By bus or rail

Greyhound and **Amtrak** run, respectively, bus and rail services into and out of Miami. For details, including station addresses, *see p214.*

Information

Miami's public transportation system is run by **Miami-Dade Transit**. For information, log on to www.miamidade.gov/transit or call 305 770 3131 (6am-10pm Mon-Fri; 9am-5pm Sat, Sun). Alternatively, visit the **Transit Information Booth** at Government Center Station, Downtown, where you can pick up route maps or, if you're very lucky, the *Miami-Dade County Transit Map*, a schematic plan showing the various transport services and their connections. Guard it with your life.

Buses

Buses – here in Miami called Metrobuses – are for the unlucky. Only the poor or near terminally aged don't drive their own car in this town. Hence buses often resemble mobile outpatient wards. The vehicles themselves are clean, air-conditioned and comfy, but they travel congested routes and often don't serve the places where visitors might want to go. The fact that there's no direct service from MIA to South Beach says it all. (On South Beach itself, however, there's the South Beach Local shuttle bus; *see p60*). For more on specific, useful routes, see the individual Sightseeing chapter introductions.

Frequency of service varies by route, time and day of the week: as often as every ten or 15 minutes or as far apart as every 45 minutes, so leave yourself lots of time, take a patience pill and try to enjoy the scenery.

FARES & BUS STOPS

A one-way bus fare is $1.25; children up to 3 feet 6 inches tall travel free. Express buses cost $1.50. Transfers cost an extra 25¢; you must ask and pay for a transfer when you get on the bus. You'll need the exact fare, but the machines take silver, crisp dollar bills and tokens (*see p247*). Bus stops are marked by a rectangular white sign with a blue and green metal marker bearing the specific bus route(s), and often by a yellow kerb stripe. Sometimes they are not marked at all, and it's just guesswork as to where to stand. Shelters are uncommon, so take a hat to keep the sun off your head.

TOKENS & PASSES

For frequent bus use, it pays to buy tokens from designated stores or Miami-Dade Transit (*see p246*). A roll contains ten tokens and costs $10, saving you $2.50 and the hassle of needing exact change. Tokens are also valid on the Metrorail (*see below*). If you're in town for a while and are planning on doing some major schlepping on public transport, consider buying a monthly Metropass for $60, which gives you unlimited travel. You can buy tokens and passes from Miami-Dade Transit at Government Center Station in Downtown Miami, and only tokens from stores throughout Miami and on Miami Beach.

Trains

There are three train lines in Miami-Dade – **Metromover**, **Metrorail** and **Tri-Rail**.

METROMOVER

Miami's Toonerville Trolley, an elevated, electric monorail that runs a very short loop around Downtown 24 hours daily, is free to travel and offers fine views of Biscayne Bay and the city. Sadly, that's about all it offers as it goes nowhere useful.

METRORAIL

A 21-mile elevated train system that runs from Hialeah (north) to Dadeland (south), with stops around every mile, Metrorail is another of Miami's expensive and underused transit systems. As on the bus, a trip costs $1.25, plus 25¢ for a transfer. Trains run every 20 minutes until midnight. Visitors might find Metrorail useful for trips to

Coconut Grove, Coral Gables and Vizcaya. Metrorail also connects to **Tri-Rail**, the Gulf Coast's intercity commuter system (*see p214*).

Taxis & limos

Taxi meters start at $1.70 and click away at $2.20 per mile, plus waiting time charges ($35 per hr). For short distances, they're affordable; for long distances, they can cost a fortune. The meter racks up $10 just travelling the length of the MacArthur Causeway. Some approximate fares from South Beach are: $16-$20 to the Design District; $18-$22 to W Flagler Street, Downtown; $25-$27 to CocoWalk in Coconut Grove; $27-$29 to Miracle Mile in Coral Gables. On top of these outrageous fares, you are also expected to tip 15 per cent; cabs carry a handy little tip calculation chart pasted inside the passenger windows.

Cabs are usually radio-dispatched, although on South Beach and Downtown you can just flag one down. Restaurants and hotels will call cabs for patrons. Note that drivers often speak little or no English. Some reliable companies are **Best Taxi Service** (305 444 4444), **Central Cabs** (305 532 5555), **Eights Cab** (305 888 8888) and **Yellow Cabs** (305 633 0503).

Limos are a dime a dozen in some areas, especially South Beach, where they're the size of ocean liners. Rates start at $50 per hour for a Lincoln Town Car and escalate to $75-$85 per hour for a ten-passenger stretch limo. Virtually all companies require a three-hour minimum rental time, and many tack on a 20 per cent 'gratuity'. Ask your hotel to recommend a limo service. You might want to consider hiring a vintage Rolls-Royce limo with chauffer, from $95 per hour – call **Vintage Limos** on 305 444 7657.

To make a complaint about a taxi, call 305 375 3677.

Driving

Like most Americans, Miamians regard driving as their birthright. But because such a large segment of the population was neither born nor raised here, many residents drive without knowledge of local traffic rules. Be sure to drive carefully and with extra alertness. In addition to the usual big-city problems, you'll encounter some uniquely local driving issues, such as drivers who change lanes without signalling, stop suddenly at the top of freeway on-ramps in merging lanes and ignore stop signs. Then there are the many elderly drivers who drive in a bizarre kind of panic but at a snail's pace, always refusing to give way. Not to mention those with their cell phones clamped to their ears, who wouldn't look back if they heard a thwack (they'd just assume it was a speed bump). Don't forget, too, that several major highways change names with mysterious frequency. And don't even get us started on the notoriously inadequate road signage.

The potentially lethal driving dangers for which Miami became notorious in the early 1990s – carjackings – have subsided to normal (for the US) levels, although you still wouldn't want to get lost in many neighbourhoods. (Generally speaking, Miami's easternmost communities are safer than the central and western sectors).

If you do find yourself lost and in need of directions, stay calm. Always stop at well-lit commercial outlets for directions, and take into account who's around. Another option is to call your hotel or your destination for directions. Don't leave valuable items visible in your car, even while you're in motion, as 'smash-and-grab' robbers approach idling cars at traffic lights.

If you break down, use your judgement about whether to leave the car and phone for help. The AAA recommends you wait until a police car passes and flag it down. If you're a member of the AAA or have affiliated membership through a similar foreign group, always call it rather than a towing service, whose rates touch on the extortionate. Emergency phones are provided on freeways. If you have a mobile phone, dial *FHP for the highway patrol. *See also p257* **Safety & security**.

Two last points: during rush hours (7-9am, 4-6pm Mon-Fri), only vehicles carrying at least two people including the driver can travel in lanes marked 'HOV' ('high-occupancy vehicles'); and Florida law allows you to turn right on a red light if the road is clear, unless a sign says otherwise.

Parking

Parking on South Beach is an ordeal, and an expensive one to boot. Invariably, you will have to use meters, parking lots (many of which have meters), garages or valet parking. For meters, you'll need rolls of quarters (it costs $1 per hr but is free from midnight to 9am) and for garages and valet services, tons of money, full stop. Finding a free meter on South Beach can be tricky, although they're more prevalent the further north you go.

Vehicle hire

There are many car rental companies to choose from as long as you have a major credit card and are over 25 years old. (Some local car rental agencies will rent to people without credit cards if they are over 25, produce a licence and a round-trip air ticket, and pay a deposit of several hundred dollars, or to persons aged 21-25 with a major credit card.)

Rental rates range wildly, depending on company and the time of the year. Do some comparative shopping by calling several of the nationals before your trip, making sure to ask about any discounts – for example, as a member of the US-based AAA – British AA members also qualify – or the AARP (American Association of Retired Persons). Booking via websites can net you extra discounts.

It's also worth researching fly-drive deals and rentals through your travel agent. These often offer the best value, especially if you're coming from outside the US; otherwise, reserve a car at the best rate you've found; you can usually cancel with no penalty.

Remember that the prices companies quote you do not include state sales tax or either collision damage or liability insurance. If your home policy or credit card doesn't cover you, grit your teeth and hand over the cash, even though it may almost double the rental bill. Driving without coverage can be financially ruinous should the unlikely happen.

National car rental companies

Alamo 1-800 462 5266/ www.alamo.com.
Avis 1-800 331 1212/ www.avis.com.
Budget 1-800 527 0700/ www.budget.com.
Dollar 1-800 800 4000/ www.dollar.com.
Enterprise 1-800 261 7331/ www.enterprise.com.
Hertz 1-866 654 3131/ www.hertz.com.
National 1-800 227 7368/ www.nationalcar.com.
Thrifty 1-800 847 4389/ www.thrifty.com.

Local car rental companies

If you want to rent a car for a day or two in the middle of your stay, you don't have to make the inconvenient and expensive trip to MIA, which is where most of the big rental

companies are based (*see p246*): there are local rental companies that will, for no extra cost, either deliver and pick up your rental car at your hotel or pick up and deliver you to their office.

Those that offer reasonably competitive rates ($30-$40 per day for a mid-size car) include **InterAmerican Car Rental** (305 871 3030). Many locals and nationals have offices on South Beach, including **Avis** (305 538 4441) and **Budget** (305 865 4447).

Scooters, cycling & blading

If you're spending much time on South Beach, consider exploring or cruising by scooter, bicycle and/or in-line skating. **Electric Rentals** even rents out those weird, clunky Segway 'people movers'. All these options (bar the Segways) are a lot cheaper than renting a car.

Beach Scooter Sales & Rentals

1435 Collins Avenue, at Española Way, South Beach (305 538 0977/ www.beachscooter.com). Bus C, H, K, W, South Beach Local. **Open** 10am-8pm daily. **Credit** AmEx, DC, MC, V. **Map** p273 B3.

Electric Rentals

233 11th Street, at Collins Avenue, South Beach (305 532 6700). Bus C, H, K, W, South Beach Local. **Open** 10am-midnight daily. **Credit** AmEx, DC, MC, V. **Map** p273 D2.

Fritz's Skate, Bike & Surf Shop

730 Lincoln Road, at Meridian Avenue, South Beach (305 532 1954). Bus C, G, H, K, L, S, W, South Beach Local. **Open** 10am-10pm daily. **Credit** AmEx, DC, Disc, MC, V. **Map** p273 A1.

Miami Beach Bicycle Center

601 5th Street, at Washington Avenue, South Beach (305 674 0150). Bus C, H, K, W, South Beach Local. **Open** 10am-7pm Mon-Sat; 10am-5pm Sun. **Credit** AmEx, DC, MC, V. **Map** p273 F1.

Resources A-Z

Addresses

On long, narrow Miami Beach, the east–west thoroughfares are numbered (the lower the number, the further south the street), with most taking the suffix 'Street'; the north–south thoroughfares all take proper names, with the majority using the suffix 'Avenue'. Figuring out cross-streets for Avenue addresses on Miami Beach is done by removing the last two digits of the street number. So, the cross-street for 1601 Collins Avenue is 16th Street, and the cross-street for 18215 Collins Avenue is 182nd Street.

Miami itself takes a more typical grid system, albeit one with a few quirks. Much of the city is divided into four quadrants: NW, NE, SE and SW. Point zero is Downtown at the junction of Flagler Street (the north–south divider) and Miami Avenue (the east–west divider). East–west thoroughfares are numbered and take the suffix 'Street', while their numbered north–south counterparts use the suffix 'Avenue'. Again, cross-streets are simple to figure and go in hundreds: 3555 SW 8th Street is at SW 35th Avenue; 360 NW 8th Street is at NW 3rd Avenue.

Age restrictions

In common with much of the US, the minimum drinking age in Florida is 21. And also in common with many major US cities, you're advised to carry a photo ID with you at all times. Bar staff, especially on South Beach, work in fear of licence infringements, and will demand ID to assuage their doubts.

Smokers, meanwhile, must be 18 in order to purchase cigarettes in Miami. Drivers need to be 18 in order to legally get behind the wheel. For more information on driving and care hire, *see pp247-248*.

Attitude & etiquette

Hot weather and an overriding reliance on the tourist industry combine to make south and central Florida generally friendly. Casual dress is necessary, thanks to the generally hot and steamy weather, and the overall vibe is similarly relaxed.

However, all of this comes with several caveats. On a fairly trivial level, workers in the service industries on South Beach can be surly: many see themselves as 'resting' models/musicians/whatevers, and they're not afraid to let their customers know they think they're too handsome/cool/talented to be doing their job.

More seriously, although the crime situation isn't as bad as it was in the early 1990s, parts of Miami are still unsafe; for more on this, *see p257* **Safety & security**. And also, despite appearances, this is still the South. While Miami Beach is relaxed on matters of race and sexuality, other parts of Florida – including the Keys before you reach Key West – are far less liberal. Choose your local bar carefully.

Business

Business services

Compunet Inc
6600 NW 27th Avenue, at NW 66th Street, North-West Miami (305 693 5553). Bus 27/Metrorail Dr Martin Luther King. **Open** 9am-5pm Mon-Fri. **Credit** AmEx, MC, V.

Kinko's
16-17 Alton Road, at Lincoln Road, South Beach (305 532 4241/www. kinkos.com). Bus M, S, W. **Open** 24hrs daily. **Credit** AmEx, MC, V. **Map** p272 C2.

Conventions & conferences

Coconut Grove Convention Center
2700 S Bayshore Drive, at SW 27th Avenue, Coconut Grove (305 579 3310/www.coconutgroveconvention center.com). Bus 6, 27, 48, Coconut Grove Circulator. **Map** p277 B4. This centre on the edge of Biscayne Bay – and just across the way from

---

Travel advice

For up-to-date information on travel to a specific country – including the latest news on safety and security, health issues, local laws and customs – contact your home country government's department of foreign affairs. Most have websites packed with useful advice for would-be travellers. *See also p254* **Passport update**.

Australia
www.smartraveller.gov.au

Canada
www.voyage.gc.ca

New Zealand
www.mfat.govt.nz/travel

Republic of Ireland
http://foreignaffairs.gov.ie

UK
www.fco.gov.uk/travel

USA
http://travel.state.gov

Miami City Hall – is home to a variety of events: shows for antiques and jewellery, guns and knives as well as concerts and trade shows.

Miami Beach Convention Center

1901 Convention Center Drive, between 17th Street & Dade Boulevard, South Beach (305 673 7311). Bus C, G, H, K, L, S, W, South Beach Local. **Map** p272 C3.
This is one of the best-designed convention centres in the US and can handle four major events at any one time. It's used for everything from the annual Boat Show to Art Basel. A massive structure, it takes up four blocks in South Beach's Deco District, minutes from the ocean-front.

Couriers & shippers

DHL

600 SW 1st Avenue, at SW 6th Street, Downtown (1-800 255 5345/ www.dhl-usa.com). **Open** 9am-6pm Mon-Fri. **Credit** AmEx, DC, MC, V. **Map** p274 F2.

Federal Express

200 Biscayne Boulevard, at SE 2nd Street, Downtown (1-800 463 3339/ www.fedex.com). **Open** 9am-7.15pm Mon-Fri. **Credit** AmEx, DC, MC, V. **Map** p274 E3.

Translators & interpreters

Language Service Bureau

Suite 307, Tower 1, 1000 Quayside Terrace (NE 107th Street & Biscayne Boulevard), Downtown (305 891 0019). Bus 3. **Open** 9am-5pm Mon-Fri. **No credit cards.**

Professional Translating Services

Suite 1800, 44 W Flagler Street, at NW 1st Avenue, Downtown (305 371 7887). Metromover Miami Avenue. **Open** 8.30am-5.30pm Mon-Fri. **Credit** AmEx, MC, V. **Map** p274 D2.

Useful organisations

Coconut Grove Chamber of Commerce

2820 McFarlane Road, at S Bayshore Drive, Coconut Grove (305 444 7270/www.coconutgrove. com). Bus 48, Coconut Grove Circulator. **Open** 9am-5pm Mon-Fri. **Map** p277 B3.

Coral Gables Chamber of Commerce

224 Catalonia Avenue, at Le Jeune Road, Coral Gables (305 446 1657/ www.gableschamber.org). Bus 24, 42, 72/Metrorail Douglas Road. **Open** 8am-5pm Mon-Thur; 8am-4pm Fri. **Map** p276 C3.

Miami Beach Chamber of Commerce

1920 Meridian Avenue, at Dade Boulevard, South Beach (305 674 1300/www.miamibeachchamber.com). Bus A, L, M, S. **Open** 10am-5pm Mon-Fri. **Map** p272 C2.

Consumer

Before leaving, check that your credit card covers you for transactions that go awry for whatever reason: many offer protective insurance against such matters. In Florida, if you encounter a problem with a particular company, contact the West Palm Beach-based **Better Business Bureau** (561 842 1918, www.bbbsouth eastflorida.org), an admirable non-profit public service organisation dedicated to monitoring the quality of businesses in many fields. The south-east Florida office serves the Miami region.

Customs

A high volume of air traffic means that getting through Customs and Immigration at Miami International Airport might take an hour or more. Travellers from countries on the Visa Waiver Program (*see p260* **Visas & immigration**) can speed the process up by correctly filling in the two forms that you should have been given by your flight attendant, one for Customs, the other for Immigration. However, the popularity of the city among drug smugglers means that searches are common. If you're stopped, be as polite and co-operative as possible; there's no point being otherwise, as you're likely only to be detained longer.

Current customs regulations allow foreign visitors to import, duty-free, 200 cigarettes or 50 cigars (not Cuban, unless the traveller is returning from a licensed visit there and the value of the cigars is less than $100) or two kilograms of smoking tobacco (all over-18s only); one litre of wine or spirits (over-21s only); and up to $100 in gifts. You can take up to $10,000 in cash, travellers' cheques or endorsed bank drafts in or out of the country tax-free, along with goods worth up to $1,000 (a flat-rate tax of ten per cent is payable on the excess). For more information, contact the **US Customs Service** (305 869 2800), or see www.cbp.gov.

Disabled

As in most of the US, disabled travellers to Miami are likely to find it relatively easy to get around. The exception may be South Beach's Deco District, where the 1930s architecture offers some tight angles and tiny lifts that can plague wheelchair users. However, even the smallest of hotels often have ramps and lifts fitted, and by federal law, all public buildings – which include museums and libraries – must have wheelchair access and suitable toilet facilities.

On the beaches, there's wheelchair access at 10th Street and Ocean Drive on South Beach, at Crandon Park on Key Biscayne and at the North Shore State Recreation Area. Most buses have specially low entrances, set spaces and grips, and both the Tri-Rail (*see p214*) and Metromover (*see p247*) are fully wheelchair accessible.

The New York-based Society for Accessible Travel and Hospitality (1-212 447 7284, www.sath.org) can offer information and services for disabled travellers in all parts of the US.

Deaf Services Bureau

1250 NW 7th Street, at NW 12th Court, Little Haiti (305 560 2866/ www.deafmiami.com). Bus 7. **Open** 8am-5pm Mon-Thur; 8am-noon Fri. **Map** p275 B2.

Miami-Dade Transit Agency Special Transportation Service

305 263 5406/www.co.miami-dade.fl.us/transit. **Open** *Office* 8am-5pm Mon-Fri.
Door-to-door transport for disabled people unable to use public services, on a shared-ride basis, available daily except 2.30-4.30am. Expect it to cost $2.50-$4 per one-way trip. You can register on the number above, but be sure to call ahead of your trip to confirm your eligibility and book your ride(s).

Miami Lighthouse for the Blind

601 SW 8th Avenue, at SW 6th Street, Little Havana (305 856 2288/www.miamilighthouse.com). Bus 6, 8. **Open** 8am-4.30pm Mon-Fri. **Map** p275 C3.

Electricity

Rather than the 220-240V, 50-cycle AC used in Europe, Miami and the United States use a 110-120V, 60-cycle AC voltage. Except for dual-voltage, flat-pin plug shavers, you will need to run any appliances you bring with you via an adaptor. Bear in mind that most US videos and TVs use a different frequency from those in Europe: you will not be able to play back footage during your trip. However, you can buy and use blank tapes.

Embassies & consulates

Miami is a major point of entry into the US, and therefore many nations have consulates in the area. Details of the UK consulate in Miami are given below; for all others, check the phone book. If your country isn't listed in it, call directory information for Washington DC (1-202 555 1212) to find your consulate there, as it'll probably be the nearest.

UK Consulate

Suite 2800, 1001 S Brickell Bay Drive, at SE 8th Street, Downtown (305 374 1522/www.britainusa.com). Bus 24, 48, 95, B/Metrorail 8th Street. **Open** 9am-1pm, 2-5pm Mon-Fri.

Emergencies

In an emergency, call 911 for an ambulance, the fire service or the police. This number is free from all phones.

For the **US Coast Guard**, call 305 415 6800 in the event of an air emergency, and 305 535 4472 for emergencies on water. For the **Poison Information Center**, call 1-800 282 3171.

For a list of helplines, *see p252* **Helplines**; for hospitals in the Miami region, *see p252* **Hospitals**; and for details on police stations in the area, *see p256* **Police stations**.

Gay & lesbian

Information on gay and lesbian Miami is available from the **Miami-Dade Gay & Lesbian Chamber of Commerce** (Suite 202, 3510 Biscayne Boulevard, Downtown, 305 573 4000, www.gogaymiami.com). The website has loads of information, including a daily calendar of events and comprehensive listings of community resources and basics, such as dining and accommodation.

For what's happening in the bars and clubs, check out *Hot Spots*, *Scoop* and *Wire*, plus *She* for events in the women's community. There's also *TWN*, south Florida's gay newspaper. All are weekly, and available from drop boxes, gay venues and bookstores. 'Outlooks', a column on gay issues written by Steve Rhothaus, runs in the *Miami Herald* every second and fourth Thursday of the month. He also has a comprehensive blog, gaysouthflorida.blogspot.com,

which has useful links to dozens of other local gay-related websites.

For general information on organisations serving the gay community, call **Switchboard of Miami** (305 358 4357, www.switchboardofmiami. org), a 24-hour crisis and information line. **Project YES** (5275 Sunset Drive, at SW 52nd Avenue, 305 663 7195, www.projectyes.org) and **Pridelines** (180 NE 19th Street, at NE 2nd Avenue, 305 571 9601, www.pridelines.org) co-ordinate services and social groups serving gay youth.

The **Miami Gay & Lesbian Yellow Pages**, the community's telephone book, has a website with listings at www.glyp.com/mmiami.html. A list of forthcoming events, as well as articles on current news in Florida, can be found at the *Miami Herald* website at www.herald.com, under the Gay South Florida link.

Health

Accident & emergency

All the hospitals listed on p252 have emergency rooms.

Contraception & abortion

Planned Parenthood of Greater Miami

1699 SW 27th Avenue (Unity Boulevard), at SW 17th Street, Coconut Grove (office 305 285 5532/ clinic 305 285 5535). Bus 27. **Open** 9am-9pm Mon-Fri; 10am-1pm Sat.
Care for men and women, including birth-control supplies, testing and treatment for sexually transmitted diseases and pregnancy testing.

Dentists

For referrals, call **AAA Referral Service** (1-800 733 6337 or 1-800 511 8663) or, for the **Dental Society**, phone 305 667 3647.

Directory

Doctors

Dade County Medical Association

305 324 8717/www.miamimed.com.
Open 9am-5pm Mon-Fri.
Phone for doctor referrals.

Hospitals

Be forewarned that in Miami, as in other parts of the US, you'll be charged a fortune for even the most basic medical care. Just a consultation with a doctor will cost you about $100. Having full insurance cover, preferably with a low excess, is the only way to feel at ease; keep the details with you and leave a copy with someone at home.

If it's not an emergency, try one of the many walk-in clinics, which are cheaper, friendlier and more numerous than hospitals. They include the **Miami Beach Community Health Center** at the Stanley C Myers Center (710 Alton Road, at 7th Street, 305 538 8835, www.miami beachhealth.com), a public clinic that charges you according to how much you earn. It's open 7am to 5pm Monday to Friday. Others can be found in the local *White Pages*.

For full-blown emergencies, dial 911 or head for the nearest emergency room. The one at **Mount Sinai Medical Center** in Miami Beach is considered the best but also charges the most.

Cedars Medical Center

1400 NW 12th Avenue, at NW 14th Street, Downtown (305 325 5511/ www.cedarsmedicalcenter.com). Bus 12, 22, 95, M/Metrorail Civic Center.
Private rooms and an international centre specialising in the treatment of foreign patients.

Children's Hospital

3100 SW 62nd Avenue, off Red Road (SW 57th Avenue) at Devonshire Boulevard, South-West Miami (305 666 6511/www.mch.com). Bus 72.
A specialist emergency room and good outpatient services.

Coral Gables Hospital

3100 Douglas Road (SW 37th Avenue), at Santander Avenue, Coral Gables (305 445 8461/www.coral gableshospital.com). Bus 37.
A 24-hour emergency department and a high-capacity outpatient unit with same-day surgery.

Jackson Memorial Hospital

1611 NW 12th Avenue, at NW 16th Street, Downtown (305 585 1111). Metrorail Civic Center.
The main county hospital.

Mount Sinai Medical Center

4300 Alton Road, at 43rd Street, North Beach (305 674 2121/ www.msmc.com). Bus C, M, R.
A well-equipped hospital, and pricey.

Opticians

Pearle Vision

7901 Biscayne Boulevard, at NE 79th Street, Miami Shores (305 754 5144). Bus 3, 16, 33, L. **Open** 9am-6pm Mon-Fri; 9am-4pm Sat. **Credit** AmEx, MC, V.

Pharmacies

Walgreens and **CVS** are the prevalent chains of pharmacies, with branches all over town, several of which are open 24 hours; see the phone book for addresses.

STDs, HIV & AIDS

HIV transmission in Miami is at epidemic proportions. The combination of a sexy tropical atmosphere with easy access to drugs, holidaymakers looking for a good time and the trend for barebacking have stymied AIDS-prevention efforts. For information on HIV and AIDS, call **CARE Resource** or **South Beach AIDS Project**.

CARE Resource

Suite 300, 3510 Biscayne Boulevard, at 35th Street, Design District (305 576 1234/www.careresource.net). Bus 9, 10, J. **Open** 9am-5.45pm Mon-Fri.

South Beach AIDS Project

Suite 200, 1234 Washington Avenue, at 12th Street, South Beach (305 535 4733/www.sobeaids.org).

Bus C, G, H, K, L, R, S, W, South Beach Local. **Open** 9am-5pm daily. **Map** p273 C2.

Helplines

For numbers for emergency services, *see p251.*

Alcohol & Drug Abuse Hotline

1-800 234 0420. **Open** 24hrs daily.
Information and referrals on alcohol- and drug-related problems.

Alcoholics Anonymous

Suite 801, 1110 Brickell Avenue, at SE 11th Street, Downtown (305 371 7784/www.alcoholics-anonymous.org). Bus 24, 48, 95, B. **Open** *Phoneline* 24hrs daily. *Office* 9am-1pm, 2-4pm Mon-Fri.
Phone for details of local meetings.

Crisis & Suicide Counselling Service

305 358 4357. **Open** 24hrs daily.
Trained volunteers are on hand round the clock.

Rape Hotline

305 585 7273. **Open** 24hrs daily.
A counselling and support service. Staff won't file a report to the police unless you ask them to do so.

Insurance

Baggage, trip-cancellation and medical insurance should be taken care of before you get on the plane. Of these, the big one is health. The US is renowned for its superb health-care facilities; the catch is that the cost will most likely put you in hospital needing treatment for shock. The majority of medical centres require you to prove you have insurance – by producing something with the company name and policy number on it – before they will treat you. Short of that, the alternative is to give them your credit card. *See also above* **Hospitals**.

Internet

Like much of the US, Miami is a very net-friendly city on many levels. Its burgeoning status as a business centre means that all but the cheapest

¿Hablas español?

Good morning/afternoon Buenos días	**Please can I have the bill?** La cuenta, por favor	**seventeen** diecisiete
Good evening/good night Buenas noches	**one** un, uno (m), una (f)	**eighteen** dieciocho
Hello Hola	**two** dos	**nineteen** diecinueve
Goodbye/see you later Adiós/hasta luego	**three** tres	**twenty** veinte
Please Por favor	**four** cuatro	**twenty-one** veintiuno
Thank you Gracias	**five** cinco	**thirty** treinta
Excuse me Perdóneme	**six** seis	**forty** cuarenta
Do you speak English? ¿Habla usted inglés?	**seven** siete	**fifty** cincuenta
Sorry, I don't speak Spanish Lo siento, no hablo español	**eight** ocho	**sixty** sesenta
I don't understand No entiendo	**nine** nueve	**seventy** setenta
How much is… ? ¿Cuánto cuesta?	**ten** diez	**eighty** ochenta
	eleven once	**ninety** noventa
	twelve doce	**one hundred** cien
	thirteen trece	**one hundred and one** ciento uno
	fourteen catorce	**five hundred** quinientos
	fifteen quince	**one thousand** mil
	sixteen dieciséis	**one million** un millón

hotels now offer some kind of internet connection in the guestrooms, be it a dataport or, increasingly, high-speed access (for which a fee is charged, sometimes hefty). WiFi, on the other hand, is not very prevalent, though there is talk of the entire beach district being wired in the near future.

Cyber cafés, too, are few and far between, though as well as the handful listed below, many of Miami's libraries also offer free internet access (including the main Miami-Dade Public Library; *see below*), although sessions are limited to 45 minutes.

CybrCaffe
1574 Washington Avenue, at 15th Street, South Beach (305 534 0057/ www.cybrcaffe.com). Bus C, H, K, W, South Beach Local. **Open** 9am-midnight Mon-Thur; 9am Fri-midnight Sun. **Cost** $6 per hr (min 30mins). **Credit** AmEx, DC, MC, V. **Map** p273 B2.

Kafka's Used Book Store & Cyberkafe
1460 Washington Avenue, at 14th Street, South Beach (305 673 9669). Bus C, H, K, W, South Beach Local. **Open** 8.30am-midnight daily. **Cost** $6 per hr; $3 per hr 8.30am-noon, 8pm-midnight. **Credit** AmEx, DC, MC, V. **Map** p273 C2.

Language

Miami is virtually a bilingual city. You'll hear Spanish spoken almost everywhere; in areas such as Little Havana and Hialeah, it's the lingua franca. You can get by with just English, especially in the major tourist areas, but if you've ever picked up any kind of holiday Spanish, dust off that phrasebook now (for some basic Spanish vocab, *see above* **¿Hablas español?**). That said, the only places you're really likely to need Spanish are small mom-and-pop style businesses in Little Havana.

Left luggage

Miami International Airport (*see p246*) has storage rooms on level two between concourses B and C, and on level one of concourse G. Prices vary depending on the size of the bags stored. Short-term lockers are located beyond the security checkpoint to the gates.

Legal help

Most Florida cops are tourist-friendly. However, if you're challenged by a police officer, do exactly as you're told and don't make any sudden movements. If you find yourself arrested and accused of a serious crime, you will be allowed one phone call, in which case your best bet is to call your consulate (for a list, *see p251*), where staff should be able to help. If you don't have a lawyer or can't afford one, the court will appoint one for you. Otherwise, you can call the **Florida Bar Association** (1-800 342 8060) for a referral.

Libraries

Miami-Dade Public Library
101 W Flagler Street, at NW 1st Avenue, Downtown (305 375 2665/ www.mdpls.org). Bus 3, 16, 95, C, K, S/Metromover Government Center. **Open** 9am-6pm Mon-Wed, Fri, Sat; 9am-9pm Thur. *Oct-June* also 1-5pm Sun. **Map** p274 D2.
Part of the Miami-Dade Cultural Center and the main branch of Miami-Dade's library system. It offers free internet access.
Coconut Grove Branch *2875 McFarlane Road, at S Bayshore Drive, Coconut Grove (305 442 8695). Bus 48.* **Open** 9.30am-6pm Mon, Wed, Thur, Sat; 11.30am-8pm Tue. **Map** p277 B3.

Passport update

People of all ages (children included) who enter the US on the Visa Waiver Progam (VWP; see p260) are now required to carry their own machine-readable passport, or MRP. MRPs are recognisable by the double row of characters along the foot of the data page. All currently valid burgundy EU and EU-lookalike passports issued in the UK since 1991 (ie ones all that are still valid) should be machine readable. Some of those issued outside the country may not be, however; in this case, holders should apply for a replacement even if the passport has not expired. Check at your local passport-issuing post office if in any doubt.

The US's requirement for passports to contain a 'biometric' chip applies only to those issued from 26 October 2006. By then, all new and replacement UK passports should be compliant, following a gradual phase-in. The biometric chip contains a facial scan and biographical data.

Though it is being considered for 2008 (when ID cards may be introduced), there is no current requirement for UK passports to contain fingerprint or iris data. The application process remains as it was, except for new guidelines that ensure that the photograph you submit can be used to generate the facial scan in the chip.

Further information for UK citizens is available by calling 0870 521 0410 or by logging on to www.passport.gov.uk. Always check the above advice still stands before travelling. Nationals of other countries should check well in advance whether their passport meets the requirements for the time of their trip, at http://travel.state.gov/visa and with the issuing authorities of their home country.

Coral Gables Branch *3443 Segovia Street, at Aledo Avenue, Coral Gables (305 442 8706). Bus 72.* **Open** 9.30am-9pm Mon-Thur; 9.30am-6pm Fri, Sat. **Map** p276 D3.
South Shore Branch *131 Alton Road, at 1st Street, South Beach (305 535 4223). Bus H, M, W.* **Open** 9.30am-6pm Mon-Thur, Sat. **Map** p272 F2.

Lost property

For items lost on **Miami-Dade Transit**, call 305 375 3366 (8.30am-4.30pm Mon-Fri). If you've lost something at **Miami International Airport**, call 305 876 7377 or visit the Lost and Found office near the entrance to concourse E on level two. Otherwise, call your nearest police station (for a list of local ones, *see p256*).

Media

Newspapers

The most widely read and most reliable newspaper, not just in Miami but in the whole of south Florida, is the *Miami Herald*. Covering both international and national news, the paper and its reporters became known across the globe in the early 1990s, when Miami was the murder capital of the US and the *Herald* set itself the task of tracking down and naming those responsible. The paper found similar fame when Al Diaz's photograph of Elián González being seized from his relatives' home in Little Havana was beamed across the world. Columnists to look out for these

days include bestselling crime novelist-cum-eco warrior Carl Hiaasen (*see p31*).

The *Herald*'s Friday edition has a 'Weekend' section with movie and theatre reviews, restaurant listings and details of pretty much everything going on in Miami. However, it merits mention that the *Herald* is the only major paper in town, and critics feel it often indulges in a civic boosterism that's uncomfortably cosy with the city's tourism establishment.

The leading alternative paper is the weekly *Miami New Times*, free from clubs, bars and drop bins. It often picks up the ball the *Herald* drops when it comes to investigative journalism. *New Times* reviewers are also more feisty than their *Herald* peers and more apt to zero in on what's new and happening.

The *Sun Post*, found mostly on Miami Beach, has increased its cultural coverage over the last few years, and it now has comprehensive arts and music information on a weekly basis (Tuesdays).

NEWSPAPERS IN SPANISH

The largest Spanish-language daily in the United States is Miami's *El Nuevo Herald*, published by the *Miami Herald*. There is some carry-over of stories from the English edition, but *El Nuevo* has its own columnists, reporters, reviewers and editorial board. Often the paper will have more complete international news than its English-language cousin.

Neither paper seems to be able to say 'boo' about Cuba without upsetting somebody in town and causing a protest outside the *Herald* building. However, that more political niche is adequately filled by other Spanish-language papers, such as *Libre* and *Diario Las Américas*, both daily.

Radio

88.9 FM WDNA Community public radio.
90.5 FM WVUM The University of Miami's station plays lots of grungy, student-style rock and alternative music.
91.3 FM WLRN An affiliate of the admirable National Public Radio; good for intelligent discussion programmes, and for jazz in the evening.
92.3 FM WCMQ Spanish music. Also known as FM 92.
93.9 FM WLVE Also called Love 94, this channel plays non-stop jazz.
94.9 FM WZTA Advertises itself as the home of 'real rock': tunes to cruise by.
99.1 FM WEDR Known as 99 Jamz, this is the main urban contemporary, hip hop and R&B station.
99.9 FM WKIS Don't be fooled by the name (Kiss FM): this is the home of good ol' country music.
102.7 FM WMXJ Plays the oldies, but not too oldies, from the Supremes to the Beatles. Better known as Magic 102.7.
105.1 FM WHQT A mix of R&B with a sprinkling of adult contemporary and soul. Locals call it HOT 105.
710 AM WAQI Radio Mambi: Spanish talk, loud, passionate and controversial.
940 AM WINZ Air America: the new left-leaning, nationwide talk radio.
1400 AM WFTL Talk, with an emphasis on entertainment. Good for reviews and tips on where to go.

Television

What with Miami being the gateway to Latin America, it's no surprise to find that it's the base for MTV's Spanish-language programming. Other Latin products made here include the variety show *Sábado Gigante*, shown in

18 Latin American countries. Attending a taping will be one of the wildest things you could do in Miami, even if – or perhaps because – you don't speak the language. For details, call 305 471 8262 (be prepared for a Spanish answerphone message).

The local public access cable station, Channel 3, while not as extreme as New York's, is still worth a look to see what the more eccentric members of the community get up to.

Money

The US dollar ($) is divisible into 100 cents (¢). Coin denominations are: the penny (1¢; Abraham Lincoln on the only copper-coloured coin), the nickel (5¢; Thomas Jefferson), the dime (10¢; Franklin D Roosevelt), the quarter (25¢; George Washington) and the less common half-dollar (50¢; John F Kennedy). You may come across the smaller 'Susan B Anthony' dollar coin, which, though not common, is valid.

Paper bills, which are, confusingly, all the same size and colour (green), come in denominations of $1 (George Washington), $5 (Abraham Lincoln), $10 (Alexander Hamilton), $20 (Andrew Jackson), $50 (Ulysses S Grant) and $100 (Benjamin Franklin). Older bills have smaller portraits, while newer bills have bigger, more cartoonish portraits.

ATMs

Automated Teller Machines (ATMs) are commonplace in Miami: all banks have them, of course, but so do many convenience stores and gas stations. The main two globally recognised card networks are **Cirrus** (1-800 424 7787 for a list of locations) and **Plus** (1-800 843 7587): if your bank card displays either of these two symbols, you

should be able to withdraw cash from ATMs. However, you will be charged for the privilege: $1.50-$3 is common for US cardholders, while holders of foreign cards should check with their banks for exact details. Some machines also have annoying upper limits to how much you can withdraw at any one time (it can be as little as $60).

Most ATMs also dispense cash advances on credit cards, with MasterCard and Visa the most widely accepted. Once again, however, prepare to be charged a handling fee for each withdrawal.

Banks

Bank hours are usually 9am-4pm Monday to Friday, and sometimes 6pm or 7pm on Thursdays, with drive-in windows open until 6pm. Larger branches open on Saturday mornings. Below is a list of some of the larger banks in Downtown Miami. All have branches elsewhere in the city; for your nearest, check the *Yellow Pages* or call the 1-800 numbers listed by each bank.

Bank of America
1 SE 3rd Avenue, at E Flagler Street, Downtown (1-800 299 2265/305 350 6350/www.bankofamerica.com). Bus 3, 16, 95, C, S. **Open** 8.30am-4pm Mon-Thur; 8.30am-5pm Fri. **Map** p274 E2.

Wachovia
1395 Brickell Avenue, at SE 13th Street, Downtown (1-800 275 3862/305 789 3900/www.wachovia.com). Bus 24, 48, 95, B/Metromover 8th Street. **Open** 9am-4pm Mon-Fri.

Washington Mutual
150 SE 2nd Street, at Brickell Avenue, Downtown (1-800 788 7000/786 425 0559/www.wamu.com). Bus 24, 48, 95, B/Metromover 8th Street. **Open** 8am-6pm Mon-Fri. **Map** p274 E3.

Bureaux de change

Bureaux de change are less common in the US than in Europe, but you will find them

Directory

in tourist areas and larger cities. They generally charge higher commission and offer lower rates than banks, which all offer currency exchange.

American Express
*100 Biscayne Boulevard, at NE 1st Street, Downtown (305 358 7350/ http://home.americanexpress.com). Bus 48, 95. **Open** 9am-5.30pm Mon-Fri; 9am-5pm Sat. **Map** p274 D3.*

Credit cards

The two major cards that are accepted just about everywhere in the United States are **MasterCard** (1-800 826 2181, www.mastercard. com) and **Visa** (1-800 336 8472, www.visa.com). **American Express** (1-800 528 4800, www.american express.com) is also prominent at higher-end places. **Diners Club** (1-800 234 6377, www.dinersclub.com) and **Discover** (1-800 347 2683, www.discovercard.com) are less ubiquitous.

Lost/stolen credit cards

If you lose or have your credit cards stolen, call the numbers below; it's a good idea to keep the appropriate number with you in case the worst happens. Always make a separate note of the numbers of your travellers' cheques, as it will speed up the process of replacing them; in fact, without the numbers, you may not get your money back at all. If you need money wired to you in an emergency, try **Western Union** (1-800 325 6000).

Lost/stolen cards & travellers' cheques
American Express
1-800 992 3404.
American Express travellers' cheques *1-800 221 7282.*
Diners Club *1-800 234 6377.*
Discover *1-800 347 2683.*
MasterCard *1-800 307 7309.*
Thomas Cook travellers' cheques *1-800 223 7373.*
Visa *1-800 847 2911.*

Tax

Sales tax in Florida is 6.5 per cent. However, be aware that hotels levy a further six per cent tourist tax.

Natural hazards

Mosquitoes

Although Miami itself has an effective control programme that ensures mosquitoes are rarely a pest, be prepared to be eaten alive the moment you pass the city limits. The Everglades and other wooded areas are the worst affected, so buy an insect repellent you like the smell of, and use it. Mosquitoes are most active after long wet periods and least active along the beach, where the sea breeze acts as an effective natural deterrent. Summer, from about May to October, is the peak season, and the public radio station, WLRN (91.3 FM), runs bulletins on mossie activity. Mosquitoes in Florida do not carry malaria, but like those of sandflies, fire ants, sealice and no-see-ums (near-invisible flies that come out at dusk on beaches and by lakes), their bites can be painful and itchy.

Weather

The Florida sun is fierce and should be avoided at its height until you are acclimatised. Protect yourself and your children throughout the day with a high-factor sun cream, a hat and good sunglasses.

Hurricane season in Florida runs from June to November, and during the course of a year there may be as few as two or as many as 20 blowing in. The majority blow themselves out or remain at sea rather than striking the mainland. Having been devastated several times in the past (including a direct hit from Hurricane Wilma in 2005),

Miami has a highly sophisticated early warning system ensuring that when the 'big one' does arrive, it is unlikely to be a surprise. The National Hurricane Center in Miami can give 24 hours warning of a possible hit, and public radio and most TV stations then give out the latest storm information and evacuation plans. Be prepared to evacuate your hotel, even if the weather does not appear threatening when the warning is issued.

Tornadoes are part of the same weather system, but despite their dramatic appearance, they are considerably less destructive. They are also less predictable, so there will be no warning. Most of Miami's buildings are robust enough to suffer only minor damage, even if they are directly in a tornado's path, so staying inside is probably the safest thing to do.

For weather updates, call the **National Weather Service Forecast Office** on 305 229 4522. For more on storm and hurricane seasons, as well as a climate chart, *see p260*.

Opening hours

Office hours in Florida are usually 9am-5pm, give or take half an hour. Shop hours vary considerably according to location: businesses in malls and other pedestrian areas are often open until 9pm or later, Sundays included. Some Miami clubs and restaurants take a breather after the weekend: the occasional restaurant closes on Sunday and/or Monday, while many clubs are dark on Monday and Tuesday.

Police stations

For emergencies, *see p251*. The numbers given on p257 are non-emergency numbers.

Coral Gables Police Department

2801 Salzedo Street, at Sevilla Avenue, Coral Gables (305 442 1600). Bus 24, 72. **Open** *24hrs daily.* **Map** *p276 C4.*

Miami Beach Police Department

1100 Washington Avenue, at 11th Street, South Beach (305 673 7900). Bus C, H, K, W, South Beach Local. **Open** *24hrs daily.* **Map** *p273 D2.*

Miami Police Department

400 NW 2nd Avenue, at NW 4th Street, Downtown (305 579 6111). Metromover Government Center. **Open** *24hrs daily.* **Map** *p274 C1.*

North Miami Beach Police Department

16435 NE 35th Avenue, at NE 164th Street, North Miami Beach (305 948 2931). Bus E, H, V. **Open** *24hrs daily.*

Postal services

First-class mail costs 39¢ within the US for letters up to one ounce, and 25¢ for each additional ounce. Postcards sent within the US require a 24¢ stamp. Overseas mail costs vary from country to country, but a postcard costs 75¢ and a one-ounce letter costs 84¢.

Post offices

Coconut Grove Post Office

3191 Grand Avenue, at Matilda Avenue, Coconut Grove, FL 33133 (1-800 275 8777/305 529 6700). Bus 42, 48. **Open** *7.30am-5pm Mon-Fri; 7.30am-2pm Sat.* **Map** *p277 B2.*

Coral Gables Post Office

251 Valencia Avenue, at Salzedo Street, Coral Gables, FL 33134 (1-800 275 8777/305 443 2532). Bus 24, 42, J. **Open** *7.30am-5pm Mon-Fri; 8am-2pm Sat.* **Map** *p276 C4.*

Downtown Miami Post Office

500 NW 2nd Street, at NW 5th Street, Downtown, FL 33101 (1-800 275 8777). Metromover Government Center. **Open** *8am-5.30pm Mon-Fri; 8.30am-1.30pm Sat.* **Map** *p274 D2.*

Main Post Office

2200 NW 72nd Avenue, Building 2210, Miami International Airport, FL 33159 (1-800 275 8777). Bus 73. **Open** *8.30am-9pm Mon-Fri; 9.30am-1.30pm Sat.*

Miami Beach Post Office

1300 Washington Avenue, at 13th Street, South Beach, FL 33139 (305 599 1787). Bus C, H, K, W, South Beach Local. **Open** *8am-5pm Mon-Fri; 8.30am-2pm Sat.* **Map** *p273 C2.*

Poste restante

You can have mail sent to you c/o General Delivery at any post office, provided you use the correct zip code and collect it within 30 days using some form of photo ID (a passport or driver's licence is preferred).

Religion

All People's Synagogues

7455 Collins Avenue, at 74th Street, North Beach (305 861 5554). Bus G, H, K, T, S. **Services** phone for details.

Christ Episcopal Church

3481 Hibiscus Street, at Grand Avenue, Coconut Grove (305 442 8542). Bus 6, 48, Coconut Grove Circulator. **Services** 9am Sun. **Map** *p277 B1.*

Coconut Grove United Methodist Church

2850 SW 27th Avenue, at US 1, Coconut Grove (305 443 0880). Bus 27/Metrorail Coconut Grove. **Services** 11am Sun.

First Baptist Church of Miami Beach

2816 Sheridan Avenue, at W 28th Street, Mid Beach (305 538 3507). Bus K. **Services** 11am Sun.

First Church of Christ Scientist

410 Andalusia Avenue, at Le Jeune Road, Coral Gables (305 443 1427). Bus 24, 72. **Services** 10am Sun. **Map** *p276 C4.*

Plymouth Congregational Church

3400 Devon Road, at Main Highway, Coconut Grove (305 444 6521). Bus 42, 48. **Services** 10am Sun.

St Patrick Catholic Church

3716 Garden Avenue, at Barry Street, Mid Beach (305 531 1124). Bus C, R. **Services** 8am Mon-Sat; 5pm Sat; 8am, 9.30am, 11am Sun. **Map** *p272 A3.*

Safety & security

South Florida acquired a well-deserved nasty reputation for tourist crime – murder included – in the late 1980s to mid '90s. Sometimes tourists were the targets, sometimes they simply got in the way of the crime wave that was sweeping the state. Tourism took a dive, and authorities moved quickly to introduce anti-crime measures. Tourist areas are now visibly policed, and precautions have been taken to reduce car crime: signage has been improved, rental cars are no longer marked and rental agencies are required to provide maps and directions. These measures have had the desired result: tourist crime has been falling.

Although paranoia is totally unjustified, you do need to be careful: don't leave your street smarts at home. Barring random occurrences, you are fine on South Beach, but elsewhere in the city, the usual urban crime thrives, and you could easily run into trouble by crossing an invisible line that only locals are wise to. Play it safe. We've tried to give safety information for all the areas we discuss, but if in doubt, stay away.

Safety tips

If your hotel has a safe, keep your valuables there. If you do carry them with you, do so discreetly and don't flash large amounts of cash around. Don't leave anything you want to keep on the beach while you swim. Keep a note of your travellers' cheque and credit card numbers separately. It's a good idea to leave a note of these with someone at home, along with other information you might need in an emergency, such as your insurers' contact number and passport number.

Keep all credit card slips, including receipts from credit sales at gas stations, and don't let anyone overhear your card number. If your hotel asked for an imprint when you checked in, insist it is destroyed when you leave. Don't let anyone you don't know into your hotel room. Call the front desk if you need to check someone is a member of staff.

If somebody threatens you and demands money or goods, quietly give them what you have. Then go straight to the nearest phone or police station to report the crime. Make sure you get a reference number for any crime you report; you will need it for your insurance.

Finally, try not to look like a tourist. Grifters target tourists with elaborate con games, while purse-snatchers look for anybody not paying attention to their bags. Awareness is the key to safety in Miami.

For more on driving safety, see p247 **Driving**.

Study

There are two main universities in Miami, the state-run **Florida International University** and the private **University of Miami**. The FIU has a strong arts programme, while UM is geared more towards science and is renowned for its medical curriculum. The **Miami-Dade Community College** is the county-sponsored public college, with its main centre in Downtown. It has good language labs, with short courses available.

Florida International University
University Park, SW 8th Street & SW 107th Avenue, Miami, FL 33199 (305 348 2363/ www.fiu.edu). Bus 8, 11.

Miami-Dade Community College
300 NE 2nd Avenue, at NE 3rd Street, Miami FL 33132 (305 237 3000/www.mdcc.edu). Bus 9, 10, K, T/Metromover College/Bayside. **Map** p274 D3.

University of Miami
San Amaro Drive, at SW 56th Street, PO Box 248025, Coral Gables FL 33124 (305 284 2271/www. miami.edu). Bus 52, 56/Metrorail University.

Telephones

Dialling & codes

Most Miami numbers still take the phone code 305, although a reorganisation of phone codes in recent years has added the 786 code into the Miami mix.

Numbers prefaced by 1-800, 1-888 or 1-877 are free – though if you dial them from your hotel you will incur a flat fee (usually 50¢-$1). You can dial most (but not all) 1-800 numbers from outside the United States, but they will be charged at international rates, as will premium-rate 1-900 numbers.

Making a call

For local calls, dial the code (305 or 786), then the seven-digit number as listed in this book. There's no need to dial a '1' first: simply dial the ten digits. For long-distance calls, dial 1 + [area code] + [the number]. Note that although Key West shares the 305 code with Miami, you still need to prefix it by dialling 1.

For international calls, dial 011 followed by the country code (Australia 61; Germany 49; Republic of Ireland 353; Japan 81; New Zealand 64; UK 44; see the phone book for others) and the number, dropping the first zero of all UK numbers. For Canada, you just need to dial the area code.

In hotels, you may have to dial 0 or 9 before all these numbers to get a line. You

will also pay a surcharge; ask how much at your hotel, as using a phone card (*see below*), credit card or payphone can work out significantly cheaper, especially when making long-distance and international calls.

Operator services

For collect (reverse charge) calls, dial the operator on 0. For police, fire or medical emergencies, dial 911. For local directory information, dial 411. For national long-distance directory information, dial 1 + [area code] + 555 1212 (if you don't know the area code, dial 0 for the operator).

Public phones

To use a public phone, pick up the receiver, listen for a dialling tone and feed it change before dialling. The vast majority of call boxes charge 35¢, although a handful around town charge only 25¢. Make sure you have plenty of change, as pay phones take only nickels, dimes and quarters. Remember, 911 calls are free.

Phone cards

Hotels charge the earth for long-distance and international calls; a phone card, available in many denominations and sold at delis, newspaper kiosks, vending machines, pharmacies and other shops, is one way around the problem.

It's worth shopping around for the longest talk-time for the lowest price. Examples include **AT&T** (1-800 225 5288), **MCI** (1-800 888 8000) and **Sprint** (1-800 366 2255), although there are plenty of smaller companies touting for custom in what is an extremely competitive field. When looking for the best deal, don't just look at the price per minute to the area you'll be calling most: also pay close attention to the small print detailing connection charges.

Mobile phones

Whereas in Europe and much of the rest of the world, mobile phones work on the GSM network at either 900 or 1800 MHz, United States GSM operates in the 800 and 1900 MHz bands. Visitors to America should therefore check with their service providers whether their phones will work in Miami. As a rule, single- and dual-band international GSM phones won't work in the US, but tri- and quad-band phones will. Travellers should also be sure to confirm (with their home service provider) that their phone has been enabled for international roaming before departure, as they won't be able to do so once they've left their home network. It's also worth checking the price of calls made (and received) while roaming abroad, as these can be very expensive with some networks.

Those without an 800-1900 MHz compatible GSM phone who would like to rent one for the duration of their stay can do so at the locations listed below, although these two are just the tip of the iceberg: check the phone book for more, call around for the best deal and always read the small print. Many hotels on South Beach also now offer mobile phone rental to guests at prices less prohibitive than you might expect. Always call ahead if you're interested in this option.

Rent a Cellular

127 SE 1st Avenue, at SE 1st Street, Downtown (305 377 2284/www.rent-a-cellular.com). Bus 3, 11, 16, 48, 77, 95, C, S/Metromover Knight Center. **Open** *9.30am-6pm Mon-Fri; 10am-3pm Sat.* **Credit** *AmEx, MC, V.* **Map** *p274 E3.*

Unicomm

1608 Washington Avenue, at 16th Street, South Beach (305 538 9494/ www.unicomm.com). Bus M, S, W. **Open** *9am-6pm Mon-Fri; 11am-4pm Sat.* **Credit** *AmEx, DC, MC, V.* **Map** *p273 A2.*

Time

Florida operates on Eastern Standard Time, which is five hours behind Greenwich Mean Time (London), one hour ahead of Central Time (Chicago), two hours ahead of Mountain Time (Denver) and three hours ahead of Pacific Standard Time (the West Coast). Daylight Savings Time, which is almost concurrent with British Summer Time, runs from the first Sunday in April (when the clocks go forward) to the last Sunday in October (when they go back).

Tipping

Tipping is standard practice here. So much so, in fact, that many restaurants add the tip on to the bill before you get it; always check before paying unless you particularly want to tip twice, which you more than likely don't. If the bill doesn't already contain a tip, add 15-20 per cent in restaurants. The quality of service in many South Beach restaurants may mean you'll have to bite your tongue when doing so.

Bartenders and food delivery workers should get a tip of 15 per cent. Cloakroom attendants, doormen and the like should be tipped a dollar or so. Bellhops and baggage attendants merit $1-$2 a bag, while hotel maids should be left $1-$2 on the pillow each night of your stay. Cab drivers, too, expect to be tipped 15 per cent, plus $1 per bag.

Foreign visitors should note, that, almost without exception, staff in the service industries in the US are paid next to nothing as a basic wage, and rely heavily on gratuities just

to get by. In other words, they feel they've got a genuine gripe if you don't cough up – and they are likely to let you know about it.

Toilets

Public restrooms can be found in large stores, shopping malls, bars, restaurants, museums, gas stations, public beaches, large car parks and railway and bus stations. Sometimes they are clean. Sometimes they rather desperately need cleaning. Bars, cafés and restaurants may ask you to buy something in order to use their facilities, but if you're feeling mean, ask to use the phone, which is often next to the restrooms, and then sneak in.

Tourist information

Visitor guides, including lists of accommodation, brochures and maps, are available free of charge from the following tourist offices (none of which, it should be noted, is located anywhere near the areas in which tourists are likely to spend time).

Coconut Grove Chamber of Commerce

2820 McFarlane Road, at S Bayshore Drive, Coconut Grove (305 444 7270/www.coconutgrove.com). Bus 48, Coconut Grove Circulator. **Open** *9am-5pm Mon-Fri.* **Map** *p277 B3.*

Greater Miami Convention & Visitors' Bureau

Suite 2700, NationsBank Building, 701 Brickell Avenue, at SE 7th Street, Downtown (305 539 3000/ www.gmcvb.com). Bus 24, 48, 95, B/Metromover 8th Street. **Open** *8.30am-5pm Mon-Fri.* **Map** *p274 F3.*

Miami Beach Chamber of Commerce

1920 Meridian Avenue, at Dade Boulevard, South Beach (305 674 1300/www.miamibeachchamber.com). Bus A, M, L, S. **Open** *10am-5pm Mon-Fri.* **Map** *p272 C2.*

Directory

Climate check

	Average high ($^{\circ}$F/$^{\circ}$C)	Average low ($^{\circ}$F/$^{\circ}$C)	Average rainfall (in)	Relative humidity (%)
Jan	73 (23)	61 (16)	2.8	81
Feb	75 (24)	61 (16)	2.1	82
Mar	79 (26)	64 (18)	2.5	77
Apr	81 (27)	66 (19)	3.2	73
May	84 (29)	72 (22)	6.8	75
June	86 (30)	73 (23)	7.0	75
July	88 (31)	75 (24)	6.1	75
Aug	88 (31)	75 (24)	6.3	76
Sept	88 (31)	75 (24)	8.0	79
Oct	82 (28)	72 (22)	9.2	80
Nov	79 (26)	66 (19)	2.8	77
Dec	75 (24)	63 (17)	2.0	82

Visas & immigration

Under the Visa Waiver Program, citizens of the UK, Japan, Australia, New Zealand and all West European countries (except for Portugal, Greece and Vatican City) do not need a visa for stays of less than 90 days (business or pleasure), as long as they have a passport that is valid for the full 90-day period, and a return ticket. An open standby ticket is acceptable. Canadians and Mexicans do not need visas but must have legal proof of their residency. All other travellers must have visas. Full details and visa application forms can be obtained from your nearest US embassy or consulate.

US Embassy in London
www.usembassy.org.uk.

US Embassy Visa Information Line
09042 450100.
Operator-assisted visa information for callers in the UK, available 8am-8pm Mon-Fri; 10am-4pm Sat; £1.20 per min.

When to go

Like many subtropical places, Miami has two seasons: rainy and dry (not to mention hot

and hotter). Miami's average minimum and maximum temperatures run from 61-73°F (16-23°C) in January to a searing, uncomfortably hot 75-88°F (24-31°C) in July and August, the height of summer.

The winter air is warm, dry and pleasant, though you may need a sweater in the evening, and the sea is still warm enough for swimming, especially for those used to chillier climes.

Summer, meanwhile, gets very hot and unpleasantly humid during the day, and sultry in the evening, with morning and late afternoon the best times for going to the beach for a dip in the jacuzzi-warm sea. June to November is hurricane season: winds are high and storms rush in during the afternoon. Most are brief, but sometimes tropical rains set in. Weather-watchers will find the dramatic display of clouds and lightning, with the possibility of a stray tornado, intoxicating.

The Season – when South Beach is at the peak of its cycle – is from the end of November to May. This is when hotel and car rental rates shoot up and most major events occur. November/December and late April/early May are good

times to visit: the weather's usually good, but prices aren't at their peak.

For phone forecasts, dial 511 followed by 4400 for Florida, 4020 for Miami, 4374 for Orlando and 4998 for hurricanes.

National holidays

New Year's Day *1 Jan.*
Martin Luther King Jr Day *3rd Mon in Jan.*
Presidents Day *3rd Mon in Feb.*
Memorial Day *last Mon in May.*
Independence Day *4 July.*
Labor Day *1st Mon in Sept.*
Columbus Day *2nd Mon in Oct.*
Veterans' Day *11 Nov.*
Thanksgiving Day *4th Thur in Nov.*
Christmas Day *25 Dec.*

Women

Women should take the same precautions in Miami as they would in any major city. In particular, to minimise the risk of someone spiking your drink, never leave it unattended in clubs and bars. For general information about safety and security, *see p257.*

Women's Chamber of Commerce of Dade County
305 446 6660.
An organisation promoting women-owned and women-run businesses.

Further Reference

Books

For more on Miami crime fiction, *see pp30-32.*

Fiction

Russell Banks *Continental Drift* (1985) A showdown ensues in Little Haiti as the American Dream implodes.
Christine Bell *The Perez Family* (1991) Mariel refugees use their considerable talents to get a sweet immigration deal. Later made into a film.
Edna Buchanan *Miami, it's Murder* (1995) The strong woman protagonist is a news reporter investigating bizarre and dangerous crimes.
James W Hall *Tropical Freeze* (1989) A pacey, readable Miami-set thriller.
Ernest Hemingway *To Have and Have Not* (1937) Hemingway is Key West's mascot, but this is his only book set there.
Carl Hiaasen *various novels* All Hiaasen's crime novels are set in Florida, and all are sharp, satirical and deliriously off the wall. Hiaasen is as good a holiday primer as a whole shelf of non-fiction.
Marjorie Kinnan Rawlings *The Yearling* (1938) Pulitzer Prize winner about a boy growing up in central Florida.
Elmore Leonard *various novels* Not all Leonard's books are set in south Florida. Those that are include *La Brava, Gold Coast, Maximum Bob, Pronto* and *Riding the Rap*.
Peter Matthiessen *Killing Mister Watson* (1991) The settlement of the Everglades, and how it led to some of south Florida's current problems.
Thomas McGuane *Ninety-Two in the Shade* (1995) A cult favourite about the quest for self-discovery of an aspiring Key West fishing guide.

Sean Rowe *Fever* (2005) In the tried and true Miami tradition of crime fiction, this former Miamian has woven a 21st-century 'tropical noir' set in south Florida.
John Sayles *Los Gusanos* (1991) The noted film director's take on Cuban Miami.
Charles Willeford *Miami Blues* (1984) The film is better known, but the book is superior in all other respects.

Non-fiction

TD Allman *Miami: City of the Future* (1987) Hugely colourful bio of the city.
Barbara Beer Capitman *Deco Delights* (1988) A photo-tour of Miami Beach's deco buildings, by the woman who played a major role in ensuring their survival.
Edna Buchanan *The Corpse had a Familiar Face* (1987) Pulitzer Prize-winning journo's in-your-face account of her years covering one of the world's edgiest crime beats.
David Leon Chandler *Henry Flagler* (1986) The lowdown on the Robber Baron who was largely responsible for establishing Miami's infrastructure.
Joan Didion *Miami* (1987) Compelling impressions of the meltdown pot.
Howard Kleinberg *Miami Beach: A History* (1994) How the Beach got the way it is today. Kinda.
Stuart B McIver *Dreamer, Schemers & Scalawags: The Florida Chronicles* (1994) The underground history of Florida's mobsters, gamblers and risk-takers.
Gary Monroe *Life in South Beach* (1989) B&W photos of the pre-renaissance Beach.
Arva Moore Parks *Miami, The Magic City* (1981) The 'official' history of the city, with many pictures.

David Rieff *Going to Miami: Exiles, Tourists and Refugees in the New America (2000)* A controversial vision of Miami alienated from the US.
Marjory Stoneman Douglas *The Everglades: River of Grass* (1947) A personal testament to the vulnerable beauty of the Everglades that kick-started the conservation programme in the 1940s.
Alexander Stuart *Life on Mars* (1996) Moving, observant and funny essays on the heart and souls of Florida from the renowned British writer.
Alfredo Triff *Miami Arts Explosion* (2006) A chronicle of Miami's burgeoning visual arts scene from the former *Miami New Times* art critic.
John Viele *The Florida Keys* (1996) A multi-volumed historical tract on the Keys.

Films

For more on Miami in film, *see p172* **Reel-life fantasies**.
The Bellboy *dir. Jerry Lewis* (1960) Lewis plays the bellboy of the title in this riotous flick filmed in Morris Lapidus's garish Fontainebleau Hotel.
The Birdcage *dir. Mike Nichols* (1996) Worth watching for the opening shot alone as the camera tracks in from the sea to the gloriously neon-lit party scene of Ocean Drive.
Get Shorty *dir. Barry Sonnenfeld* (1995) John Travolta alternates his two facial expressions in this fine adaptation of Elmore Leonard's terrific book.
Key Largo *dir. John Huston* (1948) The movie that named the island; not, as many assume, the other way around.
Miami Blues *dir. George Armitage* (1990) Another Miami-set crime-tinged flick, boasting one of Alec Baldwin's better performances.

Directory

Miami Vice *dir. Michael Mann* (2006) Vice detectives James 'Sonny' Crockett and Ricardo Tubbs take on the Florida drugs world.
Scarface *dir. Brian de Palma* (1983) Al Pacino gives a monstrous performance as a Cuban Marielito razoring rivals and nose-diving into mounds of cocaine. A Miami period piece.
There's Something About Mary *dir. Peter and Bobby Farrelly* (1998) Geeky Ben Stiller tracks down his high-school love (Cameron Diaz) to Miami. Cue crude, offensive, sexist set pieces – and gut-aching laughs.
True Lies *dir. James Cameron* (1994) Arnold in a typical Schwarzeneggerian performance. As flashy, shallow and jaw-dropping as Miami Beach itself.

TV

The Golden Girls Hilarious series about four co-habiting, cheesecake-munching retirees, which ran for seven seasons from 1985.
Miami Vice Directed by Michael Mann, this 1980s series focused on the lives and loves of Sonny Crockett and Ricardo Tubbs (played by Don Johnson and Philip Michael Thomas). Big hair, even bigger shoulder pads – and huge fun.

Music

Bacilos *Caraluna* Catchy Spanish tunes with intelligent lyrics from a group of diverse Latin rockers who met at the University of Miami.
Celia Cruz *Regalo del Alma* The patron saint of Miami's Cuban community left a gift for her fans with this last, perfect album, supported by some great young musicians from Havana.
Gonzalo Rubalcaba *Supernova* Internationally acclaimed jazz pianist Rubalcaba shines on this CD.

Gloria Estefan *Greatest Hits* Sure, she's hokey, and her new albums are forgettable attempts to keep in the game. But the Miami diva's early hits with the Miami Sound Machine are classics of crossover.
Iggy Pop *Skull Ring* The godfather of punk brought the Stooges down to his Miami Beach home for a reunion album, also featuring Sum 41 and Greenday.
Los Van Van *Live at the Miami Arena* Police in riot gear were called in to protect concert goers from the wrath of Cuban exile demonstrators at this 1999 performance of Cuba's most popular band. As this two-CD set attests, art triumphed over politics on that historic night.
Manolin Puente *Live in the US* The 'salsa doctor' attempts to cure political ills with this booty-shaking music at this Miami concert.
Ricky Martin *Ricky Martin* If you'd like to live *la vida loca*, this is the soundtrack.
Siete Rayo *Descemer* The debut album from this Afro-Cuban funk band is a knock-out. *See also p186* **Rayo hope**.
Spam Allstars Any one of the CDs (including an excellent live album) from Miami's most loved dance/funk band is worth a listen.
Trick Daddy *www.thug.com* The new generation of Miami rap. Not for the easily offended, and much the better for it.
Trina *Diamond Princess* Eve, Missy Elliot and more hip-hop luminaries join Miami's 'Baddest Bitch' for some dirty rhyming.
Various *Heart of Stone: The Henry Stone Story* Disco king Henry Stone ignited Miami's dance scene in the 1970s, sowing the seeds for the *Saturday Night Fever* sensation. This two-CD compilation features artists ranging from legendary KC & the Sunshine Band to funky R&B diva Betty Wright.

Websites

City of Coral Gables *www.citybeautiful.net* Official portal to the City Beautiful.
City of Miami *www.ci.miami.fl.us* Official link to civic and visitor information.
Citysearch *www.miami.citysearch.com* Pretty generic lifestyle and ents info with locals' ratings and a strong music section.
Florida Keys History Museum *www.keyshistory.org* Complete Keys archive from 120,000 BC – reef started forming – to date.
Greater Miami Convention & Visitors' Bureau *www.tropicoolmiami.com* The glitz big-up, followed by useful information.
Miami Beach *www.ci.miami-beach.fl.us* City admin site also takes the official temperature on the beach.
Miami Herald/ Real Cities *www.miami.com* The excellent online *Miami Herald* joined to the Real Cities network.
Miami New Times *www.miaminewtimes.com* Spruce and savvy writing on Miami's hot topics and places in this online version of the city's main free alt paper.
South Beach Magazine *www.southbeach-usa.com* The Miami 'scene': shopping, dining, real estate and so on…
State of Florida *www.myflorida.com* Everything from Gov' Jeb Bush's email address to a hospital services guide.
Critical Miami *www.criticalmiami.com* This web/blog site concentrates on political and cultural commentary and 'hedonistic pursuits', plus listings for the week. Good links to other sites too.

Directory

Index

Advertisers' Index

Please refer to the relevant pages for contact details

Place of interest and/or entertainment	▢
Railway station	▢
Park	▢
Hospital/university	▢
Metromover	Ⓜ
Neighbourhood	Kendall

Maps

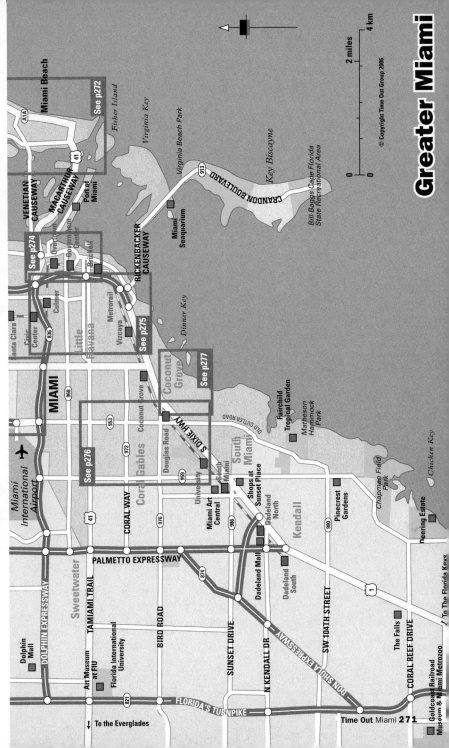

Greater Miami

Miami Beach
See p272

Fisher Island

Virginia Key

Virginia Beach Park

Key Biscayne

Bill Baggs Cape Florida
State Recreational Area

CRANDON BOULEVARD

913

Miami
Seaquarium

RICKENBACKER
CAUSEWAY

See p275

Dinner Key

VENETIAN
CAUSEWAY

MACARTHUR
CAUSEWAY

41

Port of
Miami

See p274

Overtown

Government
Center

Brickell

Metrorail

Vizcaya

Little
Havana

Civic
Center

Culmer

Santa Clara

836

MIAMI

Coconut Grove

Douglas Road

Coconut
Grove

See p277

S DIXIE HWY

OLD CUTLER ROAD

Fairchild
Tropical Garden

Matheson
Hammock
Park

Chapman Field
Park

Chicken Key

Deering Estate

953

972

Coral Gables

959

University

See p276

Miami Art
Central

South
Miami

South
Miami

Shops at
Sunset Place

Dadeland
North

986

Kendall

Pinecrest
Gardens

990

968

41

Miami
International
Airport

Sweetwater

Dolphin
Mall

DOLPHIN EXPRESSWAY

TAMIAMI TRAIL

Art Museum
at FIU

Florida International
University

821

To the Everglades

976

CORAL WAY

PALMETTO EXPRESSWAY

874

BIRD ROAD

SUNSET DRIVE

N KENDALL DR

DON SHULA EXPRESSWAY

SW 104TH STREET

Dadeland Mall

Dadeland
South

The Falls

CORAL REEF DRIVE

1

To The Florida Keys

FLORIDA'S TURNPIKE

Goldcoast Railroad
Museum & Miami Metrozoo

Time Out Miami **271**

© Copyright Time Out Group 2006

0   2 miles   4 km
0

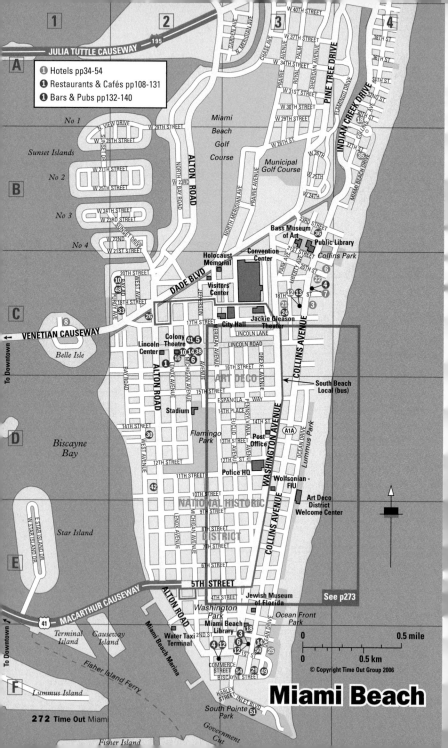

Miami Beach

A

① Hotels pp34-54
① Restaurants & Cafés pp108-131
① Bars & Pubs pp132-140

JULIA TUTTLE CAUSEWAY   195

W 40TH STREET
W 37TH STREET
CHASE AVE
GARDEN AVE
N MERIDIAN AVE
PRAIRIE AVENUE
ROYAL PALM AVENUE
SHERIDAN AVENUE
PINE TREE DRIVE
INDIAN CREEK DRIVE
FLAMINGO DRIVE
COLLINS AVENUE
MIAMI BEACH DRIVE
38TH ST
36TH ST
W 34TH STREET
W 31ST STREET
W 30TH STREET
W 29TH STREET
32ND ST
30TH ST
29TH ST
27TH ST
25TH ST

Miami
Beach
Golf
Course

Municipal
Golf Course

No 1
Sunset Islands
W VIEW DRIVE
W SUNSET DRIVE
W 28TH STREET
W 29TH STREET
NORTH BAY ROAD
ALTON ROAD
N MERIDIAN AVE
W 28TH ST
W 26TH ST
W 25TH
W 24TH

B

No 2
W 27TH STREET
W 25TH STREET
W 23RD STREET
No 3
W 24TH STREET
W 23RD STREET
No 4
W 22ND STREET
W 21ST STREET

PRAIRIE AVENUE
23RD STREET
21ST STREET
PARK AVENUE
20TH ST
18TH ST

Bass Museum
of Art   ③⑥
Public Library
Collins Park
③⑥

Holocaust
Memorial
Convention
Center

Visitors
Center
⑩
48
33
26
20TH STREET
WEST AVE
18TH STREET
JEFFERSON
DADE BLVD

LIBERTY AVE
⑫⑬
21
25
22
④
⑦
③

C

VENETIAN CAUSEWAY
⑧
Belle Isle
17TH STREET
City Hall
Jackie Gleason
Theater
Lincoln
Center
Colony
Theatre
41 ⑤
⑩ 14 38
16 ⑥
LINCOLN LANE
LINCOLN ROAD
16TH STREET
ART DECO
MERIDIAN AVENUE
JEFFERSON AVENUE
MICHIGAN AVENUE
LENOX AVENUE
DREXEL AVENUE
PENNSYLVANIA AVE
COLLINS AVENUE

South Beach
Local (bus)

To Downtown

D

Biscayne
Bay
Star Island
E STAR ISLAND DR
W STAR ISLAND DR

15TH STREET
ESPANOLA WAY
14TH PLACE
14TH STREET
Stadium
BAY ROAD
ALTON ROAD
WEST AVENUE
14TH STREET
Flamingo
Park
⑩
EUCLID AVENUE
13TH STREET
Post
Office
12TH STREET
A1A
14TH ST
WASHINGTON AVENUE
OCEAN DRIVE
Lummus Park

12TH STREET
Police HQ
Wolfsonian-
FIU
Art Deco
District
Welcome Center
⑫
11TH STREET
42
10TH ST
NATIONAL HISTORIC
DISTRICT
9TH STREET
8TH STREET
7TH STREET
6TH STREET
MICHIGAN AVENUE
LENOX AVENUE
COLLINS AVENUE

E

MACARTHUR CAUSEWAY
41
Terminal
Island
Causeway
Island
ALTON ROAD
5TH STREET
4TH STREET
Washington
Park
Jewish Museum
of Florida
Ocean Front
Park
See p273

To Downtown
Fisher Island Ferry
Miami Beach Marina
Water Taxi
Terminal
Miami Beach
Library
⑫
3
⑥⑫
54
2ND ST
18
14
50
25
29 49
COMMERCE
STREET
BISCAYNE STREET

F

Lummus Island
HARLEY STREET
INLET BLVD
South Pointe
Park
51

272 Time Out Miami

0   0.5 mile
0   0.5 km
© Copyright Time Out Group 2006

Fisher Island
Government
Cut

South Beach

Time Out Miami **273**

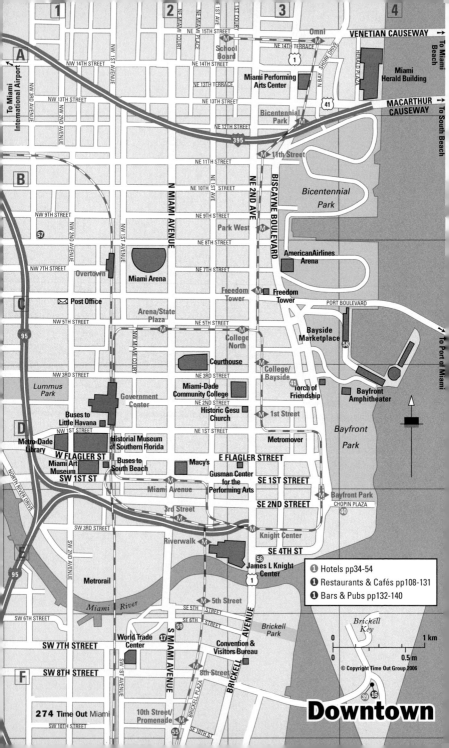

Downtown

Little Havana

Legend:
- ❶ Hotels pp34-54
- ❶ Restaurants & Cafés pp108-131
- ❶ Bars & Pubs pp132-140

Miami River

NORTH RIVER DRIVE

NW 7TH STREET

Orange Bowl

NW 6TH STREET
NW 5TH STREET
NW 4TH STREET
NW 3RD STREET

SW 7TH AVENUE

SW 22ND AVENUE

SW 17TH AVENUE

SW 12TH AVENUE

SW 8TH AVENUE

NW 6TH STREET
NW 5TH STREET
NW 4TH STREET
NW 3RD STREET
NW 2ND STREET
NW 1ST STREET

W FLAGLER STREET

SW 1ST STREET

W FLAGLER STREET

SW 1ST STREET

SW 2ND STREET
SW 3RD STREET
SW 4TH STREET
SW 5TH STREET
SW 6TH STREET
SW 7TH STREET

SW 3RD STREET
SW 4TH STREET
SW 5TH STREET
SW 6TH STREET
SW 7TH STREET

To Downtown Miami

SW 16TH AVENUE
SW 15TH AVENUE
SW 14TH AVENUE
SW 13TH AVENUE
SW 11TH AVENUE
SW 10TH AVENUE

Latin American Art Museum

SW 8TH STREET (CALLE OCHO)

Brigade 2506 Memorial

El Crédito

SW 8TH STREET

Bay of Pigs Museum

Máximo Gómez Park

Tower Theatre

SW 9TH STREET
SW 10TH STREET
SW 11TH STREET

SW 9TH STREET
SW 10TH STREET
SW 11TH STREET

SW 12TH STREET
SW 13TH STREET
SW 14TH STREET
SW 15TH STREET
SW 16TH STREET
SW 16TH TERRACE
SW 17TH STREET
SW 17TH TERRACE
SW 18TH STREET
SW 19TH STREET

SW 12TH COURT

Cuban Museum of the Americas

SW 9TH AVENUE
SW 7TH AVENUE
SW 23RD ROAD
SW 22ND ROAD
SW 21ST ROAD
SW 20TH ROAD
SW 19TH ROAD
SW 18TH TERRACE

SW 3RD AVENUE

SW 12TH STREET
SW 13TH STREET
SW 14TH STREET
SW 17TH STREET
SW 18TH STREET
SW 19TH STREET

SW 13TH AVE
SW 14TH AVENUE
SW 16TH AVENUE
SW 13TH AVE
SW 12TH AVENUE

To Downtown

SW 20TH STREET
SW 21ST STREET

SW 22ND STREET

SW 20TH STREET

SW 22ND AVENUE

SW 17TH AVENUE

SW 22ND ROAD (MEMORIAL BLVD)

SW 31ST ROAD

Vizcaya Metrorail Station

To Key Biscayne

SW 23RD STREET
SW 24TH STREET

Miami Museum of Science & Planetarium

Vizcaya Museum & Gardens

SW 25TH STREET

To Coconut Grove

SAMANA DRIVE

ALASKA DRIVE

TIGERTAIL AVENUE

SHORE DRIVE

BAYSHORE DRIVE

RICKENBACKER CAUSEWAY

0 — 400 m
0 — 400 yds

© Copyright Time Out Group 2006

Street Index

Thomas Avenue - p277 B1
Tigertail Avenue - p275 F2, p277 A3/4/B3
Trapp Avenue - p277 A4

University Drive - p276 C3/4/D3/E2
Urbino Avenue - p276 F1

Valencia Avenue - p276 C2/3/4
Velarde Avenue - p276 D3/4
Venetia Avenue - p276 A1/2
Venetian Causeway - p272 C1/2, p274 A4
Vilabella Avenue - p276 E2/3
Virginia Street - p277 A3/B3
Viscaya Avenue - p276 D3/4
Vittorio Avenue - p276 F3/4

W 21st Street - p272 B1/2/C1/2
W 22nd Street - p272 B1/2
W 23rd Street - p272 B1/2
W 24th Street - p272 B1/2/3
W 25th Street - p272 B1/2/3
W 26th Street - p272 B3
W 27th Street - p272 B1/2
W 28th Street - p272 B1/2/3
W 29th Street - p272 A2/3/B2
W 30th Street - p272 A3
W 31st Street - p272 A3
W 34th Street - p272 A3
W 37th Street - p272 A3
W 40th Street - p272 A3
W Flagler Street - p274 D1/2, p275 B1/2/3/4
W Star Island Drive - p272 E1
Washington Avenue - p272 C3/D3/E3, p273 A2-F2, p276 E4
Washington Place - p273 A3
West Avenue - p272 C2/D2/E2
William Avenue - p277 B1/2

Zamora Avenue - p276 B4